An Outer Banks Reader

An
Outer
Banks
Reader

Selected

and edited by

David Stick

THE UNIVERSITY OF NORTH CAROLINA PRESS
CHAPEL HILL AND LONDON

The paper in this book meets the guidelines for
permanence and durability of the Committee on
Production Guidelines for Book Longevity of the
Council on Library Resources.

Library of Congress Cataloging-in-Publication Data
An Outer Banks reader / selected and edited by David Stick.
p.   cm.
Includes bibliographical references (p.   ) and index.
ISBN 0-8078-2420-8 (cloth: alk. paper)
ISBN 0-8078-4726-7 (pbk.: alk. paper)
1. Outer Banks (N.C.)   I. Stick, David, 1919–
F262.096094   1998   97-40791
975.6'1—dc21   CIP

02 01 00 99 98   5 4 3 2 1

A complete list of the sources from which the pieces
in this book are reprinted can be found on pages 299–304.

Contents

Ships and the Sea

War on the Banks

Making a Living

Ones of a Kind

Visitors Leave Their Footprints

Lifestyles

Acknowledgments

All of the source material in this book was taken from the archives of the Outer Banks History Center in Manteo, or was located elsewhere by the center's curator and staff. All royalties from the sale of *An Outer Banks Reader* will go to a special fund of the Outer Banks Community Foundation, which was established for the sole purpose of providing financial support for the Outer Banks History Center.

This project has been six years in the making since it was proposed by David Perry, now editor-in-chief at the University of North Carolina Press. Without his continued encouragement and support, the book would never have reached the publication stage. The copyediting by Mary Caviness at the University of North Carolina Press and the assistance of Mary Merritt and Jack Finn is also greatly appreciated.

David Stick
Kitty Hawk
October 1997

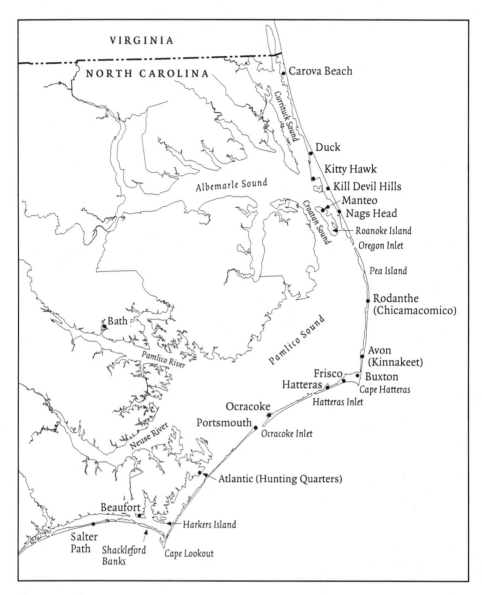

The Outer Banks

Introduction

Early maps of North America showed a strip of land that stretched far out to sea off the coast of what is now North Carolina. It's still there, a long, narrow barrier reef separated from the mainland by a succession of shallow sounds. This fragile and long-remote chain of islands, changing size and shape whenever new inlets open and old ones close, is the Outer Banks, permanent home to a rapidly increasing number of people who would rather spend the rest of their lives here than any place else in the world. Visitors often want to know why, but in truth there is no answer to the question; no single answer, that is, because each Outer Banker, native or adopted, has his or her very own reasons for considering the Outer Banks so special.

An Outer Banks Reader is my attempt to explain the appeal of this place we call home, and to do it by using the words of others rather than my own. It is the culmination of a four-year search through more than a thousand books, pamphlets, periodicals, historical documents, and other writings, seeking the ones that seemed to add color to this verbal picture of the Outer Banks. There is no intent here to include all of the geographical areas of the Banks, or all of the many different aspects of life for those residing on a barrier island. Not all authors who have written about the Outer Banks are included, nor is every person who has figured prominently in the history of the area. Certainly I was concerned about accuracy, but above all else I looked for readability. If a piece was jam-packed with facts, but sounded dull, it was thrown out. Biographical sketches of well-known people were eliminated in favor of more interesting stories about obscure individuals practically nobody ever heard of. My preference was for first-person accounts, and if the reader is sometimes surprised by my selections, then all the better for it.

In the process of searching, cutting, editing, and discarding, fewer than seventy of the nearly two hundred pieces once given serious consideration for inclusion have survived. Together they form a potpourri, covering more than four and a half centuries of observation.

The reader should understand that life on the Outer Banks isn't always idyllic, as Orville Wright made clear in a 1901 letter from Kitty Hawk to his sister back home in Dayton, Ohio, complaining that the mosquitoes had chewed clear through his underwear and socks, raising lumps all over his body "like hen's eggs." In another letter, however, he told her the sunsets at Kitty Hawk were "the prettiest I have ever seen," and he waxed poetic about the multicolored clouds.

What, then, is the Outer Banks? Who are the Outer Bankers? How did their ancestors get here, survive here, even prosper here? The selections in this anthology are my attempt to answer these questions.

First Impressions

Few travelers take the time to write down descriptions of places they see for the first time, or of the people they encounter there. Something about the Outer Banks, however, causes many visitors to feel that they had better make a record of their first impressions while the memories are fresh. This has been going on periodically for more than four and a half centuries, since 1524 to be exact, when a Florentine adventurer anchored off the Banks and sent a party ashore for water. Here is an excerpt from the account of that episode, followed by impressions of others who came later.

Contact

GIOVANNI DA VERRAZZANO   1524

Two decades after Amerigo Vespucci suggested that Columbus had found a New World, no one knew its true extent. So in January 1524, King Francis I of France sent the Florentine navigator Giovanni da Verrazzano west in search of a middle-latitude route to the Orient. Two months out, Verrazzano met "an obstacle of new land" that he reckoned "almost larger than Asia." After exploring the vicinity of Cape Fear, he sailed south, then north, confident of finding "some strait to get through to the Eastern Ocean." On the Feast of the Annunciation he anchored at a remarkable place: "We called it Annunciata from the day of arrival, and found there an isthmus one mile wide and about two hundred miles long, in which we could see the eastern sea from the ship, halfway between west and north. . . . We sailed along this isthmus, hoping all the time to find some strait . . . where land might end to the north, and we could reach those blessed shores of Cathay." He hoped in vain. The supposed isthmus was part of the Outer Banks, evidently between capes Lookout and Hatteras; the sea, Pamlico Sound. Cartographers drew these features for years, however, inspiring sailors to seek a way to the Pacific through the imaginary Sea of Verrazzano. The following excerpt of Verrazzano's report to the king is the oldest known record of a meeting between Europeans and natives of the Outer Banks.

WE . . . CONTINUED to follow the coast, which we found veered to the east. All along it we saw great fires because of the numerous inhabitants; we anchored off the shore, since there was no harbor, and because we needed water we sent the small boat ashore with XXV men. The sea along the coast was churned up by enormous waves because of the open beach, and so it was impossible to put anyone ashore without endangering the boat. We saw many people on the beach making various friendly signs, and beckoning us ashore; and there I saw a magnificent deed, as Your Majesty will hear. We sent one of our young sailors swimming ashore to take the people some trinkets, such as little bells, mirrors, and other trifles, and when he came within four fathoms of them, he threw them the goods and tried to turn back, but he was so tossed about by the waves that he was carried up onto the beach half dead. Seeing this, the native people immediately ran up; they took him by the head, the legs, and arms and carried him some distance away. Whereupon the youth, realizing he was being carried away like this, was seized with terror, and began to utter loud cries. They answered him in their language to show him he should not be afraid. Then they placed him on the ground in the sun, at the foot of a small hill, and made gestures of great admiration, looking at the whiteness of his flesh and examining him from head to foot. They took off his shirt and shoes and hose, leaving him naked, then made a huge fire next to him, placing him near the heat. When the sailors in the boat saw this, they were filled with terror, as always when something new occurs, and thought the people wanted to roast him for food. After remaining with them for a while, he regained his strength, and showed them by signs that he wanted to return to the ship. With the greatest kindness, they accompanied him to the sea, holding him close and embracing him; and then to reassure him, they withdrew to a high hill and stood watching him until he was in the boat.

Traffic with the Savages

ARTHUR BARLOWE   1584

John and Sebastian Cabot explored Newfoundland and vicinity under the English flag in the late 1490s, but England did not press a claim until 1577, when Queen Elizabeth I permitted Sir Humphrey Gilbert to investigate anew. After Gilbert disappeared on a second voyage in 1583, she reserved Newfoundland for the Crown but gave his younger half-brother Walter Raleigh a patent of discovery for the remaining parts of North America "not actually possessed of any Christian prince and inhabited by Christian people." Raleigh quickly dispatched Philip Amadas and Arthur Barlowe in two small ships to reconnoiter his huge grant. They reached the neighborhood of Cape Fear on July 4, 1584, and, according to Barlowe, coasted north "a hundred and twenty English miles" until they found a promising inlet. On July 13 they entered it, "not without some difficulty," and took possession of the territory in the name of the queen. Two days later they had their first dealings with her unwitting new subjects. The editors of the third edition of Richard Hakluyt's *Principal Navigations* modernized some spelling and typography in the following excerpt of Barlowe's account, which were simplified further for this book.

THE THIRD DAY we espied one small boat rowing towards us having in it three persons: this boat came to the island side, four harquebus-shot from our ships, and there two of the people remaining, the third came along the shoreside towards us, and we being then all within board, he walked up and down upon the point of the land next unto us: then the master and the pilot of the admiral, Simon Ferdinando, and the Captain Philip Amadas, myself, and others rowed to the land, whose coming this fellow attended, never making any show of fear or doubt. And after he had spoken of many things not understood by us, we brought him with his own good liking, aboard the ships, and gave him a shirt, and hat & some other things, and made him taste of our wine, and our meat, which he liked very well. . . . [A]fter having viewed both barks, he departed, and went to his own boat again, which he had left in a little cove or creek adjoining: as soon as he was two bow shot into the water he fell to fishing, and in less than half an hour, he had laden his boat as deep, as it could swim, with which he came again to the point of the land, and there he divided his fish into two parts, pointing one part to the ship and the other to the pinnace: which, after he had (as much as he might) requited the former benefits received, departed out of our sight.

The next day there came unto us divers boats, and in one of them the king's brother, accompanied with forty or fifty men, very handsome and goodly people, and in their behavior as mannerly and civil as any of Europe. His name was Granganimeo, and the king is called Wingina, the country Wingandacoa. . . . The manner of his coming was in this sort: he left his boats altogether as the first man did a little from the ships by the shore, and came along to the place over against the ships, followed with forty men. When he came to the place, his servants spread a long mat upon the ground, on which he sat down, and at the other end of the mat four others of his company did the like, the rest of his men stood round about him, somewhat afar off: when we came to the shore to him with our weapons, he never moved from his place, nor any of the other four, nor never mistrusted any harm to be offered from us, but sitting still he beckoned us to come and sit by him, which we performed: and being set he made all signs of joy and welcome, striking on his head and his breast and afterwards on ours, to show we were all one, smiling and making show the best he could of all love, and familiarity. After he had made a long speech unto us, we presented him with divers things, which he received very joyfully, and thankfully. . . .

After they had been divers times aboard our ships, myself, with seven more went twenty mile into the river, that runneth toward the city of Skicoak, which river they call Occam: and the evening following, we came to an island, which they call Roanoak, distant from the harbor by which we entered, seven leagues: and at the north end thereof was a village of nine houses, built of cedar, and fortified round about with sharp trees, to keep out their enemies, and the entrance unto it made like a turnpike very artificially; when we came towards it, standing near unto the water's side, the wife of Granganimeo the king's brother came running out to meet us very cheerfully and friendly, her husband was not then in the village; some of her people she commanded to draw our boat on shore for the beating of the billow: others she appointed to carry us on their backs to the dry ground, and others to bring our oars into the house for fear of stealing. When we were come into the utter room, having five rooms in her house, she caused us to sit down by a great fire, and after took off our clothes and washed them, and dried them again: some of the women plucked off our stockings and washed them, some washed our feet in warm water, and she her self took great pains to see all things ordered in the best manner she could, making great haste to dress some meat for us to eat.

After we had thus dried our selves, she brought us into the inner room, where she set on the board standing along the house, some wheat like frumenty, sodden venison, and roasted, fish sodden, boiled, and roasted, melons raw, and sodden, roots of divers kinds, and divers fruits: their drink is commonly water, but while the grape lasteth, they drink wine, and for want of casks to keep it, all the year after they drink water, but it is sodden with ginger in it, and black cinnamon, and sometimes sassafras, and divers other wholesome, and medicinable herbs and trees. We were entertained with all love and kindness, and with as much bounty (after their manner) as they could possibly devise. We found the people most gentle, loving, and faithful, void of all guile and treason, and such as live after the manner of the golden age. . . . While we were at meat, there came in at the gates two or three men with their bows and arrows from hunting, whom when we espied, we began to look one towards another, and offered to reach our weapons: but as soon as she espied our mistrust, she was very much moved, and caused some of her men to run out, and take away their bows and arrows and break them, and withal beat the poor fellows out of the gate again. When we departed in the evening and would not tarry all night, she was very sorry, and gave us into our boat our supper half dressed, pots and all, and brought us to our boat side, in which we lay all night, removing the same a pretty distance from the shore: she perceiving our jealousy, was much grieved, and sent divers men and thirty women, to sit all night on the bank side by us, and sent us into our boats five mats to cover us from the rain, using very many words to entreat us to rest in their houses: but because we were few men, and if we had miscarried, the voyage had been in very great danger, we durst not adventure any thing, although there was no cause for doubt: for a more kind and loving people there can not be found in the world, as far as we have hitherto had trial.

The Dividing Line

WILLIAM BYRD   1728

William Byrd of Westover was a prominent Virginia planter, a businessman with interests spanning the Atlantic, a patron of art and learning, owner of the largest private library in the colonies, and a multifaceted public servant. In early 1728 he agreed to lead the Virginia half of a commission appointed to survey the hotly disputed boundary with North Carolina. (An earlier attempt had failed.) Byrd and company were frustrated from the outset. Unable to employ guides in Norfolk to take them to the starting point for the survey at Old Currituck Inlet, they even had difficulty finding anyone who could tell them how to get there. In their first meeting with the North Carolina delegation, the two groups quarreled over who was in charge; then they began wrangling over whether to begin at the current or former site of the inlet, which had migrated south from its original location and had nearly closed in the process. For the next seven months this colorful group hacked and squabbled westward through 200 miles of often inhospitable terrain. The *History of the Dividing Line betwixt Virginia and North Carolina* was not published until 1841; but Byrd's trenchant remarks about his fellow commissioners, the lower classes, Carolina, and all things Carolinian quickly earned it recognition as a minor classic. Spelling and typography in the following piece were modernized for this book. Material in brackets has been added by the editor.

[March] 5.
The day being now come, on which we had agreed to meet the commissioners of North Carolina, we embarked very early, which we could the easier do, having no temptation to stay where we were. We shaped our course along the south end of Knot's Island, there being no passage open on the north.

Farther still to the southward of us, we discovered two smaller islands, that go by the names of Bell's and Church's isles. We also saw a small New England sloop riding in the sound, a little to the south of our course. She had come in at the New Inlet, as all other vessels have done since the opening of it. This navigation is a little difficult, and fit only for vessels that draw no more than ten feet water.

The trade hither is engrossed by the saints of New England, who carry off a great deal of tobacco, without troubling themselves with paying that impertinent duty of a penny a pound.

It was just noon before we arrived at Currituck Inlet, which is now so shallow that the breakers fly over it with a horrible sound, and at the same time afford a very wild prospect. On the north side of the inlet, the high land terminated in a bluff point, from which a spit of sand extended itself towards the southeast, full half a mile. The inlet lies between that spit and another on the south of it, leaving an opening of not quite a mile, which at this day is not practicable for any vessel whatsoever. And as shallow as it now is, it continues to fill up more and more, both the wind and waves rolling in the sands from the eastern shoals.

About two a clock in the afternoon we were joined by two of the Carolina commissioners, attended by Mr. S—n, their surveyor. The other two were not quite so punctual, which was the more unlucky for us, because there could be no sport till they came. These gentlemen, it seems, had the Carolina commission in their keeping, notwithstanding which they could not forbear paying too much regard to a proverb fashionable in their country, —not to make more haste than good speed.

However, that we who were punctual might not spend our precious time unprofitably, we took the several bearings of the coast. We also surveyed part of the adjacent high land, which had scarcely any trees growing upon it, but cedars. Among the shrubs, we were showed here and there a bush of Carolina Tea called Japon. . . . This is an evergreen, the leaves whereof have some resemblance to tea, but differ very widely both in taste and flavor.

We also found some few plants of the spired leaf silk grass, which is likewise an evergreen, bearing on a lofty stem a large cluster of flowers of a pale yellow. Of the leaves of this plant the people thereabouts twist very strong cordage.

A virtuoso might divert himself here very well, in picking up shells of various hue and figure, and amongst the rest, that species of conch shell which the Indian peak is made of. The extremities of these shells are blue and the rest white, so that peak of both these colours are drilled out of one and the same shell, serving the natives both for ornament and money, and are esteemed by them far beyond gold and silver.

The cedars were of singular use to us in the absence of our tent, which we had left with the rest of the baggage for fear of overloading the periaugas. We made a circular hedge of the branches of this tree, wrought so close together as to fence us against the cold winds. We then kindled a rousing fire in the center of it, and lay round it, like so many knights templars. But, as comfortable as this lodging was, the surveyors turned out about 2 in the morning to try the variation by a meridian taken from the North Star, and found it to be somewhat less than three degrees west.

The commissioners of the neighboring colony came better provided for the belly than the business. They brought not above two men along with them that would put their hands to anything but the kettle and the frying-pan. These spent so much of their industry that way, that they had as little spirit as inclination for work.

[March] 6.

At noon, having a perfect observation, we found the latitude of Currituck Inlet to be 36 degrees and 31 minutes.

Whilst we were busied about these necessary matters, our skipper rowed to an oyster bank just by, and loaded his periauga with oysters as savoury and well-tasted as those from Colchester or Walfleet, and had the advantage of them, too, by being much larger and fatter.

About 3 in the afternoon the two lag commissioners arrived, and after a few decent excuses for making us wait, told us they were ready to enter upon business as soon as we pleased. The first step was to produce our respective powers, and the commission from each governor was distinctly read, and copies of them interchangeably delivered.

It was observed by our Carolina friends, that the latter part of the Virginia commission had something in it a little too lordly and positive. In answer to which we told them 'twas necessary to make it thus peremptory, lest the present commissioners might go upon as fruitless an errand as their predecessors. The former commissioners were tied down to act in exact conjunction with those of Carolina, and so could not advance one step farther, or one jot faster, than they were pleased to permit them.

The memory of that disappointment, therefore, induced the government of Virginia to give fuller powers to the present commissioners, by authorizing them to go on with the work by themselves, in case those of Carolina should prove unreasonable, and refuse to join with them in carrying the business to execution. And all this was done lest His Majesty's gracious intention should be frustrated a second time.

After both commissions were considered, the first question was, where the dividing line was to begin. This begat a warm debate; the Virginia commissioners contending, with a great deal of reason, to begin at the end of the spit of sand, which was undoubtedly the north shore of Currituck Inlet. But those of Carolina insisted strenuously, that the point of high land ought rather to be the place of beginning, because that was fixed and certain, whereas the spit of sand was ever shifting, and did actually run out farther now than formerly. The contest lasted some hours, with great vehemence, neither party receding from their opinion that night. But next morning, Mr. M— . . . to convince us he was not that obstinate person he had been represented, yielded to our reasons, and found means to bring over his colleagues.

Here we began already to reap the benefit of those peremptory words in our commission, which in truth added some weight to our reasons. Nevertheless, because positive proof was made by the oaths of two credible witnesses, that the spit of sand had advanced 200 yards towards the inlet since the controversy first began, we were willing for peace-sake to make them that allowance. Accordingly we fixed our beginning about that distance north of the inlet, and there ordered a cedar post to be driven deep into the sand for our beginning. While we continued here, we were told that on the south shore, not far from the inlet, dwelt a marooner, that modestly called himself a hermit, though he forfeited that name by suffering a wanton female to cohabit with him.

His habitation was a bower, covered with bark after the Indian fashion, which in that mild situation protected him pretty well from the weather. Like the ravens, he neither plowed nor sowed, but subsisted chiefly upon oysters, which his hand-maid made a shift to gather from the adjacent rocks. Sometimes, too, for change of diet, he sent her to drive up the neighbor's cows, to moisten their mouths with a little milk. But as for raiment, he depended mostly upon his length of beard, and she upon her length of hair, part of which she brought decently forward, and the rest dangled behind quite down to her rump, like one of Herodotus's East Indian pygmies.

Thus did these wretches live in a dirty state of nature, and were mere Adamites, innocence only excepted.

[March] 7.

This morning the surveyors began to run the dividing line from the cedar post we had driven into the sand, allowing near 3 degrees for the variation. Without making this just allowance, we should not have obeyed His Majesty's order in running a due west line. It seems the former commissioners had not been so exact, which gave our friends of Carolina but too just an exception to their proceedings.

The line cut Dosier's Island, consisting only of a flat sand, with here and there an humble shrub growing upon it. From thence it crossed over a narrow arm of the sound into Knot's Island, and there split a plantation belonging to William Harding.

The day being far spent, we encamped in this man's pasture, though it lay very low, and the season now inclined people to aguish distempers. He suffered us to cut cedar-branches for our enclosure, and other wood for firing, to correct the moist air and drive away the damps. Our landlady, in the days of her youth, it seems, had been a laundress in the Temple, and talked over her adventures in that station, with as much pleasure as an old soldier talks over his battles and distempers, and I believe with as many additions to the truth.

The soil is good in many places of this island, and the extent of it pretty large. It lies in the form of a wedge: the south end of it is several miles over, but towards the north it sharpens into a point. It is a plentiful place for stock, by reason of the wide marshes adjacent to it, and because of its warm situation. But the inhabitants pay a little dear for this convenience, by losing as much blood in the summer season by the infinite number of mosquitoes, as all their beef and pork can recruit in the winter.

The sheep are as large as in Lincolnshire, because they are never pinched by cold or hunger. The whole island was hitherto reckoned to lie in Virginia, but now our line has given the greater part of it to Carolina. The principal freeholder here is Mr. White, who keeps open house for all travelers, that either debt or shipwreck happens to cast in his way.

[March] 8.

By break of day we sent away our largest periauga, with the baggage, round the south end of Knot's Island, with orders to the men to wait for us in the mouth of North River. Soon after, we embarked ourselves on board the smaller vessel, with intent, if possible, to find a passage round the north end of the island.

We found this navigation very difficult, by reason of the continued shoals, and often stuck fast aground; for though the sound spreads many miles, yet it is in most places extremely shallow, and requires a skillful pilot to steer even a canoe safe over it. It was almost as hard to keep our temper as to keep the channel, in this provoking situation. But the most impatient amongst us stroked down their choler and swallowed their curses, lest, if they suffered them to break out, they might sound like complaining, which was expressly forbid, as the first step to sedition.

At a distance we descried several islands to the northward of us, the largest of which goes by the name of Cedar Island. Our periauga stuck so often that we had a fair chance to be benighted in this wide water, which must certainly have been our fate, had we not luckily spied a canoe that was giving a fortune-teller a cast from Princess Anne County over to North Carolina. But, as conjurers are sometimes mistaken, the man mistrusted we were officers of justice in pursuit of a young wench he had carried off along with him. We gave the canoe chase for more than an hour and when we came up with her, threatened to make them all prisoners unless they would direct us into the right channel.

By the pilotage of these people we rowed up an arm of the sound, called the Back Bay, till we came to the head of it. There we were stopped by a miry pocosin full half a mile in breadth, through which we were obliged to daggle on foot, plunging now and then, though we picked our way, up to the knees in mud. At the end of this charming walk we gained the terra firma of Princess Anne County. In that dirty condition we were afterwards obliged to foot it two miles, as far as John Heath's plantation, where we expected to meet the surveyors & the men who waited upon them.

While we were performing this tedious voyage, they had carried the line through the firm land of Knot's Island, where it was no more than half a mile wide. After that they traversed a large marsh, that was exceeding miry, and extended to an arm of the Back Bay. They crossed that water in a canoe, which we had ordered round for that purpose, and then waded over another marsh, that reached quite to the high land of Princess Anne. Both these marshes together make a breadth of five miles, in which the men frequently sunk up to the middle without muttering the least complaint. On the contrary, they turned all these disasters into merriment.

It was discovered, by this day's work, that Knot's Island was improperly so called, being in truth no more than a peninsula. The NW Side of it is only divided from the main by the great marsh above-mentioned, which is seldom totally overflowed. Instead of that, it might, by the labour of a few trenches, be drained into firm meadow, capable of grazing as many cattle as Job, in his best estate, was master of. In the miry condition it now lies, it feeds great numbers in the winter, though, when the weather grows warm, they are driven from thence by the mighty armies of mosquitoes, which are the plague of the lower part of Carolina, as much as the flies were formerly of Egypt, and some rabbis think those flies were no other than mosquitoes.

Antebellum Nags Head

GREGORY SEAWORTHY (GEORGE HIGBY THROOP)   1849

Nags Head became a summer resort in the early 1830s, after a Perquimans County planter built a cottage there overlooking Roanoke Sound. The resort grew steadily as other well-to-do residents of the Albemarle area built their own cottages along the soundside. Soon there was a seasonal church, a community bathhouse, and a hotel said to accommodate 200 guests.

From July to September 1849, George Higby Throop, a native of upstate New York serving as tutor to the twelve-year-old son of a prominent Bertie County landowner, kept a diary of his stay in Nags Head. From the notes in his diary Throop (using the pen name Gregory Seaworthy) wrote *Nags Head, or, Two Months among the "Bankers,"* which the late Richard Walser called "the first novel dealing with contemporary times in North Carolina." In the following excerpts the reader will find many telling observations of "Sea-shore life and manners" that might apply today.

First Impressions.

My first impressions of Nag's Head were very favorable. The mere escape from the malaria, and fevers, and heat of Perquimans was quite enough to raise my spirits; but when we hove in sight of the harbor, in the gray of the morning, and saw the sun rise over Nag's Head, making still more than the usual contrast between the white sand-hills and the dark, beautiful green of its clusters of oak; when we discerned the neat white cottages among the trees, the smoke curling lazily from the low chimneys, the fishing-boats and other small craft darting to and fro, the carts plying between the shore and the dwellings, the loiterers who were eager to know who and how many had arrived, what wonder that I was prepared to be pleased with my new home? And then the dear, delightful sea-breeze, calling up old memories of a lustrum of my life in which I roamed over many a clime of "the big world." . . .

The Landing. — The House.

When you come to anchor at Nag's Head, you go ashore in the yawl belonging to the packet, or in one of the boats, or *flats* (scows), sent off by mine host of the hotel. A *row* of half a mile brings you to a little market-house, standing over the water, a few rods from shore. From this to terra firma you walk on a narrow staging of plank.

Handing my valise to a sleepy-looking black boy, I straightway set forth along the shore of the sound for my new home. Did you ever walk in the sand, worthy reader, for a considerable distance? Do you remember anything in life that so moderates any undue exuberance of animal spirits, or a chance phase of romance or enthusiasm in your feelings? Do you know anything more discouraging? Probably not. Well! saving only Provincetown, on Cape Cod, and the empire of Nantucket, and the Great Sandy Desert, there is no place where sand is more abundant; sand constituting the small portion of *terra firma* yet left at Nag's Head above the surface of the sea.

Along the interminable sand-beach did I resolutely plod my way for some two or three furlongs. My guide then turned to the left, and began the ascent of a very considerable hill. Sinking to the ankle, at times, in the sand, we at length reached the summit. Directly in front of us, but some ten or twelve feet lower, surrounded by a dwarfish growth of live-oak, was the house. It is a small story-and-a-half cottage, shingled and weather-boarded, but destitute of lath and plaster.

On the eastern side, it has a comfortable piazza, where the family gather of an evening for a social chat, and for the enjoyment of the sea-breeze. It commands a wide view of the ocean; and there is scarcely an hour of the day when you cannot see one or more vessels sailing by, brigs and schooners "wing and wing," or a "square-rigger" with both sheets aft, or else close-hauled and standing off and on. It is also the retreat, after dinner or tea, for the gentlemen to smoke; and two or three times every day you may see little Tom bringing a coal of fire on the tines of a fork for the especial benefit of the smokers. Our host makes the piazza useful in still another way; suspending on oaken hooks a goodly hammock, and enjoying a siesta with commendable zest.

The cottage contains five apartments; and they accommodate, at this present time, fifteen persons. C— occupies the north chamber with me. There being no ceiling, we enjoy the pattering of rain upon the roof; that most delicious of luxuries when one is drowsy. On the other hand, however, when we have a brisk breeze from the west, without rain, the sand comes sifting through every nook and cranny in the roof and weather-boarding; covering our beds and clothes, and filling one's hair and eyes—ay, and mouth, with a rapidity almost incredible.

Altogether, the cottage is what is sometimes called "a love of a home." Its roof rises but little above the evergreen oaks by which it is hemmed in. It is retired, quiet, snug, comfortable; and that, I fancy, is enough to say in praise of one house. We have gray-haired age; sturdy manhood in its maturity; youth and prattling infancy. We have faithful servants. We have good-humored faces—and we are happy!

The Packets.

Nag's Head would not long be known as a watering-place, or summer resort, but for the peculiar features which distinguish it from any other within my knowledge. One of these features is the fact that a very large proportion of the visitors are actual residents in private dwellings. True, there is a large hotel, and it is usually thronged from the first of July until the latter part of September. The majority of those who take up their quarters at the hotel are unmarried. Planters, merchants, and professional men usually have a snug cottage at Nag's Head, to which they remove their families, with the plainer and more common articles of household furniture, one or more horses, a cow, and such vehicles as are fitted for use on sandy roads; a buggy sometimes, but oftener a cart, resembling the convenient Canadian cart or the Nantucket "calash" (caleche). One, two, three, sometimes half a dozen servants accompany the family. Indeed, I know one gentleman who has some sixty negroes (children and invalids for the most part) living here, not far from his own residence. It costs but little, if any more, to keep them here than it would to leave them at home.

Now, to feed so many hungry mouths there must be a goodly supply of provisions. And, inasmuch as nothing can be cultivated here, the supplies must come from the plantation. As fresh vegetables are almost indispensable, it is of great importance, too, that the intercourse between Nag's Head and *home* be constant and regular.

It is this that sustains some three or four packets, which run usually twice a-week. One of these plies between Elizabeth City and Nag's Head. Another comes from Hertford; another from Edenton, and another from Salmon River, or Merry Hill; the latter being owned and employed by a wealthy gentleman for the convenience of his family and friends.

None of these packets, I believe, run less than sixty miles. They are chartered, if I am rightly informed, by a number of families; and for a stipulated sum carry them back and forth, and convey horses, furniture, provisions, and other freight during "the season." . . .

The Chapel.

———"Amoena vireta
Fortunatorum nemorum, sedes que beatas."

About a stone's throw from the hotel is a little chapel. It is a wooden structure, of small pretensions to architectural beauty, or outer or inner decoration, yet commodious, neat, comfortable. Like the dwellings around it—like almost all of them at least—it is destitute of ceiling. The weather-boards, joists, and shutters are neatly whitewashed, and the altar has latterly received a coating of white paint. This last, to give the praise where it is due, was the work of the clergymen who officiate there, Rev. Mr. F—, of Elizabeth City, and Rev. Mr. S—, of Hertford.

Its position is indeed a happy one. It stands pretty nearly in the centre of a diminutive forest of live-oak, the underwood all growing in primitive freedom and luxuriance. You approach it from several directions, through paths shaded and overhung by the evergreen foliage, and it is not until you are within a very few yards of it that you are conscious of its existence. The branches of the surrounding trees almost touch its walls.

Here, in the gray morning, so early as six o'clock, you may see mother and daughter, sire and son, quietly gathering for their morning devotions. As your eye strays inquiringly around, while waiting for the late-comers, you may see here a lady whose

"Customary suit of solemn black"

points her out as one of earth's mourners. There you discern the pale, attenuated features of some half-recovered invalid. In yet another seat, is a round-cheeked boy, or a fair-haired girl, as intent upon the liturgy, to all appearance, as was ever

Thomas à Kempis at his devotions. And, side by side with them, is gray-haired age, turning the well-worn prayer-book with hands that have lost the steadiness of younger days. And then—shall it be confessed?—you might, by sheer accident, catch the glance of a dark eye from beneath as dark a hood, and the shadow of an envious green veil, dreadfully destructive to the devotional feelings with which you may have threaded the winding, dew-bespangled paths to the little chapel. . . .

Amusements.

The amusements at all watering-places are, as far as I happen to know, much the same. There are, however, some points in which those of Nag's Head are somewhat peculiar. Gentlemen who are fond of fox-hunting bring their horses and hounds, and go galloping over the treacherous sands, much to the hazard of both horse and rider. The disciples of Walton and Stoddart can fish here without the aid of the "Complete Angler," and catch an abundant supply. Then there are excursions to the Fresh Ponds, to Roanoke Island, Kill-Devil Hills, and the New Inlet. Bathing occupies, too, and right pleasantly, many an hour that might else hang heavily upon one's hands. Then there is the drive on the beach, or, if you prefer it, the walk: alone, in the

> "society where none intrudes,
> By the deep sea,"

or with one or more companions of your own choosing. Besides these, there is a bowling-alley, where the boarders from the hotel and the residents from the hills meet at nine or ten in the forenoon, and remain until the dinner hour.

But the centre of attraction is the hotel. A siesta after the late dinner leaves you time for a short stroll about sunset; and after tea, dressing is the universal occupation. At length, sometimes as early as eight o'clock, but oftener at nine, or a later hour, the musician makes his appearance. The twang of the strings, even, as he tunes it, is enough to call the little folks around him; and it is not long before the ladies make their appearance; the sets are formed, and the long-drawn "Balance, all !" gives the glow of pleasure to every face.

Three Weddings at Hunting Quarters

NATHANIEL H. BISHOP 1874

Nathaniel H. Bishop was a man of many interests—a scientist, a naturalist, an inventor. But above all he was an adventurer, and in 1874 he set off from Quebec on a 2,500-mile trip to the Gulf of Mexico in a twelve-foot paper canoe. Bishop's innovative craft, the *Maria Theresa*, was exceptionally light despite her length, for he had designed her for easy rowing and portaging. (She also carried canvas that could serve as a sail.) Talk of Bishop's conveyance piqued curiosity along his route. At Hatteras, for instance, he received a letter from a judge who had searched Pamlico Sound for the paper canoe in order to "force upon the captain the hospitality" of New Bern.

As Bishop rowed toward Core Banks one evening he saw an object atop a sand hill, which he finally recognized as "a man on a lookout post." When Bishop had beached the canoe, the man "suddenly slid down the bank," landed at his feet, and greeted him:

> Well, now, I thought it was you. Sez I to myself, That's him, sure, when I seed you four miles away. Fust thinks I, It's only a log, or a piece of wrack-stuff afloating. Pretty soon up comes your head and shoulders into sight; then sez I, It's a man, sure, but where is his boat? for you see, I couldn't see your boat, it was so low down in the water. Then I reckoned it was a man afloating on a log, but arter a while the boat loomed up too, and I says, I'll be dog-goned if that isn't him. I went up to Newbern, some time ago, in the schooner, and the people there said there was a man coming down the coast a-rowing a paper boat on a *bet*. The *boat* weighed only fifty-eight pounds, and the *man* had a heft of only eighty pounds. When pa and me went up to the city agin, the folks said the man was close on to us, and this time they said the man and his boat together weighed only eighty pounds. Now I should think you weighed more than that yourself, letting alone the boat.

The next day, Bishop visited the little community of Hunting Quarters. It was to be a day of festivity, for an itinerant preacher was scheduled to arrive there that afternoon to fulfill the dreams of three young couples who had been waiting a long time for his visit.

I CROSSED the sound, which is here four miles in width, and coasted along to the oystermen's village of Hunting Quarters, on the mainland. The houses were very small, but the hearts of the poor folks were very large. They came to the water's edge and carried the canoe into the only store in the neighborhood. Its proprietor, Mr. William H. Stewart, insisted upon my sharing his bachelor's quarters in an unfinished room of the storehouse. My young host was hardly out of his teens. In his boyish way he kindly remarked:

"I am here all alone. Father told me, before he died, never to let a stranger pass my door but to make him share my lodgings, humble though they are; and now, any way, you're just in time for the fun, for we are to have three weddings to-night, and all the boys and girls of the neighborhood will be at Hunting Quarters."

I entered a mild protest against joining in the festivities, on the plea of not having received an invitation; at which the handsome youth laughed heartily.

"Invitation!" he exclaimed; "why, no one ever gives out invitations in Hunting Quarters. When there is to be a 'jollification' of any sort, everybody goes to the house without being asked. You see we are all neighbors here. Up at Newbern and at Beaufort, and other *great* cities, people have their ways, but here all are friends."

So we went to the little house in the piny forest, where two hearts were to be made one. The only room on the first floor was crowded with people. The minister had not arrived, and the crowd was gazing at the young groom and his pretty bride-elect as they sat in two chairs in the middle of the company, with their arms around each other, never speaking a word to any one. The heavy weight of people began to settle the floor, and as two joists gave way I struggled to escape through an open window, thinking we would be precipitated into the cellar below. But the good-natured company took no notice of the snapping timbers, only ejaculating, "She'll soon touch bottom"; and to my inquiries about the inconvenience of being pitched through to the cellar, a rustic youth, with great merriment depicted upon his countenance, replied:

"Sullers, captain, why, there ain't a suller to a buildin' within thirty miles of the Quarters. We never uses sullers hereabouts."

By my side was a young fisherman, who had got home from a cruise, and was overflowing with affection towards every girl present. "O, gals," he would cry, "you don't know how nice I feels to get back to you once more!" Throwing his arms around a bright-eyed girl, who vainly tried to escape him, he said, "O, weary mariner, here is thy rest! No more shall he wander from thee."

This sentimental strain was interrupted by an old lady, who reached her arm over my shoulder to administer a rebuke. "Sam, ye're a fool!" she cried; "ye're beside yourself to-night, and afore this paper-canoe captain, too. Ef I was a gal I'd drap yere society, wid yere familiar ways right in company."

The blow and the admonition fell harmlessly upon the head and the heart of the sailor, who replied, "Aunty, I knows my advantages in Hunting Quarters — *wimen is plenty, and men is few.*"

The crowd roared with laughter at this truism, but were quieted by the shout of a boy that the preacher was a-coming; whereupon the reverend gentleman elbowed his way through the guests to the quiet couple, and requested them to stand up. A few hurried words by the clergyman, a few bashful replies from the young people, and the two were made one. The crowd rushed outside of the house, where a general scramble took place among the boys for their girls. Then a procession was formed, headed by the clergyman, which marched along the sandy road to another house in the woods, where the second marriage was to be celebrated.

It was amusing to see the young men dash away from the procession, to run to the village store for candy at twenty-five cents per pound, containing as much *terra alba* (white clay) as sugar. With well-filled pockets they would run back to the procession and fill the girls' aprons with the sweets, soon repeating the process, and showering upon the fair ones cakes, raisins, nuts, and oranges. The only young man who seemed to find no favor in any woman's eyes invested more capital in sweetmeats than the others; and though every girl in the procession gave him a sharp word or a kick as he passed, yet none refused his candies as he tossed them at the maidens, or stuffed them into the pockets of their dresses.

The second ceremony was performed in about three minutes, and the preacher feeling faint from his long ride through the woods, declared he must have some supper. So, while he was being served, the girls chatted together, the old ladies helped each other to snuff with little wooden paddles, which were left protruding from one corner of their mouths after they had taken "a dip," as they called it. The boys, after learning that the preacher had postponed the third marriage for an hour, with a wild shout scampered off to Stewart's store for more candies. I took advantage of the interim to inquire how it was that the young ladies and gentlemen were upon such terms of pleasant intimacy.

"Well, captain," replied the person interrogated, "you sees we is all growed up together, and brotherly love and sisterly affection is our teaching. The brethren love the sisteren; and they say that love begets love, so the sisteren loves the brethren. It's parfecly nateral. That's the hull story, captain. How is it up your way?"

At last the preacher declared himself satisfied with all he had eaten, and that enough was as good as a feast; so the young people fell into line, and we trudged to the third house, where, with the same dispatch, the third couple were united. Then the fiddler scraped the strings of his instrument, and a double-shuffle dance commenced. The girls stamped and moved their feet about in the same manner as the men. Soon four or five of the young ladies left the dancing-party, and seated themselves in a corner, pouting discontentedly. My companion explained to me that the deserters were a little stuck-up, having made two or three visits on a schooner to the city (Newbern), where they had other ways of dancing, and where the folks didn't think it pretty for a girl to strike her heels upon the floor, &c.

How long they danced I know not, for the prospect of a long row on the morrow sent me to rest in the storehouse, from which I was called by a kind old couple sending for me to take tea with them at half an hour after midnight. Unwilling to wound the sensitive feelings of these hospitable people, I answered the summons in *propria persona*, and found it was the mother of bride No. 1, to whom I was indebted for the invitation. A well-filled table took up the space in the centre of the room, where a few hours before the timbers creaked beneath the weight of the curious crowd; and there, sitting on one side in the same affectionate manner I have described, were the bride and groom, apparently unmoved by the change of scene, while the bride's mother rocked in her chair, moaning, "O John, if you'd taken the other gal, I might have stood it, but this yere one has been my comfort."

A Visit to Ocracoke

CARL GOERCH   1956

Ocracoke Island had been a summer resort for many years, perhaps since colonial times, when Carl Goerch made his first trip there in 1913. For the remainder of his life the island was his favorite vacation spot. Soon after founding *The State* magazine in 1933 he began making regular mention of Ocracoke in its pages and on his radio program, thus serving as an unpaid publicist for the island, which was little known in the interior. In 1956 he compiled *Ocracoke*, a popular book drawn from his writings and recollections of nearly half a century. In the chapter reprinted here he describes Ocracoke as it was when most tourists were repeat visitors of long standing, and even the few, hardy day-trippers were more interested in fishing than in sunbathing.

OCRACOKERS eat supper early. Visitors at hotels and boarding houses have to do the same thing if they want to be fed. There's none of this foolishness of keeping dining rooms open until nine o'clock in the evening. You eat at six, if you want a hot supper, or else you don't eat at all.

No, I'll take that back. Sometimes fishermen remain out on the beach until after the regular supper hour. They may not return to their hotel 'til nine or ten o'clock but they still can get something to eat.

It was left on the table for them. Left there at six o'clock. Naturally everything is

stone cold (although you can get a cup of hot coffee) but food tastes good at Ocracoke regardless of whether it is hot or cold—especially after you've been standing
out in the salt air for several hours and are thoroughly weary.

We'll take it for granted that you arrived on the island on the mail boat. By the
time you get to your hotel or boarding house it's five o'clock. You unpack and clean
up a bit. Promptly at six the supper bell rings. It may have been on your program
to take a drink or two, relaxing after the boat trip, and then sitting down to your
evening meal at about eight o'clock. There's no objection to your taking a drink,
if you do it privately, nor is there any objection to your relaxing, but you'll have to
attend to this before six o'clock.

And another thing; you don't have to study over a lengthy menu when you get
into the dining room. You'll find the food has already been placed on the table. The
waitress comes up to you and asks: "What'll you have to drink?"

That's the only choice you have.

If you're on the island in the summertime, it's still light outside after supper,
so you decide to take a walk and see what the place looks like.

You follow the ten-foot paved road and head for Silver Lake, a couple of hundred yards distant around a bend in the highway. Stumpy trees grow on either side
of the road. Some of these are yaupons. A form of tea is made from the leaves and
this is still relished occasionally by some people living on the Outer Banks. Visitors also.

The houses are entirely of frame structure, nicely painted and, for the most
part, neat in appearance. Oleander trees grow in many of the yards. So do zinnias,
hydrangeas and other blooms. Most of the yards are fenced in and the fences are
in good repair.

When someone decides to build a new house nowadays he has to order the necessary lumber from Washington, New Bern, Beaufort or some other point on the
mainland. Long ago, however, many homes on the island were built of lumber salvaged from wrecked ships.

Occasionally, as you walk along, you meet a car or truck, or else a vehicle approaches from behind. This means you have to step off the pavement and stand in
the sand on either side in order to let the jeep or truck pass. The occupants give
either a slight wave of the hand or a cordial nod.

You observe this same friendliness on the part of everyone you meet along the
road, young and old alike. All of them have a brief word of greeting, and none
seems especially curious about who you are or what your business might be. If you
want to stop someone and engage in a conversation about things pertaining to the
island, he'll stay with you as long as you want him to.

Their attire is along simple lines. In the summertime most of the men wear a T-shirt and pair of duck trousers. Shoes are generally worn, although when mariners are working on a boat or along the docks or maybe around the house, the shoes very often are discarded. And I for one don't blame them for doing so because, to my way of thinking, shoes are superfluous on the island as an item of wearing apparel.

It just naturally feels good to walk through the sand, barefooted, and many visitors take off their shoes on arrival on the island and never put them on again until they are ready to leave.

The women wear plain dresses. Twenty-five years or so ago they, too, frequently went barefooted while going from one place to another, but you don't see that any more. Sunbonnets may still be seen, and wide-brimmed hats are popular because they help keep off the rays of the sun.

Sundays, when folks go to church, you'll find everyone dressed up just as they are in your own town.

People on the island dress with one principal thought in mind—comfort. They don't go in for anything fancy in the way of apparel. I've never seen an Ocracoke woman of mature years dressed in slacks or shorts, and I've never seen an Ocracoke man wearing Bermuda shorts or other type of summer attire so much in vogue at more sophisticated resorts.

As you start walking around Silver Lake you come to what might best be described as the down-town business section of Ocracoke. Here are the post office, the ice and electric plant, three stores, storage tanks for gasoline and diesel fuel, most of the docks and, just a short distance away, the Coast Guard station. All on the north side of the lake.

If you're hungering for conversation you usually can find several small groups of men sitting in front of the stores or on the docks.

It's a rather busy scene. Customers are entering and leaving the stores. Men are at work on boats tied up along shore. The engines in the power and ice plant offer a background of noise of which one soon loses consciousness.

Altogether there are four small stores on the island and their stocks of merchandise consist principally of things to eat. Also a sizable quantity of marine supplies. One can buy a limited number of articles of wearing apparel. Also soft drinks, tobacco and cigarettes, toilet accessories and so on, but that's about all. Most of the population manage to get to the mainland at least once a year and these expeditions are in the nature of intensive shopping trips. Washington, Beaufort and Morehead City are favored with most of this patronage.

Time and again, as you walk along, you can't help but be impressed with the attention property owners give to the cultivation of flowers. Near the southern end of the village you'll see several yards with a most beautiful profusion of blossoms of a wide variety. Practically everyone has at least a few flowers growing in the front or at the sides of their homes.

The lighthouse property, with its well-kept grounds and buildings, is one of the principal points of interest on the island. It is the oldest in service along the Atlantic coast.

Farther along you'll see vestiges of Pamlico Inn, for many years the most popular hostelry on the island. Operated by Captain Bill Gaskill and his family, it was known far and wide for its fine seafood. Captain Bill died about twenty-two years ago. Storms blew down the hotel. The water tank and a few pilings out in the water are just about all that's left.

At the extreme southerly end of the village is what is known as Springer's Point. It was here that the pirate, Edward Teache, is supposed to have had a hideout, and it was close by that he was killed by Lieutenant Maynard. It is also here that Blackbeard is supposed to have buried some of his treasure.

There's been a lot of digging throughout the years in this locality, but thus far no money has been found. As a matter of fact, those folks, who have done some research work in connection with the history of Ocracoke, are doubtful that Teache ever had a place of residence at Springer's Point.

Another outstanding spot of interest is the Coast Guard station, a large frame structure, painted white, in close proximity to the little channel which serves as an outlet for Silver Lake into the sound. Usually you'll find one or more Coast Guard boats tied to the piers in front of the station. It is located across the lake from the light house.

Children on bicycles . . . ponies wandering around loose and grazing in front yards . . . sea gulls floating aloft in the southwesterly breeze . . . the chug-chug of motors in boats . . . quacking of ducks and geese as they cross your path . . . all combine to create an atmosphere that is different from anything you'll find elsewhere along our coast.

By the time you have finished your walk you'll have a pretty good idea of what Ocracoke is like and your first impression in most instances will be favorable. That is, if you like simple living without any of the fancy frills that you will find at the average summer resort.

The Natural Environment

Few people associate the Outer Banks with agriculture, but some early European visitors were impressed by the ease with which the natives grew a variety of crops using the most primitive methods. Thomas Harriot, the scientist sent to Roanoke Island by Sir Walter Raleigh in 1585, described in detail the techniques employed by the Native Americans and the crops they produced. Many who followed wrote of the great plenty of other things, good, bad, and neutral, ranging from fish and wildfowl to mosquitoes and ghost crabs.

Native Agriculture

THOMAS HARRIOT   1585–1586

Two years before the Lost Colonists landed, 107 men under Ralph Lane established the first English colony in America on the north end of Roanoke Island. Among those based here from July 1585 to June 1586 was the versatile young scientist and mathematician Thomas Harriot, who was responsible for studying the new land, its products, and its inhabitants. He was notably interested in agriculture, and two native crops attracted much of his favorable attention. One was maize, or Indian corn; the other an aromatic leaf called uppowoc that would soon bring wealth to England and her colonies and misery to the world. Although sailors jettisoned an unknown quantity of Harriot's notes in haste to leave the island, he wrote a comprehensive, albeit too-flattering description of the area for Sir Walter Raleigh and other backers of the venture. Published in 1588 and again, with illustrations, in 1590, Harriot's *Briefe and True Report of the New Found Land of Virginia*, the source of the following passage, stood for nearly 200 years as the most accurate and influential treatise on the natural history of North America. The editors of the third edition of Richard Hakluyt's *Principal Navigations*, from which this excerpt is taken, modernized some spelling and typography, which were modernized further for this book.

COMMODITIES for victual are set or sowed, sometimes in grounds apart and severally by themselves, but for the most part together in one ground mixedly: the manner thereof, with the dressing and preparing of the ground, because I will note unto you the fertility of the soil, I think good briefly to describe.

The ground they never fatten with muck, dung, or any other thing, neither plow nor dig it as we in England, but only prepare it in sort as followeth. A few days before they sow or set, the men with wooden instruments made almost in form of mattocks or hoes with long handles: the women with short peckers or parers, because they use them sitting, of a foot long, and about five inches in breadth, do only break the upper part of the ground to raise up the weeds, grass, and old stubs of corn stalks with their roots. The which after a day or two days drying in the sun, being scraped up into many small heaps, to save them labor for carrying them away, they burn into ashes. And whereas some may think they use the ashes for to better the ground, I say that then they would either disperse the ashes abroad, which we observed they do not, except the heaps be too great, or else would take special care to set their corn where the ashes lie, which also we find they are careless of. And this is all the husbanding of their ground that they use.

Then their setting or sowing is after this manner. First for their corn, beginning in one corner of the plot, with a pecker they make a hole, wherein they put four grains, with care that they touch not one another (about an inch asunder) & cover them with the mold again: and so throughout the whole plot making such holes, and using them after such manner, but with this regard, that they be made in ranks, every rank differing from other half a fathom or a yard, and the holes also in every rank as much. By this means there is a yard spare ground between every hole: where according to discretion here and there, they set as many beans and peas; in divers places also among the seeds of macocquer, melden, and planta solis.

The ground being thus set according to the rate by us experimented, an English acre containing forty perches in length, and four in breadth, doth there yield in crop or offcome of corn, beans and peas, at the least two hundred London bushels, besides the macocquer, melden, and planta solis; when as in England forty bushels of our wheat yielded out of such an acre is thought to be much. . . .

There is an herb which is sowed apart by itself, and is called by the inhabitants uppowoc: in the West Indies it hath divers names, according to the several places and countries where it groweth and is used: the Spaniards generally call it tobacco. The leaves thereof being dried and brought into powder, they use to take the fume or smoke thereof, by sucking it through pipes made of clay, into their stomach and head; from whence it purgeth superfluous phlegm and other gross humors, and openeth all the pores and passages of the body: by which means the use thereof not only preserveth the body from obstruction, but also (if any be, so that they have not been of too long continuance) in short time breaketh them: whereby their bodies are notably preserved in health, and know not many grievous diseases, wherewithal we in England are often times afflicted.

This uppowoc is of so precious estimation amongst them, that they think their gods are marvelously delighted therewith: whereupon sometime they make hallowed fires, and cast some of the powder therein for a sacrifice: being in a storm upon the waters, to pacify their gods, they cast some up into the air and into the water: so a weir for fish being newly set up, they cast some therein and into the air: also after an escape of danger, they cast some into the air likewise: but all done with strange gestures, stamping, sometime dancing, clapping of hands, holding up of hands, and staring up into the heavens, uttering therewithal, and chattering strange words and noises.

We ourselves, during the time we were there, used to suck it after their manner, as also since our return, and have found many rare and wonderful experiments of the virtues thereof: of which the relation would require a volume by itself: the use of it by so many of late men and women of great calling, as else, and some learned physicians also, is sufficient witness.

Market Gunning

H. H. BRIMLEY   1884

Commercial hunters once provided a sizable number of the ducks, geese, and swans consumed in eastern cities, and much of that supply of wild game came from the sounds of North Carolina. This was particularly true of Currituck Sound, which freshened appreciably between 1795 and 1830, inducing the growth of vast quantities of the kinds of brackish-water grasses favored by wildfowl. By the 1880s Currituck had become a renowned hunting center.

Many recreational hunters coming to Currituck were members or guests of the private shooting clubs that occupied much of the land adjacent to the sound. Others came down on their own and stayed with local families who could provide room, board, equipment, and guides. But despite their number and enthusiasm, recreational hunters killed far fewer birds than were taken for the market.

Over a period of more than half a century, zoologist Herbert H. Brimley made numerous visits to Currituck County, ever on the lookout for new or better wild-fowl specimens for the exhibits he prepared for the State Museum in Raleigh. His observations appeared in many articles and several books, including the posthumous compilation *A North Carolina Naturalist*, from which the following selection was taken.

MY FIRST DIRECT knowledge of Currituck Sound was in February, 1884. . . .

Reaching Currituck was not easy in those days as that section of the State then possessed no railway facilities. By rail to Norfolk was the first lap; thence by steamer up the Elizabeth River, through the Albemarle and Chesapeake Canal and North River into Currituck Sound. The canal was again entered at the south end of Coinjock Bay, my getting-off place being the settlement of Coinjock. From there, across Church Island to the Midyette place on the sound was by ox-cart.

My business there was to collect and preserve specimens of waterfowl for exhibition purposes at the State Exposition that was to be held during the whole of the following October at the old State Fair Grounds near Raleigh.

My headquarters being situated about the center of the market-hunting industry, most of the specimens secured were purchased from the professional gunners. But I did some personal collecting, as on "Bluebird" days the market hunters would not bother to go out, when I would secure the loan of a battery and pick up a few specimens that way.

The gas boat was unknown in those days, all boat movement being by sail or man-power. The sail-boats were . . . canoes roomy enough to carry five or six head of cattle, or horses, and they were used by the duck-hunters in carrying their batteries to and from the shooting grounds, with the stand of decoys, occupying one or more skiffs and towed by the canoe.

These crafts were built up of three dug-out pieces dowelled together, the inside framing assisting in fastening the three units to tight, waterproof joints. They were heavy but safe and seaworthy, their sail-plan being the more or less standardized sprit-sail and jib rig, perhaps the most handy and convenient rig ever used on a comparatively small sail-boat.

The skiffs were never rowed or paddled, as the shallow waters of the sound made poling a much more efficient method of propulsion.

There were ducks and geese on the sound in those days. One afternoon I tried to count roughly the number of Canada Geese in a straggling line of flocks that was crossing Church's Island for their night's resting place in Coinjock Bay. My estimate was well above the ten thousand mark, and that flight represented only a small part of the myriads frequenting the sound both north and south from my viewpoint.

My host, Uncle Ned Midyette, owned four batteries and employed the gunners to man them, two men constituting the crew of each. He also employed a boy to do odd jobs around the house whose first duty every morning was, as soon as light enough to distinguish objects, to take his gun and inspect several miles of shoreline to pick up crippled ducks that had swum ashore during the night, it being a well-known habit of ducks to come ashore, when wounded. . . .

The following are the approximate prices the gunners were getting for their fowl, cash on the spot by the regular buyers, all prices per pair except as otherwise noted: Canvasback, $1.00; Redhead, 50 cents; "common duck," 30 cents; small ducks, as Teal, Ruddy, Bufflehead, etc., 25 cents, with four ducks constituting a pair! Canada Geese brought 50 cents each.

At that time, of course, no refrigeration facilities were available, though a small amount of icing may have been done. The usual method, however, was to allow the fowl to hang up over night to cool off, they being packed in barrels the next morning and shipped to Norfolk by steamer. . . .

Batteries have been outlawed for a number of years now, and it may be a matter of interest—particularly to the younger generation—to submit a description of an old-time battery and its outfit as used on Currituck Sound in the eighteen eighties.

Another name for the device was "sink box," which is far more descriptive than the name commonly used, which means hardly anything in this connection.

The box itself was a coffin-shaped affair, of such dimensions as to afford a fairly close fit, both in length and width, for an average sized man lying on his back, its depth being such that no part of the occupant could be seen when the box was viewed from the side.

When in use, a small pillow, or cushion, raised the head until the eyes were on a level with the rims of the box. At this same level a rigid deck some three feet wide was attached on all four sides and sloping slightly down towards the water, with flexible floating wings attached to all sides of the fixed deck, and with a particularly long extension at the head end. These wings, rising and falling with the motion of the surface water, tended to keep it from running up the fixed deck and so into the box. An added precaution against this most uncomfortable possibility consisted of strips of sheet lead an inch or two wide that were tacked along their inner edges, so that they could be turned slightly by their outer edges whenever the surface became rough-enough to warrant such procedure. When finished, the whole upper surface of the complete battery was painted a flat slaty-gray, which made it almost invisible a short distance away.

At its best, a battery was always a clumsy affair and awkward to handle, and setting one out and taking it up again on a cold, windy day was no job for weaklings.

It was securely anchored by the head, with a dragging anchor of lighter weight out over the tail end, the latter to prevent too much swinging sidewise.

Possibly, 150 decoys was about an average "stand" for a single battery. I have seen much larger stands used as well as many not so large. The best arrangement of the decoys is . . . with the bulk of the decoys concentrated about at right angles to the box on the left side of the man lying therein. For a left-handed gunner, the arrangement would be reversed. The remainder of the decoys should gradually taper off in width and be more widely scattered down wind from the larger concentration near the battery.

Movable ballast was used to sink the battery to its most effective level in the water, the ballast consisting of cast iron decoys, weighing about twenty-five pounds each. The number of iron ducks used was variable, perhaps ten being an average. . . . They were painted in keeping with the wooden decoys, and each iron decoy was fastened with a stout line to one of its wooden brethren, so that if the weather should turn rough enough to threaten water in the box, some of the iron ducks could be slid overboard and thus raise the battery to a safer level.

The professional gunners, and some experienced amateurs, would take two guns with them in the box. The thirty-two-inch barrels made it easier to rest the muzzles on the foot-board, which should always be done for reasons of safety. The guns usually used by the market gunners were double-barreled ten gauge weapons, with thirty-two-inch barrels, and hammers. Automatics and repeaters came along at a later date.

I have tried this method of shooting on a number of occasions but have nearly always had better shooting from a blind, though the battery was a deadly method of taking water-fowl when practiced by experienced professionals. There is a Chesapeake Bay record of more than five hundred ducks killed in one day's shooting by a market hunter using two guns in his battery. On Currituck, bags of a hundred a day from a battery were not rare enough to get one's name in the paper.

A now-deceased friend of mine, a crack shot on ducks, substituting for a market hunter at his request, once averaged about 130 a day for three successive days, and that was well within the present century.

I never saw or heard anything to make me believe that "punt" guns had ever been in general use on Currituck Sound, at least in comparatively recent years, as they had been in some parts of Chesapeake Bay. But, some years later, the State Museum was given the choice of purchasing one or both of two guns of this type, from a resident of Currituck County. We secured the better of the two, which is now on display in the Museum. Our specimen is a flintlock, weighing nearly one hundred pounds. The barrel is eight feet long, with a bore of one and a half inches. The standard load for this weapon would have been about one pound of shot driven by an ounce and a half to two ounces of black powder. Larger swivel guns, breech-loaders, were used in later years, some of them being handsomely finished pieces to be used with nitro powders. So far as I can learn, no gun of this more modern type ever found its way to Currituck. . . .

It goes almost without saying that a majority of the inhabitants of the shores of the sound made most of their winter's income directly or indirectly from the commercial hunting of wildfowl.

The Hungry Horde

JACK DERMID   1952

Beachcombers wading along the intertidal zone of the ocean beach in daylight are afforded an opportunity to view firsthand the frenzied activity taking place with each change of tide and each new wave. One moment a potpourri of shells and crustaceans washes up on the shore, only to be drawn back out toward the sea again as the very same wave recedes. Sand fleas exposed by an incoming wave burrow frantically beneath the sand before the next wave arrives, while shorebirds scutter along the beach, feasting on creatures too small or quick to be seen by the human eye. As all this goes on, ghost crabs sleep deep in the sand, waiting until sunset to emerge from their hiding places and begin their nightly feeding rampage under cover of darkness. Occasionally, however, man with his flashlight or his automobile headlights startles and temporarily blinds multitudes of ghost crabs. In the following piece Jack Dermid, the author of numerous articles for *Wildlife in North Carolina*, describes his first encounter with the hungry horde.

"IT'S UNBELIEVABLE!" Ken Wilson and I exclaimed in unison. Other words failed to come, and we repeated the same expression over and over. We had to pinch ourselves to make sure we were awake—to make sure that the spectacle before us was not a dream.

We were standing on the beach near Corolla in Currituck county on a warm July night with the beams of our flashlights trained along the water's edge. The sand was literally swarming with ghost crabs. Each light reflected from the eyes and the backs of hundreds, even thousands, of scampering individuals. The little armored monsters were everywhere except under our feet, where they respected a "no crab's land" of several yards in diameter. Our astonishment wore off slowly, for this was the greatest concentration of a single species that Ken or I had ever observed.

To count them one by one would have been impossible, but Ken, being a Commission biologist, wanted to take a census. Most of the crabs were gathered in a tight band extending about ten yards up the beach from the ocean. Each crab occupied about a square foot of space, and all we needed to determine was the length of the band to estimate the total population. We started hiking up the beach. The crabs melted before us as we walked, closing again behind us as we passed, just like a flock of sheep making room for a horseman riding into their midst.

Soon we tired of hiking. We directed our lights up the beach and, as far as we were concerned, the crabs extended on to infinity. Their light brownish-gray, ghost-like bodies contrasted sharply with the dark, wet sand. We concluded that there were more than 150,000 individuals in the mile we covered.

Why were the crabs so abundant? What were they doing? All sorts of questions filled our minds. We turned off our lights, stood quietly, and listened. Above the lazy surf a din of snapping, scraping, popping noises was audible. The crabs were busy feeding. It seemed miraculous that enough food was available to satisfy such a horde even at the edge of the bountiful sea. Close observation revealed that the crabs were dining largely on a small clam of the genus *Donax*. As the water receded from each wave, crabs rushed into the swirling sand to make a capture. They retreated above the water line and extracted the clam without breaking its shell. How the crabs managed to open the tiny bivalves with their pinchers without crushing them remains a mystery to Ken and me. We watched crab after crab, but none would perform in the beam of our lights.

The next morning we returned to the scene of the gigantic feast. The beach was practically deserted; only an occasional ghost crab watched us with its periscope-like eyes. Maybe the spectacle of the previous night had really been a dream born of mosquitos and heat. But evidence was there to the contrary. The dunes were riddled with tracks, and down near the water in areas not yet reached by the rising tide, we found the empty shells of victims where the sand had been torn up by thousands of sharp feet.

Creatures of the Shoals

RACHEL CARSON   1955

The publication of Rachel Carson's *Silent Spring* in 1962 gave readers throughout the world an awareness of how seriously mankind was disrupting the balance of nature. By this stage in Carson's career, she had already helped teach a generation about biology, especially marine biology, by means of lucid books such as *Under the Sea-wind* (1941) and *The Sea Around Us* (1951) and various titles written for the U.S. Fish and Wildlife Service, which employed her most of her working life. Eight years before *Silent Spring*, she described in prose equally understandable to the layperson the great diversity of life in the narrow transitional zone that she named the "edge of the sea." Research for the book bearing this name as its title, partially under-written by a Guggenheim Fellowship, took her to Bird Shoal, in the teeming tidal estuary separating Shackleford Banks from the town of Beaufort. Here, as at many other spots that she investigated along the Atlantic "rim of sand," she found a multitude of species living, feeding, reproducing, and dying in and under the water.

DOWN ALONG THE line of barrier islands that stands between the mainland and the sea, the waves have cut inlets through which the tides pour into the bays and sounds behind the islands. The seaward shores of the islands are bathed by coast-wise currents carrying their loads of sand and silt, mile after mile. In the confusion of meeting the tides that are racing to or from the inlets, the currents slacken and relax their hold on some of the sediments. So, off the mouths of many of the inlets, lines of shoals make out to sea—the wrecking sands of Diamond Shoal and Frying Pan Shoal and scores of others, named or nameless. But not all of the sediments are so deposited. Many are seized by the tides and swept through the inlets, only to be dropped in the quieter waters inside. Within the capes and the inlet mouths, in the bays and sounds, the shoals build up. Where they exist the searching larvae or young of sea creatures find them—creatures whose way of life requires quiet and shallow water.

Within the shelter of Cape Lookout there are such shoals reaching upward to the surface, emerging briefly into sun and air for the interval of the low tide, then sinking again into the sea. They are seldom crossed by heavy surf, and while the tidal currents that swirl over or around them may gradually alter their shape and extent—today borrowing some of their substance, tomorrow repaying it with sand or silt brought from other areas—they are on the whole a stable and peaceful world for the animals of the sands.

Some of the shoals bear the names of the creatures of air and water that visit them—Shark, Sheepshead, Bird. To visit Bird Shoal, one goes out by boat through channels winding through the Town Marsh of Beaufort and comes ashore on a rim of sand held firm by the deep roots of beach grasses—the landward border of the shoal. The burrows of thousands of fiddler crabs riddle the muddy beach on the side facing the marshes. The crabs shuffle across the flats at the approach of an intruder, and the sound of many small chitinous feet is like the crackling of paper. Crossing the ridge of sand, one looks out over the shoal. If the tide still has an hour or two to fall to its ebb, one sees only a sheet of water shimmering in the sun.

On the beach, as the tide falls, the border of wet sand gradually retreats toward the sea. Offshore, a dull velvet patch takes form on the shining silk of the water, like the back of an immense fish slowly roiling out of the sea, as a long streak of sand begins to rise into view.

On spring tides the peak of this great sprawling shoal rises farther out of the water and is exposed longer; on the neaps, when the tidal pulse is feeble and the water movements sluggish, the shoal remains almost hidden, with a thin sheet of water rippling across it even at the low point of the ebb. But on any low tide of the month, in calm weather, one is able to wade out from the sand-dune rim over immense areas of the shoal, in water so shallow and so glassy clear that every detail of the bottom lies revealed.

Even on moderate tides I have gone so far out that the dry sand rim seemed far away. Then deep channels began to cut across the outlying parts of the shoal. Approaching them, I could see the bottom sloping down out of crystal clarity into a green that was dull and opaque. The steepness of the slope was accentuated when a little school of minnows flickered across the shallows and down into the darkness in a cascade of silver sparks. Larger fish wandered in from the sea along these narrow passages between the shoals. I knew there were beds of sun ray clams down there on the deeper bottoms, with whelks moving down to prey on them. Crabs swam about or buried themselves to the eyes in the sandy bottoms; then behind each crab two small vortices appeared in the sand, marking the respiratory currents drawn in through the gills.

Where water—even the shallowest of layers—covered the shoal, life came out of hiding. A young horseshoe crab hurried out into deeper water; a small toadfish huddled down in a clump of eelgrass and croaked an audible protest at the foot of a strange visitor in his world, where human beings seldom intrude. A snail with neat black spirals around its shell and a matching black foot and black, tubular siphons—a banded tulip shell—glided rapidly over the bottom, tracing a clear track across the sand.

Here and there the sea grasses had taken hold—those pioneers among the flowering plants that are venturing out into salt water. Their flat leaf blades pushed up through the sand and their interlacing roots lent firmness and stability to the bottom. In such glades I found colonies of a curious, sand-dwelling sea anemone. Because of their structure and habits, anemones require some firm support to grip while reaching into the water for food. In the north (or wherever there is firm bottom) they grasp the rocks; here they gain the same end by pushing down into the sand until only the crown of tentacles remains above the surface. The sand anemone burrows by contracting the downward-pointing end of its tube and thrusting downward, then as a slow wave of expansion travels up the body, the creature sinks into the sand. It was strange to see the soft tentacle clusters of the anemones flowering here in the midst of the sands, for anemones seem always to belong to the rocks; yet buried in this firm bottom doubtless they were as secure as the great plumose anemone blooming on the wall of a Maine tide pool.

Here and there over the grassy parts of the shoal the twin chimneys of the parchment worm's tubes protruded slightly above the sand. The worm itself lives always underground, in a U-shaped tube whose narrowed tips are the animal's means of contact with the sea. Lying in its tube, it uses fanlike projections of the body to keep a current of water streaming through the dark tunnel of its home, bringing it the minute plant cells that are its principal food, carrying away its waste products and in season the seeds of a new generation.

The whole life of the worm is so spent except for the short period of larval life at sea. The larva soon ceases to swim and, becoming sluggish, settles to the bottom. It begins to creep about, perhaps finding food in the diatoms lying in the troughs of the sand ripples. As it creeps it leaves a trail of mucus. After perhaps a few days the young worm begins to make short, mucus-coated tunnels, burrowing into thick clumps of diatoms mixed with sand. From such a simple tunnel, extending perhaps several times the length of its body, the larva pushes up extensions to the surface of the sand, to create the U-shape. All later tunnels are the result of repeated remodelings and extensions of this one, to accommodate the growing body of the worm. After the worm dies the limp, empty tubes are washed out of the sand and are common in the flotsam of the beach.

At some time almost all parchment worms acquire lodgers—the small pea crabs whose relatives inhabit the burrows of the ghost shrimps. Often the association is for life. The crabs, lured by the continuous stream of food-laden water, enter the worm tube while young, but soon become too large to leave by the narrow exits. Nor does the worm itself actually leave its tube, although occasionally one sees a specimen with a regenerated head or tail—mute evidence that it may emerge enough to tempt a passing fish or crab. Against such attacks it has no defense, unless the weird blue-white light that illuminates its whole body when disturbed may sometimes alarm an enemy.

Other little protruding chimneys raised above the surface of the shoal belonged to the plumed or decorator worm, *Diopatra*. These occurred singly, instead of in pairs. They were curiously adorned with bits of shell or seaweed that effectively deceived the human eye, and were but the exposed ends of tubes that sometimes extended down into the sand as much as three feet. Perhaps the camouflage is effective also against natural enemies, yet to collect the materials that it glues to all exposed parts of its tube, the worm has to expose several inches of its body. Like the parchment worm, it is able to regenerate lost tissues as a defense against hungry fish.

As the tide ebbed away, the great whelks could be seen here and there gliding about in search of their prey, the clams that lay buried in the sands, drawing through their bodies a stream of sea water and filtering from it microscopic plants. Yet the search of the whelks was not an aimless one, for their keen taste sense guided them to invisible streams of water pouring from the outlet siphons of the clams. Such a taste trail might lead to a stout razor clam, whose shells afford only the scantiest covering for its bulging flesh, or to a hard-shell clam, with tightly closed valves. Even these can be opened by a whelk, which grips the clam in its large foot and, by muscular contractions, delivers a series of hammer blows with its own massive shell.

Nor does the cycle of life—the intricate dependence of one species upon another—end there. Down in dark little dens of the sea floor live the enemies of the whelks, the stone crabs of massive purplish bodies and brightly colored crushing claws that are able to break away the whelk's shell, piece by piece. The crabs lurk in caves among the stones of jetties, in holes eroded out of shell rock, or in man-made homes such as old, discarded automobile tires. About their lairs, as about the abodes of legendary giants, lie the broken remains of their prey.

If the whelks escape this enemy, another comes by air. The gulls visit the shoal in numbers. They have no great claws to crush the shells of their victims, but some inherited wisdom has taught them another device. Finding an exposed whelk, a gull seizes it and carries it aloft. It seeks a paved road, a pier, or even the beach itself, soars high into the air and drops its prey, instantly following it earthward to recover the treasure from among the shattered bits of shell.

Coming back over the shoal, I saw spiraling up out of the sand, over the edge of a green undersea ravine, a looped and twisted strand—a tough string of parchment on which were threaded many scores of little purse-shaped capsules. This was the egg string of a female whelk, for it was June, and the spawning time of the species. In all the capsules, I knew, the mysterious forces of creation were at work, making ready thousands of baby whelks, of which perhaps hundreds would survive to emerge from the thin round door in the wall of each capsule, each a tiny being in a miniature shell like that of its parents.

A History of Blues

JOEL ARRINGTON   1984

Bluefish are a puzzle. Sometimes they migrate north for the summer and south for the winter in huge schools, more or less as expected. Sometimes they keep to their apparent schedule but steer so far out to sea that surf and pier fishermen catch only a few. Sometimes they arrive at the appointed places at the appointed times but in far smaller or larger numbers than usual. For years scientists, anglers, commercial fishermen, and environmental activists have looked for patterns in the comings and goings of *Pomatomus saltatrix*, but no one really understands the movements or the population dynamics of this popular gamefish. One thing is predictable, however: every fall surf fishermen hoping to take advantage of a bluefish blitz line the beach at Cape Hatteras as far as the eye can see. In the following piece from *Wildlife in North Carolina* Joel Arrington, one of the fortunate handful who make a tidy income by writing about fishing, recounts his first blitz and tries to make some sense of his baffling quarry.

THE FIRST BIG bluefish I ever saw hit trolled spoons in the rain on Wimble Shoals out of Oregon Inlet in May of 1969. They weighed about 12 pounds apiece and I was amazed. After years of saltwater fishing in North Carolina I had never caught a bluefish larger than about three pounds; nor in my ignorance had I even heard of such jumbo blues anywhere. Previously the biggest I had seen were six-pounders some of us had caught on a headboat out of Montauk, New York, in 1960.

The big bluefish we boated that spring day presaged an angling era on the Outer Banks and in the western Atlantic Ocean generally that has not run its course to this day. We had no way of knowing that big bluefish populations would continue to expand and that the pursuit of them by hordes of new anglers would change the nature of surf fishing on the Outer Banks for the next 15 years and more.

I should not have been surprised at the size of those fish we caught on Wimble Shoals. If I had been better read on blues, I would have known that the big fish have a history of population surges, sudden disappearances and long absences, and that a few large blues had been caught by sport fishermen in North Carolina through the '60s. However, not until 1970 were the runs major, the anglers who experienced them numerous, nor was the publicity about them extensive.

It must have been Outer Banks publicist Aycock Brown who first used "blitz" to describe the way hundreds, perhaps thousands, of big blues congregate in the surf zone and trap bait and sometimes larger fish against the beach. A bluefish blitz has come to be the single most memorable angling experience of many Outer Banks surf fishermen, the holy grail sought by thousands of hopeful pilgrims to the Banks lured by accounts of wild fishing and blood in the water.

The first one I participated in was a dandy.

Actually, it was speckled trout that lured me to Nags Head in November of 1970. I learned on arriving that there had been a few scattered bluefish and striped bass caught in recent days north of Kitty Hawk. For some forgotten reason, however, we began the first morning at Oregon Inlet and caught just a few, maybe three, blues in the 18-pound class, the biggest I had ever seen and the first from the surf. But action ended quickly and we moved north, looking for birds.

I remember that the weather was ideal, with highs in the 60s, light northeasterly wind. In fact, it had been blowing gently from the northeast for several days and the surf had cleared to emerald green. The beach was littered with countless thousands of man-o-war jellyfish whose floats popped under our tires. We drove up from the inlet and arrived at the stretch of beach north of Jennette's Pier just as the blues and stripers moved in.

There were only a few at first, with birds working over them—gulls over the bluefish, terns over the stripers. We caught all the blues we wanted and two striped bass in just a little while and sat back in the car to watch the show. Gradually the birds increased and apparently word had been spreading like wildfire, because more and more anglers arrived on the beach. Some walked over the dunes from the road, others drove. By this time, some of the early anglers had accumulated stacks of sandy bluefish on the beach and excited drivers, intent on the now thousands of squalling gulls and scores of wildeyed anglers, ran over them and kept going as if nothing had happened. Many of these people were men, women and children who had never caught a big fish in their lives, people from Elizabeth City and Norfolk who had heard about this most amazing thing that was happening on the beach at Nags Head and had picked up freshwater tackle, anything, however inadequate, and rushed to get in on the bonanza. They cast bait and lures of every description, but it made no difference whatever, because the blues hit anything, with no hesitation, and ran off with miles of line as they snapped and cut monofilament right and left. People were screaming and cursing and bleeding from fingers incautiously thrust into fishes' mouths. Soon the riot ended when the tide turned and gradually the fishing tapered off

Some of these fish weighed 20 pounds and a little more. You hear a lot of people say, these days, that they caught some "20-pound blues," but they didn't actually weigh them. Fish approaching 20 pounds were rare after 1972 and only recently have a few more than usual been showing up in tournaments. In 1970 and again the following fall, they were commonplace. Recently fall-run blues have averaged about 16 pounds, spring-run about 12.

There is no doubt that the resurgence of bluefish in the '70s accounted in large measure for the vast increases in Outer Banks beach traffic that occurred subsequently and continues today. Red drum and speckled trout could not have attracted the numbers of people that bluefish did because they are too hard to catch. Here, after all, was a big fish that assaulted the beach in great numbers, was fast, strong, ravenous and utterly undiscriminating between lure types or baits. Why, anyone could catch them. At least that's what people thought and the idea sold a lot of beach buggies and motel rooms.

But they were only partly right. Despite much publicized blitzes, big bluefish over the years have proven to be not so universally available to sports fishermen and not so easy to catch when they are about. Even veteran anglers make trips to the coast in season and never see a bluefish. Before December of 1965, when a mini-blitz occurred on Hatteras island, big bluefish were last recorded in numbers on the Outer Banks in 1935. Now their renewed presence here and elsewhere in the western Atlantic after 30 years of total absence added a new dimension to surf, pier and inshore fishing. Without them, North Carolina coastal angling in the last 20 years would be much the worse.

Bluefish occur in many of the earth's oceans, along the shores of North and South America, Africa and even in the Pacific. In eastern America, they generally are distributed from Massachusetts to Florida, with smaller fish in the Gulf of Mexico. In years when populations are large, a few range to Nova Scotia and Cuba. There are blues off Venezuela, Brazil and Uruguay.

Bluefish everywhere, not just in North Carolina, display wild and mysterious fluctuations in abundance over a period of years. Hal Lyman in *Successful Bluefish-*

ing . . . quotes one Zaccheus Macy in his Account of Nantucket to the effect that bluefish were abundant for five years around the Massachusetts island when settlers first arrived, then suddenly disappeared in 1764. Big blues have reportedly done this in over 200 years of fishing records.

Numbers of theories have been put forward to explain these population variations, but none is totally convincing. Lyman offers his own: Since bluefish have been present in the western Atlantic during this cycle longer than any other period in recorded history, and since bluefish are known to be susceptible to parasites that proliferate only when the population reaches a certain density, perhaps, he suggests, heavy fishing pressure these days is keeping the population cropped below the critical level at which disease or parasites can spread and wipe out all but a few survivors. Under Lyman's theory, the population crash never occurs and we continue to enjoy good fishing.

It is a good idea, but there are other possibilities, too. In the past, perhaps the fish have gone somewhere else — to Africa or South America. We don't know, but research goes on.

At one time it was thought, without much evidence, that there was only one race of bluefish in the western Atlantic and that migrations were principally north and south. Tagging studies have revealed, however, that the situation is much more complicated than that. There are at least two, possibly three or more, distinct races. One, called the "southern spring spawners," breeds off the mid-Atlantic coast at the edge of the Gulf Stream. Another, the "northern summer spawners," breeds closer to shore between Chesapeake Bay and Cape Cod. Young of these northern fish move southward in the fall to spend their first winter off the Carolinas, then move into the sounds in the spring. From then on, these fish apparently migrate north in the spring and back again in the fall. Just how far they migrate and how far offshore they move is still largely unknown.

Young of the "southern spring spawners" move southward offshore and contribute to the Florida winter fishery. Apparently there is yet another race that breeds off Florida.

All this is quite complicated, and may prove to be even more so as additional studies are made. Researchers have concluded that bluefish are more oceanic than formerly thought, rather than associated with inshore waters, and that movements are less predictable.

For several years, there was a commercial fishery in the winter off Cape Fear, and whenever weather permitted, sports fishermen could run the 35 or so miles from Southport or Carolina Beach Inlet to the fishing grounds near the Frying Pan Shoals navigation tower. Those fish failed to show up in the winter of 1981–82 and only a few have returned since. Similarly, sportfishing success in spring and fall is largely dependent on whether any numbers of blues move close to shore where anglers can get at them, either from pier, surf or boat. Factors such as currents, turbidity, presence of bait and temperature are so complex that fishing success is highly unpredictable even though we may know from recent catch records that the fish population level is high.

The largest bluefish recorded as a sportfishing catch is attributed to James Hussey of Tarboro. His fish was caught off Hatteras Island on January 30, 1972, and, at 31 pounds, 12 ounces, no other records even come close. No other listing of the International Game Fish Association even exceeds 25 pounds. Hal Lyman reports an old handline catch of 45 pounds from Northern Africa, but the U.S. has a virtual monopoly on world sportfishing records. The exceptions are a 17-pound, 10-ounce fish from the Canary Islands in 1981 and a 24-pound, 3-ounce fish from the Azores in 1953.

Some of these bigger fish are quite old, as fish go. Growth rates slow down as bluefish reach about six years, so that a 15-pound fish is likely to be about 10 years old, a 17-pounder about 14. Bluefish tend to be thick and heavy in the fall, big-headed and rakish in the spring. Some blues caught at Oregon Inlet in the spring of 1983 were exceptions, however, being heavy for their length and weighing, some of them, over 18 pounds.

Such fish are a challenge to catch on light tackle. Wherever anglers can find a concentration of big bluefish in relatively clear water and cast to them with line testing under 17 pounds, the level of sport increases exponentially. One of these locations is Cape Lookout shoals in April and November. Spring bluefish usually come into shallow water near the cape to feed and warm themselves. Sometimes, early in the morning, they can be found on the shoal west of Cape Lookout jetty basking like largemouth bass on a bed. These fish are not easy to entice to a lure, but they can be caught. Light-tackle angler Tom Earnhardt uses a large white popping bug and picks up the lure noisily and casts it repeatedly to goad the fish into striking. Fair weather in the fall produces calm seas and clear water on cape shoals where bluefish may be in packs stalking menhaden, mullet and other bait. These fish will readily take any surface lure over 3 inches in length and they show a preference for a noisy one, like the Arbogast Scudder.

The most interesting bluefish angling I have seen occurs at Oregon Inlet in May and June. Guide Vernon Barrington of Wanchese showed me schools of blues up on the extensive shoals south of the inlet and stretching along the western side of Hatteras Island. We cast to them with 8-foot spin rods and pencil poppers with great success and one year even teased some close to our boat with a hookless popper so that Chico Fernandez could get one on fly. He was fishing 6-pound test leader and caught an 11-pound fish.

Although many North Carolina bluefish are caught from boats out to the edge of the Gulf Stream, particularly around wrecks, most are hooked from piers and the surf. The fall run usually begins in October with a few fish caught from the beach north of Kitty Hawk. Oregon Inlet frequently is a hot spot for weeks at a time and sometime in early November the first fish appear at Cape Hatteras Point. This spot, the hub of surf fishing in the mid-Atlantic, may very well be the most consistent producer of bluefish in the world—if you can stand the crowds. Through the winter, blues may appear whenever there is mild weather at Hatteras Inlet, Ocracoke Inlet, along the Core Banks and at Cape Lookout shoals. Less frequently the big fish come to the shore south of Lookout.

In the spring, usually by mid-April, there are jumbos in the surf zone of Core Banks and particularly on Cape Lookout shoals. May and the first two or three weeks of June are tops for Oregon Inlet. In summer only a few stragglers are left around the inlets. However, there are smaller blues weighing up to 5 or 6 pounds near inlets all along the coast from spring through fall. Some of the most enjoyable late summer fishing I know is for 2- to 5-pound blues on 8-pound line and topwater plugs beside marsh islands near Outer Banks inlets. These snappers come into the inlets on failing tide and work upcurrent into the sounds, slashing bait they trap against a bank or shoal. They are spectacular surface strikers and tough fighters.

If the big blues behave true to form, they will suddenly be gone one day, just as they always have. I look on their continued presence as a gift. Although we had more speckled trout before the blues came back, I'm not sure there was a connection. If the great bluefish disappearing act occurs again, I, for one, will miss them.

Man versus Nature

The Indians who met the first transatlantic explorers and colonists appear to have accepted nature's handiwork without trying very hard to change it. The original Bankers seem to have shared with other Native Americans the belief that human beings are only tenants of the land whose inherited responsibility is to leave it more or less as they had found it. Not so the Europeans who usurped the Indians' homeland in the process of "civilizing" them. Here are a series of accounts of the continuing conflict on the Outer Banks between these busy late arrivals and the forces of nature.

The Opening of Oregon and Hatteras Inlets

C. O. BOUTELLE AND WILLIAM L. WELCH   1846

The inlets that breach the Outer Banks are forever changing in size, shape, and location. Major changes usually occur during tempests such as hurricanes, when the storm surge floods the low-lying islands, often causing new inlets to open and old ones to close. Most storm-bred inlets remain open only a short while, but some, like the pair created by the hurricane of September 7–8, 1846, last for decades, even centuries.

C. O. Boutelle, the assistant superintendent of the U.S. Coast Survey, was running a base line on Bodie Island when the storm struck. His account of the opening of two small channels from sound to sea, one of which soon closed while the other widened and deepened to become Oregon Inlet, was published in the annual report of the Coast Survey for 1846 and is excerpted in the first piece below.

Hatteras Inlet was initially the more significant of the 1846 inlets. By 1862 it was large enough and stable enough to accommodate a large Federal fleet en route to Roanoke Island. While stationed at Hatteras in the summer of 1864, William L. Welch heard some history of the inlet from Redding R. Quidley, a local pilot. It was almost twenty years, however, before Welch set out to learn more about the circumstances of its opening and began writing to Quidley. The selections from their correspondence that make up the second piece are taken from the *Bulletin of the Essex Institute.*

Both inlets have remained open ever since and are at this writing the northernmost inlets on the North Carolina coast.

Oregon Inlet   C. O. BOUTELLE

. . . ON THE MORNING of the September gale, the sound waters were all piled up to the southwest, from the effects of the heavy northeast blow of the previous days. The weather was clear, nearly calm, until about 11 A.M., when a sudden squall came from the southwest, and the waters came upon the beach with such fury that Mr. Midgett, within three quarters of a mile of his house when the storm began, was unable to reach it until four in the afternoon. He sat upon his horse, on a small sand knoll, for five hours, and witnessed the destruction of his property, and (as he then supposed) of his family also, without the power to move a foot to their rescue, and, for two hours, expecting every moment to be swept to sea himself.

The force of the water coming in so suddenly, and having a head of two to three feet, broke through the small portion of sea beach which had formed since the March gale, and created the inlets. They were insignificant at first—not more than 20 feet wide—and the northern much the deepest and widest. In the westerly winds which prevailed in September, the current from the sound gradually widened them; and, in the October gale, they became about as wide as they are now. The northern one has since been gradually filling, and is now a mere hole at low water. West of the line the men waded across it in chaining; and at the bar our boat would not float over with the men in her. During the time I remained at Bodie's Island, it filled sensibly.

In the March gale, the *ocean* broke through the sea beach, and inundated many of the lower parts of the island—such as the sand flats, &c.; but in the September gales it was the sound alone that overflowed the whole island, leaving only the tops of the highest sand knolls bare. Comparing the elevations of certain places, which Mr. Midgett pointed out as just above water, with the known heights of points on the base near them, I came to the conclusion that the water rose to the mean height of 5.5 feet above the lower sand flat. The waves ran very high, and broke over the top of a post seven feet above the flat.

Hatteras Inlet   WILLIAM L. WELCH

THE LETTER OF Mr. Quidley, received in April through Col. Whitford and Gov. Jarvis, was dated at Hatteras Inlet, N.C., Apr. 7, 1884, and says:

> I will say in regard to your request, that Hatteras Inlet was cut out by a heavy gale, a violent storm on the 7th of Sept., at night, 1846. The first vessel that passed through into Pamlico Sound, was the schooner *Asher C. Havens*, on the 5th day of Feb'y, 1847, Capt. David Barrett, Commander: I was pilot of said schooner, conducted her through all safe. No other vessel had ever passed through the Inlet.
>
> The first vessel that ever crossed over the bar of Hatteras Inlet was in Jan., '47. I was then a licensed pilot for Ocracoke Inlet, got on board to pilot the schooner into Ocracoke, wind came ahead, I went into Hatteras Inlet for harbor, stayed all night, went out next morning and went into Ocracoke. I cannot give any correct report what time the first vessel passed out, it was not long after the first passed through; the second vessel passed through

about two weeks after the first, it was a small steamer bound through Core Sound, I piloted it through.

In another letter . . . Mr. Quidley says:

I was licensed to pilot at Ocracoke Inlet in 1831; I then lived at Hatteras and when I piloted a vessel in at Ocracoke, which very often would be two, three, or four a week, and walked home to Hatteras, there was nothing to cause me or any one, to have any idea that there would be an inlet there, sooner than any other part of the beach; there was no water passed over the place except in those heavy easterly gales, when as a general thing it passes over nearly all our beach from Hatteras to Ocracoke. The day the inlet was cut out, there were several families living where the inlet is now . . . but to their great surprise, in the morning they saw the sea and sound connected together, and the live oaks washing up by the roots and tumbling into the ocean. I was well acquainted with the growth of the land where the inlet now is, I lived with my brother where the inlet is now. I have worked with him cutting wood and chopping yopon, where now, I have no doubt there is three or four fathoms of water; the growth was live oak principally, did not grow tall, but large trunks and spreading limbs. I had an old uncle lived about where the inlet is, who had a fine fig orchard, and many peach trees on his lot, with fine potato patch and garden.

Again he writes:

Since I wrote you last, I have conversed with the two oldest men living on this portion of the Banks (one is in his 75th year, the other in his 72d), both born and raised where the inlet is now.

John Austin, the eldest, says he remembers his grandfather very well; he says he has heard the old gentleman say, there was an inlet about six miles southwest of where the inlet is now; he states that the old man said there was an English vessel, a ship, ran on the bar of said inlet, and was lost, and the wreck sanded up and the beach made down to it and finally closed up the inlet; Mr. Austin's grandfather's name was Styron; died Mch. 7, 1825, aged 86 yrs.

The other man I talked with was William Ballance. He says his father died in 1826, 68 years old; he says he heard his father say that he had seen a piece of wreck standing up, right at, or near the place that Austin speaks of as being the place where the inlet was, and had been told by older people, that it was the stern post of the vessel that closed up the inlet. This place

that they speak of is about five or six miles from this inlet we have now, between two points known now as "Shingle Creek" and "Quake Hammock."

In a letter . . . dated Sept. 29, 1884, he says:

The Shingle Creek is about five miles from Hatteras Inlet, is 40 or 50 yds.
wide, makes up through a portion of marsh and a low growth of woods or
bushes to the beach, but not through the beach; and a little to northeast
of it there is another creek, about like the one just named, called the "Old
Inlet Creek," which I think might take its name from being somewhere near
where the inlet was. The "Great Swash" is a level place of beach, nothing
growing on it but some grass or sedge next to the sound side, and extends
about a mile to next growth of woods called "Knole": the Quake Hammock
is a small clump of woods lying between Shingle Creek and Great Swash.

I cannot give the exact time that vessels left off passing through Ocracoke. I was one of the first Commissioners of Navigation appointed for
Hatteras Inlet, I think in 1852; there has been but very little passing through
Ocracoke Inlet since 1855; there is no vessel pass through there now except
perchance, that a vessel goes in case of distress of weather, or head winds,
and draws light draught of water, 4 or 5 feet.

The Worst Light in the World

DAVID D. PORTER   1851

The massive shoals that stretch out from Cape Hatteras toward the Gulf Stream
have snared innumerable vessels and made this area the scourge of coastal mariners. Early efforts to warn vessels of the danger included placing buoys on the
shoals and beacons along the shore, but all were ineffectual. Lightships anchored
at the outer end of the shoals seldom remained there for very long, and the ninety-
foot sandstone tower erected in 1802–3 near the point at Cape Hatteras was too
low to be seen beyond the shoals, even in clear weather.

In 1851 the newly formed Lighthouse Board sought opinions concerning navigational aids on the east coast from the captains of packets and mail steamers that
regularly traveled the coastal shipping lanes. David D. Porter, a once and future
naval officer serving as captain of a coastal packet, sent in the following assess-
ment of the Cape Hatteras Light, published twenty years later in a compilation of
lighthouse documents. The board may not have appreciated his frank comments,

but its reaction, whatever it was, seems to have had no bearing on his career. Porter later served with distinction in the Civil War, became superintendent of the U.S. Naval Academy, and rose to the rank of full admiral.

SIR:

I have received your communication of May 29, with enclosed act of Congress relating to light-houses, and hasten to lay before the board such information as I possess on the subject. I also do it with great pleasure, as our light-houses as at present arranged are so wretched that any seafaring man must desire a change: and I am confident that the intelligent gentlemen composing the board will have great satisfaction, at the close of their labors, in feeling that they have conferred the greatest benefit on commerce by making a complete revolution in the present disorganized system of light-houses.

There is at the present moment two million eight hundred thousand invested in steamships alone, which pass Cape Hatteras light twice a month, all of which vessels run for the light and pass Hatteras shoals close aboard. This amount of property is invested in twelve steamships of the first class—four Charleston and Savannah ships, and four for Chagres; eight of these vessels take the inshore route, passing all the lights as far as Charleston or Savannah, and thence proceeding to New Orleans, keeping the coast on board as far as Carysfort reef and Tortugas. . . .

I know nothing of the lights on Capes Henlopen, May, and Henry, and will proceed to speak of Hatteras light, the most important on our coast, and, without doubt, the *worst* light in the world. Cape Hatteras is the point made by all vessels going to the south, and also coming from that direction; the current of the Gulf Stream runs so close to the outer point of the shoals that vessels double as close round the breakers as possible, to avoid its influence. The only guide they have is the light, to tell them when up with the shoals: but I have always had so little confidence in it that I have been guided by the lead, without the use of which, in fact, no vessel should pass Hatteras. The first nine trips I made I never saw Hatteras light at all, though frequently passing in sight of the breakers: and when I did see it, I could not tell it from a steamer's light, excepting that the steamer's lights are much brighter. It has improved much latterly, but is still a wretched light. It is all important that Hatteras should be provided with a *revolving* light of great intensity, and the light to be raised fifteen feet higher than at present.

Twenty-four steamships' lights of great brilliancy pass this point in one month —nearly at the rate of one every night . . . and it can be seen how easily a vessel may be deceived by taking a steamer's light for a light on shore.

There is very much required off the point of Hatteras shoal a fog-bell that can be heard at some distance. I have no doubt that a buoy could be so fixed, that it would stand the heaviest gales. It would be great guide to vessels in foggy weather, which continues, more or less, throughout the year. There are fog-bells located in the English channel, where they are quite as much exposed as one would be at Hatteras.

The Sand Wave

JOHN R. SPEARS   1890

Some early descriptions of the Outer Banks tell of large areas of lush forest from which settlers cut the timber they needed to build their homes, outbuildings, and boats. In time, livestock was turned loose to graze at will, and in areas where old inlets had closed or where salt water from ocean overwash had killed the trees and other stabilizing vegetation, the growth of new grass and bushes was inhibited by the grazing cattle, horses, and sheep. Though logging and grazing contributed to the denudation of large areas of the Banks, the greatest damage was caused by the migratory sand hills that formed near the ocean and, driven by northeast winds, moved westward, burying the living forests in their way. The following piece, taken from *Scribner's Magazine*, described one such wave as it crossed the northern part of Hatteras Island late in the nineteenth century.

IT IS ON THE island of which Cape Hatteras is the most prominent feature that the traveller will find a sand-wave which, by its extent, by the speed with which it is moving, and by its power for distressing a simple community, will excite simultaneously his wonder and his compassion.

Fifty years ago Hatteras Island, from inlet to inlet, a distance of over forty miles, was almost completely covered with a prodigious growth of trees, among which live-oak and cedar were chief in size and number. Growing everywhere in this forest were grape-vines of such great length and extent that the boys of that day (the white-haired men of this) were in the habit of climbing into the tree-tops and crawling from tree to tree, often for a distance of over one hundred yards, on the webs the vines had woven.

The population was sparse then, but it has been increasing in such ratio as families of from nine to nineteen children may give. The people then, as now, were of simple habits, living on corn-meal, fish, oysters, pork, and tea made from the leaves of the yapon shrub; but they had to have a little money for clothing and tobacco. To obtain this they cut and sold the live-oak and the cedar.

Thus it happened that spaces along the sea-side of the island were denuded by the axe, and then burned over by the fires the fishermen built when the bluefish and the mackerel came swarming into the beach. In time, and especially during the great demand for live-oak for Yankee clippers, just before the war, these spaces were enlarged, until at last there was a permanent widening of the whole beach north of the cape.

It was then that the northeast wind, on a bright day, picked up the sand just beyond the edge of the surf, and tossed it back inland in a fine spray, when it fell down at the feet of the laurel, and the young cedar, and the young live-oak and the pine, and the yapon. With each fine day the pile of sand in the shrubbery grew, until the shrubbery withered under the breath that fanned it, and finally died. Where the green trees had stood in a sandy loam, a sand-ridge arose, which, receiving the breath of life from the northeast gale, started on a mission of death. This wave was of extended length, but its pathway was short. It reached, with the exception of a few short breaks, from the cape to Loggerhead Inlet, a distance of about thirty miles, but the journey it was to make must end at the Sound, and the island was on the average only a little over half a mile wide, though at Kinnakeet it is barely one mile from sea to sound.

The wave's progress was at first very slow, because it was of small height; it was scarce entitled to be called a wave, it was but a sand-ripple. But its speed of travel increased with each year, for every inch that was added to the narrow, sandy desert along the sea increased the area on which the wind could get a firm hold of the sand. Foot by foot, yard by yard, rod by rod the wave travelled inland.

. . . In places where the timber was scattered, the progress of the wave was so rapid that within twenty years from its starting the narrower parts of the island had been crossed. . . .

But two settlements exist north of the cape—Kinnakeet and Chicamicomico. Kinnakeet lies in a grove a mile long and half a mile wide at its widest place. Half the island has been crossed by the sand-wave at its widest place. At Chicamicomico the grove is not over a quarter of a mile wide, and consists of scattered clumps of brush separated by stretches where the wave has entirely crossed the island. Some idea of the time which will elapse before every vestige of these two groves will be gone, can be had from a single measurement which I made at Kinnakeet. The Pastor of the Methodist Episcopal church (the only denomination on the island) pointed out a dead cedar which had just been reached by the advancing wave during the first week of January. In May, when I saw it, the crest of the wave was thirty-one long steps further inland. It had travelled through the thickest part of the grove one hundred feet in five months, and the Sound but half a mile away.

It was in the Kinnakeet cemetery that this measurement was made. In the old days a spot was selected for the burial of the dead in a little hollow that was surrounded by great live-oaks and cedars, and covered with myrtles. The vine-covered branches arched and met overhead and shut out the sunshine until the soft light of evening prevailed at noon-day. Here shallow trenches were dug, and the loved ones laid to rest where the roar of the surf, modified by the intervening trees and shrubs, was as musical as the light was soft and soothing. But thoughtless greed destroyed the protecting oaks and cedars, and now the desolating sand-wave is upon the hallowed spot. Indeed, one corner has been crossed by it. The laurel and the yapon are withered and dying. The hot glare of the sun beats down where once only the cooling shade was known. The hot sand is filling in between the tiny mounds and burying them and the cedar head-boards, carved by unaccustomed hands, with names and dates and scriptural words of comfort in rude letters, many feet under the yellow sand, but not forever. Where the wave has passed, it is not content with uncovering the mounds that marked the graves, but because they, too, are of sand it scoops them up, and, digging deeper and deeper, at last exposes the coffins and even the bones of the dead. The vain efforts which the living make by driving stakes and building little huts to prevent the desecration are pitiful. The blast that uproots tree-trunks is not to be stayed by anything that this people can do.

Though but a few years must elapse before the island north of the cape will be uninhabitable, save as the families of the life-saving crews live in huts on the desert, the people as a whole are almost heedless of the inroads which the sand-wave is making. They are a contented race. One day of hard labor will yield a return that will supply a family with the necessaries of life for a week. Not that the islander very often does a hard day's work; he takes the greater part of a week to accomplish what he might do if he had to, in twelve hours. He fishes, he tongs for oysters, and he sells the surplus to dealers who come to him for it. Having food and raiment, he is therewith content. If his attention is by any chance called to the sand-wave, he languidly says that it won't reach the Sound in his time, or that when he "kain't stan' it no longer dowd doubt I will hev t' move"; and that is the end of the matter in his mind.

Yet the time will soon come when this simple people must be driven from their homes, pursued by a fate as irresistible as the deluge of old, leaving behind them all the associations of their race, of their customs, and of their occupations; leaving the bones of their dead to whiten in the burning sun, or to be lifted from their resting-place and tossed about by the merciless wind. Powerless against this tidal wave of sand they must flee away and hide themselves from its fury in a part of the island below the cape, where stunted groves may yet protect them in the years to come; or to wander Ishmael-like on the mainland. Steadily, stealthily onward creeps the relentless wave, and calmly, idly waiting, these people accept their doom.

Project Nutmeg

CAPTAIN HOWARD B. HUTCHINSON, USN   1949

In 1946 the United States moved its tests of nuclear weapons from New Mexico to the Marshall Islands. Despite the useful data gathered in the South Pacific, the Atomic Energy Commission proposed resuming Stateside tests, and on October 7, 1948, its military liaison ordered a secret report on desirable sites to be finished by the end of the year. Code name: Nutmeg. The research staff (a part of whose report appears below) saw promise in the arid parts of several western states and in the lower Outer Banks. Within a year, the Soviet Union tested an atomic weapon, and the AEC was suddenly in too big a rush to bother condemning land on the Banks, which follow-up inquiry had shown to suffer erratic weather and other drawbacks. The Banks were saved, to the detriment of Nevada and its neighbors. Even so, powerful men had given serious consideration to a study which threatened the lower banks and its people with relocation, radiation, and ruin. (Consider that Bikini, one of the Pacific islands bombarded in the 1940s, is still too hot for human habitation.)

NEVADA, Arizona, and New Mexico seem to offer the optimum conditions as to meteorology, remote available land and logistics. It would seem expedient to choose a site in New Mexico; a state conditioned to nuclear [deleted by censor].

If the fall-out element over the eastern part of the United States cannot be accepted, sites can be chosen on the coast of Maine or on the coasts of Delaware, Maryland or Virginia. Meteorology is favorable for removing the waste out to sea during two-thirds of the year between 20% and 30% of the time.

If fall-out upon the waters of the Atlantic is not acceptable because of second order effects upon its fisheries, sites can be chosen along the southeastern seaboard between Cape Hatteras and Cape Fear. In this region population is not dense, meteorology is favorable during two-thirds of the year between 20% and 30% of the time; and the waters of the Gulf Stream will remove the waste products to the open Atlantic with no possibility of second order effects through biological processes.

8. *Pamlico-Core Sound Area.* Upon request of the Chief, Armed Forces Special

Weapons Project, the United States Air Forces provided aerial photographs of the coastal regions of North and South Carolina. The photographs have been examined and have been compared with . . . U.S. Coast and Geodetic Survey Charts. . . . It seems probable that several areas are suitable for test sites between Cape Hatteras and Cape Lookout along this coast. The coast, in this region, consists of more or less continuous sea strands or beaches, extending roughly northeast-southwest, with the Atlantic Ocean containing the Gulf Stream on the seaward side and with the shallow extensive Pamlico Sound and the long narrow Core Sound on the landward side. Possible test sites are described below.

a. *Cape Hatteras.* . . . To the northwestward of Cape Hatteras and extending northward and westward are 100 square miles of sand flats. Most of these flats are exposed at low tide. . . . Cape Hatteras is made up of old strand lines and is apparently building seaward. There are Coast Guard installations and the Light House as well as about 50 buildings in the total area. About half the total area is covered with vegetation while the remaining area is beach sand and sand dunes. A road exists along the island southward from Oregon Inlet. Rollinson Channel crosses the flats from Pamlico Sound to the little hamlet of Hatteras, some 7 miles to the west. Rollinson Channel has a controlling depth of 6 feet at mean low water. Avon Channel crosses the flats to Avon some 7 miles to the north. Avon Channel has a controlling depth of 5.5 feet at mean low water. Cape Hatteras is a possible site for nuclear tests. It is relatively accessible by water, yet could be easily placed "out of bounds" for security control.

b. *Ocracoke Island.* . . . extends for some 15 miles between the ocean and Pamlico Sound. It has a width ranging from a quarter to a half mile and is bordered on its landward side by some 45 square miles of sand flats. These flats contain Howard Reef, Clark Reef and Legged Lump, composed of hard sand. The aerial photographs show a road along the entire length of the strand. There are but one or two installations on this island, except the little village of Ocracoke on the southwest end at Ocracoke Inlet. Ocracoke Inlet has a controlling depth of 10 feet at mean low water. It is extensively buoyed and lighted. Ocracoke village has a boat basin and two piers.

c. *Portsmouth Island, Portsmouth Bank, and Core Bank.* Extending from Ocracoke Inlet to Cape Lookout, in a southwesterly direction, is some forty miles of sea strand. . . . Between this strand and the mainland extends Core Sound through which exists a dredged channel having a controlling depth of 6.5 feet at mean low water. Core Sound has an average width of three miles or more. It is believed that an exceptionally favorable site for nuclear tests could be constructed on Portsmouth Bank. If a site were chosen at about 34°-55′N, 76°-14′W, a radius of 10,000 yards can be swung without including any important installations, yet there are plenty of adjacent points for observation of the tests. This place is of easy access by water from the Beaufort–Morehead City rail terminus. It is adjacent to the town of Atlantic, opposite Drum Inlet, open to the sea. Atlantic has an air field. The large Marine Corps Air Base of Cherry Point, North Carolina, is 25 miles west of Atlantic. The Beaufort–Morehead City air field is 18 miles southwest of Atlantic. The extensive Cedar Island area, as well as Portsmouth Bank, is apparently under government control since it is called a "danger area" on the aeronautical charts. This last described area seems to hold the most promise for sites on the southeastern Atlantic seaboard because from here southward to Florida, the strand-like islands, separated from the mainland by sounds, are replaced by marshy islands integral with the mainland. It is believed the Pamlico-Core Sound area should be investigated first, at least, for continental test sites, when the desire is paramount to avoid fall-out of radioactive waste upon the population or the commercial fisheries of the nation.

Man's Impact on the Barrier Islands of North Carolina

ROBERT DOLAN, PAUL J. GODFREY,

AND WILLIAM E. ODUM 1973

Scientists paid little attention to the Outer Banks until the development explosion of the 1950s and 1960s. Since then a flood of studies, reports, impact statements, and scholarly essays has told anyone who would read them what is happening to the Outer Banks, why it is happening, and, in some cases, why it should not happen. Some of their authors even agree with one another.

Robert Dolan began a serious study of wave action on Bodie Island in the late 1950s and has been called on frequently since then by the National Park Service and other agencies to undertake a variety of research projects in the area. With associates Paul J. Godfrey and William E. Odum, the University of Virginia geologist set down some of his thoughts on the effects of development in a 1973 article for *American Scientist*, excerpted here.

FROM A geological point of view, the Outer Banks of North Carolina are one of the most dynamic areas under the jurisdiction of the National Park Service. The barrier islands undergo continual change in position. Because oceanic overwash plays an essential role in this process, an unbalanced situation is developing wherever artificial barrier dunes have been built or encouraged. . . . Further compounding the seriousness of the situation has been the false impression of safety and stability offered by the barrier dune. Numerous structures, including motels, restaurants, beach cottages, park facilities, and a United States naval station at Cape Hatteras, have been built immediately behind the barrier dune in the mistaken belief that it would provide permanent protection from encroachment by the sea. Instead, the beach has steadily narrowed, and the barrier dune has subsequently eroded away, leaving these structures with little protection from extreme storms.

The opening and closing of inlets, together with oceanic overwash, creates serious problems in maintaining a permanent highway down the center of the Outer Banks. In the past it has been necessary to clear the highways when covered with sand deposited by overwash, and the highways have been rerouted several times when erosion destroyed the dunes and threatened them. Bridges have been abandoned and roads built where inlets have closed.

In other cases it has been necessary to fill in recently formed inlets and replace the destroyed highway. The Ash Wednesday storm of 1962, for example, opened a new inlet between Buxton and Avon which required $700,000 to close, in addition to almost $1 million to rebuild the dune system and replace the roadway. The same storm destroyed segments of over 20 kilometers of the artificial barrier dune system, which also had to be rebuilt.

Although the present system is undependable, endangered, and expensive to maintain, alternatives are even more expensive and somewhat questionable in terms of application and economics. One approach has been to attempt to maintain the beaches by constructing groins at right angles to the beach or by dredging sediments and pumping them into the beach. The cost of groin fields commonly runs into millions of dollars, and yet they have not been very effective on the Outer Banks at Hatteras Lighthouse. . . . Dredging and beach nourishment may cost $700,000 per km, and in most cases this too is only a temporary measure.

Another suggestion has been to build a reinforced dune system at critical sites by forming sea walls of sand bags and filling the center with loose sand. . . . A structure such as this, estimated to cost about $3 million per km, ignores the basic fact that once the beach is gone, nothing will stop heavy surf action for very long. A better solution, and clearly the more desirable from both an ecological and geological standpoint, would be to construct an elevated highway on the sound side of the islands. Although this would allow natural processes to take place with little resultant damage, the costs would surely be prohibitive.

Survival of the natural beach environment along coastal North Carolina requires a strategy of submission and rebuilding. Man has attempted to draw a line and prevent the sea from passing. The results have been unexpected and negative. Because the Cape Hatteras portion of the Outer Banks has already been developed to the point where it would be virtually impossible to remove the highway, it must be maintained. However, as the system continues to narrow, new instances of overwash, erosion of the artificial barrier dunes, and inlet formation can be forecast. Many of the structures which have been built in the proximity of the beach will be lost, and the highway will require relocation in several places within a few years.

The Cape Lookout section of the Outer Banks presents an entirely different situation. The islands from Portsmouth Island south to Cape Lookout and then west along Shackleford Bank are undeveloped. There are no highways, utilities, and permanent settlements to protect. Placement of a permanent roadway down the island would require a continuous artificial dune system for protection and stabilization.

The National Park Service plan is to leave Portsmouth Island, Core Banks, and Shackleford Banks in a natural state. Rather than building a highway the length of the islands, which would surely lead to management problems similar to those that now exist within the Cape Hatteras National Seashore Recreation Area, the plan is to construct several visitor centers on the sound side to be served by ferry traffic from the mainland. Maintenance costs for this type of development will be low although usage will be high. This is, in effect, a limited-use national seashore with no attempt to interfere with or control natural biophysical processes.

Within the past fifteen years the National Park Service has become the public's manager of most of the nation's remaining natural barrier islands, and if the present trend of acquisition continues, several new areas will increase this responsibility significantly. All of these seashore and lakeshore areas can be classed as high-stress environments, but the barrier islands are perhaps more delicately balanced than most.

In addition, most of the water-oriented land holdings under National Park Service jurisdiction are classed as recreation areas rather than national parks or wilderness areas, so that they are subject to additional stress via development, heavy visitation, and a wide range of recreational uses. The National Park Service handbook categorically states:

Outdoor recreation shall be recognized as the dominant or primary resource management objective. Natural resources within the area may be utilized and managed for additional purposes where such additional uses are compatible with fulfilling the recreation mission of the area. Scenic, historical, scientific, scarce, or disappearing resources within recreation areas shall be managed compatible with the primary recreation mission of the area.

For these reasons it is particularly important that the National Park Service be supported for cautiously charting the course of development and land use within the newly acquired national seashore and lakeshore areas. The Outer Banks of North Carolina serve as an excellent case study of the geologic, ecologic, and political/economic implications of large-scale manipulations of these systems.

Saving Nags Head Woods

MICHAEL GODFREY   1981

Nags Head Woods is one of the great natural treasures of the Banks and must be seen repeatedly in all seasons to be appreciated. Standing east of Albemarle Sound and just above the former site of colonial era Roanoke Inlet, it acts as a filter for plants, animals, seeds, and eggs borne seaward by the Roanoke, Chowan, and other rivers. Thus it abounds in species seen almost nowhere else east of the Piedmont. In addition, it is virtually the farthest outpost for northern species such as the red-backed salamander. For centuries this amazing diversity survived scattered settlement, intermittent agriculture, and advancing sand hills. But in recent decades commercial and residential development missed the Woods by the width of a bulldozer blade. Recognizing the unique value of this place, concerned citizens and, eventually, the Nature Conservancy turned more than 1,100 acres of public and private land into an ecological preserve secure from the threat of exploitation. This capsule history of the effort to preserve the woods originally appeared in *Wildlife in North Carolina*.

SQUINTING INTO the milky haze at 5,500 feet over Albemarle Sound I hand Massengale a chart. Can he see a shoreline off to our right? Yes. Good. Thanks. Preoccupied, he folds the chart, wrong of course, and flips it absently into the back seat. While I retrieve it the aircraft begins to bank right, the nose drops and the airspeed whistles. Massengale looks at his white knuckles as if surprised to see them on the wheel, more surprised to see them instinctively bring us back to level flight.

The pilot is inwardly pleased. Nothing annoys quite like a passenger consumed with his own concerns and unaware that he is in mortal peril. Let 'em participate!

"What do you see?"

"Nothing."

Tom Massengale is Director of the North Carolina Nature Conservancy. He organized the chapter in 1977. Nationally, the Conservancy has preserved 1.7 million acres of America's critical natural habitats, many of which would by now otherwise view the sun through an asphalt filter. The North Carolina chapter is one of the most successful. Massengale is a wheedler, a cajoler, a coordinator of the good offices, intentions and energies of others. He has orchestrated the preservation of much of North Carolina's natural heritage which now stands safe, 130,000 acres so far. As if acres tell the story. . . .

A white strand somehow separates itself from the haze. It cuts the wind-screen just below the second screw in the divider. That would be the beach at Nags Head. The milky business below it is Roanoke Sound; that above it, the Atlantic Ocean. Massengale sees it now.

"There's the Woods!" He jams his finger into the plexiglass, shakes it and starts gathering up real-estate plats, apple cores and briefcases.

The nose angles downward and the airspeed whistles again. We can see a dark band on the Sound side of the Outer Banks. At each end of it is a white knob. The knob at the north end is Run Hill. Jockey's Ridge anchors the south end. The lush, five-mile corridor of greenery connecting them is Nags Head Woods. It is a Nature Conservancy Preserve, though the work of preservation is far from complete. This is the 19th time we've made this flight in the past two years, another move in the chess match to secure the Queen of North Carolina's natural areas.

For those who like their aesthetics quantified—and there's no other way to raise money to preserve a tract or to convince the government that it's worthy of being named a National Landmark—there is a hefty document by Henrietta List and Tom Atkinson which catalogues the goodies. Nags Head Woods contains:

- 33 of the 37 woody communities on the Outer Banks, in most cases the best examples remaining.
- Southernmost occurrence of woolly beach heather (*Hudsonia tomentosa*).
- Northern limit for the green orchid (*Habenaria repens*).
- The only pools in North Carolina containing all genera of duckweed: *Wolffia*, *Wolfiella*, *Lemna*, and *Spirodela*.
- At least 17 species which are on the Cape Hatteras National Seashore Park list of rare and endangered plants.
- Unusually large specimens of American holly, dogwood, hop hornbeam, live oak, pignut hickory.

Now we're getting to the point. What is Nags Head Woods, anyway? Some kind of condominium development bulldozed out of the dune scrub?

The fact is Nags Head Woods is a real woods. It's not a tangle of maritime shrubs and salt-stunted runts. It's a forest of tall pines, oaks and hickories. There are also hollies and beeches—huge ones you'd expect in an Appalachian cove. But this woods is not in Appalachia. It's at the seashore. In flora and fauna, Nags Head Woods is the most diverse forest on the Atlantic seacoast.

The dunes begin on the west side of Route 158 By-pass, behind the beach at Nags Head. They are dry, hot and only loosely vegetated. There are stunted wads of greenery that, had fate been kinder in distributing the seeds, would have been trees—pines and oaks. Here the sand impoverishes them; the salt spray knocks them flat.

A quarter mile inland from the surf the oaks and pines begin to look like trees, though they don't act their age. A 40-year-old pine may be only 3 inches across. The sand underfoot is knit by the rare woolly beach heather, a pioneer on northern dunes. Its spreading cedarlike clumps lace into the sand at scattered locations between Cape Cod, Massachusetts, and Atlantic Street, Nags Head, North Carolina 27959.

The dunes steepen abruptly. Each becomes a little mountain 50 or 60 feet high with a slope of up to 70 degrees (for reference, 90 degrees is vertical). There is no pattern to them, no ranks marching as before a prevailing wind. The sand is heaped at random and steeper of slope than seems prudent.

It's hard not to notice also that the dunes are forested. We stand amid tall, straight pines, oaks and hickories. Nearer Roanoke Sound there are beeches 2 and 3 feet in diameter towering in the coves of sand just as they would on the Blue Ridge Scarp. Our sense of place is tricked by this dislocation, this importation of a cove forest cathedral to the seashore. It's not like a whole system of values is threatened, though, for this exact ecology occurs nowhere else on earth.

Freshwater pools nestle between the dunes. There are dozens of them varying in size from wet-weather puddles to ten-acre Fresh Pond, until recently the only source of water for the towns of Nags Head and Kill Devil Hills. The depth may be a few inches or many feet; the bottoms are of organic muck underlain by sand. Some of the ponds are vegetatively sterile. Others host some of the world's most unusual plant communities. They may be ringed with littoral zones of submerged and emergent greenery like the water violet and *Hydrocotyle ranunculoides*, a coastal rarity with no common name. Here is a pond carpeted in a green iridescence of watermeal, mosquito fern (a real fern, aquatic, free-floating, fingernail-sized), the duckweeds *Wolfiella floridana* and *Spirodela polyrrhiza* and the yellow flowered aquatic carnivore *Utricularia biflora*. In broad perspective these ponds boil and seethe with a broth of plants, frogs, fish, herons, turtles, muskrats, snakes, otters—numerous beings that gurgle, make bubbles, squawk and plop off logs. A palmful skimmed from the surface sparkles with minute greenery and vibrating invertebrates.

There are also snakes, and some like the cottonmouth moccasin and Eastern diamondback rattler are poisonous. Visitors should be watchful, especially in the warmer months.

There is another feature more striking even than the trees, or the steep dunes. The Woods are cool—mercifully shaded and 15 degrees cooler than outside.

"Why, Henrietta?" I once asked the resident expert on Nags Head Woods.

She is Henrietta List, a self-taught naturalist who helped bring the Woods to The Nature Conservancy's attention, awakened the Outer Banks to the treasure hidden in the dunes and is now the curator and ranger-in-residence of the Nags Head Woods Ecological Preserve. Henrietta's knowledge of the Woods is encyclopedic—from the state's largest live oak to the toads, ticks, and cottonmouths. She counts the deer herd, scuffs up the bobcat scats, leads the boy scouts in hell-for-leather charges into old trash heaps and on broad sweeps against the scattered droppings of *Swinus americanus*, posts the signs on the Preserve's boundaries, deals with the vandals, welcomes the visitors, and interprets their surroundings.

"Why the trees?" she mused, "Why the pools, the cool air? There's a lens of fresh water under the dunes. Where the depressions between the dunes are deep enough, the water is visible. It moistens the roots and nourishes the trees so that they don't know they're growing in a desert. The trees take up water through their roots and release it through their leaves as vapor. Evaporating, the water absorbs heat and cools the air."

Henrietta talked about the oasis effect and about the conflict in the currents offshore. The Virginia Coastal Drift brings cooler water from the north. It accounts for the goosebumps on the swimmers at Nags Head and for the moderate climate there.

The warmer Gulf Stream flows up the coast from the south, depositing subtropical maritime species along the way—the cabbage palm at Cape Fear, the American alligator at Cape Lookout, the yellow-lipped snake, the cotton mouse, the green anole, the squirrel treefrog and a galaxy of plants including the longleaf pine and the green orchid in the vicinity of Nags Head. Realms of life coming from the north and from the south meet at an oasis. The result is an explosive diversity unequaled on the Atlantic coastline.

"The irregular dunes and steep slopes?" she asked. "Who knows! Theories abound. Maybe the inlet that opens once or twice a century south of Jockey's Ridge salted up the sound, killed the forest, destabilized the sand and let the southwest winds play with it."

We circle the huge active dune at Run Hill, checking the wind sock.

"You land this thing, Massengale. I'm going to catch a little sleep." Instantly the cockpit is a blur of floating papers and flying apple cores. The whole bucket of land-preservation paraphernalia rolls to a stop beneath the Wright Brothers monument.

A real-estate developer who has a project in the middle of Nags Head Woods is here to meet us. The economics of the times suggests he sell out. If somehow the development can be bought or at least put into friendly hands, the thinking goes, the disturbance can be minimized, the development's private trash dump can be deactivated and control can be gained over the southernmost access to the Preserve—an important measure against vandals and firewood thieves. The unmentionable other side of the coin is a takeover by an insensitive developer who will bisect the Woods and freshwater pond system with a grid of roads and bulldozed lawns, expanding southward.

There are 1,800 acres in the Nags Head Woods designated (but not yet dedicated because of the large number of owners with divergent views) a National Natural Landmark. The Nature Conservancy holds about 300 acres. Henrietta has just cut a deal with the town of Nags Head to manage its 260 adjacent acres as the Preserve is managed. Next southward is the development. Then comes a series of private holdings including a still-active farm in some lowland next to the marsh. There are old homesteads, roadways and graveyards.

Putting the pieces together was seen as an impossibility from the first talks of preservation. Yet today the northern third, the part containing most of the ponds and many of the unique and irreplaceable habitats, is safe because Massengale, List & Co. brought together the resources and the people of goodwill. The developer wants almost $1 million for his 56 acres, not the "bargain sale" Massengale had hoped for. The developer suspects—hopes fervently—that the Conservancy has rich friends. Promising at first, his scheme was burdened with the requirement to operate a sewage-treatment plant and it has become a nightmare.

We stop by the Woods for a stroll on the way back to the airport. Henrietta talks about Nags Head Woods becoming one of the most visited sanctuaries in America, rivaling the great Audubon preserves at Four-Hole Swamp in South Carolina and Corkscrew Swamp in Florida as a center of learning, research and interpretation.

Clouding Henrietta's dream is a debt of $200,000 on what has already been acquired. She and Tom are pleased with what has been accomplished but aware that the remainder is vulnerable. Henrietta wants a visitor's center, interpretive facilities and some means of acquiring the 400 unprotected acres of ponds, marsh and forest as they become available. And what is to be done with the developer?

"We did have some rich friends," says Tom, "mostly from outside North Carolina. They helped a lot, particularly at a time when the project had little grass-roots support at home. The Conservancy gave it number one priority nationally and some strong donors came through. The Mary Flagler Cary Charitable Trust gave

$600,000, the Goodhill Foundation provided $280,000, the Z. Smith Reynolds Foundation of Winston-Salem gave $100,000 and the Elizabeth City Foundation donated $5,000. An anonymous friend wrote a check for $50,000. With individual donations, the total raised so far is $1.04 million. There has been a trend of generosity on the part of the landowners in the Woods, some of whom donated their land or sold it at bargain prices.

"But time goes on and priorities shift. We have to realize that Nags Head Woods is a North Carolina project. It is this State's most significant natural heritage location and it's up to North Carolina's people to preserve it."

Henrietta leads the way up the near-vertical loose sand. We emerge from boughs of oak puffing and backsliding, gaining the summit of Run Hill lurching on all fours. Our tracks lead out of the only forest in North America being eaten by a live dune. On our left the glacier of sand is edging into one of the ponds. Candles of oak and pine, the uppermost twigs of trees 70 feet tall, poke from the dune crest, gasping for CO_2.

"You can't see that anywhere else in the world," says Henrietta quietly.

Grapevines lace the nearly obliterated treetops. Behind us against the sky loom ghostly sentinels of grapevines, their roots in the loam now beneath fathoms of sand.

"Nor that," she notes.

On our right the dune marches into the marshes of Roanoke Sound. An osprey launches from a sand-killed skeleton of oak, plunges into a tidal creek and lumbers aloft. It pauses midstroke to shake like a beagle and to streamline the fish.

To Henrietta List it is inconceivable that someone—if not everyone—in North Carolina isn't going to step up and do what has to be done about Nags Head Woods.

Cape Lookout National Seashore: A Return to the Wild

MICHAEL E. C. GERY 1992

As conceived in 1933, Cape Hatteras National Seashore was to include most of the land on the Outer Banks from the Virginia line to Beaufort Inlet. It was to fulfill a dual purpose: parts were to be made easily accessible for recreational use by vacationers and day visitors; the rest was to remain as close as possible to its natural state. But the first national seashore, centered at Cape Hatteras, came into being two decades later in several parcels virtually separated by growing, thriving resort towns and villages. Its total area had been reduced to roughly one-third of that originally proposed. Recreation was accommodated in high style, but not preservation, the other original purpose of the park. Consequently the National Park Service, under increasing public pressure, acquired all the land, ocean to sound, between Ocracoke Inlet and Beaufort Inlet for a new national seashore in which nature would take priority. The following, from the pages of *Outer Banks Magazine*, is a recent description of Cape Lookout National Seashore—so close to Cape Hatteras, yet so different.

BY BOAT. It's the only way on, the only way off. No bridges have ever linked Cape Lookout to land, and none ever will, for the Cape Lookout National Seashore is one of the last wild places left on the Atlantic seaboard. Perhaps wild isn't the word. Abandoned is more descriptive. Here, there's an eerily tidy ghost of a town, rusting skeletons of half-buried beach jalopies, and horses left behind. More than 20 years ago, the last two residents gave up trying to live in Portsmouth Village, a town that once numbered nearly a thousand.

Since 1976, the United States government has owned all 28,500 acres of Portsmouth Island, North and South Core Banks, and Shackleford Banks. Its mission: to return them to the wild. These remote barrier islands, an Outer Banks anachronism, comprise the Cape Lookout National Seashore.

If Cape Lookout has been abandoned by its residents, it still has not lost its fascination for a few hardy adventurers. People come now just for birding or shelling, to walk the silent paths of Portsmouth Village, to study marine biology, or just to spend the day sailing or paddling a kayak. Last summer, more than a dozen artists stayed two weeks just for the inspiration and camaraderie of it all.

Located just south of Ocracoke, the seashore extends 22 miles down North Core Banks to New Drum Inlet, then 22 miles down South Core Banks to Cape Lookout Point. At the point, the nine-mile Shackleford Banks angles sharply, forming an east-west orientation with ocean sunsets.

At their narrowest, the barrier islands measure 600 feet from Atlantic Ocean to Core Sound, and a mile and three-quarters at their widest. From any hummock you can see the ocean and sound at the same time.

All told, the seashore extends for 55 miles, uninterrupted by roads or power lines. At night, the only light is by candle or constellation, by Coleman lantern's glow tempered by tent or tarp, and by the occasional electric generator.

Dispersed along low barren beaches are a few dozen fishing shacks built right on the beach, newer yet spartan Park Service cabins, and a handful of summer cottages once owned by seasonal residents who now hold 25-year leases or lifetime rights to their use. Other structures include the Cape Lookout Lighthouse and adjacent Keepers Quarters at Lookout Bight, and an inactive Coast Guard Station at Cape Point.

At the northern end of the banks, Portsmouth Village is the crown jewel of Cape Lookout National Seashore. The 250-acre village is listed on the National Register of Historic Places. You can get there by boat from Ocracoke, then amble past the two dozen buildings, imagining the days when Portsmouth was the largest town on the Outer Banks. One residence and the Methodist Church are open to the public, and a ranger station occupies one of the houses near the empty Coast Guard station. Also in the vicinity are seasonal private homes which the Park Service owns and leases to occupants who were here in the 1960s. Portsmouth Village remains frozen in time. But the lure of the Core Banks always has been the wild, ever-changing beach.

Comparing Cape Lookout National Seashore to Cape Hatteras National Seashore, where he was once superintendent, Cape Lookout Park Superintendent William Harris makes the distinction between a structured versus unstructured park experience.

At Cape Lookout, there are no special programs, no campgrounds, no lifeguards. National Park Service policy is to let nature take its course, while maintaining historic sites and essential accommodations for people to enjoy it all safely. Even with limited access and limited facilities for visitors, yet still they come. In this, the era of the eco-tourist, Cape Lookout is proving to be especially irresistible, as people search for that increasingly rare commodity: unadulterated, unadorned beach.

In 1981, the National Park Service recorded 56,409 visitors to Cape Lookout National Seashore. Ten years later, more than 317,000 annual visitors were recorded at Cape Lookout (compared to 2.1 million visitors to Cape Hatteras National Seashore that same year). Despite Cape Lookout's increasingly larger draw, the total numbers remain relatively small, especially when spread over a year's time and across 55 miles of wide, open spaces.

In the 1970s, half the visitors stayed either at crude fish camps or in tents and vehicle campers; the other half stayed only for the day, arriving by ferry or private boat. Today, it is the day visitors who largely account for Cape Lookout's growing popularity.

While life at Cape Lookout can be rugged, its raw beauty and isolation have drawn a special group of people to its shores. In 1991, "Volunteers in the Park" served as Cape Lookout caretakers and hosts. The VIPs also helped the Park Service patrol the beaches, conduct bird counts, communicate by radio, and perform other services. The Park Service plans to continue the program in 1992.

During the VIP program's first year, three couples stayed for three months each in one of the restored houses in Portsmouth Village; to the south, two couples lived in the lighthouse keepers' quarters.

The first couple to live at the keepers' quarters were writer Edna "Golly" Moses and her daughter Demaris Anderson. They stayed for a six-month sojourn.

Demaris Anderson, an artist, worked with the Park Service to sponsor a two-week session called "Artists in the Park." In August 1991, 13 artists from throughout the Southeast gathered for the solitude, the inspiration, and the challenge of capturing the magnificent lighting reverberating between the vastness of sea and sky. Anderson has arranged regional exhibits of the paintings and photography those two weeks inspired, and she hopes to continue the program.

George and Doris Stein also served as VIPs at the Cape Lookout Keepers' Quarters, in the fall of 1991. Retired and living in Raleigh, the Steins once had a summer place in Marshallberg, a Down East village across the sound from South Core Banks. Their great pleasure in those days was to take their Boston Whaler over to the banks for the day.

During their residency at the keepers' quarters, the Steins watched 100 baby loggerhead turtles hatch in one evening from mounds of beach sand, and then slowly crawl into the sea. They saw dozens of gannets blown errantly to shore after Hurricane Grace. They met all kinds of people. And most of all, they met fishing people.

If Cape Lookout National Seashore is an ocean beach theme park, the theme is surf fishing. As Don Morris has said—and Don Morris has made his living on the Core Banks since the 1940s—"That old hard fisherman is what carries the ball here." That old hard fisherman comes each spring and fall, usually with buddies. They pay Don Morris or Alger Willis to ferry them, along with their vehicle, to the banks. Then they set up camp and fish. They love how hardy it is. They love being away from everything except the beach, the ocean, and their camp.

"The fishermen are in a group all their own," VIP George Stein said with affection and admiration.

"One group from out near Charlotte said they've been coming here since 1950. They all say they've been coming over for 40 years," Stein explains.

"But these fellas set up a camp out at the Point. It's a plywood structure with plastic sheeting for the roof. They build a kitchen and a bar. They bring an ice chest with 600 pounds of ice. They have a hydraulic lift on the back of the vehicle. That's how they get the ice chest down to the ground. They have everything in there you want to drink. Eight o'clock in the morning they're drinking beer. I asked them, 'What time does the bar open?' They said, 'The bar is open from 5 to 5.'

"One guy was sitting there with a sand wedge and a putter. So I asked him about the sand wedge and the putter, and he said, 'We have a golf course out here.' They had a five-hole golf course out there in the sand, from one sand dune to the other!"

With no water, no public facilities, and certainly no PGA-approved golf courses, visitors to Cape Lookout National Seashore do have to prove their resourcefulness. But visitors can call on a couple of old-timers who know the banks like the backs of their hands.

Atlantic is a "Down East" village an hour's drive north of Beaufort. There, Don Morris operates the Morris Marina, Kabin Kamps and Ferry Service, Inc. His is one of nine mainland businesses with a National Park Service contract to run a ferry.

Morris ferries people, and up to five vehicles per trip, to and from a landing on the banks north of New Drum Inlet. He is also responsible for two dozen rental beach cabins.

"I've been doing this since long before the Park Service came in," he says. "I started working with my daddy doing this in 1946."

In 1961, the State of North Carolina offered Don Morris' father $20 for each of his 960 acres of Core Banks beach. "He took it," Capt. Morris says, "and he was glad to have it." Later, the state turned over the Morris property and everything else along the banks to the federal government. I asked Don Morris what he thinks about that.

"Let me put it this way," he said from the helm of his *Green Grass* ferryboat, squinting at the shining beach as we approached. "What would that beach be worth today?

"Supposing the state hadn't come, and we had developers out here and surveyors to run streets and lots, and we built condos onto it, and it was done all over, up and down the banks.

"The man who could afford one of them condos was in good shape," said Morris. "But how about the man who couldn't afford one? He would have lost all privilege on this beach. He wouldn't be able to use it.

"So, looking at it from the standpoint of it being a national seashore and giving the public a privilege to use it, I think it is one of the best things that ever happened.

"But looking at it from the standpoint of private enterprise, we were shitted."

In the 1940s and 1950s, the Morrises carried plenty of wealthy sportsmen to the beach. "We had some people who could afford better, but for the fisherman, this was the best he could do. If you are going to a place, it doesn't make any difference how much money you have. You can only buy what a man's got for you once you get there." In other words, no clubhouse, no hotel, no restaurant, no telephone.

Taking care of tourists in those days was primitive business. Don Morris, back in 1946, went to work at age 16. His father had begun rebuilding some beach cabins wrecked by the 1944 hurricane. Young Don was put out there from April through October to work for the tourists.

"When I first started working with my daddy," Don Morris remembers, "he gave me an A Model Ford out there and he said, 'Son,' he said, 'This is all we got.'

"And it was nothing but the chassis and a steering wheel with no wheel, just three spokes. The brake pedal was on the floorboard. The whole top was cut off. It was just a chassis with a bed built on it, with a box there for me to sit on and steer with those three spokes. We had a five-gallon can on that bed to hold water for the radiator. The starter was gone off it. You had to crank it.

"And my daddy says, 'This is all we got. But we have to do the best we can with what we got.' So I said, 'Yessir.'

"And he said, 'I want you to carry these people down the beach and go back and get them and pick them up. Let them fish as long as they want to. Meet the boat when I bring her over. Take the trash out. Clean the cabin out when the party moves out. This is your job.'

"Well, I had to work. I was 16 years old.

"There was one time we had but one battery for the truck and the boat. Put the battery in the boat to go over, put the battery in the truck to haul the supplies out for the party. And you come back from the beach and put the battery back in the boat and go back across."

Today, old cars lie half buried, their rusted hulks creating a kind of abstract metal sculpture rising up from the sand. As late as the 1960s, people commonly bought a car for $50 or $100, usually with bald, tubed tires, and they took the cars over by ferry, let the air out of the tires until the walls sagged, and drove on the beach. If the car died, the owner would leave it, figuring he had gotten his money's worth.

The Park Service estimated in the mid-1970s that some 2,500 junk vehicles were on the beach, forming dunes of their own. Government helicopters lowered huge magnets onto the sand to airlift the skeletons.

The Cape Lookout Mobile Sport Fishing Club, a now-inactive group dedicated to preserving sport fishing on these banks, took it upon themselves to remove old vehicle hulks from the North Core Banks a few years ago. They used forklifts and dumpsters, then had Marine Corps helicopters draw off the dumpsters in big nets.

Abandoned vehicles on the beach, a ghostly village home to none, horses left to fend for themselves. Why is Cape Lookout such a lonely outpost?

That same delicious edge of danger and unpredictability, which today draws people hungry for a taste of nature unadorned, is precisely what drove the residents of Cape Lookout from her shores.

Life at Cape Lookout was hard.

Shackleford Banks, the island which runs perpendicular to Cape Lookout, was home to some of the hardiest bankers, including those who practiced "shore whaling" from about 1750 until the 1890s. . . .

By 1895, the whale oil and bone market faded, as indeed did the whales themselves. But it was the weather that ultimately sent the islanders packing.

After the devastating hurricane of 1899, what was left of Diamond City, named after the diamond pattern of the lighthouse, was literally moved to the mainland. Within a three-year period, all its residents had deserted the island. Many dismantled their houses, shipped them to Harkers Island, and rebuilt them there. By 1902, only the whalers' sheep, cattle, and horses remained; some of their livestock's descendants still roam the banks.

Further up the banks, Portsmouth villagers persevered longer. But merciless hurricanes in 1933 and 1944 finally drove most people away. In 1956 the population was 17, and in 1971 the last two residents left.

While economic struggle was a primary reason for the abandonment, former resident Sarah Roberts Styron said in a 1978 interview, "People were tired of cleaning up after the hurricanes." And Lionel Gilgo, who left Portsmouth in 1942, added, "They didn't want their caskets buried in water. They had to stand on the caskets to keep them down long enough to cover them with sand. . . . Naturally nobody wanted to leave, but they were so disgusted with losing everything they had once, sometimes twice, every year. We soon got tired of it and were glad to get away from it."

As day visitors today enjoy the stunning natural beauty of Cape Lookout National Seashore, we would do well to remember that while these islands harbor no grudges, neither do these fickle islands hold lasting friendships. They are nature, at its wildest, best loved as a romantic fling—an escape, however brief, from the world these barrier islands hold at bay.

Ships and the Sea

Mariners have long known the reputation of Cape Hatteras and the adjacent coast as the Graveyard of the Atlantic. Here is a selection of true stories of Outer Banks shipwrecks, of efforts to prevent them, and of valiant attempts to rescue those unfortunate enough to have been involved. They include a report by a passenger on a steamer lost off Cape Hatteras in 1812; an account of the sinking of the Civil War ironclad Monitor; stories of the exceptional bravery and fortitude shown by several members of the U.S. Lifesaving Service and Coast Guard; and most of what is known about the ghost ship of Diamond Shoals. There is even a recap of what happened at Oregon Inlet when the ship hit the span.

Shipwreck off Hatteras

SARAH KOLLOCK HARRIS 1812

In December 1812, the wife of Hillsboro judge Edward Harris booked passage on an unidentified ship bound from New York City to New Bern by way of Ocracoke Inlet. Weather permitting, the passage should have taken two or three days, four at the most. But the weather failed to cooperate, and after three weeks at sea and a number of futile attempts to clear Cape Hatteras, the vessel was wrecked a short distance north of the cape.

Mrs. Harris was accompanied on the voyage by her younger sister, Lydia, and two servants, all of whom survived the harrowing experience. By the end of February she had recovered sufficiently to send a letter to another sister with a graphic description of the voyage, the wreck, the rescue by residents of Hatteras Island, and the subsequent stay in what she described as "a miserable little hut about a mile from shore." The letter found its way into the diary of educator Margaret Anna Burwell and thence under her name into the *North Carolina Booklet*, from which the following piece is taken.

WE SAILED FROM New York Saturday, December 1st, with a favorable wind, which continued only until the next day about noon. On Monday the wind shifted 'round, and from that hour till the day of our shipwreck (24th December), severe gales, head-winds and dead calms alternated. Much did we suffer. I think I was more dreadfully sick than on any former voyage. . . .

The Saturday night after we left New York we had a tremendous gale, and were in imminent danger. The wind blew so violently that we were driven at the rate of ten miles an hour . . . without a single sail up. It thundered tremendously, and as I lay in my berth I saw the vivid flashes of lightning playing over the companion way. Rain, hail and snow succeeded each other, and had not a kind Providence endowed our captain with great firmness and presence of mind in a critical moment we must all have been lost. . . . Almost every other night we had severe gales; repeatedly we were driven into the Gulf stream when we were anticipating crossing the bar in a few hours. Sixteen days and nights we lay in that dangerous place; our wood gave out, provisions grew short, and the patience of the crew was nearly exhausted. When the passengers were entertaining the most sanguine hopes of landing in New Berne in a few hours, suddenly a head wind would spring up and blow us back into the Gulf. . . .

The evening of the 23d a most tremendous gale came on after a dark and disagreeable day. We were then approaching Cape Hatteras. Captain Pike was on deck the whole evening, and, I verily believe, acted a faithful and prudent part. The mate, who was the brother of our captain, was very sick in his berth. The lead was hove, we were in soundings, the wind blowing directly on shore. Under such circumstances, Captain Pike justly deemed it dangerous to proceed further towards the Cape or to lie there. Accordingly he turned about and made off again to sea. The lead was constantly hove till near midnight, when we were out of soundings, and then the vessel was laid to. All danger, we thought, was over, and we lay quietly down to sleep. Alas! we are often in the greatest danger when we think ourselves most secure. Before daylight the wind suddenly changed. This raised heavy opposite seas and so strong was the current that it drove us with irresistible violence towards the shore. About five o'clock on the morning of the 24th *we struck*. Conceive, if you can, my dear Mary, the horrors of that moment! In an instant we were all out of our berths; the captain flew on deck, the vessel began to fill with water and inclined much on one side, which was soon overflown. Down the cabin stairs rushed the captain, exclaiming, "By the eternal God, we're on the breakers!" Oh, what a sound was that! I pulled dear Lydia toward Mr. Davis, a gentleman who had been shipwrecked about a year previous, and who had promised assistance should any misfortune befall us. "Do, Mr. Davis, endeavor to save this poor child!"

He replied with a look of despair that froze me with horror, "Mrs. Harris, nothing can be done; we are all lost, there is no hope!"

Shrieks of anguish resounded through the vessel; it thumped violently on the breakers, and in a few moments was turned over nearly on its beam ends.

The gentlemen stood around like statues of despair, deeming all efforts to save themselves or us useless. Mr. Davis held my hand with one of his, with the other he held a candle, when a heavy sea broke over the vessel, shivered the skylight to atoms, rushed into the cabin and extinguished the light. The cabin was nearly filled with water. Mr. Griswold came toward me and said: "Mrs. Harris, you had better get the ladies, Miss Haines and Miss Henry, into your room, theirs is fast filling with water."

I entreated him to bring them in, and to their incessant cries of "Can nothing be done to save us?" Mr. Davis replied, "If Mrs. Harris will consent to my leaving you, I will go on deck and see if anything can possibly be done." I quickly withdrew my hand and urged him to go.

They now discovered that we were not, as had been apprehended, on the shoals of Cape Hatteras, but near the beach, though at such a distance they could not jump on it. The breakers ran too high to permit them to swing ashore, and the long-boat had long ago burst from its holdings and floated off. All they could do, therefore, was to cling to the shrouds, though almost dead with the intense cold, in the feeble hope that our situation might be discovered and we receive assistance.

Soon after Mr. Davis left, I begged Mr. Griswold also to go, as he could do nothing for us while below, and, perhaps, on deck, he might be able to do something.

He also went, leaving Miss Henry, Miss Haines, Lydia, my two servants and myself in my state room—every man was then above. Scarce had Mr. Griswold left us when an awful wave rushed in, swept down the cabin stairs, the stove, the bell and every thing in its way. All communication with those on deck seemed now cut off; heavy seas were constantly rushing in upon us and we all thought ourselves drowning. I entreated the dear girls with me to commit their souls to God, before whose tribunal, I thought, they would in a few moments stand. . . .

Not a sound was heard by us from the deck, so loud and awfully roared the breakers, and I verily thought that the captain, sailors and passengers had all been swept overboard. I thought we were all alone in the shattered vessel, and at such a distance from any human beings that we could not be descried. . . .

At this instant a heavy sea came over, burst open our door, completely overwhelming us, and for some time I thought we were drowning. My mouth and eyes filled with water; it was a minute or two ere I could speak. I gasped for breath, and as soon as I could give utterance to my thoughts, said, "My dear girls, the next wave will probably seal our fate."

We then sat in awful stupefaction awaiting death, but, O, my sister, it was death in such an awful form! I looked out at the door—naught could be seen but the awful breakers rolling over the remains of the vessel and smoking like a vast building in flames. The cabin was several feet deep in water, on which were floating trunks, baskets, mattresses and bedding. Crash! crash! went the broken vessel continually. The hold broke open with violence, and boxes, barrels, etc., were bursting out. The berth in which we sat began filling with water; the planks beneath our feet began to separate, displaying the roaring waves, which seemed gaping to swallow us. . . .

Upwards of an hour we remained in this state—a state of horror which no pen, no tongue can describe. One must have been in a similar situation to have any adequate idea of what we endured; our bodily anguish was lost in the agony of mind.

At length, when hope was extinct, when we had nearly ceased to think of this world, and bent our eyes only on eternity, another wave burst open the door and Miss Haines rapturously exclaimed, "Oh, there is a man coming to our relief!" I thought she was deceiving herself, and trembled for her mistake; but in an instant a large, intrepid negro was seen by us all making his way over the scattered remnants of the vessel to our room—quickly passed on discovering that we were alive (which he had not expected), and made up to the dead-lights, which, with wonderful strength, he pushed out with his arm (although they had withstood the force of so many waves), and then handed Miss Haines, Miss Henry, Lydia, myself and the remaining servant out of the cabin window to some men who stood on the beach to receive us, for we had by this time drifted so near the shore that when the surf retreated the men could run down to the vessel, secure one and retreat before the returning surf endangered their lives. Thus were we all saved—except the mate, a young man, brother of Captain Pike, who, in attempting to swim ashore, was drowned before his brother's eyes while making ineffectual efforts to rescue him. The remainder of the crew stood on the broken deck, clinging to the shrouds, till the inhabitants of the island ran down and took them. They were so benumbed that they could not stand up. . . .

We were taken with our wet night-clothes on and nearly perished with cold (you recollect how cold it was) to a miserable little hut about a mile from the shore. I was carried like a corpse by two men, one holding my head, the other my feet. My night-cap had been washed from my head, and my long hair trailed on the sand. . . .

And now, my dear sister, how shall I describe our sensations when we were a little revived and found ourselves in safety on land? We thought not of the losses we had sustained, we only lamented poor Pike's untimely fate. . . . The inmates of the wretched dwelling to which we were carried prepared some food for us, but my heart was too full to permit me to eat. The succeeding night four ladies, four sailors and two negroes slept before the same fire—miserable were our accommodations, but we felt only gratitude.

. . . Had the vessel struck one hour sooner, it is said, we must all have perished, as the crew of one that struck a mile from us did. Had I complied with the earnest entreaties of the girls and gone on deck, we must have been drowned, for the men could scarce preserve their hold when the waves beat upon them. They afterwards told me that Captain Pike, in his deep concern for us, once said, "Let us try and get the ladies on deck, they will all perish in the cabin." He ran to the binnacle for this purpose, but was happily prevented by some of the gentlemen. . . . When the vessel struck, her broadside was to the shore, but after the gentlemen were taken off and her main deck had given away, she suddenly turned her stern to the shore. Thus we could be taken through the cabin windows, the only way by which we could be saved. Had we been on the shores of Cape Hatteras (as we at first thought), doubtless we should all have perished, but we struck on the shoals eight miles north of the Cape. The wretches on this island are a disgrace to humanity. I could not have believed that so much depravity was in human beings. Exulting in the calamity which has thrown us among them, though pretending to sympathize in our distress, they would steal the wet clothes which we took from our backs and hung out to dry, and everything belonging to us which they could lay their hands on. They were really a set of harpies watching for their prey, and would actually take it from before our eyes and destitute as we were. Ere we left the island they stripped us of every thing they could.

You, my dear sister, as well as myself, lost a number of valuable articles by our shipwreck, among which were the following: A keg of excellent currant wine, Josephus and some other valuable books, an elegant lace hat and a feather for your beaver, three honeycomb hats for the children, corresponding indispensables, coral and bells for Sarah Kollock, a hat like her mantle, aprons, handkerchiefs, and scarlet cloth capes for the children, dolls, little stockings and kid gloves, a handsome pair of moccasins for Judge Nash, aprons and bombaset frocks for the children, glass for your pictures, garden seed, &c., &c. I lost, besides my trunk of clothes, a large box of books, one of sweetmeats, pickles, bedding, and a number of other articles; but our lives were preserved, and we desire to be thankful for this unmerited mercy.

The Foundering of the USS *Monitor*

WILLIAM FREDERICK KEELER 1863

The Federal warship *Monitor*, whose radical design earned her the nickname "cheese box on a raft" and the contempt of traditionalists, was not designed to be an oceangoing vessel. She was towed from New York City, where she had been built, to her first assignment in Virginia. In a shakedown cruise on Chesapeake Bay, water flooded her engine room and pilothouse and threatened to sink the un-orthodox vessel. After her famous contest with the Confederate ironclad *Virginia* (formerly *Merrimack*), the Federal transport *Rhode Island* towed her south for a new assignment in South Carolina. As the *Monitor* prepared to depart Hampton Roads, her acting paymaster, William F. Keeler, wrote to his wife, "You will not be long without a letter from me & I hope to make it interesting." Unlike sixteen of his shipmates, Keeler survived the sinking of the *Monitor* off Cape Hatteras to keep this promise. His account of the last hours of the *Monitor* is reproduced below from a volume of his letters not published until a century later.

Washington, D.C.
Jan'y 6th, 1863

Dear Anna,

Another chapter has been added to my eventful life. The *Monitor* is no more. What the fire of the enemy failed to do, the elements have accomplished.

We left Hampton Roads Monday afternoon (Dec. 29th) at 2 o'clock in tow of the side wheel gun boat *Rhode Island*. We were attached to her by means of two large hawsers, one 11 inches, the other 15 inches in circumference and from 250 to 300 feet in length.

Everything passed quietly & pleasantly that afternoon & evening; a smooth sea & clear skies seemed to promise a successful termination of our trip & an opportunity of once more trying our metal against rebel works & making the "Little *Monitor*" once again a household word.

Tuesday morning cloud banks were seen rising in the South & West & they gradually increased till the sun was obscured by their cold grey mantle. The wind which in the morning was quite light continued to increase till the middle of the afternoon when it blew quite heavy, the sea rolling with violence across our deck rendering it impossible to remain on it without danger of being swept off.

We amused ourselves for an hour or more by watching two or three large sharks who glided quietly along by our sides observing us apparently with a curious eye as if in anticipation of a feast. We made no water of consequence; a little trickled down about the pilot house & some began to find its way under the turret rendering it wet & cheerless below.

At 5 o'clock P.M. we sat down to dinner, every one cheerful & happy though the sea was rolling & foaming over our heads the laugh & jest passed freely 'round; all rejoicing that at last our monotonous, inactive life had ended & the "gallant little *Monitor*" would soon add fresh laurels to her name.

It was dark when I returned to the top of the turret. We were now off Hatteras, the Cape Horn of our Atlantic coast. The wind was blowing violently; the heavy seas rolled over our bows dashing against the pilot house &, surging aft, would strike the solid turret with a force to make it tremble, sending off on either side a boiling, foaming torrent of water.

Word came from the engine room that we were making water, more than the ordinary pumps (which had been kept working) would throw out; it sounded ominously.

Orders were given to start the Worthington pump, which for a time kept the water down, but again the report, "the water is gaining on us, Sir."

As a last resort the large centrifugal pump, of a capacity of three thousand gallons per minute, was started & once more the water diminished, but it was of short duration.

The opening through which the water was rushing was rapidly enlarged by the constant beating of the sea, which was now at times rolling over the top of the turret. Again came the report that the water was gaining & had risen above the engine room floor.

It was the death knell of the *Monitor*. The storm continued to increase in fury.

In order to understand our situation & contrast it with our passage from New York to Hampton Roads last spring, it will be necessary to bear in mind that in the latter case "the sea was on our beam" as sailors term it, that is, the waves would come up on our side, rolling onto us on one side & off on the other.

Now we were going "head on," or in other words were crossing them at right angles. As we were unable to carry our boats at sea they had been sent on board the *Rhode Island* & nothing whatever remained to support us in the water, were we obliged to trust ourselves to the treacherous element.

But our brave little craft struggled long & well. Now her bow would rise on a huge billow & before she could sink into the intervening hollow, the succeeding wave would strike her under her heavy armour with a report like thunder & a violence that threatened to tear apart the thin sheet iron bottom & the heavy armour which it supported.

Then she would slide down a watery mountain into the hollow beyond & plunging her bow into the black rolling billow would go down, down, down, under the surging wave till naught could be seen but the top of the black "cheese box" isolated in a sea of hissing, seething foam, extending as far as we could see around us. Then as she rose slowly & sullenly under the accumulated weight of waters, the foam pouring in broad sheets off the iron deck, a wave would roll over the bow & strike the pilot house with a force that would send the water in torrents on to the top of the turret, where our little company were gathered.

From behind the iron breastwork which surmounted the top of the turret, a circle of anxious faces were gazing over the expanse of angry waters & awaiting with anxiety the report from the pumps. It came as I have stated.

About this time too it was found our smaller hawser had parted; a disaster which no human agency could remedy; as well might one stand under Niagara, as to attempt to breast the waves which were rolling over our decks.

It was with the greatest reluctance that our Captain now gave the order to make the signal for assistance.

Every pump was at work & gangs of men had been organised to bail, more however with the design of keeping them employed & preventing a panic, than with the hope of any good result. The water was already a foot deep on the engine room floor & was fast deepening in the Ward Room. From its rapid influx it was very evident that but a short time would elapse before it would reach the fires & then the iron heart of the *Monitor* would cease to beat.

Every expedient which human ingenuity or skill could suggest had been tried in vain & all that remained was to save the lives of those on board.

At the order our signal flashed upon the darkness, lighting up the tumultuous sea for miles around. Our consort stopped & attempted to come alongside, but with the two vessels connected with the hawser it was found impossible.

At the call for a volunteer to go forward & cut it (a task involving almost certain destruction), one of our officers seized a hatchet & going cautiously forward holding on the life line, which was stretched around the deck, with a few blows severed the connection while the waves were rolling high over his head & returned in safety to the turret.

We hailed our consort as soon as sufficiently near, "Send your boats immediately, we are sinking." A hoarse unintelligible reply was all that we could get amid the roar of the elements. Again & again it was repeated & signal after signal flashed out amid the storm as we saw no sign of boats, & the same unintelligible response induced us to believe that they understood neither our signals or our hail.

Words cannot depict the agony of those moments as our little company gathered on the top of the turret, stood with a mass of sinking iron beneath them, gazing through the dim light, over the raging waters with an anxiety amounting almost to agony for some evidence of succor from the only source to which we could look for relief. Seconds lengthened into hours & minutes into years.

About this time the report was brought from the engine room that the water had reached the furnaces & the fires were being extinguished. Our Commander's orders were given calmly & coolly & met with a ready & cheerful response from officers & men; no one faltered in obedience, but a ready aye, aye sir, met every order. Some however obeyed mechanically, while others worked coolly & resolutely as if realising that our safety depended upon the prompt & ready execution of every order.

After an hour that seemed an eternity to us, boats were seen approaching; what a load was taken from our anxious hearts—with what interest we watched as they toiled & struggled slowly over the heavy seas, now hidden from our sight in a watery hollow, then balanced on the foaming crest of a mountain wave.

Hoping to be able to get off in one of the approaching boats & to take with me the books & accounts of the vessel, I started for my State room to gather them up. I passed down the turret ladder, felt my way around the guns & making a mis-step fell from the top of the berthdeck ladder to the deck below.

A dim lantern swinging to & fro with the motion of the vessel, just served to make the nearest objects visible in the thick darkness, rendered more dense if possible by the steam, heat & gas which was finding its way in from the half extinguished fires of the engine room.

I passed across this deck, down into the Ward room, where I found the water nearly to my waist & swashing from side to side with the roll of the ship, & groped my way through the narrow crooked passage into my State room. It was a darkness that could be felt. The hot, stifling, murky atmosphere pervaded every corner.

After groping about for a little time, I collected what books & papers I deemed it important to save, but found they made so large & unmanageable a mass that the attempt to save them would be utterly useless & would only endanger my life, as my whole physical energies would be required to get me safely over the wave washed deck & into the boats.

I took down my watch, which was hanging on a nail near by & putting it in my pocket, took out my safe keys with the intention of saving the Government "green backs." The safe was entirely submerged; in the thick darkness, below the water & from the peculiar form of the lock I was unable to insert the key. I desisted from the attempt & started to return.

My feelings at this time it is impossible to describe, when I reflected that I was nearly at the fartherest extremity of the vessel from its only outlet & this outlet liable to be completely obstructed at any moment by a rush of panic stricken men, & the vessel itself momentarily expected to give the final plunge.

Everything was enveloped in a thick murky darkness, the waves dashing violently across the deck over my head; my retreat to be made through the narrow crooked passage leading to my room; through the Ward room where the chairs & tables were surging violently from side to side, threatening severe bruises if not broken limbs; then up a ladder to the berth deck; across that & up another ladder into the turret; around the guns & over gun tackle, shot, sponges & rammers which had broken loose from their fastenings, & up the last ladder to the top of the turret.

I reached the goal & found our consort close alongside, so near in fact, that I expected every instant to see her thrown against our iron side, & both vessels go down together.

Her launch was under her quarter & was crashing & grinding most fearfully between the two vessels; its crew had leaped upon our deck to escape being crushed with the boat & for a time it seemed as if we had but received an addition to our imperilled number.

Ropes were thrown from over her bulwarks, which towered far above us but none of the crew seemed to have the courage & resolution to make the perilous passage of the deck & seize them.

Fortunately she remained but a short time in this position; she forged slowly ahead clear of our iron mass, leaving her launch tossing & pitching against our side with a violence that threatened its instant demolition; it was necessary that she should receive her living freight without delay & leave the dangerous spot, but the embarkation was an undertaking of the most perilous nature, as sea after sea was sweeping the deck with resistless violence. Already two or three of our number had been swept off & those who remained seemed to hang back fearing to make the effort.

It was a scene well calculated to appall the boldest heart. Mountains of water were rushing across our decks & foaming along our sides; the small boats were pitching & tossing about on them or crashing against our sides, mere playthings on the billows; the howling of the tempest, the roar & dash of waters; the hoarse orders through the speaking trumpets of the officers; the response of the men; the shouts of encouragement & words of caution:

"the bubbling cry
Of some strong Swimmer in his agony";

& the whole scene lit up by the ghastly glare of the blue lights burning on our consort, formed a panorama of horror which time can never efface from my memory.

Upon the order from Capt. B. to "lead the men to the boats," I divested myself of the greater portion of my clothing to afford me greater facilities for swimming in case of necessity & attempted to descend the ladder leading down the outside of the turret, but found it full of men hesitating but desiring to make the perilous passage of the deck.

I found a rope hanging from one of the awning stanchions over my head & slid down it to the deck. A huge wave passed over me tearing me from my footing & bearing me along with it, rolling, tumbling & tossing like the merest speck. I was carried as near as I could judge ten or twelve yards from the vessel when I came to the surface & the back-set of the wave threw me against the vessel's side near one of the iron stanchions which supported the life line; this I grasped with all the energy of desperation & drawing myself on deck worked my way along the life line & was hauled into the boat, into which the men were jumping one by one as they could venture across the deck.

We were soon loaded and shoved off but our dangers were not yet over. We were in a leaky, overloaded boat, through whose crushed sides the water was rushing in streams & had nearly half a mile to row over the storm tossed sea before we could reach the *Rhode Island*.

This, after a hard long struggle, was accomplished & we found ourselves under the weather quarter of our consort in imminent danger of being swamped as she sunk in the hollow of the sea. The ends of ropes were thrown to us from the high bulwarks over our heads, which the more active of our number seized & climbed up; others grasped them firmly & were thus drawn over the side.

In my exhausted state & with my crippled hand I could do neither of these, but watching my opportunity till I saw a loop, or what a sailor would call a bight of a rope, let down, I passed it under my arms & was drawn on board the *Rhode Island* to receive the congratulations & hospitalities of her officers, & I assure you they were not deficient in either.

Other boats soon came alongside bringing the remainder of our officers & crew & a little before one o'clock on the morning of the 31st the *Monitor* disappeared beneath the surface.

On mustering the officers & crew, four officers & twelve of the crew were missing. Those who escaped did so without receiving any serious injury with the exception of our surgeon, whose fingers on one hand were so badly mashed by being caught between the boats as to render partial amputation necessary.

One of the *Rhode Island*'s boats was still absent & we spent the remainder of the night & the next day in search of it, when we proceeded to Wilmington where the vessel was ordered; from there we were ordered to Beaufort & thence to Hampton Roads where we received every kindness & hospitality that friendship & our destitute condition could suggest.

During all the time we were standing on the sinking ship, & while whirling over & over in the water, I am not aware that the idea occurred to me that I might be lost. Although I fully realised the danger, I looked forward with just as much confidence to being saved as if it were a fact already established.

When we left Hampton Roads we felt convinced that if we should encounter a severe gale we should go to the bottom & had it not been for shewing a want of confidence in our vessel & a tendency to create a panic among the men, all the officers would have transferred their effects to the *Rhode Island*: as it was we got on board of her perfectly destitute & had it not been for the kindness & generosity of her officers we should have fared poorly indeed.

I still hope to visit Charleston in an iron clad.

Yours truly,
W. F. Keeler

The Wreck of the USS Huron

JOE A. MOBLEY 1877

In 1874 the U.S. Lifesaving Service opened its first seven stations on the North Carolina coast, extending from Currituck Beach to Little Kinnakeet. They were too widely spaced to offer punctual help to most vessels in distress, and were manned only from December 1 to March 31 with an inadequate complement driven to exhaustion by constantly maintaining the watch in their lookout towers and patrolling the beach. Lacking horses, the early lifesavers often wore themselves out pushing and pulling heavy equipment through deep sand before making their first attempt at a rescue. In addition, almost as soon as these stations were in operation, complaints were heard about political appointees—surfmen, and even keepers, lacking in maritime experience and knowledge. Disaster was inevitable and not long in coming.

In November 1877, ninety-eight men died when the USS Huron ran aground and broke up a few miles from the unmanned Nags Head station. The resulting furor caused a rapid reform of the Service and inaugurated a long period of spotty improvements in equipment and staffing. But right up to the absorption of the Service by the newly created Coast Guard in 1915, no station on the North Carolina coast was fully manned twelve months a year.

THE UNITED STATES warship Huron was unique in several ways. She was one of eight new warships, authorized by Congress in 1873, the construction of which marked an end to the nation's "old navy" built of wood and iron. Five of the mandated vessels were wooden gunboats, and three—Alert, Ranger, and Huron—became the last iron warships ever constructed by the United States Navy, which in 1882 began building its ships of steel. The Huron also could claim the distinction of being one of the last United States warships to use both sail and steam power and smoothbore guns.

Workmen laid the keel of the Huron at the Delaware River Shipbuilding Company in Chester, Pennsylvania, in 1873. She was completed and commissioned on November 15, 1875. The navy designated her and her sister ships as third-rate gunboats, meaning that they carried a third less armament than a first-rate ship. As a sloop of war, the 541-ton Huron had iron plating and schooner-rigged sails (although her sail arrangement was scheduled to be changed to a barkentine rig like that of the Alert and Ranger). A two-cylinder, back-acting compound engine supplied her steam power. The Huron's ordnance included five large smoothbore guns, a Gatling gun, and an assortment of small arms. She also carried a number of small boats: two launches, a cutter, a whaleboat, a dinghy, a gig, and two life rafts called balsas.

After commissioning, the *Huron* served two years with the North Atlantic Squadron, as well as in Mexican waters and surveying the northern coast of South America and the islands of the Lesser Antilles. Commander Charles C. Carpenter served as her first captain, and Commander George P. Ryan succeeded him in September 1876. In November 1877 the ship departed New York, where she had been overhauled, bound for Havana, Cuba, with orders "to make a reconnaissance of the coast of Cuba, determining the doubtful points in positions, in coastline and in outlying dangers."

The *Huron* stopped en route at Hampton Roads, Virginia, on November 17 to complete outfitting. While in port, Commander Ryan received word from the secretary of the navy to await the arrival of a draftsman from Washington, D.C., who would assist in the survey of the Cuban coast. The draftsman, John J. Evans, arrived, and the *Huron* got under way on November 23 with 132 men on board. In setting his course southward, Commander Ryan chose to sail close to the North Carolina shoreline to avoid traveling against the Gulf Stream or taking the time-consuming and longer alternative of going out beyond the stream. As in so many cases off the coast of the Old North State, that decision proved fatal.

Like an ominous precursor of disastrous events, a storm with gale-force winds struck in late afternoon and tore away the *Huron*'s staysail, forcing the crew to set a storm sail and reef up most of the other sails. After passing Currituck Lighthouse and before reaching Bodie Island light, the officers on duty—hindered by darkness, rough seas, and dense fog—failed to vary their course accurately according to the configuration of the North Carolina coastline. As a result, the *Huron* ran too close to the shore and suddenly, without warning, struck hard aground near Nags Head.

At first the officers thought that they had struck a shoal-covered wreck eight to ten miles out to sea. None realized how close to the beach their vessel really was until it was too late. When he finally saw the North Carolina coastline through the fog, Commander Ryan cried, "My God! How did we get in here?!"

In the midst of howling winds and crushing waves breaking over the steamer's decks, an attempt to back her off the shoal failed. Water poured into the engine room as collapsing spars and rigging fell through the hatch covers. The crew rushed to put the cutter overboard, but damage to its hull quickly sank it. Some of the sailors tried without much success to cut away the sails and masts and throw the guns into the water to lighten the ship in the hope that she would drift off the shoal that imprisoned her. The shooting of flares to summon help from the beach produced no response as the violent waves continued to beat upon the vessel unmercifully. The Huron ultimately turned at an angle on her port side, and the majority of the crew "gathered together on the upper side of the forecastle, suffering much from the cold and exposure." Others hung or lashed themselves to rigging and the bowsprit. Commander Ryan and a subordinate officer perished when they unsuccessfully attempted to launch another lifeboat. The tremendous swells churning across the deck continued to tear away the grips of the clutching sailors and hurl them to their deaths.

The hopes of the wretched crew rose when just before dawn on November 24 they sighted a moving light on shore. They shouted with all that was in them both in jubilation and in an effort to summon their anticipated rescuers. Their hopes were soon dashed, however, for the light belonged merely to some fishermen who had earlier spotted the flares fired from the Huron and walked to the beach to investigate. But without lifesaving equipment the people ashore had no means to launch a rescue and could only stand by and watch the horrible scene unfold.

The ultimate and tragic irony was that the Nags Head Lifesaving Station stood only two-and-one-half miles south of the disaster. But in keeping with the Lifesaving Service's then current operating procedure, it remained closed and locked until the next month, when the active season began. The keeper apparently was at his home on Roanoke Island. The local inhabitants had no authority to break into the station to obtain the beach apparatus and had no training in its operation, even if they had tried to use it.

Sunrise found the Huron survivors still huddled in the forecastle or clinging to halyards, spars, rigging, or the bowsprit. But as they grew more fatigued and the cruel sea fiercer in its attack on the wreck, more of them lost their lives to the unrelenting bombardment of wind and water. Almost every wave breaking over the vessel washed someone overboard, tumbling the helpless victims head over heels like rag dolls before finally drowning them.

Growing higher and higher, the seas carried executive officer S. A. Simmons over the side twice, and both times he clambered back aboard. Then, as if in angry retaliation for his tenacity, a third surge tossed him from his perch and drowned him. Sweeping over the entire ship, one large wave snatched away and drowned twelve men at once.

The seas around the wreck continued to climb, swelling from six to eight feet in depth. Realizing that the ship soon would be entirely swamped and that no help was likely from shore, Ensign Lucien Young called for volunteers to help him launch the one balsa remaining on the littered deck. Amid the wreckage, he and Seaman Antonio Williams eventually wrestled the balsa over the side and crawled down into it. After they cut the three-inch line by which they lowered the raft, they became entangled in the collapsed rigging and were struck several times by the spars as they washed up against the ship. The balsa then drifted toward the stern of the *Huron*, where a heavy surf capsized it. Damaged spars and other wreckage pinned both men underwater and nearly drowned them, but they somehow freed themselves and grasped the raft. They remained in the water and tried to swim and simultaneously steer the balsa to avoid its turning over again, but another large swell tossed them a second time. Ensign Young captured the raft and pushed it toward Williams, who had been thrown about ten feet by the wave. Williams pulled himself into the raft and stood up, looking desperately for a point of reference. The seaman sighted a number of telegraph poles on shore, which he mistook for the masts of fishing boats, and the two men began to steer toward them. They capsized twice more but finally and miraculously hit the beach about three-quarters of a mile north of the *Huron*. Near the site where they landed, Young and Williams discovered two other seamen, alive and lying in the surf, too exhausted to move further. They pulled them on shore, rested briefly, and then hurried down the beach in search of assistance to rescue the sailors remaining on the wreck.

Meanwhile, aboard the *Huron* other members of the crew, realizing that any chance for rescue from shore was fast slipping away, attempted to swim to safety. Cadet Engineer W. T. Warburton lowered himself into the water, where the current immediately seized him. Drifting north, he managed to stay afloat and eventually washed aground about a mile north of the disaster. There a strong undertow caught him and nearly dragged him back out to sea. Luckily two local residents pulled him from the water. Some other sailors, swept from the vessel as seas continued to wash men overboard, reached shore safely. Among the fortunate few to make it alive was Master William P. Conway. Williams and Young encountered him emerging from the surf as they hurried along the beach toward the group of locals gathered to view the wreck. The ensign asked the bystanders to patrol along the shoreline to look for victims who might make the beach and assist them if possible. He also dispatched a rider on horseback to the telegraph station at Kitty Hawk to send a message to Washington for help from the navy. It was then about seven o'clock in the morning.

Young asked the Bankers why they had not used the lifesaving equipment at the station to aid the *Huron* crew. They responded that they found the station locked and were afraid to break into it without official permission. Young then persuaded five volunteers to go with him to the station. They broke into the building and dragged out the beach apparatus equipment, which they placed in the horse-drawn cart of Dare County Sheriff Brinkley, who had just arrived at the site. Back on the wreck the mainmast fell across the smokestack and into the water. Then two other crewmen, Master W. S. French and Captain of Guard Michael Trainor, attempted to swim to safety. Trainor reached the beach, where two men pulled him from the water. French, however, disappeared, and his body was never recovered.

Ensign Young, Sheriff Brinkley, and the volunteers did not arrive at the scene of the wreck until about eleven o'clock. As they drew near, they saw the mizzenmast fall. No one alive remained aboard the vessel, which was almost completely submerged. Sometime in perhaps late morning or early afternoon Nags Head keeper B. F. Meekins, who had been summoned from Roanoke Island, arrived at the site. "On Saturday morning, November 24, 1877," Meekins later reported, "I was informed that a man-of-war was wrecked on the coast about three miles above my station. I hastened to the wreck and summoned T. T. Toler, J. T. Wescott, W. W. Dough, James Howard, Willis Tillett and Bannister Gray for my crew and was soon ready for action." Whatever time Meekins and his men finally arrived, there remained nothing to be done but to search for victims in the surf and care for the survivors. Meekins subsequently recorded in his log that his lifesavers helped to resuscitate three sailors from near death. For a while, the exhausted and battered survivors lay exposed on the beach. The bodies of the recovered dead were laid in a row. Persons on the beach began helping the still-living victims to a nearby fishing shack, where a fire and blankets warmed them. Cadet Engineer Warburton later recalled: "I was taken to a shanty, where I found a fire lighted and a dry blanket. . . . I had no idea how long I was in the water. I was so bruised that I couldn't move when I got ashore and was obliged to remain in the shanty 'til later in the afternoon. When Mr. Conway decided to move the party to the lifesaving station, I was carried in Sheriff Brinkley's cart."

As Sheriff Brinkley transported the men to Nags Head Station, they were provided with food, clothing, and bedding. The surfmen and volunteers continued to search for more survivors and bodies. Their efforts ultimately revealed that of the 132 men who had left Hampton Roads aboard the Huron on November 23 only 34 remained alive. The four officers—Young, Conway, Warburton, and Assistant Engineer R. G. Denig—spent the night of the twenty-fourth at Brinkley's house, and the thirty crewmen stayed at the lifesaving station.

In the meantime the distress message sent by the United States Signal Service operator at Kitty Hawk to Norfolk and Washington had excited a response from the Navy Department, which telegraphed Baker Brothers, a Norfolk wrecking company, to dispatch their wrecking steamer B & J Baker to Nags Head. The navy also ordered three of its steamers—Swatara, Powhatan, and Fortune—to the scene.

The ships arrived off Nags Head early on the morning of the twenty-fifth. Aboard the B & J Baker was John J. Guthrie, superintendent of District No. 6, who had hastily departed his headquarters at Portsmouth, Virginia, and joined the vessel at Old Point Comfort. The wrecking ship's passengers also included

Henry L. Brooke, a reporter for the Norfolk *Virginian*. The steamers remained off-shore for a considerable time because the rough waves and surf made a landing with a boat too hazardous. But at three o'clock in the afternoon Captain E. M. Stoddard, commanding the B & J *Baker*, ordered a boat lowered over the side. The launch carried Stoddard, Guthrie, Brooke, six seamen as oarsmen, and Stoddard's dog. Once under way, the boat made toward the beach in "good style" until it reached a point about one hundred yards south of the *Huron* and two hundred yards from the shore. There it surmounted a huge wave and "shot ahead." A second large breaker, however, arose behind and overtook the launch and "in a twinkling hoisted the surfboat broadside on, and catching it on the crest of the waves, threw it bottom upwards about ten feet in the air."

Stoddard, Brooke, and a seaman managed to catch hold of the capsized boat and held on until dragged through the surf to the beach. Another of the oarsmen managed to swim to shore and the frightened dog swam back to the B & J *Baker*. But Guthrie and four seamen drowned, thus bringing the death toll of the *Huron* incident to 103.

Fortunately for the *Huron* survivors, a naval relief party with supplies and medical assistance had arrived about one o'clock, via the inland canal from Norfolk. Even earlier the small steamer *Bonita* had tied up on the sound side of Nags Head, and its captain offered to take the victims to Norfolk. Late in the afternoon the battered and bedraggled survivors—some walking, others riding in carts—crossed over from the ocean side to a wharf on the sound, boarded the *Bonita*, and departed for Norfolk, leaving behind the corpses of many of their comrades.

For a number of days after the wreck of the *Huron*, bodies continued to wash ashore along the North Carolina and Virginia coasts, some more than thirty miles away. Search parties temporarily buried some of the deceased. Keeper B. F. Meekins of Nags Head Station noted that "the bodies who were thrown on shore by the waves were taken the best care of possible. There were two bodies lashed to the wreck. These I took off and buried."

On November 27 Lieutenant Commander J. G. Greene and a naval detachment arrived at Nags Head and began retrieving and preparing for shipment to permanent burial sites the corpses of the drowned *Huron* crew. Their task lasted two weeks. Deterioration and the loss of personal effects by the victims made their job difficult. Only tattoos identified some of the sailors whose features had badly decomposed.

A public outcry followed the *Huron* catastrophe. Many of the leading East Coast newspapers recounted the grisly details of the incident and began attacking the Lifesaving Service for a lack of professionalism and diligence in North Carolina. "The disaster might have been greatly lessened had our lifesaving station been what it should have been," declared a Boston editorialist. "This branch of our service has proved to be sadly weak and undisciplined, and more organization is needed all along the coast." How was it, some newspapers asked, that such a tremendous loss of life occurred only a short distance from a lifesaving station? "The ship struck within two hundred yards of the shore, and two miles of a life-saving station that was one in name and name only," the Norfolk *Virginian* angrily noted. That the stations were not even opened for the year and would not be opened for another week when the *Huron* went down especially engendered alarm and concern among members of the press and their readers. Editors immediately began calling for a longer active season. The Elizabeth City *Economist* complained: "The ill-fated *Huron* teaches us that the 1st of December is too late for the commencement of the duties of the Lifesaving Service. In the name of humanity . . . let the service begin on the first day of November." The Norfolk *Landmark* went even further and proclaimed: "The crews should be on duty all year, had the station been manned . . . all of the [*Huron's*] officers and men would in all probability be living today." The *Virginian* sarcastically observed that

> unfortunately for them the government of their country had decided that no shipwreck occurring before the first of December should be expected or provided for. . . . Had the station in the vicinity of which the *Huron* struck been properly manned and in efficient working order, there is little doubt that many, perhaps all, of the lost might have been saved from the wreck. As it was, for hours the poor fellows battled for life against the sea, in sight of a government institution ordained for the purpose of their rescue, while no rescue came. . . . If our vessels and our merchants are expected to navigate our coast the year round, why in the name of common sense are the means intended for their assistance limited to one-half the year? The lesson taught is a grievous one. It convicts some one, whether Congress or the Executive Department, of a grievous blunder, one that has brought sorrow and desolation to a hundred homes.

In response to such outcries, the Lifesaving Service could only plead a lack of funding to establish a sufficient number of stations, opened for adequate periods, and to pay for qualified keepers and surfmen and proper equipment and training. Even *Harper's Weekly* expressed dismay at the seeming lack of preparedness displayed by the service. In a December 1877 issue of the magazine, a satirical Thomas Nast cartoon portrayed an exasperated Uncle Sam standing at Nags Head looking over the *Huron* wreck and musing: "I suppose I must spend a little on Lifesaving."

The Wreck of the Bark Josie Troop

ANONYMOUS 1889

By the late 1880s twenty-five Lifesaving Service stations had been commissioned from the Virginia line to Cape Lookout. On average they stood seven miles apart. Surfmen patrolled the beach continuously throughout the active season, most often on foot, in search of vessels in distress. Except during emergencies, nearly every station had two on patrol at a time, one to the north, the other to the south. Surfmen from adjacent stations would meet at a halfway house (usually nothing more than a drafty shack), exchange tokens or punch a clock, then trudge back.

When a surfman spotted a stricken vessel, his first duty was to signal the survivors that help was at hand. His second was to rush back to the station with a firsthand report so that the keeper and crew could respond with the appropriate rescue gear. If the vessel was close to shore and some of the occupants were able-bodied, the lifesavers could fire them a line with a Lyle gun, pass a breeches buoy—a life ring with a canvas seat—and haul them ashore one by one. As the following narrative from the annual report of the Lifesaving Service shows, a breeches-buoy rescue was rarely an uneventful operation.

AN APPALLING disaster, resulting in the loss of eleven lives out of a total crew of seventeen, was that to the British bark Josie Troop, of Saint John, New Brunswick, February 22, 1889, which occurred a short distance south of the Chicamicomico Station, (Sixth District,) coast of North Carolina.

At about half-past 7 o'clock in the evening of the date named, as the north patrolman was returning over the beach on horseback he discovered the bark in the breakers. Putting spurs to his horse he dashed up to the station, which was between him and the vessel, alarmed the lifesaving crew, then galloped on down the shore and burned two Coston signals to apprise the people on board that assistance was close at hand.

The wind was blowing fresh from the north-northwest with a furious sea running, making an impassable surf along the beach. The station crew immediately ran out the apparatus cart, summoned by telephone the men of the adjacent stations, and in twenty minutes time had their gear opposite the vessel. She was lying, as near as could be judged, between five and six hundred yards from the beach, head on, but slowly swinging broadside to, and working to the southward. A tar barrel was aflame near the forecastle and a torch was burning on the poop deck. The gun was at once placed in position and efforts were made to reach the bark with shot-lines, but they fell short owing to her extreme distance from the shore, until but one line remained of the supply the lifesavers had with them. The keeper dispatched a surfman to the station with the horse and cart, with directions to bring to the scene all the shot-lines in store. In the meantime the company, reinforced by the crews of the two adjacent stations and a number of people from the neighboring hamlet of Chicamicomico, followed the rapidly disintegrating craft as she pounded through the heavy breakers down the beach, and when the cart returned made several further attempts to throw lines over her but to no purpose. Finally the vessel came within range of the smallest line in use, which was fired off, but before the report of the gun had died away the mainmast fell with a crash, the lights on board were extinguished, and utter darkness closed over the scene. The line, however, ran out so rapidly that the beachmen were obliged, in order to prevent its escape altogether, to fasten on another. When the latter was nearly exhausted the strain suddenly ceased and the line came to a standstill. The slack being hauled in it was found that the first line had parted a few feet from its union with the other. It is quite evident that the line fired must have fallen across some part of the wreck, probably the mainmast, and was drawn off when the spar went over the side.

It was now between 10 and 11 o'clock at night. The life-savers, discouraged, unable to get even a glimpse of the distressed vessel, and hearing no sound from her, were fearful that the fall of the mainmast betokened a complete collapse. Large quantities of wreckage coming ashore south of the scene of operations seemingly confirmed this apprehension. All the men, except enough to successfully work the apparatus if occasion required, were sent down the beach to render prompt assistance to any that might possibly wash in from the wreck. This patrol was kept up for a distance of two miles, during the entire night, without result.

The keeper with his chosen assistants remained opposite the spot where the bark had disappeared, vainly straining their eyes to obtain even a shadowy outline of her. Finally, at about 2 o'clock in the morning (23d), a portion of the after part of the vessel (which latter, it appears, had by this time broken into three pieces), consisting largely of the upper works, suddenly loomed into view within two hundred yards of the beach. As quickly as possible a line was fired across it. The whip was at once hauled off and made fast to the stump of the mizzenmast, after which the hawser was sent aboard and set up. Then the six sailors who had taken refuge on the top of the after cabin were conveyed ashore in the breeches-buoy. The first man rescued had his throat cut, his head badly battered by some blunt instrument, and his feet gashed. It was subsequently ascertained that the wounds were self-inflicted in a frenzy of fear of death by drowning. The shipwrecked men were conducted to the station and cared for, while the life-savers kept watch on the beach in hope of being able to succor others of the crew. This hope, however, was dispelled, as the light of day slowly brought into view all the parts of the vessel, except a portion of the hull, strewn in fragments along the shore. The bottom of the hull, buried under its load of chalk, remained where the vessel had finally fetched up and gone to pieces.

From the testimony of the survivors it was learned that the bark was bound from London, England, to Philadelphia, Pennsylvania, by the southern trade-wind passage, with a cargo of seventeen hundred tons of chalk. Some days prior to the disaster she had encountered thick and stormy weather, the last observation to determine her position having been taken February 17th. Since that time she had been run by dead reckoning. In the forenoon of the 22d, while the vessel was being kept to the westward, the captain, thinking that he was nearing the North Carolina coast, and expecting by midnight to raise the Cape Hatteras or some more northerly light, took soundings which resulted in an ascertained depth of twenty-five fathoms. The bark was immediately put about on the off-shore tack and a course shaped to the northeastward until some time in the afternoon. During this run she logged not more than twelve miles. The craft was then worn round and steered to the westward until she struck. The lead had not been used while standing inshore. Orders had been given to tack ship at 8 o'clock in the evening, but forty minutes before that hour she was in the breakers, when, according to the captain's calculations, she should have been thirty-six miles at sea. A tar barrel and some oakum were then ignited, and as soon as the answering signals on shore were seen the men were got aft to the cabin by the first mate and steward, who considered it the safest part of the vessel and clear of the seas that were sweeping the forward decks with great force. Ten minutes after the bark stranded she gave a heavy lurch, and the captain, who was trying to clear away one of the boats, was washed overboard. As time passed and none of the lines fired by the life-savers came aboard ten of the crew stole forward, where the large open boats were kept. No sooner had they done so than the mainmast went over the side and the craft began to break up amidships, thus cutting off all communication between the two groups of men. It is quite certain that those forward were carried overboard with the foremast, upon which they had sought refuge. This fell at about 1 o'clock in the morning. The vessel finally broke up and the first mate and his five companions were rescued from the cabin in the manner already described.

All the evidence gathered by the investigating officer concerning this affair, which included sworn statements of the survivors, the keepers and the station crews, and a number of citizen eye-witnesses, shows that everything was done that human ingenuity could devise to save the lives so unnecessarily sacrificed that night off Chicamicomico. Had the lead been used continuously from the time the vessel was first found to be in twenty-five fathoms of water until the light of which they were in search had been sighted, it would not now be necessary to record in these columns the wreck of the *Josie Troop* and the melancholy loss of the captain and ten of her crew. It is probable that to the neglect of this, the most important duty of the navigator when approaching land, is attributable the loss of more life and property than to any other of the many causes of shipwreck by stranding.

As soon as possible after the men were taken from the wreck the keeper of the Nag's Head station was requested by telephone to send a boat at once to Manteo for a physician. This was done, and by using a relay of station horses he was enabled to reach Chicamicomico early in the afternoon. The wounded man's throat was sewed up, and his bruises were dressed, as were those of the other men. The sailors were kept at the station and cared for as well as the facilities of the place admitted of until the morning of March 3d—eight days—when they were put aboard a small schooner chartered by the superintendent of the district, acting for the British consul at Norfolk, Virginia, for transportation to that city. It was learned that the wounded seaman bore the trip without disadvantage and that there was every promise of his ultimate recovery. All attested the unvarying kindness shown them while at the station. The following statement, expressing their gratitude and praise of the work of the lifesaving crew, was handed to the keeper:

CHICAMICOMICO STATION, March 2, 1889.

This is to certify that in my opinion the captain and crew of this station, assisted by the captains and crews of New Inlet and Gull Shoal stations, did all in their power to save the lives of myself and crew of the bark *Josie Troop*, which went ashore here on the night of February 22. It would have been impossible for any crew of men to have done more. Also for the kind treatment we have received from Captain J. H. Wescott and his crew during our stay here, their kind attention to the injured men (the steward and seamen) being beyond praise. In fact, the kindness of all the officers is beyond description and a credit to the nation they are serving. Their conduct throughout is beyond commendation and will never be effaced from our memory.

Yours truly,
ROBERT E. HUNTER,
First Mate, Barque *Josie Troop*,
Saint John, New Brunswick.

Wreck of the Schooner *Sarah D. J. Rawson*

ANONYMOUS 1905

The U.S. Lifesaving Service, never a branch of the armed forces, had its own medal of honor authorized by Congress in 1874. In fact, it had two medals, one gold and the other silver, to be awarded for "extreme and heroic daring in saving life from the perils of the sea." Lifesavers stationed on the Outer Banks received more than their share of these prestigious awards, but none deserved such recognition more than the men of the Cape Lookout station who responded to the wreck of the schooner *Sarah D. J. Rawson* on the dangerous outer reaches of Lookout Shoals on February 10, 1905. While saving the lives of her crewmen, the lifesavers endured twenty-eight hours of extreme privation at the oars of their open lifeboat. For the "unflinching heroism" extolled in the annual report of the service, from which the following piece is taken, Joe Salter, Bill Salter, Jim Salter, Bob Salter, Herman Salter, Horatio Salter, Ben Salter, and Keeper Adam Salter received gold medals.

THE THREE-MASTED schooner *Sarah D. J. Rawson*, of 387 gross tons burden, and carrying a crew of 7 men, all told, sailed from Georgetown, South Carolina, for New York, with a full cargo of lumber, on February 2, 1905. At 5.30 P.M. of the 9th, following, while standing to the northward under short canvas in a SSE. gale, with a thick fog and rough sea, the vessel stranded in the breakers on the south side of Lookout Shoals, and, with her cargo, became a total loss.

As soon as the schooner struck the master gave orders to take in sail. While the crew were performing this work, a heavy sea swept the decks, carrying Jacob Hansen, a Norwegian seaman, into the raging surf, where he soon disappeared and was seen no more. The same sea struck the master and 3 other seamen, and it was only by the most desperate efforts that they were able to cling to the vessel. The schooner gradually worked up on the shoal and lay somewhat easier, but the violent onslaughts of the seas breaking over her soon carried away her boat, together with deck houses fore and aft, started her deck load of lumber, and her spars began to fall. The crew, powerless to do anything for the vessel, sought refuge in the highest part of the wreck, their situation gloomy and almost hopeless.

At Cape Lookout Life-Saving Station, about 9 miles N. by W. from the place of the disaster, a vigilant lookout had been maintained during the day, the keeper in person visiting the tower during the morning and forenoon, and a surfman constantly on watch, but a thick mantle of fog covered the ocean, shutting the doomed vessel from view. At noon, just as the lookout had been relieved, the keeper again climbed into the tower, and at 12.05 P.M., while scanning the sea with the glasses, he caught, through a rift in the fog, a glimpse of the schooner's topmost spars. Knowing from her bearings that she probably was upon the shoal, he immediately called away the lifeboat, every member of the crew promptly responding.

Though the testimony taken in this case shows that the men were nearly all more or less ill, there having been an epidemic of influenza at the station, not one shrank from what all knew must at best be a long and wearisome pull in wintry weather over 18 miles of rough sea. The wind being favorable, a light WSW. breeze, the surfmen made sail, and with 8 men at the oars were off to the wreck within twenty-five minutes of the time it was discovered by the keeper, and at 4 P.M. reached the scene of the disaster. The schooner lay upon her starboard side in the midst of a seething mass of breakers, her bowsprit, foremast, main topmast, and deck houses fore and aft gone, and her stern to the mizzen rigging carried away. She was surrounded by wreckage and lumber, which, pitching and beating about in the breakers, threatened the safety of the lifeboat and the lives of its crew. The crew of the *Rawson*, 6 in number, could be seen by the surfmen, and though the latter repeatedly attempted to make their way through the mass of débris, they could not approach the wreck nearer than about 200 yards, when they would be beaten back. The master of the schooner, watching his would-be rescuers, stated that he momentarily expected to see the lifeboat pitched end over end in the turbulent sea, and this, without doubt, would have occurred, but for the cool and skillful management of the keeper and crew.

Night soon came on and the lifesaving crew anchored near the edge of the breakers, hoping, as stated by the keeper, that in case of the schooner's going to pieces they still might be able to rescue some or all of the sailors. They maintained a vigilant lookout, frequently fending off fragments of wreckage that menaced their boat, until after midnight, when the wind increased in force, hauling to NW. with the weather still thick, and much colder. The crew then shifted the lifeboat to an anchorage about 500 yards to windward, in order, as the keeper states, that should worst come to worst they might be able to weather the shoal and put to sea. Throughout the long, tedious night the surf men suffered greatly in their open boat from exposure, fatigue, and hunger, but the keeper maintained his post, giving encouragement to his crew, and urging them not to fall asleep, for fear of disastrous results in their debilitated condition.

At dawn they returned to the wreck and found that, while her remaining masts had gone by the board, a portion of the hull remained intact, and the crew had survived the perils of the night. The sea was still running very high, and the keeper decided to defer the attempt to rescue the crew until the tide turned, when he rightly judged that conditions would improve. At about 11 A.M. the wind and sea moderated somewhat, and the life-savers pulled to a position about fifty yards to windward of the wreck . . . and anchored. By veering carefully upon the cable, and steadying the boat with the oars, they dropped in among the breakers and débris as far as possible, and succeeded in throwing a heaving line on board the schooner. Then one of the seamen bent the line about his waist, jumped into the sea, and was hauled into the lifeboat. His companions followed his example, and, one by one, all hands were rescued — drenched, chilled, and nearly exhausted, but safe. The surfmen removed their own oil coats, wrapping them about the shipwrecked men, and without mishap made the return trip to the station, arriving at about 5 P.M. The crew of the *Rawson* had been forty-eight hours without food or water, and the life-saving crew had spent twenty-eight hours in an open boat, without food, and with no other nourishment than cold water, their limbs cramped with cold and the lack of room to move about, and their bodies aching from maintaining so long a sitting posture. That the wrecked crew had not succumbed to their terrible ordeal is doubtless due to the fact that the vessel lay so nearly on her beam ends as to afford them something of a lee from the wintry NW. wind sweeping over them.

The rescued men were furnished food and shelter at the station, also with clothing from the supplies of the Women's National Relief Association, but this stock becoming exhausted the surfmen supplemented it from their own stores. The master of the *Rawson* was cared for part of the time by a personal friend, whom he found in command of the schooner *Lottie W. Russell* at anchor in Lookout Bight. No member of the crew had suffered serious injury, though one seaman was afflicted by an attack of rheumatism and when removed from the station was transported upon a stretcher.

On the 12th instant the revenue cutter *Seminole* arrived in Lookout Bight, and the following day at 2 P.M. took the crew of the *Rawson* on board and carried them to Wilmington, North Carolina.

The loss of one life at this disaster occurred a very short time after the vessel struck, when all hands were in extreme jeopardy, and it was impossible for any-one to lend a helping hand to the drowning man as he was carried to his death in the breakers. Had the weather been clear and the schooner plainly visible from the life-saving station it would have been impossible for the life-savers to reach the scene in time to be of any assistance to the unfortunate seaman.

On the other hand, the keeper without doubt discovered the *Rawson* at the first instant that she became visible at the station. No other eye sighted her, no one but the life-savers went to the rescue; the shipwrecked men lost their boat soon after the vessel struck, and not many hours elapsed after the rescue before the vessel broke up and disappeared. Hence all hands must have been lost, and the fate of the *Sarah D. J. Rawson* and her crew would never have been known but for the un-flinching heroism of the crew of the Cape Lookout Life-Saving Station.

The Ghost Ship Mystery of Diamond Shoals

JOHN HARDEN 1921

Hundreds of ships of all kinds have come to grief in the waters off the Outer Banks. Wind and wave have deposited some on the beach nearly intact, reduced others to flotsam a few tantalizing feet from shore, and beaten others to pieces on shoals far from land. Fires, explosions, structural faults, mechanical failures, torpedoes, and mines have claimed many ships. Mutinous or incompetent crews have added to the toll, as have captains who sailed confidently into closed inlets and uncharted waters. A few ships have simply disappeared at sea, but of all the mischances that have ever occurred on or near the Outer Banks, none is so strange as that which befell the *Carroll M. Deering*.

John Harden, while serving as executive secretary to Governor R. Gregg Cherry in the 1940s, collected unusual stories and broadcast them in a radio program called "Tales of Tarheelia" over a Raleigh radio station. In the following piece, based on one of his programs and published in 1949 as part of *The Devil's Tramping Ground and Other Stories*, Harden deals with the most baffling shipwreck in the history of the Outer Banks.

MANY WEIRD puzzles exist in the seafaring history of Eastern North Carolina. Legends of ships and men abound along our colorful Tar Heel coast country. For the locale of this ghost ship mystery we go to the Hatteras section of the Outer Banks, long known to the men of the sea as "the graveyard of ships."

It was a midwinter morning in February, 1921, and the gray light of a waking dawn edged up over the rim of the Atlantic. The first rays pointed ominously to North Carolina's Cape Hatteras shore. There, on the outer Diamond Shoals — dreaded by seamen the world over — was a strange sight. A five-masted schooner, under full sail with her prow cut deep in the sand, was heaving mightily against the restraining land.

The morning watch at the near-by Cape Hatteras coast guard station was momentarily stunned by the eerie spectacle. There had been no storm. The last watch to scan the shore and sea before darkness closed in the night before had reported all clear and calm, with neither sail nor smoke in sight. No light had been shown during the night, and no distress signals had been sent up.

What ship was this? Where did she come from? How could she possibly have grounded? Why had not the crew given some sign of the ship's distress?

But the coast guard acts as it questions, and a power lifeboat, launched at the Hatteras station, soon pulled up on the strange craft stuck firmly there on the Diamond Shoals. The coastguardmen found that the ship was the *Carroll M. Deering*, a new and apparently seaworthy vessel. Her spreading sails, set full to catch the wind, were of new cloth. But no one greeted the coastguardmen from the deck. Her jibs and topsails, still unfurled, indicated that there had been no attempt to float the ship off the shoals.

The rescue boat could get no nearer to the nest of shoals than a quarter of a mile because the sea was running strong; so the little coast guard crew studied the *Carroll M. Deering* from a distance. They noted that she seemed to be stripped of her lifeboats and that a ladder hung over her port side. The rescuers estimated that the ship would have a crew of at least ten men. They circled the stranded schooner for more than two hours, but still there was no sign of life from on board and still no distress signals.

Nor was there any response to calls—only the whistle of the chill and penetrating February winds through the ship's rigging and the roar of the waves on the dread shoals. A boiling surf frothed and spumed like lava spouting from a vexed volcano as the vessel bit deeper into the sand with every curl of a new breaker. Finally the coastguardmen returned to the beach for further instructions. The ownership of the *Carroll M. Deering* was checked in the Marine Register and it was found to be a $200,000 schooner of 2,114 tons built at Bath, Maine, the previous year. Her owners were notified of her plight, and a cutter from Wilmington was dispatched to the scene. Coast guard crews from two other near-by stations were also rushed in to help.

When the rough sea subsided about the shoals, the coastguardmen returned to the amazing ship, still sitting there in her spreading white sails and tugging at the sand that held her bottom fast. The schooner was still intact but now quite high out of the water on the shoals. The sea was comparatively calm. The coastguardmen climbed aboard.

What they found after they scrambled up the side and over the ship's rail was so strange that it is still a favorite topic at the firesides of the people of the coast country. The coastguardmen saw why no distress signals had gone up from the ship as she plowed into the shoals the night before. There was no man on board to send up a signal. She ran ashore because there was no helmsman to guide her. The entire crew of the *Carroll M. Deering* had vanished!

Only one living thing was found as the ship was searched from stem to stern—a lean gray cat; and the only sound not made by sea or creaking timber was the faint and pitiful mewing of the cat, coming from the galley. What a story that cat could have told had she been a modern Puss-in-Boots instead of an ordinary ship's cat!

Most of the ship's papers, charts, and nautical instruments were missing. The steering apparatus was smashed, apparently by a sledge hammer that was propped casually against the wheel. The rudder swung free, allowing the vessel to drift with the current. The ship's stores, signal flags, and gear were stowed intact. The bunks were all made up, a meal was cooked, the tables set, and food—only partly consumed—was left on the plates. Other food was in the pots on the icy-cold stove. Everything was shipshape and there was no evidence of violence. Lights still burned in the ship's salon.

While the men on board pondered the strange case of the wandering, crewless schooner, the coast guard on shore was getting information to piece together the events of the *Carroll M. Deering's* last cruise. In August, six months before, the schooner had cleared Newport News, Virginia, with a cargo of coal, bound for Rio de Janeiro by way of Lewes, Delaware, under the command of Captain William Merritt of Portland, Maine. Merritt's son was first mate. The vessel was but a few days underway when Captain Merritt was taken sick; so she put in at the Delaware Breakwater, at Lewes,—and Captain Merritt was transferred from the ship to a hospital. His son went with him. There was some suggestion in subsequent investigations that Captain Merritt had been having trouble with the crew, which had been signed on at Norfolk, and pleaded ill health as an excuse to leave the ship.

At any rate, a new master and first mate came aboard. The captain who took over at Lewes was William B. Wormell of Boston, a hardy but likable skipper who had weathered roaring typhoons in the China Sea and defied the furies of the North Atlantic in every type of windjammer that floated. He came down from New York and brought a trusted and competent first mate with him. This delay was such that it was early September before the *Deering* proceeded on its run to Rio. After a comparatively calm trip, she tied up at the South American port and discharged her cargo of coal. Since there was nothing scheduled to transport back to the United States, she cleared Rio de Janeiro "light" on December 3. On the trip home she called at Barbados, where Captain Wormell found orders awaiting him to proceed without cargo to Norfolk. While at Barbados, Captain Wormell complained to his ship's agents at Bridgetown, Barbados, of the unruliness of the crew and mentioned his own ill health.

The crew, in addition to the American mate, consisted of a Finnish boatswain, a Negro steward, and six Danish sailors. Cafe loungers at Barbados were reported to have overheard a heated argument in which the mate of the *Deering* threatened to "'get the old man" before the vessel reached Norfolk, referring presumably to Captain Wormell.

On January 9, 1921, when the *Deering* left Barbados in her backwash, she had cleared a port for the last time. At 1:00 P.M. on January 23, she passed the Cape Fear lightship, off the lower North Carolina coast. Then, six days later, she passed the Cape Lookout lightship. . . . The distance between these two lightships is only eighty miles. The *Deering* was six days in sailing that distance.

The captain of the Cape Lookout lightship reported later that when the Deering passed him a man stood on the deck and hailed him through a megaphone, notifying him that the Deering had lost her anchors in a storm when coming up the coast, and asked that boats watch for her as she approached Norfolk. When the captain of the Cape Lookout lightship testified at later hearings, his description of the man who signaled him from the deck of the Deering did not tally with the appearance of Captain Wormell. The lightship captain said, too, that the man did not look or act like a ship's officer. Also, he added, crewmen were scattered about the ship in such a way as to indicate lack of discipline.

Back on the Deering, stuck fast on the shoals, a fine-toothed-comb search was being made through the cabin, forecastle head, steerage, and holds. Little was found to throw light on what happened aboard the ship during the last hours before she was beached. But there ensued one of the most exhaustive investigations in maritime records. . . .

The strange vessel was salvaged, and all her usable sails, furniture, and other gear were sold at public auction. Wreckers then left the Carroll M. Deering to the mercy of the wind and waves. The elements started their grim business of gnawing her into nothingness. The stranded vessel began to go to pieces there off Hatteras on March 21. The stern beached about twelve miles from the cape. This wreckage consisted of a poop deck, counter, port side, deck house, and after house. Hundreds of sea gulls chose this wreckage for a roost and scores of them built nests there. The nights were made hideous with their shrill cries. There was talk of spirits walking the boards of the Carroll M. Deering, and the presence of this remnant of the mystery ship soon became a nightmare to the natives of the beach near by. Finally they appealed to the government. United States Coast Guard Headquarters ordered that the Carroll M. Deering's remains be blown up. But this order was destined never to be carried out; while the coast guard cutters at Norfolk made ready to put out to sea with dynamite to blow up the stranded piece of wreckage, a sudden storm came up and within a few hours a howling northeast gale was piling the sea up high on the beach at Hatteras. Tremendous waves hit the derelict ghost ship, and she groaned and whined under their terrific beating. Soon her timbers began to loosen and she went to pieces rapidly.

The next day, when the wind was no more than a breeze and the sea was smooth and oily, hundreds of birds, made homeless by the blow that disintegrated their wreck, circled and recircled the spot, screeching and crying. Some said these noises were the cries of departed spirits hovering over the scattered remains of the schooner. All that remained of the ghost ship was timber scattered for miles along the beach.

It has been many years since some grim spectre took over the wheel of the trim and sturdy Carroll M. Deering and veered the crewless vessel off her course into a port of doom. As the seasons have come and gone, innumerable theories about the *Deering* and her fate have been propounded—each as plausible as another and each as absurd. But throughout the investigations, and in all the years since, no theory has been overlooked and no angle scoffed at. No possible clue has been thought insignificant. Yet the deeper the probe the deeper the mystery of the missing crew.

When first news of the mysterious schooner was flashed over the world, a young woman in Boston, Miss Lulu Wormell, daughter of the ship's Captain William B. Wormell, said she was positive that the ship had fallen into the hands of twentieth-century pirates and that her father and his crew had been murdered at sea. In subsequent investigations she made out a pretty good case.

On the chart that was salvaged from the ship, Miss Wormell said she could identify her father's handwriting up to January 23, the day the ship passed the Cape Fear lightship, and that after that the entries were made by a different hand. It was six days after January 23 that the captain of the Cape Lookout lightship said the *Deering* passed his ship and that he was hailed by the man on deck who did not look or act like a ship's officer.

The captain of the Cape Lookout lightship also testified that a steamer passed his station shortly after the *Deering* and refused to stop when he flagged an international code signal, "Have important message." He stated that he then blew his No. 12 chime whistle which could be heard for five miles; contrary to the unwritten law of the high seas, the steamer still refused to stop. The lightship captain said he wanted to notify the steamer that the *Deering* had lost her anchors.

The most important evidence against the modern buccaneering theory is that the ship carried no valuables, not even a cargo. It seems unreasonable that pirates would have risked their necks simply for the personal belongings of a ship's crew. Besides, there was no evidence of a topsy-turvy search of the ship for things of value. A note found in a floating bottle, indicating that the *Deering* had indeed been the victim of pirates, was produced but was later proved to be a fraud.

Other theories included that of a mass suicide at sea, with a suggested possibility that the crew had contracted some dread tropical disease and that the men had sacrificed their lives to prevent a fatal epidemic in the States. But such a theory would contemplate finding bodies and did not explain the missing lifeboats.

Also suggested, perhaps by the indication of mutiny that came from the reportedly overheard conversation at Barbados, was the possibility that the crew murdered the captain, set the ship adrift, landed in the open boats and burned them on some beach. But many who had sailed with Captain Wormell said he was a sociable individual and highly popular with his subordinates.

Then there is the theory—perhaps the most plausible of all—that the crew abandoned the ship in lifeboats for some reason and were picked up by the steamer *Hewitt*, known to have been at a position near the *Deering* at the time. The *Hewitt* was carrying a cargo of sulphur to New York. A few days after the *Deering* went aground there was a great flash of fire off the New Jersey coast and high billows of smoke hung in the air. The *Hewitt* never reached New York and it became evident that her cargo had exploded. Perhaps both crews, then aboard, were lost—perhaps.

The *Deering* investigation was finally brought to a close with the terse statement of one of the federal government officials. He said, "We might just as well have searched a painted ship on a painted ocean for sight of the vanished crew." What happened aboard the ship from the time she cleared a South American port until she put in at Hatteras, a ghost ship in full sail without captain or crew, will never be known.

Meanwhile the *Carroll M. Deering*, which once swept down the ocean highways with her snow-white canvas towering away to the royal yards, and which once surged bravely through the raging gales and biting blasts of ill-tempered seas, has finally broken up and rotted away in the death clutches of a treacherous sand bar—taking with her into oblivion one of the most baffling secrets of the ocean that washes our Carolina coast.

When the Ship Hit the Span

JOHN ALEXANDER AND JAMES LAZELL   1990

Oregon Inlet is a microcosm of the Outer Banks—a limited resource with which divergent groups wish to do many things all at once, usually at taxpayers' expense. Commercial and sport fishermen care mostly about getting through it. Hatteras Islanders and the tourists who support their economy desire a reliable means of crossing it. The U.S. Army Corps of Engineers has been trying for years to make it halt and stand at attention. An unsteady alliance of environmentalists, academics, and Interior Department officials hopes to let it evolve as naturally as it can with a bridge overhead and dredges scouring the channel. Once in a while events remind us just how limited a resource the inlet is and how fragile are the works of man. In their book *Ribbon of Sand*, John Alexander and James Lazell described one such event, which occurred early in the morning of October 26, 1990.

CAPTAIN WILLIAM CLIETT, skipper of the dredge *Northerly Island*, had decided to knock off operations. His 200-foot dredge, owned by North American Trailing

Co. of Chicago, was under contract with the Army Corps of Engineers to maintain a navigation channel through the constantly shifting shoals of Oregon Inlet. The vessel was part of an annual $4.4 million Corps program to dredge 700,000 cubic yards of sand from the inlet. It was also a bit player in a much larger debate over whether Oregon Inlet should be stabilized with a pair of mile-long jetties costing more than $100 million of taxpayers' money. The *Northerly Island* was not to remain a bit player for much longer.

According to the captain's subsequent account, the weather forecast called for twenty-five- to thirty-five-knot winds that night, with accompanying choppy seas. Captain Cliett and his crew of nine did not consider the forecast particularly ominous or unusual. He chose to anchor for the night in his usual spot east of the two-and-a-half-mile Bonner Bridge, which has spanned the inlet since 1963. But the forecast proved too benign. Within hours the weather turned foul. Cliett later said seas were running three to five feet, the winds were slicing forty-five to fifty-five knots—gale-force level—with gusts well above that mark, and the current surging to at least six knots. Subsequent investigation has shown that this storm, though short-lived, was one of the most severe of the past fifty years. . . .

At about 10:30 P.M., Captain Cliett realized the dredge's anchor was dragging. He ordered the vessel's engines at full power and directed that the ship's ballast tanks be pumped full of water to keep the barge stranded. . . . The gale was easterly. But the current and tide were causing the shoal to erode, and the dredge continued its inexorable sideways drift toward Bonner Bridge. The Coast Guard would later rule that the captain may have been negligent because he failed to drop a second anchor during the ship's grounding. Cliett, who was later absolved of any responsibility after an inquiry, argued that forces far more powerful than any under his control had commandeered his ship.

At 12:50 A.M., Cliett notified the Coast Guard to close the bridge to traffic. Twenty minutes later, the *Northerly Island* crashed into the bridge. Four of the dredge's terrified crew members climbed up the ship's superstructure and made their way onto the bridge. They were carried to safety by Dare County sheriff's deputies just minutes before the span collapsed. The officers watched in horror and amazement as the red-and-white dredge severed the bridge and catapulted 370 feet of the two-lane highway into the inlet. A fiery explosion caused by ruptured electrical cables lit up the gale-swept sky. Astonishingly, no one on board or on the bridge was injured.

Thus did the vessel commissioned to keep the inlet open temporarily close it. But much more than the bridge was severed that night. The structure had been the only direct link connecting the roughly 5,000 residents of Hatteras Island to the amenities of Nags Head, Manteo, and the mainland beyond. Before the bridge was built, rugged Hatteras residents were accustomed to living in isolation for long periods. The only link to Nags Head in those days was a long, circuitous ferry ride across the sound side of Oregon Inlet. But the bridge's advent made the drive to Nags Head an easy one. Hatteras residents took jobs to the north. The bridge also opened Hatteras Island to tourists and developers. The bridge even served as a handy conduit for electrical and telephone lines to the island. It was, symbolically, Hatteras's umbilical cord to the outside world.

When the cord was cut that gusty night in October, it revived the worst fears of Hatteras people. Not only were they plunged into darkness and cold with the loss of electric power, their economic lifeline had been tossed over, too. Autumn is the prime time for fishermen to make their pilgrimage to the Outer Banks. But with Bonner Bridge gone, the only access to the island was by ferry from Ocracoke, or by a new, makeshift ferry service across Oregon Inlet. The new ferries, up and running within nine days of the bridge's collapse, required an hour or more to traverse the inlet. The ferries' zigzag path covered six and a half miles; they frequently ran aground in the inlet's shifting shoals. Whereas the bridge could accommodate a continuous stream of traffic amounting to an average of four to eight thousand a day, a single ferry could carry a scant thirty-four cars each trip.

Wholly dependent on tourism, the island's economy plummeted. Attendance at the Cape Hatteras Lighthouse in November dropped by some 7,000 visits from the previous November. Motels, restaurants, and charter boats stood empty. As if the islanders had not been punished enough, two weeks after the bridge's collapse a tornado skipped across the island. The capricious twister's seventy-five-mile-an-hour winds destroyed three new homes and about a dozen mobile homes, and ripped part of the roof off Bubba's Bar-B-Que in Avon. Cinder blocks lifted from the restaurant's walls crushed a car in the parking lot.

Well-schooled in the art of survival, the Bankers shrugged their shoulders and waited. A few old-timers welcomed the serendipitous return to the slower pace of prebridge days. Initial predictions were that repair of the bridge would consume at least six months. But an unusually mild winter and round-the-clock repair work brought the structure back into service by mid-February 1991—less than four months after its collapse.

Apart from its immediate impact on Hatteras Island, the bridge's collapse enflamed an old debate about the Oregon Inlet jetties and may have hastened its resolution—much to the consternation of geologists and conservationists. Twenty years before, Congress had authorized construction of mile-long jetties at either end of Oregon Inlet. The jetties were intended to stabilize the inlet and permit easier passage for commercial and recreational boats. But like a lot of grandiose schemes on the Outer Banks, this one had gone nowhere—until the bridge's collapse distilled the political glue that just may stick the jetty plan together.

Among the most enthusiastic backers of the jetties is a handful of commercial fishermen based in Wanchese, a fishing community on Roanoke Island. In 1976, the state of North Carolina began constructing a seafood industrial park in Wanchese. The park was intended to serve as a major seafood processing center for trawlers working off the Outer Banks, and thus as a generator of jobs and economic growth in the region. The park's economic viability was predicated on construction of the jetties, which the fishermen said would stabilize the inlet and permit safe passage between the shoals and under Bonner Bridge. But the jetties' high price tag—more than $100 million at that time—and persistent environmental concerns stymied the project.

Absent the jetties, the seafood park lost money every year. Seafood processors deemed it too risky an investment because of the inlet's unpredictable shoals. On many days of the year, fishing boats were simply unable to navigate the inlet's shallow waters. Some of the fishing trawlers wrecked and ran aground. Alarmed, the owners of these modern, high-tech vessels hauled their catch to seafood processors in Cape May, New Jersey, and New Bedford, Massachusetts. By mid-1991, only two processing plants were operating in the Wanchese park.

Wanchese fishermen, backed by the Army Corps of Engineers, seized on the bridge's collapse as evidence for their case. Had the jetties been in place, there would have been no need for the dredge, and thus no opportunity for the accident. But the bridge's temporary demise also invites a different interpretation: that man's attempts to keep the inlet open—whether by dredging, jetties, or other means—are ultimately futile.

That Oregon Inlet is shifting is not in dispute. Like the birds that nest there, the inlet is migrating south—and at a rate of 100 feet per year. Opened by a fierce hurricane on September 7, 1846, Oregon Inlet has behaved as inlets are supposed to: longshore currents are shifting its location from north to south, while a combination of currents, wind, and wave action is filling the inlet in. The net transport of sand south from the inlet has been estimated at 710,000 cubic meters per year. The inlet has also been moving landward at a rate of five meters per year. The effect of these factors is that the northern tip of Pea Island is disappearing and exposing the southern end of Bonner Bridge to severe wave action.

Even as the debate over the jetties raged during 1990–91, state officials constructed a smaller, 2,500-foot stone revetment and groin at the inlet's south end at a cost of $15 million. Much of this structure caps the present north end of Pea Island, but some 800 feet extend out to sea. Its purpose is to protect the bridge from powerful waves and to prevent the land to which it is attached from washing away. The north end of Pea Island had been eroding at a rate of 180 feet a year. A single, ferocious northeaster in March, 1989, ripped away 200 feet of the island's north tip in one night. The same storm destroyed beach houses in Nags Head and Kitty Hawk and caused more than $4.5 million in damage up and down the Banks. But that is a rather ordinary storm for the neighborhood. The Pea Island project had long been blocked by the Interior Department, which manages the Pea Island National Wildlife Refuge on which the groin was to be built. But strong state political pressure and the realization that the highway might be separated from the bridge presumably persuaded officials to relent and grant a permit for the groin.

The argument against groins and jetties is that, far from preventing erosion, such man-made devices contribute to erosion by blocking sand transport and starving beaches downstream. In the case of the Oregon Inlet jetties, geologists such as Stan Riggs think the consequences of the jetties are obvious: they will deny the natural flow of sand to Pea and Hatteras islands and accelerate the erosion that is already carving into both islands. At the same time, the historical tendency of the Banks to move landward, and of Oregon Inlet to shift dramatically south and west, makes it an ultimate certainty that the jetties will not perform their intended function for long. The pace of the inlet's abandonment of Bonner Bridge may be slowed and slightly altered by the jetties, but it will not be stopped—especially if a violent storm on the magnitude of the 1846 hurricane should sweep through. "The dynamics of that system are such that you cannot build a structure like that without some consequences," says Riggs. "It is going to change the [beach] profile, it is going to change the sediment flow, and anybody who thinks any differently has got his head in the sand."

Protecting the bridge is only the subplot in an even larger drama, just as the inevitable tendency of Oregon Inlet to close is part of the larger barrier island dynamic. As the inlet shoals up, pressure builds elsewhere for a new inlet to open. Several miles south of Oregon Inlet . . . is the site of a former inlet, "New Inlet." . . . It made Pea Island an island. . . . Indeed, in the centuries before Oregon Inlet opened, at least a dozen inlets opened and closed between False Cape, Virginia, and Cape Hatteras. There is little reason to suppose that, unlike every one of its ancestors, Oregon Inlet can be frozen in its tracks and prevented from closing, or another "new" inlet from opening.

Bonner Bridge is not the only man-made structure jeopardized by this natural process. The highway that winds south from it to Hatteras is threatened, too. Now that the islands' dune systems are no longer stabilized, the highway is increasingly exposed to overwash from the ocean side. Whether or not a new inlet opens again south of Oregon Inlet, storm surges will inevitably spill over the highway at other low, narrow points along Hatteras Island. Even if Bonner Bridge is protected, the possibility of frequent highway washouts is real. . . .

Opposition from geologists, environmentalists, and officials of the Cape Hatteras National Seashore has not deterred advocates of the jetties. On the eve of his hard-fought reelection in November 1990, Senator Jesse Helms announced that the jetties would be built after all. The Interior Department withdrew its opposition to the jetties in exchange for having a voice in the system's design. Helms cited the accident at Bonner Bridge as the impetus for the sudden evaporation of top Interior Department opposition to the jetties. The fact that Helms was joined in his lobbying by senior elected officials from across the state contributed to the department's apparent change of heart.

But Helms's announcement did not guarantee that the jetties will be built. The Interior Department and the Corps of Engineers have commissioned a team of scientists . . . to review all the issues surrounding the Oregon Inlet controversy. That review could still sway any final decision. The project must also win budget approval from the White House and from Congress in a time of federal cutbacks. . . .

The uncertainty is not in the science, but in the politics of the Oregon Inlet dispute. If . . . scientists can prove that the jetties would have an adverse impact on the beaches of the Cape Hatteras National Seashore, will the government decide to abandon the project? Or will the perceived short-term economic benefits associated with the jetties override long-term environmental concerns that are not just environmental or aesthetic but ultimately financial as well?

The Pea Island Lifesavers

DAVID WRIGHT AND DAVID ZOBY   1995

The Outer Banks has a proud traditional association with the U.S. Lifesaving Service and its successor, the U.S. Coast Guard. Nowhere is this tradition more revered than in the small black community on Roanoke Island, which has provided these agencies far more than its share of able men with family names such as Etheridge, Meekins, Collins, Bowser, and Berry. Many were assigned to integrated stations during the very early days of the service, and since World War II many others have done duty in a variety of ethnically diverse Coast Guard units. But during the intervening years, all or nearly all billets open to the black lifesavers of Roanoke Island were concentrated at Pea Island, the only all-black station; and the highest position in public life to which any local black man could reasonably aspire was the office of its keeper. David Wright and David Zoby developed an interest in the Pea Island station while they were graduate students of English at Virginia Commonwealth University. Their ground-breaking research has resulted in several publications, including the following piece from *Coastwatch* magazine.

THE SURFMEN of the Pea Island Lifesaving Station built a reputation on hard work, bravery and skill. Along the Outer Banks and East Coast, they were a respected crew, known for assisting more than 30 vessels in distress, rescuing more than 200 people and losing only seven mariners.

But the lifesavers' skill wasn't all that set them apart from other surfmen along the coast. The Pea Island station was manned completely by blacks — the country's only such station.

Today locals, white and black, are quick to remark on the excellent reputation of the lifesavers. At the time the first black keeper was appointed, however, the idea was not wholeheartedly embraced. The first all-black Pea Island crew battled more than the ocean's tempests. They fought amid a sea of prejudice and waves of hostility in the local community.

Life on the Outer Banks in the late 19th century was hard, particularly after the devastation of the Civil War. Commercial fishing was limited, tourism nearly unheard of and poverty as widespread as the beaches were barren. As a result, everyone wanted a job with the federal government.

. . . However, the U.S. Lifesaving Service, which was officially established in 1871 under General Superintendent Sumner Kimball, did not receive federal money to build stations along the Outer Banks until 1874. These first seven stations were manned by a keeper and six surfmen. Their orders were clear: Come to the assistance of any vessels or persons in need.

Black watermen along the Outer Banks enlisted in the Lifesaving Service. Integrated rosters, called "checkerboard" crews, were common along the coast with as many as 19 blacks serving in North Carolina stations from 1874 to 1879. Black surfmen, however, served only in the lowest ranking positions on the duty roster and often doubled as the stations' cooks. Despite their low ranks, visiting Northern inspectors remarked that several of the black surfmen were among the best in the district.

Early service along the barrier islands was fraught with difficulties. With so few stations, the length of patrols was often as much as 15 miles — too long to be expedient in reporting disasters and rendering aid. At the outset, lifesavers were employed for only four months of the year, December through March, after which the stations were padlocked. Consequently, lifesaving operations often had little effect in saving lives. The situation was ripe for disaster.

Between 1876 and 1878, the disasters came in quick succession. Three highly publicized maritime shipwrecks occurred off the Tar Heel coast. More than a half million dollars in property was lost. But more importantly, 211 people died.

Kimball turned his attention to the Outer Banks to determine why people were dying along an area manned by lifesavers. He learned the problem ran much deeper than long stretches of beach and short seasons. Nepotism was ruining the service.

During an 1875 tour of the Carolina stations, government inspectors found 15 surfmen, including four keepers, unqualified to serve. One was a blacksmith, another a teacher, and neither had any knowledge of the sea. Another had been hired even though he was physically unable to perform the tasks demanded of a surfman.

Kimball successfully appealed to Congress in 1878 for more funds to expand the number of stations in the district and lengthen the active season. But improvements in hiring were slow. All too often, keepers and crews were hired for reasons other than ability.

In the early morning of Nov. 30, 1879, the schooner *M&E Henderson* came ashore two miles south of the Pea Island station on what appeared to be a clear morning. Inexplicably, aid from the station arrived late. Four men were lost; the three survivors found their way ashore unassisted by the lifesavers.

Inspectors from Washington, D.C., already troubled by incompetency in the Carolina service, found the keeper's report of the incident misleading.

Upon further investigation, inspectors learned that the Pea Island station keeper and other surfmen may have been absent from the station when the *Henderson* came ashore. The keeper and his men frequently left the station understaffed, often to go hunting.

Kimball realized that district incompetence might compromise the fledgling Lifesaving Service as a whole. So he approved radical changes to ensure adequate service in North Carolina. In January 1880, he authorized the transfer of Richard Etheridge, a black man who held the number six surfman position at the Bodie Island station, to Pea Island as keeper.

Although the appointment of a black man to a position of authority was becoming increasingly unpopular in the post-Reconstruction South, the choice of Etheridge as keeper was a natural one. In his report, Frank Newcomb, one of the two Northern inspectors, described Etheridge as follows:

"Richard Etheridge is 38 years of age, has the reputation of being as good a surfman as there is on this coast, black or white, can read and write intelligently, and bears a good name as a man among the men with whom he has associated during his life."

The other inspector, Charles Shoemaker, added: "I am aware that no colored man holds the position of keeper in the Lifesaving Service . . . and yet . . . I am fully convinced that the interests of the Lifesaving Service here, in point of efficiency, will be greatly advanced by the appointment of this man to the Keepership of Station No. 17."

Etheridge was a proven leader. Born on the beaches near Oregon Inlet, he had grown up by the water, learning the secrets of the sea and the tides along the Outer Banks.

When the Union Army opened its ranks to blacks during the Civil War in 1863, Etheridge enlisted. He served in the 36th U.S. Colored Troops, fought at the Battle of New Market Heights and was eventually promoted to regimental commissary sergeant.

Etheridge was a man committed to justice. While fighting for the emancipation of slaves, he also engaged in the struggle behind Union lines to end mistreatment of blacks. In 1865, he drafted a letter to the commissioner of the Freedmen's Bureau on behalf of his fellow black soldiers of the 36th to protest Union injustices at home on the Outer Banks.

". . . [T]he white soldiers break into our houses, act as they please, steal our chickens, rob our gardens, and if any one defends their-Selves against them, they are taken to the gard house for it."

In 1866, a year after the war ended, Etheridge left the military. He returned to the Outer Banks, where he married and resumed his life as a fisherman.

Etheridge joined the Lifesaving Service during its first years, serving at the Oregon Inlet station in 1875 and later at the Bodie Island station, where Newcomb and Shoemaker found him occupying the lowest ranking position on the duty roster.

The former keeper at Pea Island had hired a checkerboard crew, but Etheridge's would be all black. The day he arrived to assume the keepership, the white surfmen abandoned the station, unwilling to serve under a black man. To complete Etheridge's crew, Newcomb decided to transfer black surfmen from other district stations to Pea Island.

But more resistance was to come. Prominent whites in the area tried to intimidate the black lifesavers out of the service. They warned the surfmen that the Northern inspector had no intention of keeping them at Pea Island, but rather was scheming to force them out of the stations entirely. One man, Joseph Case, did not know whom to trust; he resigned. But Newcomb and Etheridge were eventually able to hire a full crew, filling the empty positions with black watermen. These men served the remainder of the spring season.

In late May [1880], just after the stations closed for the inactive season, the Pea Island station burned to the ground. Newcomb, suspecting arson, immediately launched an investigation.

He quickly learned that the Outer Banks community as a whole condemned the station's burning. Only a few people had a vested interest in removing Etheridge and his crew. Although the most logical suspect was the previous Pea Island keeper, the testimony of people who had been on the island that day pointed elsewhere.

Two brothers who . . . served at the Bodie Island station were reportedly in the vicinity of the station on the night of the fire. Newcomb pursued that line of investigation.

He found it odd that the brothers, who were aware of the fire as it burned, did nothing to notify nearby Lifesaving Service officials. While the brothers were under questioning, their story conflicted with testimony of other witnesses.

One of the brothers was the highest ranking surfman at Bodie Island and a candidate for keeper of a station; the other brother and a third suspect had served as substitutes but sought full-time positions in the service. They had interest in removing the black crew.

In fact, the brother who held the highest rank had been heard commenting "[t]hat it would be an easy matter for a surfman who had a falling out with his Keeper, to set a station on fire, or . . . injure the property in such a manner as to throw blame on the Keeper and cause his dismissal from the Service."

Newcomb reported to Kimball: "The inference is that . . . [the third suspect] was employed by [the brother who was only a substitute] to set the station on fire, the object being, to secure the removal of the present colored Keeper, thus enabling [the brother] to succeed him and giving [the third man] a situation as surfman in the station." According to Newcomb, the higher ranked brother had devised the scheme.

Although Newcomb felt strongly that these men were involved in burning the station, Kimball chose not to pursue the matter further. Kimball was aware of the risk he had taken in appointing Etheridge. He feared that prosecuting the brothers might damage the fragile infrastructure he was trying to build in the already troubled district.

The burning of the Pea Island station did not mark the end of the all-black crew. Instead, the station thrived. The season following the fire, the crew worked from the stables. A few months later, they rebuilt their station.

Etheridge ran his station with military rigor. He followed orders to the letter and expected the same of his men. He drove them like soldiers, relentlessly drilling them with the lifesaving equipment, quizzing them on their knowledge of procedure and ensuring that the station was kept in impeccable condition. The Pea Island crews became known for their daring in the surf and their commitment to duty, often under perilous circumstances.

Their most daring effort came on the night of Oct. 11, 1896, when the schooner E. S. Newman ran aground south of the station during a hurricane. The Newman's captain had beached the schooner in the hope of saving his crew, which included his wife and 3-year-old daughter. The storm was so violent that Etheridge had canceled patrols for the night for fear of losing one of his men to the wind and surf that swept across the inundated beach.

From the observation tower, surfman Theodore Meekins sighted a light off the coast. Etheridge immediately mustered his crew and led them two miles to the wreck. Once there, they realized that their lifesaving equipment was inoperable in the extreme conditions. Reacting quickly, Etheridge ordered that a line be tied between two men and that those men swim the line to the ship. Ten trips were made back and forth to the beach, one by one transporting the crew of the Newman to safety.

Over the generations, serving at the Pea Island station became a time-honored tradition among the young black men of Roanoke Island. William Bowser grew up hearing the stories of the Newman and other rescues from his grandfather, who had served under Etheridge. He always knew that he, too, would someday be a surfman.

"It was in my blood that I would go to Pea Island," says Bowser. "That's all we had on our minds. We all wanted to be just like them."

War on the Banks

In addition to being involved in the major American wars —
the Revolution, the Civil War, World War I, and World War II —
the Outer Banks has been the scene of other brutal conflicts, not all
of them dignified by a formal declaration of war.

Of Captain Teach Alias Blackbeard

CAPTAIN CHARLES JOHNSON (DANIEL DEFOE) 1718

A quick tally of the writings that Blackbeard the Pirate has inspired, the treasures he is believed to have hidden on the Outer Banks, or the living Bankers who claim descent from him or his crewmen suggests that he plied local waters for decades with a fleet as large as the Royal Navy. The truth is, however, that Edward Teach, or Blackbeard, was not born in North Carolina or even in North America, and his activities around the Outer Banks lasted less than a year. During his brief stay he worked closely with Tobias Knight, secretary to Governor Charles Eden, if not with the governor himself. At the same time Teach caused the citizenry grave concern, for, contrary to legend, piracy was not widely practiced in North Carolina or by North Carolinians. Indeed, the pilots and stockmen of the Outer Banks could not prosper in a nursery of cutthroats. Likewise the planters and merchants lining the sounds and rivers to the west needed safe maritime commerce in order to thrive. When Blackbeard's outrages became intolerable, Bankers and mainlanders jointly appealed for relief not to their own government but to Governor Alexander Spotswood of Virginia. The piece below, which relates his bold response to their petition, is taken from *A General History of the Pyrates* (1724), written under one of many pseudonyms of the author of *Robinson Crusoe*. Some spelling, punctuation, and typography were modernized for this book.

CAPTAIN TEACH, alias Blackbeard, passed three or four months in the river, sometimes lying at anchor in the coves, at other times sailing from one inlet to another, trading with such sloops as he met, for the plunder he had taken, and would often give them presents for stores and provisions he took from them; that is, when he happened to be in a giving humour; at other times he made bold with them, and took what he liked, without saying, *by your leave*, knowing well, they dared not send him a bill for the payment. He often diverted himself with going ashore among the planters, where he reveled night and day: By these he was well received, but whether out of love or fear, I cannot say; sometimes he used them courteously enough, and made them presents of rum and sugar, in recompence of what he took from them; but, as for liberties (which 'tis said) he and his companions often took with the wives and daughters of the planters, I cannot take upon me to say, whether he paid them *ad valorem*, or no. At other times he carried it in a lordly manner towards them, and would lay some of them under contribution; nay, he often proceeded to bully the governor, not, that I can discover the least cause of quarrel betwixt them, but it seemed only to be done, to show he dared do it.

The sloops trading up and down this river being so frequently pillaged by Blackbeard, consulted with the traders, and some of the best of the planters, what course to take; they saw plainly it would be in vain to make any application to the governor of North Carolina, to whom it properly belonged to find some redress; so that if they could not be relieved from some other quarter, Blackbeard would be like to reign with impunity; therefore, with as much secrecy as possible, they sent a deputation to Virginia, to lay the affair before the governor of that colony, and to solicit an armed force from the men of war lying there, to take or destroy this pirate.

This governor consulted with the captains of the two men of war, *viz.* the *Pearl* and *Lime*, who had lain in James River, about ten months. It was agreed, that the governor should hire a couple of small sloops, and the men of war should man them; this was accordingly done, and the command of them given to Mr. Robert Maynard, first lieutenant of the *Pearl*, an experienced officer, and a gentleman of great bravery and resolution, as will appear by his gallant behaviour in this expedition. The sloops were well manned, and furnished with ammunition and small arms, but had no guns mounted.

About the time of their going out, the governor called an assembly, in which it was resolved to publish a proclamation, offering certain rewards to any person or persons, who, within a year after that time, should take or destroy any pirate. . . .

The 17th of November, 1718, the lieutenant sailed from Kecoughtan, in James River in Virginia, and, the 31st in the evening, came to the mouth of Ocracoke Inlet, where he got sight of the pirate. This expedition was made with all imaginable secrecy, and the officer managed with all the prudence that was necessary, stopping all boats and vessels he met with, in the river, from going up, and thereby preventing any intelligence from reaching Blackbeard, and receiving at the same time an account from them all, of the place where the pirate was lurking; but notwithstanding this caution, Blackbeard had information of the design, from His Excellency of the province; and his secretary, Mr. Knight, wrote him a letter, particularly concerning it, intimating, that he had sent him four of his men, which were all he could meet with, in or about town, and so bid him be upon his guard. These men belonged to Blackbeard, and were sent from Bath Town to Ocracoke Inlet, where the sloop lay, which is about 20 leagues.

Blackbeard had heard several reports, which happened not to be true, and so gave the less credit to this advice, nor was he convinced till he saw the sloops: Then it was time to put his vessel in a posture of defence; he had no more than twenty five men on board, though he gave out to all the vessels he spoke with, that he had forty. When he had prepared for battle, he set down and spent the night in drinking with the master of a trading sloop, who, 'twas thought, had more business with Teach, than he should have had.

Lieutenant Maynard came to an anchor, for the place being shoal, and the channel intricate, there was no getting in, where Teach lay, that night; but in the morning he weighed, and sent his boat ahead of the sloops to sound; and coming within gun-shot of the pirate, received his fire; whereupon Maynard hoisted the king's colours, and stood directly towards him, with the best way that his sails and oars could make. Blackbeard cut his cable, and endeavored to make a running fight, keeping a continual fire at his enemies, with his guns; Mr. Maynard not having any, kept a constant fire with small arms, while some of his men labored at their oars. In a little time Teach's sloop ran aground, and Mr. Maynard's drawing more water than that of the pirate, he could not come near him; so he anchored within half gun-shot of the enemy, and, in order to lighten his vessel, that he might run him aboard, the lieutenant ordered all his ballast to be thrown overboard, and all the water to be staved, and then weighed and stood for him; upon which Blackbeard hailed him in this rude manner: *Damn you for villains, who are you? And, from whence came you?* The lieutenant made him answer, *You may see by our colours we are no pirates.* Blackbeard bid him send his boat on board, that he might see who he was; but Mr. Maynard replied thus; *I cannot spare my boat, but I will come aboard of you as soon as I can, with my sloop.* Upon this, Blackbeard took a glass of liquor, and drank to him with these words: *Damnation seize my soul if I give you quarters, or take any from you.* In answer to which, Mr. Maynard told him, that he expected no quarters from him, nor should he give him any.

By this time Blackbeard's sloop floated, as Mr. Maynard's sloops were rowing towards him, which being not above a foot high in the waist, and consequently the men all exposed, as they came near together, (there being hitherto little or no execution done, on either side) the pirate fired a broadside, charged with all manner of small shot—a fatal stroke to them! The sloop the lieutenant was in, having twenty men killed and wounded, and the other sloop nine: This could not be helped, for there being no wind, they were obliged to keep to their oars, otherwise the pirate would have got away from him, which, it seems, the lieutenant was resolute to prevent.

After this unlucky blow, Blackbeard's sloop fell broadside to the shore; Mr. Maynard's other sloop, which was called the *Ranger*, fell astern, being, for the present, disabled; so the lieutenant finding his own sloop had way, and would soon be on board of Teach, he ordered all his men down, for fear of another broadside, which must have been their destruction, and the loss of their expedition. Mr. Maynard was the only person that kept the deck, except the man at the helm, whom he directed to lie down snug; and the men in the hold were ordered to get their pistols and their swords ready for close fighting, and to come up at his command; in order to which, two ladders were placed in the hatchway for the more expedition. When the lieutenant's sloop boarded the other, Captain Teach's men threw in several new fashioned sort of grenadoes, *viz.* case bottles filled with powder, and small shot, slugs, and pieces of lead or iron, with a quick match in the mouth of it, which being lighted outside, presently runs into the bottle to the powder, and as it is instantly thrown on board, generally does great execution, besides putting all the crew into a confusion; but by good Providence, they had not that effect here; the men being in the hold. Blackbeard seeing few or no hands aboard, told his men, that they were all knocked on the head, except three or four; and therefore, says he, *Let's jump on board, and cut them to pieces.*

Whereupon, under the smoke of one of the bottles just mentioned, Blackbeard enters with fourteen men, over the bows of Maynard's sloop, and were not seen by him till the air cleared; however, he just then gave a signal to his men, who all rose in an instant, and attacked the pirates with as much bravery as ever was done upon such an occasion: Blackbeard and the lieutenant fired the first shots at each other, by which the pirate received a wound, and then engaged with swords, till the lieutenant's unluckily broke, and [Maynard] stepping back to cock a pistol, Blackbeard, with his cutlass, was striking at that instant, that one of Maynard's men gave him a terrible wound in the neck and throat, by which the lieutenant came off with only a small cut over his fingers.

They were now closely and warmly engaged, the lieutenant and twelve men against Blackbeard and fourteen, till the sea was tinctured with blood round the vessel; Blackbeard received a shot into his body from the pistol that Lieutenant Maynard discharged, yet he stood his ground, and fought with great fury, till he received five and twenty wounds, and five of them by shot. At length, as he was cocking another pistol, having fired several before, he fell down dead; by which time eight more out of the fourteen dropped, and all the rest, much wounded, jumped overboard, and called out for quarters, which was granted, though it was only prolonging their lives a few days. The sloop *Ranger* came up, and attacked the men that remained in Blackbeard's sloop, with equal bravery, till they likewise cried for quarters.

Here was an end of that courageous brute, who might have passed in the world for a hero, had he been employed in a good cause; his destruction, which was of such consequence to the plantations, was entirely owing to the conduct and bravery of Lieutenant Maynard and his men, who might have destroyed him with much less loss, had they had a vessel with great guns; but they were obliged to use small vessels, because the holes and places he lurked in, would not admit of others of greater draught; and it was no small difficulty for this gentleman to get to him, having grounded his vessel, at least, a hundred times, in getting up the river, besides other discouragements, enough to have turned back any gentleman without dishonour, had he been less resolute and bold than this lieutenant. The broadside that did so much mischief before they boarded, in all probability saved the rest from destruction; for before that, Teach had little or no hopes of escaping, and therefore had posted a resolute fellow, a Negro, whom he had bred up, with a lighted match, in the powder room, with commands to blow up, when he should give him orders, which was as soon as the lieutenant and his men could have entered, that so he might have destroyed his conquerors with himself: And when the Negro found how it went with Blackbeard, he could hardly be persuaded from the rash action, by two prisoners that were then in the hold of the sloop.

What seems a little odd, is, that some of these men, who behaved so bravely against Blackbeard, went afterwards a pirating themselves, and one of them was taken along with Roberts; but I do not find that any of them were provided for, except one that was hanged; but this is a digression.

The lieutenant caused Blackbeard's head to be severed from his body, and hung up at the bowsprit end, then he sailed to Bath Town, to get relief for his wounded men.

The Rendezvous at Hatteras

WILLIAM MORRISON ROBINSON JR.   1861

Hatteras Inlet was opened by a hurricane in the fall of 1846. Less than fifteen years later, at the outbreak of the Civil War, it had become the deepest and most strategically located inlet on the Atlantic coast between Cape Lookout and Chesapeake Bay. For mariners not familiar with its meandering channels, however, navigation of the inlet was hazardous, which made it an ideal base for privateers. After North Carolina seceded from the Union in May 1861, it took advantage of the inlet by forming its own little state navy consisting of a side-wheel steamer, the *Winslow*, and three propeller-driven former canal boats, which soon became known as "The Mosquito Fleet." A home base was established in a deep slough back of Hatteras Inlet, from which the smaller craft patrolled the nearby sounds while the *Winslow* was darting in and out of the inlet in pursuit of unescorted vessels traveling along the coast. In a period of a few months the *Winslow* was reported to have captured sixteen ships, mostly laden with supplies, earning for Hatteras Inlet the reputation of being "the principal rendezvous for the Confederate Privateers." The following account of these activities is taken from Robinson's book *The Confederate Privateers*.

THE ADVANTAGE OF geographical nearness to an enemy, or to the object of attack . . . is nowhere more apparent than in that form of warfare which has lately received the name of commerce-destroying, which the French call *guerre de course*. This operation of war, being directed against peaceful merchant vessels which are usually defenseless, calls for ships of small military force. Such ships, having little power to defend themselves, need a refuge or point of support near at hand; which will be found either in certain ports of the sea controlled by the fighting ships of their country, or in friendly harbors. The latter give the strongest support, because they are always in the same place, and the approaches to them are more familiar to the commerce-destroyer than to his enemy.

The value of this geographical advantage is well illustrated by the Confederate use of Hatteras Inlet. This inlet offered the safest and most reliable escape from the terrible seas off the North Carolina capes into the peaceful waters of the sounds. Hatteras is at the point of maximum outward swing on the great bow that the North Carolina coast presents to the surging Atlantic Ocean. The American coasting ships and the West Indian trade passed within its lights, and the lookouts in the lighthouses exercised surveillance over the transit-trade.

"A sail to the northwards," "several sail in sight," and so forth were the signals for the Confederate sea-dogs to dash forth.

The first armed vessels to utilize the natural advantages of Hatteras were the gunboats of the North Carolina navy. Immediately, following her secession, and prior to her admission into the Union of the Confederate States, the Old North State had organized an army and navy. The latter consisted of the *Winslow*, a side-wheel steamer, mounting two guns, and the two canal towboats, the *Raleigh* and the *Beaufort*, carrying one gun each. The *Winslow*, Lieutenant Commanding Thomas M. Crossan, N.C.N., being the fastest of the squadron, usually got the pickings.

The first prize came to the North Carolinians in May, and was the brig *Lydia Frances*, of Bridgeport, Connecticut, bound from Cuba to New York, with a cargo of sugar. A little later the bark *Linwood*, while returning to her home port, New York, with coffee from Rio de Janeiro, fell into their hands; as also did another bark, carrying flour, lard, and white pine, and the schooner *Willet S. Robbins*. In the latter part of June the *Winslow* captured the chartered transport *Transit*, Master Knowles, of New London, Connecticut, returning northward after having carried provisions and munitions to the United States forces at Key West. The *Transit*, a schooner of 193 tons, costing about $13,000, was safely taken into New Berne by H. Seawell, prize master. A few days later, on July 3, the *Winslow* took the schooner *Herbert Manton*, of Barnstable, Massachusetts, coming up from Tunas de Zaza, Cuba, with 175 hogsheads and 45 tierces of sugar and 70 hogsheads of molasses on board, and valued at $30,000.

On June 25, while cruising in the Gulf Stream some thirty miles southeast of Cape Hatteras, the energetic *Winslow* recaptured the hermaphrodite brig *Hannah Balch* from the enemy's prize crew. This brig had been captured by the U.S.S. *Flag* five days before, while attempting to run the blockade into Savannah: but it seemed predestined that she should deliver her cargo of molasses to a Confederate port.

A fortnight later the little North Carolina cruiser again assisted Confederate commerce. Seeing a sail off Ocracoke bar, she gave chase; and, at length, opened fire upon the fleeing vessel. Thereupon the schooner *Charles Roberts* surrendered. However, the apprehension on the one side and the pleasant expectation on the other were soon ended. The boarding officer found the prize to be a Confederate vessel with a cargo of West Indian molasses for Wilmington. The *Winslow* then made amends by conveying the schooner to her destination.

Shortly afterward, the North Carolinians made another prizeless capture. The schooner *Priscilla* was taken into New Berne; but, her Maryland ownership becoming established, she was released and allowed to complete her voyage to Baltimore. By her the Confederate Government sent home a number of the seamen brought in on the captured merchantmen.

About the last of July the North Carolina naval forces were transferred to the Confederate States navy. It was also at this time that the privateers began to rendezvous at Hatteras.

The first of them was the saucy-looking *York*, formerly the pilot boat *Florida* of Norfolk. This little schooner was of only 68 tons burden, mounted one 8-pounder rifle, and carried about thirty men. She fitted out in her home port, under Captain John Geoffrey, and came down into the North Carolina sounds by way of the Albemarle Canal. The *York* was singularly unfortunate. On July 23, she captured the brig *B. T. Martin*, three days out from Philadelphia, bound for Havana, and laden with staves and a complete sugar mill. The capture was effected about 110 miles eastward of Hatteras. A prize crew was put on the brig and the brig's people taken on board the privateer.

The next day, the prize crew, on what seems to have been a scare, beached the brig some twenty or thirty miles north of the cape. The privateersmen, assisted by the natives, began to strip the prize of her sails and rigging and to land the cargo. The work of unloading and dismantling the *Martin* was about completed when the U.S.S. *Union* put in an appearance and began to shell the wreckers, who fled precipitately into the woods. The cruiser then landed five or six boat parties, which burned the brig and the salvage piled near by.

The *York*'s career ended in disaster on August 9. She was now under the command of Captain T. L. Skinner. On Thursday, the day before, she had recaptured the Texan schooner *George G. Baker*, at a point about seventy-five miles northeast of the rendezvous. This schooner was, at the moment of recapture, in charge of a prize crew from the U.S.S. *South Carolina*, which had taken her in the Gulf of Mexico for violation of the blockade and was sending her to New York for adjudication. Captain Skinner had put four men on board and ordered them to take the prize into Hatteras. Early on Friday morning, with the lighthouse on the Cape in sight, the privateer and her prize discovered that they were being chased. The *York* attempted to run into an inlet but her enemy, the U.S.S. *Union*, intervened, and she then tacked and stood directly in for the land. After running the vessel ashore, the privateersmen set fire to her in several places and made their escape, carrying away with them the captured prize crew. The *Union* remained by the little letter of marque until she burned to the water's edge, and then gave chase to the *Baker*, which in the meantime was beating seaward. About 3:30 in the afternoon the enemy again took possession of the schooner. The Confederate prize crew was thrown into double irons, and a second United States prize crew continued the interrupted voyage to New York.

Closely following the *York* came the *Mariner* to the rendezvous at Hatteras. This privateer was a small screw-steamer, single masted, fitted out at Wilmington under the command of Captain B. W. Berry. She mounted one 6-pounder rifle and two 12-pounder smooth bores, and carried about thirty men. On July 25, she captured and brought in her only prize, the schooner *Nathaniel Chase*. It was the same day that the *Gordon* arrived with her first prize in tow.

This new letter of marque was of Charleston outfitting. She had been a packet running on the Charleston-Fernandina line, and was a fast side-wheel steamer of 519 tons. She carried fifty men and mounted three very fair pieces of ordnance. Her commander, Captain Thomas J. Lockwood, at the commencement of the war the master of a sister ship, the *Carolina*, likewise belonging to the Florida Steam Packet Company, had been handed his commission on July 15.

On the morning of the seventeenth, the *Gordon* left Charleston and stood up the coast of the Carolinas. She met with no interference from blockading vessels except in the vicinity of Cape Romain. . . . After eluding the enemy, Captain Lockwood again put to sea. At seven A.M., on the twenty-fifth, while some forty miles off Hatteras, he fell in with the brig *William McGilvery*, of Bangor, Maine, freighting Cuban molasses to Boston. To advise the Yankee skipper that his presence was desired on board the steamer, a shot was fired in his direction. It fell short, and the brig paid it no heed. But a second shot passed disconcertingly between the head stays and the foresail, and Master Hiram Carlisle hove to. The privateer steamed alongside, and ordered the obstinate skipper to come on board with his papers. This he declined to do until Captain Lockwood threatened to sink his brig under him. All hardheadedness then disappeared, and Carlisle discreetly complied without further ado. The papers showing the *McGilvery* to be a lawful prize, the *Gordon* carried her into Hatteras Inlet to join the goodly company of prizes assembled there.

The *Gordon* was on the wing again without loss of time; and soon fell in with the schooner *Protector*, of and for Philadelphia, with luscious fruit from the beautiful Cuban port of Matanzas. This prize hove to promptly when a shot went hurtling across her bow. Making fast to her with a towline, the privateer returned to the rendezvous.

On the thirtieth, while cruising off Cape Lookout, the *Gordon* was seen by a United States man-of-war, which gave chase; but the privateer showed a clean pair of heels and made into Beaufort, North Carolina. Here she remained three days and then returned to Hatteras.

The privateer *Gordon* and the C.S.S. *Winslow* were the leading vessels on the station, and got the prizes. The smaller public- and private-armed ships, however, did not fail to carry on. The routine on these lesser war vessels may be exemplified from the log of the *Beaufort* — a little gunboat which later played a gallant part in all the fleet actions in the James River from the memorable March 8, 1862, to the fall of Richmond in April, 1865. . . .

The first schooner taken on the fourth by the *Gordon* was the *Henry Nutt*, from Key West for Philadelphia, having on board a quantity of logwood and mahogany. After placing a prize crew on board, the *Gordon* towed her into Hatteras, and then returned to the hunting ground. There the guns of the privateer soon persuaded the schooner *Sea Witch*, of and for New York, from Baracoa, Cuba, to bring her cargo of tropical fruit into the inlet — for the delectation of the North Carolinians.

The activities of the Hatteras gentlemen had become a thorn in the side of the United States commercial interests. On August 9, six marine insurance companies addressed a joint petition to the Hon. Gideon Welles, Secretary of the United States Navy, reciting that their loss "is and has been very heavy," and concluding: "Any project by which this nest of pirates could be broken up would be hailed with gratitude by all interested in commerce."

How the impunity with which the Confederate gunboats and privateers operated out of Hatteras against Union shipping humiliated officers of the United States Navy is attested by a letter to Secretary Welles, dated August 10, and written by a lieutenant on board the sloop-of-war *Cumberland*. He wrote:

I trust in bringing this communication to the notice of the Department, that I may not lay to myself the charge of officiousness; but if I err in so doing, it will be considered in the light of an excess of zeal for the public service.

It seems that the coast of Carolina is infested with a nest of privateers that have thus far escaped capture, and, in the ingenious method of their cruising, are probably likely to avoid the clutches of our cruisers.

Hatteras Inlet, a little south of Cape Hatteras light, seems their principal rendezvous. Here they have a fortification that protects them from assault. A lookout at the lighthouse proclaims the coast clear, and a merchantman in sight; they dash out and are back again in a day with their prize. So long as these remain it will be impossible to entirely prevent their depredations, for they do not venture out when men-of-war are in sight; and, in the bad weather of the coming season, cruisers cannot always keep their stations off these inlets without great risk of going ashore.

Let eight or ten tugboats be chartered, of not more than 7 feet draft— some less—armed with a 32-pounder and carrying in tow a man-of-war launch with its gun and crew. A steamer of the *Iroquois* or *Seminole* class, with a smaller gunboat, can silence the battery from the outside. Let the fleet of steamers enter the inlet, and cruising in couplets, explore Albemarle and Pamlico sounds. In three weeks there will not be a vessel left that can be productive of harm.

These tugboats should be paddle-wheel, not propellers, as the latter draw too much water, carry 20 men, and may be equipped sufficiently for the service in forty-eight hours. Let them be officered temporarily by the officers of the Atlantic fleet, and in three weeks nothing more will be heard of Carolina privateers.

But the United States Navy Department had its own novel plans under way for the closing of the North Carolina inlets. The intention was to seal the entrances to the sounds by sinking in them old vessels loaded with stone. To cover these operations a joint army and navy force was being organized in Hampton Roads. By the middle of August the expedition was ready, but the prevalence of high winds and rough seas delayed the sailing until near the end of the month.

In the meantime, the Confederates, unaware that their day was drawing to a close, continued their forays. But United States flags—due to transfers of registry or to lack of cargoes—were rapidly becoming scarce, and most of the ships overhauled were flying British colors. After her two captures on the fourth, although remaining almost continuously at sea, the *Gordon* saw only two enemy merchant-men and they were under convoy of men-of-war. Then on the twenty-seventh, when putting out from the rendezvous, the privateer made ten ships in the off-ing, which were supposed to be United States vessels. Seven of them appeared to be steamers and three sailing vessels. Captain Lockwood thought it best to give such an assemblage a wide berth, and stood for a southward cruise. That night, Tuesday, he put into Wilmington, where he remained two days. Early Friday morn-ing, he left the Cape Fear and steamed for home. Passing Bull's Bay he saw a large man-of-war and upon arriving off the Charleston bar he found two more. But they were "not keeping up the blockade—at least, they were unable to keep out the *Gordon*," said her captain to a news reporter shortly after coming to an anchorage in Charleston harbor, on the afternoon of that same Friday, August 30.

On the morning of the twentieth, the *Winslow* brought in the last of the Hat-teras prizes, the steamer *Itasca*. Exactly a week later the Fortress Monroe expedi-tion, which the *Gordon* had sighted, appeared within sight of Cape Hatteras Light, and, during the afternoon, anchored to the southward of the cape. Surf boats were hoisted out and preparations were made for landing troops on the next morning.

Col. William F. Martin, commanding Forts Clark and Hatteras, which guarded the inlet, was an interested spectator of these proceedings. With the aid of his glass he made out the formidable proportions of the expedition, which consisted of the screw frigates *Minnesota*, 47 [guns], flagship to Commodore Stringham, and *Wabash*, 46, the sailing sloop *Cumberland*, 24, the screw sloops, *Susquehannah*, 15, and *Pawnee*, 9, the gunboats *Harriet Lane*, 5, and *Monticello*, 8, the steam transports *Adelaide* and *George Peabody*, and the army tug *Fanny*. There were two regiments of infantry volunteers and a company of artillery regulars on board the transports, under command of Brigadier General Benjamin F. Butler. In addition there was the flotilla of stone ships.

It so happened that none of the public- or private-armed vessels of the Confed-eracy were that day on the station. Colonel Martin, whose garrison consisted of about 850 men, at once sent a courier by small boat to the camp on Portsmouth Island at Ocracoke Inlet for reinforcements.

With daylight the next morning the enemy landed troops at a point up the beach, well screened from the forts. A little before nine the squadron stood in and opened fire at long range upon Fort Clark, the smaller and nearer of the two Confederate works. The Confederates returned the fire, but were outranged. By noon all the artillery ammunition in Fort Clark having been expended, the garri-son spiked its guns and withdrew to the larger stronghold. Upon Fort Hatteras the bombardment was continued until nightfall.

During the afternoon Commodore Samuel Barron, C.S.N., commanding the naval defenses of North Carolina and Virginia, arrived in the *Winslow*, accompanied by the *Ellis*. That night a great gun was landed from the little flagship and was mounted in the fort on a navy carriage, doing splendid work during the next morning's battle. Colonel Martin, an infantryman, was completely exhausted, and persuaded Commodore Barron to accept the sole command. Thus did the old naval officer, in singleness of patriotism, essay the rôle of coast artilleryman.

The enemy's landing party had been busy during the night, and with the morning the defenders of the fort found themselves fired upon not only from the sea, but also from a battery of naval howitzers planted on the land side. All the morning the enemy's squadrons, from a position just beyond the reach of the greatest elevation of the Confederate guns, poured a flood of shells into the fort. A regiment arrived from Portsmouth, but too late to be of any assistance. Toward noon Barron called a council of war, which "unanimously agreed that holding out longer could only result in a greater loss of life, without the ability to damage our adversaries." A white flag was then displayed, and the garrison surrendered unconditionally.

The *Winslow* and the *Ellis* escaped into the inland waters; but Hatteras, an incomparable sally port upon the extensive navigation which must pass that way, was permanently lost to the Confederate commerce-destroyers.

Lincoln Hears the News

CARL SANDBURG   1861

The easy capture of Hatteras Inlet by Federal forces under General Benjamin Butler in early 1861 was a turning point in the Civil War. It gave the Union a notable victory and a much-needed boost in morale close on the reverses of First Bull Run and Big Bethel, it provided the first Union foothold on Confederate soil outside Virginia, and it contributed materially to the success of President Lincoln's blockade. But even though the gateway to the sounds of North Carolina had come under Union control, the victors disagreed about what to do with the captured Confederate forts Hatteras and Clark. Butler's superiors saw no need to maintain a presence on the Outer Banks and gave him clear orders to sink two sand-filled schooners in Hatteras Inlet, rendering the passage useless to Confederate privateers and blockade-runners—and to the blockading squadron. Butler regarded an open Hatteras Inlet as an asset to the Union and chose not to carry out these orders. Instead, he ordered soldiers to leave the channel clear and to hold the two forts, while he took off for Washington to explain himself. In the following extract from *Abraham Lincoln: The War Years*, Carl Sandburg recounts how Lincoln authorized Butler's amphibious expedition and later, flushed with success, quickly forgave his insubordination.

LINCOLN ASKED quickly, "You think we are wrong, do you?" "Yes," said Butler, "in this: you are making this too much a party war. You must get the Democrats in it." Butler pointed to the election for Congressmen coming next year. "And if you get all the Republicans sent out as soldiers and the Democrats not interested, I do not see but that you will be beaten." And Lincoln replied, according to Butler, as if he had not thought of it before: "There is meat in that, General. What is your suggestion?" Then on hearing Butler's proposals Lincoln authorized Butler to enlist 6,000 men in sixty days in New England, Butler to command the division and follow his own devices. As officers he would choose all Democrats, Butler assured Lincoln, and "if you put epaulettes on their shoulders they will be as true to the country as I hope I am." Lincoln, according to Butler, told Butler to go ahead and arrange the presidential order to be signed: "Draw such an order as you want, but don't get me into any scrape with the Governors about the appointments of the officers if you can help it."

Butler headed an expedition of ships and men to Hatteras Inlet in August at a cost of one man killed for five of the enemy, captured fortifications controlling a long line of seacoast, 715 prisoners, 1,000 muskets, 30 cannon, several ships, and 150 bags of coffee. The victory won, he decided to disobey orders and not sink two sand-laden schooners in the inlet. He also decided that his disobedience would be approved if he could get to Washington himself immediately with the news. He arrives at Postmaster General Blair's home opposite the White House late at night to find Blair in his study with the Assistant Secretary of the Navy, Gustavus Vasa Fox. They were glad to hear the news and asked Butler to step across and tell the President. "We ought not to get him up at this time of night," said Butler. "Let him sleep." "He will sleep enough better for it," was Fox's idea.

At the White House it took them about fifteen minutes to find the watchman and wake him. Butler remarked that it would have been a good night for the enemy to kidnap a President. Lincoln was called, and as Butler told it: "He immediately came in in his night shirt; and he seemed very much taller in that garment; and Fox was about five feet nothing. Fox communicated the news, and then he and Lincoln fell into each other's arms. That is, Fox put his arms around Lincoln about as high as the hips, and Lincoln reached down over him so that his arms were pretty near the floor, and thus holding each other they flew around the room once or twice, and the night shirt was considerably agitated." Butler lay on the sofa and roared.

The Chicamacomico Races

EVERT A. DUYCKINCK   1861

A month after the capture of Hatteras Inlet by Federal forces, a detachment of approximately 600 men, mostly from Colonel W. L. Brown's Twentieth Indiana Volunteers, finally occupied the northern end of Hatteras Island. Arriving by boat opposite the village of Chicamacomico, the men found the sound so shallow that they had to wade more than half a mile to shore. Once on dry land, they set up a base that they named Live Oak Camp.

When the Confederates on Roanoke Island learned of this development, they decided to attack the camp, even if it meant seriously weakening their own position. They settled on a pincerlike maneuver: one unit (the Third Georgia Regiment) would land above Chicamacomico, and a second (Colonel Shaw's Eighth North Carolina Regiment) would land below. But when Colonel Brown saw the first of the Georgians wading ashore, he abandoned the camp and retreated down the beach toward Cape Hatteras. Local residents, most of whom had held no strong allegiance, were suddenly forced to choose a side. The following account of this half-comic engagement comes from the *National History of the War for the Union*, published the following year.

IT WAS ABOUT 9 o'clock when the attack upon the Indianians was made. Armed only with their muskets, and with not a day's provisions on hand, they were drawn up along the shore, prepared to receive the foe. Without returning to his encampment Colonel Brown commenced the retreat. It was a march of fearful severity. One of the Indianians who participated in its hardships has described it. "The sun was shining on the white sand of the beach, heating the air as if it were a furnace. The men had neither provisions nor water. The haste in which they had rushed to repel the enemy had prevented this, and it was too late to go back to camp. It was a march I shall never forget. The first ten miles was terrible. No water, the men unused to long marches, the sand heavy, their feet sinking into it at every step. As the regiment pushed along man after man would stagger from the ranks and fall upon the hot sand. Looking back, I saw our Colonel trudging along with his men, having given up his horse to a sick soldier. But the most sorrowful sight of all was the Islanders leaving their homes from fear of the enemy. They could be seen in groups, sometimes with a little cart carrying their provisions, but mostly with nothing, fleeing for dear life; mothers carrying their babes, fathers leading along the boys, grandfathers and grandmothers straggling along from homes they had left behind. Relying on our protection, they had been our friends, but in an evil hour we had been compelled to leave them.

"We still toiled on, the heat most intense, and no water. Hunger was nothing in comparison with thirst. It was maddening. The sea rolling at our feet and nothing to drink. I started to take a scout to watch the movements of the enemy's vessels. I skirted the Sound for some ten miles. In every clump of bushes I would find men utterly exhausted. The enemy's vessels were now nearly opposite, steaming down the Sound to cut off our retreat. I would tell them this, but they would say, 'they did not care, they would die there,' so utterly hopeless did they seem.

"Near sunset I caught sight of the army drawn up in line of battle on the beach, about a mile distant. Soon joining them, I found that the enemy were reported in force in front. After some delay, the army marched by the right flank, skirmishers ahead, until we reached the narrow inlet about five miles above Hatteras light-house, and here our great danger was at once seen. The fleet of the enemy had drawn up in line, so as to sweep the beach, and render a passage impossible, but had neglected to land their men. It was now near twilight. The clouds in the west reflected the bright tints of the sun, and showed us the enemy in the foreground. In the east heavy gray clouds lowered, and our uniforms corresponding, hid us from their view, as we silently stole along, the roar of the surf drowning the foot-steps of the men and the commands of the officers, yet every little while we would watch, expecting to see the flash of the enemy's cannon or hear the report of the bursting shell in our little band. It was a narrow escape, and a providential one, and our Colonel was affected to tears at the danger we had passed. At midnight we reached Hatteras Lighthouse, having made a march of twenty-eight miles. Here we found water, and using the lighthouse as a fort, we encamped for the night, and woke up next morning feeling like sand-crabs, and ready, like them, to go into our holes, could we find them."

Thus closed the events of the 4th with the escape of the fugitives. The 5th was to witness a bitter and unexpected revenge from the guns of the fleet. Colonel Hawkins, on making his preparations to meet the returning troops, had also given information to Captain J. L. Lardner . . . in the command of the steam-frigate *Susquehanna*, of the state of affairs. Besides his vessel, the United States steamer *Monticello*, Lieutenant D. L. Braine commanding, was then in the inlet. Captain Lardner immediately brought both vessels to Hatteras Cove, where he found the retreating Indianians in the morning gathered round the lighthouse after their exhausting night vigil. He supplied them with food and remained for their protec-tion, sending the *Monticello* along the coast to watch the movements of the enemy, who, having effected a landing, were reported to be in force some miles above at

Keneekut. The errand was thoroughly accomplished. Its striking incidents are thus related in the official report of Lieutenant Braine . . . "I stood through the inner channel of Hatteras shoals at 12 ½ P.M., and stood close along shore to the northward, keeping a bright look-out from aloft. At 1 ½ P.M. we discovered several vessels over the woodland Keneekut, and at the same time a regiment marching to the northward, carrying a rebel flag in their midst, with many stragglers in their rear; also two tugs inside flying the same flag. As they came out of the woods of Keneekut, we ran close in shore, and opened a deliberate fire upon them at a distance of three-quarters of a mile. At our first shell, which fell apparently in their midst, they rolled up their flag and scattered, moving rapidly up the beach to the northward. We followed them, firing rapidly from three guns, driving them up to a clump of woods in which they took refuge, and abreast of which their steamers lay. We now shelled the woods, and could see them embarking in small-boats after vessels, evidently in great confusion, and suffering greatly from our fire.

Their steamers now opened fire upon us, firing, however, but three shots, which fell short. Two boats filled with men were struck by our shells and destroyed. Three more steamers came down the Sound and took position opposite the woods. We were shelling also two sloops. We continued firing deliberately from 1 ½ P.M. to 3 ½ P.M., when two men were discovered on the sea-beach making signals to us. Supposing them to be two of the Indiana regiment, we sent an armed boat and crew to bring them off, covering them at the same time with our fire. Upon the boat nearing the beach they took to the water. One of them was successful in reaching the boat—private Warren O. Haver, Company H, 20th regiment Indiana troops. The other man—private Charles White, Company H, 20th regiment Indiana troops—was unfortunately drowned in the surf.

"Private Haver informs me that he was taken prisoner on the morning of the 4th; that he witnessed one shot which was very destructive. He states that two of our shells fell into two sloops loaded with men, blowing the vessels to pieces and sinking them. Also that several officers were killed, and their horses seen running about the track. He had just escaped from his captors, after shooting the captain of one of the rebel companies. He states that the enemy were in the greatest confusion, rushing wildly into the water striving to get off their vessels. Private Haver now directed me to the point where the rebels were congregated, waiting an opportunity to get off. I opened fire again with success, scattering them. We were now very close, in three fathoms water, and the fire of the second shell told with effect. Six steamers were now off the point, one of which I recognized as the *Fanny*. At twenty-five minutes past 5 we ceased firing, leaving the enemy scattered along the beach for upwards of four miles. I fired repeatedly at the enemy's steamers with our rifled cannon—a Parrott 30-pounder—and struck the *Fanny*, I think, once."

Twenty-nine of the Indiana regiment, in addition to those captured on the *Fanny*, were missing in this retreat. . . . The Georgia regiment, on landing, dragged their guns with them through the heavy sand in the pursuit, so that they had themselves a taste of the hardships which they were inflicting on the fugitives. . . . The entire expedition then returned to Roanoke Island, stopping on their way to gather the spoils left at Chicamacomico.

The Battle of Roanoke Island

GEORGE WASHINGTON WHITMAN   1862

As the Civil War heated up, Roanoke Island became the key to northeastern North Carolina. Although its Confederate defenders expected a Union push from the south after the fall of Hatteras Inlet, they dug in on the *north* end of the island where there was high ground overlooking Croatan Sound.

By late morning February 7, 1862, most of the Federal fleet had passed into Croatan Sound and the naval battle was enjoined— just where the Confederates had expected. In late afternoon, however, the invading fleet withdrew and began debarking troops several miles south of the main fortification, at Ashby's Harbor (now Skyco). Throughout the afternoon and evening the landing continued until approximately 7,500 Union soldiers commanded by General Ambrose Burnside were ashore. Before sunrise the next morning they began passing through a swamp the Confederates considered impenetrable and soon captured the little three-gun battery built at the last minute to control the only road running the length of the island. As the conquering Union forces advanced toward the north end of the island, some 3,000 Confederates manning the larger forts surrendered or fled.

Although the Battle of Roanoke Island was neither long nor unusually bloody, it enabled the Burnside Expedition to gain control of most of the northeast quadrant of the state before summer. The following account, from a collection of letters put together in 1973 by a Duke University doctoral candidate, has none of the polish we might expect of Walt Whitman's brother; but its wealth of detail makes up for its stylistic shortcomings. In the interest of readability, a few spellings have been changed, and paragraph breaks and punctuation have been inserted.

Roanoak Island North Carolina Feb 9th

Dear Mother

I wrote you last when we arived at Hateras Inlet nearly a month since but dont know as you received it as I hear the leters did not leave there untill we left to come here, which was on Wednesday last. This island is on Palmico Sound about 45 miles from Hateras and is about 12 miles long and 4 wide.

We left Hateras with a fleet of about 70 vessels only 15 or 16 of which was fighting crafts. The rest were tow boats, old steamboats, and schooners. We had about 13000 Infantry on board the transports and came to anchor near hear on Thursday afternoon.

On Friday Morning we got under way, the gunboats taking the lead, and as soon as we got within range the gunboats opened fire on the Batteries here, and they blazed away back. It was a fine sight, the shells bursting all around the batteries and sending up a column of sand 20 feet high and the Batteries throwing shot and shells like blazes. The Staten Island Ferry boat *Hunchback* which had some heavy guns on board was shot through and through but she anchored and stuck to it like a good fellow. They kept it up untill dusk and then hauled off for the night.

About 5 O Clock in the afternoon our regiment landed, one of the gunboats throwing shell to cover us, one of the Mass regts landing just about the same time. We were on board of an old stern wheel steamboat which took us up so close that we jumped on shore we had to wade about 200 yards through mud and water up to our knees and then found a spot not very dry but we stoped there for the night. We built fires and tried to dry ourselves as well as we could, took our suppers of hard crackers, and then laid down for the night. About 11 O Clock it comenced to rain, not very hard but enough to make it very unpleasant. I stuck it out until my blanket got wet through, and then got up and stood around the fire until morning. We had breakfast of good crackers, put more crackers in our haversacks and then fell in for a march.

We moved off in two Brigades, we being the second, numbering all told about 7300 men with a battery of 5 howitzers. We struck directly into the woods and soon heard the firing comence on the right of the first Brigade. We were in a wagon path and all around us was a thick wood almost as thick as the woods around Deer Park. We kept on, the first Brigade driving the enemy untill we got into a thick swamp where the mud and water was over the top of my boots and the bushes was so thick that we had the greatest difficulty in getting through. We kept on however untill we drove them chock into their Batery which was one of the celebrated masked Bateries we have heard so mutch about. Our regiment worked around on their right flank through a thicket that you would think it was imposible for a man to pass through. It was mighty trying to a fellows nerves as the balls was fly-ing around pretty thick cutting the twigs off overhead and knocking the bark off the trees all around us, but our regiment behaved finely and pressed on as fast as possible. We were under fire about an hour and a half before our regiment dare fire a shot for fear of shooting our own friends as we could not see 10 yards on either side.

As soon as our regt got sight of the Batery Gen Reno who is our Brigadeer Gen-eral gave the order to charge and away we went, the water flying over our heads as we splashed through it. I was in my position on the left flank of our regt when I heard the order to charge so that when I reached the Battery our colors and the flag of the 9th New York and the 21st Mass were planted there. Ours were there first however but it was mighty tight between us and the others. When the other regts came in you can bet there was some tall shouting but there was nary a rebel in sight for as soon as they saw us start on a charge they started to run. One of the rebels lay there dead by his gun. Another lay badly wounded. A few feet further in the bushes lay an old man with beard perfectly white, dead. Here and there heaps of knapsacks, haversacks, and clothes, guns, and amunition. I picked up this paper and envelope inside the Battery, and as I wanted a pair of drawers I found a new pair and a lot of hankerchiefs which I lost again.

We soon formed again and started after the rebels, quite a number of whome had broke for the shore about a mile off. The way was pretty well strewn with blan-kets an coats thrown off by the rebels as they ran. A few of them escaped in boats but we got 40 or 50 there. Among the rest was Mr. O Jennings Wise, son of Gov Wise of Virginia, who was badly wounded and I believe died to day. He came to the Island yesterday morning with 600 of the noted Wise Legion. He was a fine looking young fellow and plucky. We took these prisoners to a house near by and started off in the woods to look for more game and we found it. After traveling about an hour we found two dead rebels lying in the woods and farther on lay another just dying, the top of his head being shot off. A little way from these we met a dozen rebels with a white flag. We took care of them and soon met another party with a flag. They said they came from a large force and wanted to make terms for a surender. Our general told them unles they made an unconditional surender at once he would order his forces to fire, but they had had enough for one day and stacked their arms and wilted without a strugle.

They numbered about 1600 men and had cleared a space of a couple of hun-dred acres of land in the woods and erected splendid barracks for I should think 20,000 men. The buildings have floors and fire places and shingle roofs. I have not counted the buildings but should think there was 75 or 80, some 25 or 30 of which are about 100 feet by 50, and a good many first rate log houses and a large hospital

Building. Quite a quantity of stores were found in some of the buildings consisting of bacon, rice, crackers, all of which we took peacable posession of and we have slaughtered hogs enough in the woods to keep us all in fresh pork last night and today with a small stock for tomorrow. We are living now like fighting cocks and prisoners have been comeing in and giving themselvs up, and squads of them have been taken by our pickets all day so that we must have some 2500 to night. I have seen 1 or 2 Colonels and lots of captains and other Officers among them. They have been working here, the prisoners say, for the last 5 months puting up these buildings and I give them credit for haveing built tip-top quarters.

The loss of our regiment was remarkable small, I think not over 10 killed and 10 or 12 wounded. I think the loss on our side not more than 40 killed and 70 or 80 wounded. It is a miracle to me that our loss was so small when I think how the bullets wized around our heads. The enemy had a great advantage in knowing the ground and could pick his position while we had to follow without knowing were we were going. They thought they would tole us up to the Bateries and then slaughter us as they did at Bethell. They say they did not think we would go in that water and fight. The Batery was made of turf and had 4 guns. We whiped them fair and square on their own ground and they say we are a good deal smarter than they thought we were. It was rather a sickening sight to see the wounded brought along the road but I expected sutch things so that it did not effect me mutch and after a while we would pass them lying in the bushes and think nothing of it. I was as calm and cool during the whole affair as I am at any time and I was perfectly surprised to see how well our troops acted. Our Generals too, Reno and Foster, acted first rate. Burnside and Pratt I believe was not on shore. They were atending to the forts on shore. Pratts Brigade I believe did not land untill the fleet silenced some of the Bateries. The fleet went to work yesterday morning about the same time that we did, knocked tar out of some of the Batteries on the shore, and scared the rebels so that they left others before the fleet fired a shot into them.

I went down to one of their Batteries this afternoon and was surprised to see how large and well aranged it was. It was made of turf, the parapet which shields the guners being about 15 ft thick and 8 or 9 feet high with embrasures to rain the guns out. It mounted 10 guns, 2 of them being 32 pound Parrot guns, rifled, and the others heavy smoothe bore guns. I could see from there three other Forts, one they say just like the one I was in, another mutch larger and mounting 18 large guns. And I believe there are some others that I have not seen. . . .

So Mammy I think we done a pretty good days work yesterday marching 15 or 16 miles and fighting with boots filed with water for 4 hours. . . . Wish Walt if he is home, or Jeff would send me some papers. Often it is a great treat to get a sight of a New York Paper. I would like one giveing a description of the battle I supose you

will see a good acount of it as I saw 2 or three reporters in the field yesterday. . . .
Good night Mother.

G. W. Whitman

The only efects I feel of my work yesterday is a little stiffness in my legs from walking.

The Mirlo Rescue

JOHN ALLEN MIDGETT 1918

Less than three months before the end of World War I, the British tanker *Mirlo* struck a German mine off Wimble Shoals. The resulting explosions tore the ship in two. Its cargo of gasoline spewed burning from ruptured tanks, and gale winds pushed the conflagration west, barring the desperate survivors from shore. The watch at Chicamacomico Coast Guard Station saw the first explosion, and within a half hour Keeper John Allen Midgett and a crew of five had put to sea in the power surfboat. In the next four hours they saved forty-two of the fifty-two officers and men of the doomed ship. Great Britain decorated Midgett and his crew for heroism in 1920, but the United States postponed recognition another decade. Here is Keeper Midgett's matter-of-fact account of one of the most daring maritime rescues ever effected on the Outer Banks.

AT 4:30 P.M., August 16, 1918, the lookout reported seeing a great mass of water shoot up in the air which seemed to cover the after portion of a steamer that was about seven miles from this station and heading in a northerly direction. A great quantity of smoke rising from the after part of the ship was noticed, but continuing her course for a few minutes when she seemed to swing around for the beach and then heading for the shore.

The fire was now seen to shoot up from the stern of the steamer and heavy explosions were heard. I called all hands, including the liberty man, and started with power surfboat No. 1046; wind NE, moderate heavy sea on beach; had some difficulty in getting away from the beach; cleared the beach at 5:00 P.M. and headed for the burning wreck.

When about five miles off shore, I met one of the ship's boats with captain and 16 men in it. I was informed that their ship was a British tank steamer, the *Mirlo*, and that she was torpedoed which caused the fire, explosion and loss of ship.

Upon inquiry, I was informed that two other boats were in the vicinity of the fire and that one was capsized and that he feared all the crew of that boat had perished in the burning sea.

I directed the captain of that boat where and how to go and wait my arrival, but not to attempt a landing as the sea was strong and there was danger of him capsizing his boat without assistance. I then headed for the burning mass of wreckage and oil.

On arrival, I found the sea a mass of wreckage and burning gas. There were two great masses of flames about 100 yards apart, with the sea for many hundreds of yards covered with burning gas and oil. And in between the two great flames, at times when the smoke would clear away, a lifeboat could be seen bottom-up, with six men clinging to it. The heavy swell was washing over the boat.

With some difficulty I ran our boat through the smoke, floating wreckage and burning gas and oil and rescued the six men from the burning sea. They informed me that at many times they had had to dive under water to save themselves from being burned to death; all had burns, none serious. They informed me they had seen some of their crew sink and disappear in the burning sea. These six men seemed to know nothing of the other boats, they being lost sight of in the fire and smoke that were rising from the burning gas and oil.

I headed our boat before the wind and sea in hope of finding the missing boat, and in a short time, the third boat with 19 men was sighted. It was overloaded and so much crowded that the men in it could not row; and it was drifting with the wind and sea. The boat was about nine miles SE of this station.

I ran along side, took her in tow, and proceeded to where I had directed the first boat to be. This boat was soon reached and taken in tow. With 36 men in the two boats being towed and six men in the station boat, in addition to my own crew, I was heading for my station when the wind began to fresh from the NE and the sea rising on the beach. It was now dark, and for safety's sake, I decided to make a landing. I had the ship's two boats anchored about 600 yards off shore and began transferring the shipwrecked crew to land in the station boat where I was met by other members of my crew that were left on shore, and also by Keeper and crew from Station No. 180, who assisted in landing the crew. Four trips were made in the station boat.

I put the surfmen in the ship's two boats and had them landed. As fast as the crew were landed, they were taken to the station and to Station 180. I landed in station boat last trip at 9:00 P.M. and had all boats put up on beach out of danger of the sea. I arrived at my station at 11:00 P.M. All shipwrecked men were given medical aid and their burns dressed, and were given some dry garments. Members of crew were furnished with supper and given a place to sleep.

I Wore a Dead Man's Hand

AYCOCK BROWN AND KEN JONES   1942

The surprise attack on Pearl Harbor pushed the United States into a global conflict ill-prepared to face Japan, much less Germany. Not long after the Third Reich declared war, Admiral Karl Dönitz sent U-boats to our poorly guarded Eastern Seaboard. In the first six months of 1942, the handful of submarines involved in Operation Drumbeat cut a frightful swath through Allied shipping, sinking more than five dozen vessels in North Carolina waters alone. Before long the area around Cape Hatteras earned an unflattering nickname, Torpedo Junction. Up and down the Outer Banks, gunfire and explosions punctuated the rumble of the surf, burning ships illuminated the nighttime horizon, oil fouled the waters, and debris littered the beach.

Aycock Brown, a mountain man who moved to the coast and went native, became a widely recognized publicist while promoting Morehead City, Beaufort, Atlantic Beach, and Ocracoke. For the last twenty-six years of his career he managed the Dare County Tourist Bureau and helped create a booming tourist industry on the northern Banks. During World War II he served as a civilian agent of U.S. Naval Intelligence. In this article that he cowrote in 1955 for *Male* magazine, Aycock described one of his least-enviable duties in that position: identifying bodies washed ashore or recovered at sea.

"WHERE IS IT?" I looked dully through red-rimmed eyes at Lieutenant George H. Meekins, commander of the Cape Hatteras Coast Guard Station.

"In there," the lieutenant replied, jerking his head toward the station's equipment house. "And I'm not going with you. We've had that thing around here too long already. I hope you'll take it away. We can't stand the stink, and that's all there is to it." He turned grimly away as I walked toward the shed.

It didn't make any difference, for as a civilian agent of Naval Intelligence I'd come to Cape Hatteras to identify a man whether I had assistance or not. The man would most likely be one of three things: a member of the British or American military, a British or American seaman, or an enemy agent. I had to know which and the subject himself couldn't tell me in his present condition.

The gloom of the unlighted interior and the smell of death that was days, perhaps weeks old, cut sharply, like a knife, across the threshold of the equipment house. Outside, the fresh air stirred with a living rustle, and the bright summer sun reflected from clean white sand. Stepping through the door, I saw the dim outline under a tarp on the floor in the furthest corner. I crossed quickly to it, raised one edge of the canvas, and contemplated the job before me.

The man's face was disfigured to a degree which rendered it a mask stamped with a vacant horror. The body was naked, and there were no dog tags or other identifying discs. The hand was missing from the stump of the left wrist, which stuck out awkwardly and stiff almost on a line with the shoulder. The knees were drawn up as if locked in bitter protest against an unbearable cramp. But all of this was as nothing compared with the right hand which held my fascinated gaze.

The right arm was thrust upward and partly out until the hand was just below the chin. And the black, bony fingers were gnarled and twisted into claw more forbidding, more frightening, than anything I've ever seen. My job was going to be a tough one, because, quite apparently, finger prints would be the only possible means of identification.

Unlimbering my portable fingerprint kit, I reached for the dead man's hand. As I touched it, a shudder of revulsion passed through my whole body, and I drew back with a quick, spasmodic gesture. But that one touch had told me one thing I needed to know. Those fingers, bent as they were into an iron claw, could never be printed. Again I forced myself to shake hands with the dead, and this time I had a crazy notion: Maybe the fingers would come off!

The fingers wouldn't come off. But as I stood there holding it I became aware of another value: despite the rigidity of the bones, the skin of the fingers was loose! Could I . . . ? Yes, I could, and I did! Fighting back an understandable disgust and an unreasoned fear, I slid the skin casings from those five fingers, one by one. Then, holding them in the palm of my hand, I bolted through the door and back into the world of reality where the truck waited to drive me to my plane.

Then there was another problem.

I had the skin finger casings, complete with the finger nails, but how could I preserve them until I found an opportunity to finish the rest of my weird experiment in post mortem fingerprints? Alcohol? Sure. But I didn't have any alcohol— or did I? After all, there was my bottle of bourbon. In they went!

As I flew back in the plane with my bottle. I thought about other grisly things I'd had to do to identify the dead. And no matter how I did it it was important that it be done—at all costs. There were reasons.

For instance: Still classified as "secret" in Navy archives in Washington are many details of the raids made by enemy submarines (principally German, although a Jap or two came to the party) along the coast of North Carolina immediately following our entry into World War Two. While the Navy finally released a list of 79 vessels—aggregating 425,850 tons sunk, and a total death roster of 843 merchant seamen and gun crews within the jurisdiction of the Fifth Naval District with headquarters at Norfolk—the actual totals were considerably greater than those officially acknowledged.

A number of acute problems arose from this situation. Most important was the opportunity for espionage. Enemy submarines could and did take prisoners from torpedoed Allied shipping. What would be simpler than landing spies and saboteurs using the official identification of captured American or British seamen.

It was a near-perfect setup, and there was only one defense against it: We had to identify and learn the fate of every single man aboard every vessel sunk off our Atlantic Coast.

It was in pursuance of this near-impossible job that I had gotten into a bitter argument with the Navy sometime before this trip with the dead man's fingers. I claimed a British warship had been sunk, because I had two corpses from her right in front of me to prove it. The Navy said "no such thing." Records showed her to be very much alive, active and out on a war mission. But let me tell you the details.

It all started when the 6,000-ton British tanker, the *San Delfino*, loaded with high octane gasoline and headed toward Britain, was torpedoed and sunk some 20 miles north of Diamond Shoals lightship.

Although the *San Delfino*'s master managed to launch boats and rafts before she went down in the night, there was considerable loss of life in the disaster. The survivors, picked up at sea by surface craft, were taken directly to Norfolk for interrogation by the Office of Naval Intelligence. Some days later I received an urgent call to go to the morgue at Morehead City to try to identify two bodies. I found the bodies in excellent condition—fully clothed, and with identification papers. One was a British seaman. The other was a member of the British Army gun crew aboard the tanker.

With identification complete and my report on its way through channels I turned next to the job of "burying the dead reverently," as my orders read.

The honor guard and firing squad were not difficult to secure; the American Legion post at Morehead took care of that. But where was I to find two British flags? It so chanced at the time that the United States was painfully short of small surface craft, and Great Britain had loaned us some sturdy North Sea trawlers which had been converted into corvettes. One of these small vessels, HMS *Bedfordshire*, was coaling at Morehead, and Captain Estess, commanding the Naval Section base there, suggested that I try the *Bedfordshire* for the flags I needed.

"Where's the officer of the deck?"

"That's 'im up there; Sub-leftenant Cunning'im," a seaman answered.

I turned toward the bridge to see a handsome, young, black bearded giant smiling down at me. He waved, and I climbed up beside him and explained my problem. "I'd not only like to have a couple of flags," I told him, "but if you could spare a few British seamen to represent His Majesty, I think that would be fine too."

"Terribly sorry, old man—terribly!" smiled the sub-leftenant with warmth. "The flags you may have, and welcome! But I can't let you have any men, because our orders are to sail as soon as we've filled our bunkers. But how's for a spot of something or other while I have the jacks brought up?"

Tom Cunningham and I had a drink and a talk and we were very merry for a brief time. I wished that I could meet him again after the war. It's not very often that you make friends like him so readily. Finally, with the British battle ensigns tucked beneath my arm, I went ashore and arranged the burial.

Six weeks later, I was back on another case.

"I don't see how you'll ever identify this pair!" said Captain Homer Gray, commanding the Coast Guard station on Ocracoke Island. I had been summoned to look at two bodies picked up at sea by a patrol boat and brought to the Ocracoke station. Homer and I stood in the boathouse, and he held up one corner of a dirty tarpaulin, revealing the bodies of two men. They were nude, in rather bad shape, and there was little apparent means of identification. But as I looked at the faces of the two men, the strength seemed to flow out of my body.

"I'm afraid it will be easy to identify these men," I said. Homer looked at me.

"I know this man," I said finally, when I could control my anger at an enemy who fired torpedoes. With my foot I indicated the nearer of the two bodies. "He's Sub-leftenant Tom Cunningham, of HMS *Bedfordshire*." The same Cunningham I'd talked and drank with in borrowing the British flags.

"We'd better notify the Fifth District." said Homer, letting the tarp fall back into place. But, when I had the Fifth Naval District on the line, they wouldn't believe me!

"You must be crazy!" said the officer at the other end. "We know where the *Bedfordshire* is."

"Maybe you do," I told him, "but I'd advise you to double check!"

Minutes later the Fifth District rang up again, and this time they were excited. "Our British liaison officer has lost the *Bedfordshire*! Are you sure of your identification?"

"Positive!" I assured them sadly. And the facts, subsequently established, bore me out. The *Bedfordshire* had disappeared like magic from the face of the sea. There was no wreckage; no survivors.

But as I sat on the plane, thinking about Cunningham, and regretting that men such as he must die as he did, I knew the man whose fingers I had pickled in my bourbon would not be so easy to identify. Yet, as I said, for reasons of security that might save hundreds of lives, he had to be identified somehow.

Natural circumstances had, of course, compelled the burial, unidentified, of the body George Meekins had sent me in to look at when I'd visited his Cape Hatteras Station. When I'd slipped the skin casings off those talon-like fingers, I'd really had only a glimmering—not a cogently formed plan—of what I'd do with them. Pickled in the bourbon, however, they haunted me. Like most robust North Carolinians I had a proper respect for a crock of prime drinking whiskey, and while I don't mind donating a dram or two for the furtherance of the legitimate purposes of the U.S. Navy, I hate to waste the stuff. But, in addition, there were the aspects of security.

I strode into the sick bay of the Naval establishment at Morehead City, holding my bottle of bourbon aloft with its freight of fingers, and shouting loudly for a pair of surgical rubber gloves. I'd decided upon a plan; resolved to take the plunge in stride; and although the whole thing was, I confess, ghoulish beyond normal tolerance, I was determined to carry it off as if it was routine.

A pair of rubber gloves was forthcoming at once, and a little knot of Navy corpsmen clustered about. But as I fished the finger casings from the bourbon, one by one, and placed them on a pad of raw cotton to dry, a sudden lack of enthusiasm swept the gathering. Only two corpsmen were left when I was ready for the second step in the experiment, and that pair didn't look any too healthy.

Donning the gloves, I carefully slipped the finger casings over the rubber-protected fingers of my own left hand. It was slow, delicate work, for the skin of the dead man's fingers was extremely fragile. When the casings were thoroughly dry, I inked each finger tip and pressed it gently upon the finger print blank I'd previously set out. The result was as perfect a set of prints as I've ever made.

These fingerprints were forwarded to the Office of Naval Intelligence, Fifth Naval District, and by them in turn to the FBI in Washington. In due time, through channels from London, came the name of our man. From the *San Delfino*.

When next I visited the Hatteras station I had another talk with Lieutenant Meekins. He and his men made a tombstone of concrete with the seaman's name cut in it.

He shall remain anonymous, however, out of respect for the feelings and comfort of his family. They would, I am sure, rather not know what we had to do to identify him. But if they did, I'm also sure they would admit it was worth it.

Making a Living

Until modern times the residents of the Outer Banks were among the most self-sufficient people in America. This was more the result of necessity than of choice, for these barrier islands were distant from the centers of commerce and trade, and few of the residents had any measurable wealth. Anyone who wanted something done most often had to do it himself. Residents of Shackleford Banks became whalers, rowing out to sea in little homemade boats to capture the giant mammals as they migrated along the coast. Until well into this century the raising of livestock was a profitable enterprise as well, for no fencing and little other overhead was required on the island ranges. In recent times Bankers have taken up more conventional work; but if something breaks down, the man of the house—who may hold several jobs—can usually figure out a way to repair it. And for that matter, the woman of the house can too.

The Petition of Legal Pilots of Ocracoke Bar

JOHN WILLIAMS ET AL. 1773

Until this century it was possible to survive on the Outer Banks by hunting, fishing, trapping, beachcombing, bartering, keeping a few head of livestock, and tending a vegetable garden. But just about anyone who wished to raise his standard of living without moving away had to take up a maritime occupation. Sometimes local men shipped out for Europe or the West Indies on merchant vessels. More often they piloted ships through the shifting inlets or practiced lighterage (removing cargo to smaller craft so that heavily laden ships might cross the bar) or transshipment (transferring cargo between ships on opposite sides of the bar). The area was sparsely populated and attracted free blacks, many of them experienced watermen. By the late eighteenth century, mainlanders were sending slaves out to the Banks to take piloting business from residents of all colors. Although race relations were usually calm, white pilots were not timid about asking the colonial government for help in suppressing black competition, as this piece from the *Colonial Records of North Carolina* attests. Some spelling and typography have been modernized for this book.

TO HIS EXCELLENCY Josiah Martin Esquire, Captain General, Governor and Commander in Chief in and over the Province of North Carolina,

The petition of legal pilots of Ocracoke Bar humbly sheweth that your petitioners under the sanction of an act of Assembly of this province have settled at Ocracoke Bar in order to attend and carry on the business of their calling at great costs and expense as well for the benefits resulting thereby as for the advantage of mariners and traders of the province in general.

Notwithstanding which sundry Negroes as well free men as slaves to considerable number by unjust and unlawful means take upon themselves to pilot vessels from Ocracoke Bar up the several rivers to Bath, Edenton and New Bern and back again to the said bar to the great prejudice and injury of your petitioners contrary to law and against the policy of this country and to trade in general.

Your petitioners therefore humbly beg leave to observe to Your Excellency that the pilotage at the said bar at present no ways answer the salutary ends intended by law as great confusion and irregularity daily insue from the insolent and turbulent disposition and behavior of such free Negroes and slaves.

Under those circumstances your petitioners humbly pray Your Excellency would please take this matter into consideration and prevent the like for the future by denying license or branch to any such free Negro or slave whatsoever.

And your petitioners as in duty bound will ever pray &c

John Williams	Adam Gaskins
Geo. Bell	Richard Wade
John Bragg	William Styerin
William Bragg	Simon Hall

The Wild Horses, Their Qualities and Habits

EDMUND RUFFIN   1856

Cattle, sheep, goats, horses, and swine were important to the local economy from the mid-1600s until the abolition of free range in the 1930s. Few pens and dipping vats are visible now, and only a few horses have survived in the wild. So it was probably inevitable that recent immigrants, unaware of three centuries of intermittent breeding and continual exploitation by natives, would associate feral (not "wild") horses with Spanish explorers or the Raleigh colonists.

One of the earliest descriptions of the Banker horses was written by Edmund Ruffin, a vehement defender of slavery, states' rights, and secession who was reputed to have fired the first shot of the Civil War. But he is probably better known as an "agricultural experimenter" and as a writer on agriculture and other subjects. He traveled extensively in eastern North Carolina during the two decades preceding the Civil War, and in 1861 the state of North Carolina, as part of its agricultural and geological survey, published his *Sketches of Lower North Carolina*, from which the following is excerpted.

EXCEPT AT AND NEAR Portsmouth, and where actual residents have possession, there is no separate private property in lands, on this reef, from Ocracoke to Beaufort harbor. But though there are no land-marks, or means for distinguishing separate properties, every portion of the reef is claimed in some manner, as private property, though held in common use. If belonging to one owner, the unsettled land would be valuable, for the peculiar mode of stock-raising in use here. But under the existing undefined and undefinable common rights, the land is of no more value to one of the joint-owners, or claimants, than to any other person who may choose to place breeding stock on the reef.

There are cattle and sheep on the marshes of this portion of the reef, obtaining a poor subsistence indeed, but without any cost or care of their owners. On the other hand, the capital and profits are at much risk, as any lawless depredator can, in security, shoot and carry off any number of those animals. But horses cannot be used for food, (or are not—) and cannot be caught and removed by thieves— and, therefore, the rearing of horses is a very profitable investment for the small amount of capital required for the business. There are some hundreds of horses, of the dwarfish native breed, on this part of the reef between Portsmouth and Beaufort harbor—ranging at large, and wild, (or untamed,) and continuing the race without any care of their numerous proprietors. Many years ago I had first heard of similar wild horses on some of the larger sea-islands of Virginia. . . . But I had supposed that the stock, (in the wild state) had ceased to exist there—and did not suspect that wild horses, and in much greater number, still were on the narrow sand-reef of North Carolina.

In applying the term wild to these horses, it is not meant that they are as much so as deer or wolves, or as the herds of horses, wild for many generations on the great grassy plains of South America or Texas. A man may approach these, within gunshot distance without difficulty. But he could not get much nearer, without alarming the herd, and causing them to flee for safety to the marshes, or across water, (to which they take very freely,) or to more remote distance on the sands. Twice a year, for all the horses on each united portion of the reef, (or so much as is unbroken by inlets too wide for the horses to swim across,) there is a general "horse-penning," to secure, and brand with the owner's marks, all the young colts. The first of these operations is in May, and the second in July, late enough for the previous birth of all the colts that come after the penning in May. If there was only one penning, and that one late enough for the latest births to have occurred, the earliest colts would be weaned, or otherwise could not be distinguished, as when much younger, by their being always close to their respective mothers, and so to have their ownership readily determined.

The "horse-pennings" are much attended, and are very interesting festivals for all the residents of the neighboring mainland. There are few adults, residing within a day's sailing of the horse-pen, that have not attended one or more of these exciting scenes. A strong enclosure, called the horse-pen, is made at a narrow part of the reef, and suitable in other respects for the purpose—with a connected strong fence, stretching quite across the reef. All of the many proprietors of the horses, and with many assistants, drive (in deer-hunters' phrase,) from the remote extremities of the reef, and easily bring, and then encircle, all the horses to the fence and near to the pen.

There the drivers are reinforced by hundreds of volunteers from among the visitors and amateurs, and the circle is narrowed until all the horses are forced into the pen, where any of them may be caught and confined. Then the young colts, distinguished by being with their mothers, are marked by their owner's brand. All of the many persons who came to buy horses, and the proprietors who wish to capture and remove any for use, or subsequent sale, then make their selections. After the price is fixed, each selected animal is caught and haltered, and immediately subjected to a rider. This is not generally very difficult—or the difficulties and the consequent accidents and mishaps to the riders are only sufficient to increase the interest and fun of the scene, and the pleasure and triumph of the actors. After the captured horse has been thrown, and sufficiently choked by the halter, he is suffered to rise, mounted by some bold and experienced rider and breaker, and forced into a neighboring creek, with a bottom of mud, stiff and deep enough to fatigue the horse, and to tender him incapable of making more use of his feet than to struggle to avoid sinking too deep into the mire. Under these circumstances, he soon yields to his rider and rarely afterwards does one resist. But there are other subsequent and greater difficulties in the domesticating these animals. They have previously fed entirely on the coarse salt grasses of the marshes, and always afterwards prefer that food, if attainable. When removed to the main land, away from the salt marshes, many die before learning to eat grain, or other strange provender. Others injure, and some kill themselves, in struggling, and in vain efforts to break through the stables or enclosures in which they are subsequently confined. All the horses in use on the reef, and on many of the nearest farms on the mainland, are of these previously wild "banks' ponies." And when having access to their former food on the salt marshes, they seek and prefer it, and will eat very little of any other and better food.

These horses are all of small size, with rough and shaggy coats, and long manes. They are generally ugly. Their hoofs, in many cases, grow to unusual lengths. They are capable of great endurance of labor and hardship, and live so roughly, that any others, from abroad, seldom live a year on such food and under such great exposure. The race, of course, was originally derived from a superior kind or breed of stock; but long acclimation, and subjection for many generations to this peculiar mode of living, has fixed on the breed the peculiar characteristics of form, size, and qualities, which distinguish the "banks' ponies." It is thought that the present stock has suffered deterioration by the long continued breeding without change of blood. Yet this evil might be easily avoided, by sometimes exchanging a few males from different separated parts of the whole coast reef. It would be the reverse of improvement to introduce horses of more noble race, and less fitted to endure the great hardships of this locality. Such horses, or any raised in other localities, if turned loose here, would scarcely live through either the plague of blood sucking insects of the first summer, or the severe privations of the first winter.

On the whole reef, there are no springs; but there are many small tide-water creeks, passing through and having their heads in marshes, from which their sources ooze out. Their supply must be from the over-flowing sea-water. I could not learn, and do not suppose, that these waters, even at their highest sources, are ever fresh. Water that is fresh, but badly flavored, may be found any where, (even on the sea-beach,) by digging from two to six feet deep. The wild horses supply their want of fresh water by pawing away the sand deep enough to reach the fresh-water, which oozes into the excavation, and which reservoir serves for this use while it remains open.

The Last Whale Killed along These Shores

GRAYDEN PAUL AND MARY C. PAUL 1898

Whaling became an exciting and lucrative undertaking for the residents of Shackleford Banks between the Civil War and the turn of the century. Those engaged were shore whalers, but instead of waiting for dead or dying whales to wash up on the beach, as their distant forebears had done, they kept close watch during migrations; and when a whale appeared, they launched their little boats and rowed out to do battle. Whaling was seldom the richest source of income for the area; but it supplemented other earnings, and for a while it gave some watermen a decent income. One Shackleford Banker, Absalom Guthrie, reported that he had participated in killing fifty-two whales in his career. The following account of the end of this short-lived industry appeared three-quarters of a century later in a collection appropriately titled *Folk-Lore, Facts and Fiction about Carteret County*.

IT WAS APRIL 3, 1898. The sun came up over the Atlantic Ocean with a burst of glory. The first thing to catch its early morning rays was Cape Lookout Light house, which towers 165 feet above the sand dunes of Carteret County. As it cast its shadow westward, it fell across a lovely strip of sand dotted with cedar, yaupon, and sea myrtle. This was Shackleford Banks.

Here lived a sturdy race of people—the Guthries, Moores, Davises, Lewises, Chadwicks, Willises, Royals, and Roses. With their bare hands they eked a meager living from the surf, oyster rocks, and clam beds; and with their bare hands, they would attack and kill the world's largest living creature, the Leviathan of the deep, the mighty whale.

This is how they did it, as told by an eye witness, Stacy Guthrie, whose father, Devine Guthrie, built the boats. . . .

Look-outs were posted along the beach, and when a whale was sighted, they came running up the beach, shouting at the top of their voices, "Whale! Whale!, thar she blows!" At that moment pandemonium broke loose. Men, women and children came running from every direction, shouting, "Whale! Whale! Man the boats!" They grabbed hold of the three 18-foot whale boats, and literally carried them into the surf where eight men scrambled aboard each boat—six oarsmen, one helmsman in the stern, and a harpoon man in the bow. These boats were made of wood lap-streak siding, oak and cedar ribs and knees, and sharp at both ends. They were sturdy enough to stand severe pounding of the surf, and an occasional slap of a whale's fluke.

Now the whales when undisturbed, follow a set pattern. They blow (or come up to breathe) three times in a row at fifteen minute intervals, then they submerge for one hour. Therefore, Captain Guthrie was surprised when he saw the whale three times in less than five minutes, and gave a warning shout, "Look out boys! Thar's three whales out thar!" And to everyone's amazement, they discovered there was a bull, a mother, and a calf.

The way of the sea is cruel indeed. They had to first attack the calf, knowing that the bull would run at the first sight of danger, but that the mother would stay and protect her baby, though it cost her her life. So they thrust a harpoon in the fleshy part of the calf, with no intent to kill it, as they had no cash value; but so they could get a better chance at the mother. Captain Stacy says that if you wound a calf so badly it can't rise for air, the mother will take it in her fluke, and hold it above water so it can breathe. When she knows it is dead, then she will head for the briny deep.

In this case, they did not kill the calf, but all three boats attacked the mother whale with the fury of desperate men, knowing that food for their babies depended on the death of this monster.

To kill a whale, you have to hit its vital organs which the whalers refer to as "her life." To do this, you aim about two feet under the water just aft of her spout. When she goes down, you follow by the whirlpools caused by her tail when she swims. A good boat crew can usually row as fast as she swims. When she rises and blows, they are there ready for another thrust of the harpoon, and a shot from the gun which carries an explosive head. If the water is clear when she blows, you know you have missed the mark. If it is tinted with blood, you are getting close, and if it is solid blood, you have hit "her life," and you had better stay clear, for she then goes in her death struggle, slapping with her tail so hard it would smash your boat like a match box.

This time, however, the men had done their work well. Slowly the great fish began to calm down, the whirlpools and foaming waves subsided. Then, with one mighty last effort, she thrust herself half out of the water, then settled back beneath the surface. All the boats started closing in to where the whale had disappeared from view, and as they neared the spot, the great hulk rose slowly to the surface, motionless as a log. Then all the men stood up, held their oars straight up in the air, and gave three loud whoops, telling the people anxiously watching along the shore, that the battle was over, and the victory won. That was also the signal for the women to head for home and "put on the pot."

At this point in the story, Captain Stacy was all fired up, but I just had to interrupt him with a question. I asked, "How come that whale to float? I thought all fish sank to the bottom when first killed." At that question, the fight went out of Captain Stacy's face and voice, and his eyes, which had been staring through the youpons and cedars, across the sand dunes, far out into the ocean, shifted toward me, and a smile lit up his face, as he answered, "You know, Grayden, God had a lot to do with that. Did you know that a whale was the first living creature, and the largest that God ever created? (Genesis 1:21) Yet He gave man dominion over it, (Genesis 1:26) and He marked it so there would be no mistake about who made it. He put 365 bones in its mouth for the days of the year; but the strangest thing of all is why a whale, as its life comes to an end, gradually turns toward the setting sun; but I know for sure that every whale killed along these shores died with its nose headed due sou'west."

To get this monster ashore was a herculean task. When the people on the beach got the signal that the whale was dead, Captain Devine Guthrie went out in a sail boat (sharpie), to give a hand. The three whale boats were fastened together, and tied to the whale. They began to move it slowly toward the shore. When Captain Guthrie reached the scene, he fastened on to the lead boat and spread all the sails he had.

Nature smiled on those weary men, as a gentle breeze sprang up from the southwest, and the tide started coming in. It was necessary to beach the whale when the tide was at its peak, so that when the tide went out, the men could wade out, start cutting away the thick outer layer of flesh, or blubber, which has a very high oil content.

Before they started this tremendous job, all the men took a short nap and ate a hearty meal of "Conch Stew, Hard Crabs and Jumping Mullets." Now "Conch Stew" to a Core Sounder, is like spinach is to "Pop-Eye." The men went about their task with superhuman strength.

They cut the blubber in chunks about eight by twelve inches, which the women and children toted ashore in washtubs, and dumped into large iron kettles or "try pots." A roaring fire was already briskly burning under the kettles. It took thirty or forty people from three to four days to finish the job. The most important part was cooking the oil just right. If it was cooked too fast, it would turn dark, if too slow, it would smell and spoil. Only the old and experienced hands could do this work.

The oil, when finished, was poured out in pork barrels, and wooden vats, to cool. A merchant came over from Beaufort and sampled it, and made an offer. Then the oil was sealed in wooden barrels, hauled across Shackleford Banks, with a yoke of oxen, loaded on sail boats and brought over to Beaufort, where the crew was paid on the average of one thousand dollars for the total products of the whale.

This, divided among the thirty or forty men, amounted to about $35 per man. The average kill along the Shackleford Banks was one or two whales per season. The money from the whales supplied these hardy families with gun powder and shot for hunting ducks, geese, and loons. These wild fowl, with conchs, crabs, fish, oysters and escallops, along with collards, sweet potatoes and corn from their garden patches, made a satisfactory diet for them.

All in all, life was good. The sea was cruel, yet gave these hardy souls an adventurous, stimulating living.

Yaupon Factory

H. H. BRIMLEY　1903

The cured leaves and twigs of yaupon, a member of the holly genus (*Ilex vomitoria*), were the most common ingredients of black drink, a social and medicinal beverage esteemed by many Indian societies of the southeastern and central states. As the scientific name of yaupon implies, Indians sometimes induced vomiting by taking large quantities of black drink, often with seawater or other emetics added. Unadulterated yaupon tea seldom causes gastric upset when drunk in moderation, however, and it was the caffeinated beverage of choice in the coastal region of the Carolinas and Georgia through the colonial era. Eastern North Carolinians continued drinking yaupon tea as late as the Great Depression, but only on the Outer Banks did processing yaupon retain any economic importance past the turn of the century. The following piece was written during the last days of commercial yaupon processing, but it was not published in *The State* magazine until a half century later.

ON HATTERAS BANKS is a manufacturing establishment that so far as I know is the only one of its kind in the country. It is owned and operated by an old colored man who, strange to say, is the only one of his kind in the neighborhood or I should say that he and his family are the only ones, as he has several children who assist . . . in his occupation. His establishment is devoted to the gathering and curing of Yopon Tea.

What is Yopon? the reader may ask and what is done with the tea? Yopon is a shrubby plant and grows abundantly on the sandhills of the ocean beaches along certain areas on the South Atlantic seaboard. It is supposed to possess certain mild medicinal qualities but besides that, it is used as a beverage by many of the older people living within its habitat, although not nearly so extensively as formerly.

The younger element find the teas and coffees of commerce much more palatable and, now that they are within the reach of pretty much everybody in price and are found on sale at even the most remote country stores, the consumption of the product of the Yopon tree has fallen to quite a low ebb compared with what it was only a very few years ago. . . .

The following is a brief description of the methods now pursued in the gathering and curing of the tea, the particulars being gleaned at firsthand directly from the proprietor of the factory at the establishment itself. . . . The only effort required in the collection of the product is the labor necessary to go out and cut what quantity is needed at one curing. It is not even essential to cut with any great degree of discrimination as the bushes are trimmed after reaching the factory, anyway, and anything not suitable can be very easily eliminated there.

It is quite probable that in former times most of the more well-to-do families prepared the leaves themselves, or at least had it done on the premises, as heaps of round stones, similar to those now used in the sweating process, may still be found around many an old homestead in the section where the plant grows. There were also men in every community who carried on the preparation of the leaves as a regular business but, until I came across such a factory still in working order and turning out the product regularly, I was under the impression that the business was as extinct as the Dodo.

On Hatteras Banks, several miles west of the Cape and right alongside the high road between Frisco and Buxton, I came across old man Scarborough's Yopon tea factory and from the manufacturer himself secured the details of the process as well as permission to photograph the plant.

The Yopon, Yapon or Yaupon is an evergreen shrub . . . sometimes almost reaching the dignity of a shrubby tree and along on the sandhills of the ocean's border for the whole length of the coast line of the south Atlantic States it grows in thickets more or less dense and plentiful, it being one of the most characteristic tree growths of the region. . . . Its original uses seem to have been largely medicinal, its action being both purgative and emetic. Now, however, perhaps from the fact that as a beverage it is used in a weaker infusion than when used medicinally, the original idea is to a great extent lost sight of, although not entirely, as old man Scarborough expatiated to me on the smooth and easy way in which the drinking of his tea would remove fevers from the system with a guarantee of no bad after-effects. . . .

In the process of manufacture, the bushes are first cut and hauled to the chopping trough, there being no particular size of limb or bush selected, although the most of those seen would run from three-quarters to an inch and a half in diameter where cut off. Then the twigging knife comes into play. . . .

Standing alongside the trough, the bushes are picked up in the left hand and, with the twigging knife in the right, all the small twigs, with leaves attached, are lopped off, twigs up to at least an eighth of an inch in diameter being taken. So it will be seen from this that the young wood is used as well as the leaves in this make of tea. This work of twigging continues until a pile of raw material has accumulated sufficient to make a charge for the hogshead. Meanwhile a fire has been built and the rocks put in the coals to heat. The rocks used will probably average some six or eight pounds each in weight, and they are cared for carefully between firing as they are imported goods, no rock of any description being a natural constituent of the soil hereabouts. While this heating is going on the cutting up of the twigs in the chopping trough is started. This trough is some twelve feet long by two feet wide by nine inches deep, with the bottom made of one heavy piece of timber hewn flat on its upper side and strongly supported. Standing alongside it the operator with his broad axe chops steadily into the piled up mass of twigs and leaves, cutting and stirring until the twig lengths are all reduced to one or two inches. This work is continued with fresh material in the trough until the whole charge has been worked over, when the sweating of the tea has to be looked after.

The "hogshead" . . . is a hollow cypress log measuring on the inside about three and a half feet in diameter by five feet deep, and something over half its depth is let into the ground and by so doing bringing its top to a convenient height for working at. Possibly the question of the prevention of radiation of heat may have had something to do with this practice of partly burying the sweating receptacle. The inside of the hogshead is smooth and clean and its bottom is built of plank.

From the fire the hot (but not too hot) stones are raked and lifted by means of the rock hook . . . and a layer of them is spread over its bottom. On top of these is quickly shovelled a thick layer of the product of the chopping trough and another pile of clean, hot stones on top of that. Then more chopped leaves and twigs and more rocks until the hogshead is fully charged, then it is tightly covered and the work is over for the time being.

After the sweating caused by the heat and moisture has gone on for thirty-six hours the cover is removed and the cured tea taken out and spread on an elevated plank platform to thoroughly dry out. When properly dried it is shovelled into sacks and barrels and packed away in the storehouse to await a sale. One charging of this hogshead produces about thirty bushels of dried tea, the bushel being the unit by which it is measured and sold. And it is apropos of this large unit of measurement that they tell the tale of an English ship running down to speak to a Kinnekeeter (a schooner hailing from Kinnekeet, a nearby settlement) to ask if they could not spare them a little tea. And the Kinnekeeter's reply was a sock-dollager, being to the effect that they could not, being nearly out themselves and having only about seven bushels left!

The sale of old man Scarborough's goods is now mostly on the mainland to which he freights it in his skiff and the regular price is twenty-five cents a bushel or in trade two bushels of tea for one of corn, little or none of the latter being grown on the banks. This tea works being now the only source of supply for those who still use this medicinal beverage, it is sad to think what will become of the users when the old man is gone as I don't imagine there is enough in it to strongly tempt the younger generation to continue the business.

The storehouse held about a hundred bushels when I visited the place. . . . We had some that night at supper: I tried it straight, I tried it with milk and I tried it with enough sugar to make shoal water in the middle of my cup, but one of the boys looked at my cupful so wistfully that I could not resist the dumb appeal and I let him finish it up.

A Record Catch

OLD TRUDGE (CARL GOERCH) 1944

Seine fishing from the beach was big business on the North Carolina barrier islands for many years. By the mid-twentieth century haul seiners had forsaken the traditional carts for stripped-down trucks, which carried the crew and towed a dory already loaded with net. Setting the net—by trailing it from the stern of the dory as the crew rowed through the breakers, then down the beach, and back to shore again—was the easy part. Hauling a net even partially filled with fish was something else again, and usually required all hands. Yields were occasionally spectacular, but no one could have been prepared for what happened on Bogue Banks in October 1944, when a crew landed what has been described as the largest catch in the history of North Carolina: 200,000 pounds (100 tons) of spot in a single set. This may well have been the last big hurrah for beach fishermen, few of whom bother with this grueling occupation anymore in the face of mounting antagonism from vacationers, organized anglers, and government regulators. Carl Goerch, founder and long-time editor of *The State* magazine, published this account of the massive haul in the November 4, 1944, issue under his often-used pen name.

SEVERAL YEARS AGO, a friend of ours, who is a great fisherman, told us about a dream he had had the night before.

"I dreamt that I was fishing down at Morehead," he said. "I caught so many fish that it wasn't long before the bottom of the boat was covered with them. I kept on catching them until the boat was completely filled. Then the boat started sinking, and just as I was about to drown, I woke up."

That was a lot of fish: no question about it. But if our friend had been in the vicinity of Morehead City last week, he would have seen a sight that would have made his dream fade into utter insignificance.

He would have seen the water black with fish. He would have seen enough fish to swamp a dozen boats. He would have seen a crew of twenty-five men work for three days, shoveling the fish into net-baskets and loading them into large trucks. He would have seen fish dragged up on the beach by the tens of thousands. In other words, he would actually have seen more fish than he could possibly have dreamt of in all his life, even though he might have had the D.T.'s.

The first we heard about it was when our friend, Tony Seamon, called us up from Morehead City last Monday morning. . . . Tony is proprietor of the Sanitary Fish Market down there. And that, as you probably know, is the place where you get the best seafood dinner in North Carolina.

"You better come down here," said Tony.

"Why?" we inquired.

"They have made the biggest haul of fish that's ever been seen in these parts," he said. "It sure is a sight to behold."

Well, as luck would have it, we had a friend who was going down to Cherry Point, near Morehead, so we got him to take us down there with him. We met Tony at the Sanitary Fish Market and he took us in his car over to the beach. On the way, he told us about what had taken place.

"The fishermen put out their net Saturday afternoon," he said, "and yesterday they found out that they had caught a tremendous quantity of fish. They worked all day long and got out more than 120,000 pounds. They'll probably get close to 70,000 pounds out of the net today, and there's no telling how many more fish are inside the net. It may take them two or three days to finish the job."

"Where did all this happen?" we asked him.

"Off the beach at Salter Path," he told us. . . .

When we reached Atlantic Beach, Tony turned to the right and we drove along the new sand-clay road in a westerly direction. In about fifteen minutes we parked alongside the road and got out. We had to walk a hundred yards or so to get to the beach. As we climbed to the top of the last sand dune, we obtained our first view of the fishermen.

More than twenty men were at work. In addition, there were about a hundred spectators, including many women and children. Some of the men were up to their knees in the water, dipping out fish with large wire-shovels. These were being placed into net-baskets, each of which was handled by two men. Just as soon as about a hundred pounds of fish had been shoveled into the baskets, the men waded ashore with them, and the fish were heaved into a large five-ton truck. It took about an hour to fill the truck to its capacity limit. When this had been accomplished, the truck drove off, and another one took its place. The loaded truck headed for Morehead, where the fish were iced, placed in other trucks, and carried to Norfolk, Philadelphia, Atlanta and various other markets.

This had been going on all day Sunday. Sunday night several men remained on the beach in order to keep watch and make sure that a storm didn't damage the net. Incidentally, the fishermen were not only lucky in the size of their catch, but also lucky so far as the weather was concerned. If a storm had come up while the fish were in the net, chances are that most of them would have got away.

The men couldn't work too fast, because if they did, the ice-plant at Morehead would have been unable to handle the fish, and they would be spoiled.

When we arrived on the scene, the net was almost on the beach, and we commented on the fact that we had arrived just in time to take some pictures.

"Just in time!" exclaimed Tony. "Why, they haven't even begun to empty the net. That's just one of the small nets that you're looking at. There's the big net, out at sea."

Sure enough, about a hundred yards from the beach we could see the floats of another net. This net was 500 yards long. On Saturday afternoon, one end of it had been made fast to a stake on the beach. Then the net had been placed in a dory. The boat was rowed slowly out to sea, and the net was gradually paid out. It was made fast about three hundred yards out from the beach. The wind and tide caused it to bulge in the form of a semi-circle.

Sunday morning, a couple of fishermen went out again in the boat. They observed immediately that a tremendous number of fish were in the semi-circle. They went back to shore and got another net. This was made fast to the other one at the outer point. It was dropped into the water as the boat was rowed toward shore. And thus all openings were closed and the fish were securely imprisoned in the net.

Under normal circumstances, the net would have been brought in slowly, but such a course couldn't be considered in this particular case. You can imagine what would have happened if the fishermen had tried to drag in a quarter of a million pounds of fish. The net would have broken under the strain, and it would have been a case of good-bye fish.

So smaller nets were brought into play. These nets were carried out and brought back to the beach within the area included in the big net. In each of these hauls there were approximately 40,000 pounds of fish.

The men were displaying a lot of enthusiasm and vigor in their work. There were frequent shouts and outbursts of laughter. Their task was a strenuous one, but they didn't seem to mind it. The reason for this was that they knew they were going to be well paid for what they were doing. . . .

A large fishing net, such as the one used in this case, costs about $800. Well, to be perfectly frank about it, nobody at Salter Path has got that much money to spend for a net. So the thing is worked out on a cooperative basis. A wholesale fish-merchant supplies the net. The net is worked by a crew of men. The merchant pays a certain price to the fishermen for all the fish they catch. He, in turn, ices them and ships them out in trucks to various jobbers. The jobbers sell them to the retailers, and the retailers sell them to you.

The Belhaven Fish & Oyster Company furnished the net that was used in making this record catch. The fishermen received four cents a pound for the spots. There were twenty-five men in the crew. Slightly more than 200,000 pounds of fish were caught. Multiply this by four, and you get $8,000. Divide this by 25, and you'll see that each of the men will get around $320 for his share of the catch.

Maybe $320 isn't regarded as very much money in New York, Philadelphia or Chicago, but we're telling you right now that in Salter Path it's a sizable fortune. A family can live on it very nicely for a year or so and enjoy all the comforts of life.

We said a little while ago that there were a number of women among the spectators on the beach. They were watching proceedings with lively interest, and you can readily understand why. Those baskets and truckloads of fish meant new dresses, new hats, new shoes, new curtains and a lot of other new things. Unless we miss our guess, Salter Path is going out on a spending spree the like of which never before has been seen in the community.

"I ain't going to eat another fish for six months," one of the fishermen smilingly told us.

"What are you going to eat?" we asked.

"Pork chops!" he exclaimed, licking his lips.

We've heard of all kinds of sprees, but this was the first time we ever have heard of a pork-chop spree.

You've probably been out in a boat, fishing, with several other fellows. In many instances you've observed that some one chap catches most of the fish while the others catch scarcely anything. And you've wondered why.

Some of the fishermen along the Bogue banks are doing some wondering along the same line in connection with this big haul of fish. Their nets were not far away, but they didn't have any such luck. The net directly west brought in about 100 pounds; the one directly east brought in about 400 pounds. Nobody can explain why all the fish headed for this particular net of the Belhaven Fish & Oyster Company.

We stayed on the beach for about an hour, watching the men at their work. Then we walked back to Tony's car and headed for Morehead.

Have you ever driven along the highway directly behind a truck loaded with cotton-seed? If you have, you've observed on the road little pieces of cotton that have jolted off the truck as it rolled along. We saw something of the same nature on our way back to Morehead; only this time it wasn't cotton-seed—it was spots that had flipped themselves out of the truck or had been jolted out.

We followed a trail of fish all the way back to town.

All this happened Monday afternoon. On Wednesday, Tony called us up and said that the job had been completed.

"How many fish altogether?" we asked.

"Better than 200,000 pounds," he said. "They finished up yesterday afternoon. But there were plenty of more fish in the net."

"Why didn't they get 'em out?"

"Well, you see; the sharks were trying to get into the net and eat the fish. They made several holes in the net, and a good many of the fish got out through these holes. The fishermen decided to pull in the big net before the sharks destroyed it completely. So they did, and it's all over now."

All over—except a little financial transaction in which those twenty-five fishermen are keenly interested.

Pumping and Grinding

TUCKER LITTLETON 1980

Nineteenth-century visitors to the Outer Banks must have had difficulty figuring out why there were so many windmills. Almost all of them were post windmills, designed primarily for grinding corn. So why were there so many of them on the isolated barrier islands of the Outer Banks where practically everybody fished for a living and nobody grew a significant amount of corn? In time visitors no doubt learned that it was common practice for fishermen to sail across the sounds with boatloads of surplus fish to trade with the mainland farmers for corn. If the fishermen happened to have a big haul of shrimp—one product of the sea that few residents would eat until recently—the farmers would take that in trade also, for use as fertilizer. Tucker Littleton of Swansboro, part-time preacher and rest-of-the-time historian, carried on a determined search for coastal windmill information, identifying more than sixty-five that had been in operation at one time in Carteret County alone. The following article describing post windmills and their operation appeared in the October 1980 issue of *The State*.

DURING THE EARLY years of the Civil War, Charles F. Johnson was a part of the Union campaign against the North Carolina sounds. Johnson, who wrote an account of his war experiences and observations in the Outer Banks region entitled *The Long Roll*, was astounded at the number of windmills dotting the North Carolina coast. He wrote that in the northern part of the Tar Heel coast he had seen more windmills than he had "supposed were in existence in the whole country. . . ." While my research has shown that Johnson was not exaggerating, I find it hard to understand how so many windmills could have been so soon forgotten. But today's Tar Heels are largely unaware that there were ever windmills on our coast, and many of my inquiries regarding windmills have been greeted with such replies as, "You've got to be kidding!"

Nevertheless, the historic coastal windmills, almost totally belonging to the type called "post mills," reached their greatest abundance during the mid-1800's and then rapidly declined near the end of the nineteenth century. By the beginning of the twentieth century, perhaps not more than a dozen of the historic windmills remained; and by 1920 apparently every vestige of the old post mills had disappeared from the Tidewater region.

Only recently has a visible reminder of the age of the windmills reappeared on the Tar Heel coast. Mrs. Lynanne Westcott of Manteo, N.C., was determined that the windmill would not be completely forgotten, and she has undertaken at Nags Head the long and expensive task of restoring the windmill to a segment of the Outer Banks landscape. Mrs. Westcott's new windmill is an exact replica of the typical nineteenth-century windmill once so popular on our coast. Every detail has been authenticated, and this memorial to the age of windmills . . . offers a genuine educational experience to both out-of-state tourists and native Tar Heels.

While Mrs. Westcott's windmill is intended to represent primarily the Outer Banks windmills of the nineteenth century, it could just as well represent the entire period of the existence of the post mill inasmuch as the post mill when it passed out of use was virtually unchanged in architecture and operation from its earlier known ancestors. The earliest authenticated reference to a windmill in western Europe is that of a post mill in France in 1180 A.D. The first reference to a windmill (post mill) in England occurred in 1191 A.D., and it was this type of windmill which the English colonists first introduced to the New World. The first windmill in America was a post mill erected in 1621 by Governor Yeardley on his plantation in Virginia near the falls of the James River. Ten years later the first windmill built in the Massachusetts Bay Colony was a post mill.

In North Carolina the General Assembly in 1715 passed "An Act to Encourage the Building of Mills" and provided that two acres should be laid out for anyone building a water mill or a half-acre for anyone building a wind mill "to grind wheat and Indian corn." In *The Hatterasman* Ben Dixon MacNeill asserted that the first windmill built in North Carolina was located at Avon (formerly Kinnakeet) in 1723, but he failed to document that claim. So far, the earliest documented reference to a North Carolina windmill I have found is a 1748 deed which mentions "Old Windmill Point," which was incorporated in 1758 as Nixon's Town (Nixonton) in Pasquotank County. . . .

In 1786 George Bell, living at what is now Marshallberg in Carteret County, deeded to his grandson, Stephen Bell Foot, two acres of land "on the point," one acre of which was specified as being for a mill. Further up the coast in Carteret County, John Gray Blount and John Wallace, probably as early as 1790, had two windmills—one at Portsmouth for grinding corn and one at Shell Castle Island for pumping water. In 1793 John Norcom advertised in the State Gazette of North Carolina (Edenton) that his windmill, not then three years old, was for sale. At Beaufort in 1796 Samuel Leffers advertised a windmill for sale situated on the mouth of Taylor's Creek adjoining the easternmost boundary of Beaufort and fronting Old Topsail Inlet. The mill was described as in good repair and having all new bolting machinery.

Apparently the windmill was inevitable for the North Carolina coast. For centuries, the watermill and the windmill were the only complex machines known to European peoples of the Old World and the New, and the grinding of wheat and corn in large quantities required the use of one or the other type of mill. On the Outer Coastal Plain, where large areas of low, flat land dominate the landscape, only the windmill was feasible. The low coastal lands were exposed to constant winds that provided the free power for operation of the windmills, and local shipwrights and sailmakers possessed the needed skills for building the wooden mills and preparing their sails. Thus all the mills on the barrier islands and most of those on the mainland next to the larger sounds were windmills. With very few exceptions the windmills on the North Carolina coast north of the present Onslow-Pender County line were grist mills, and south of that line they tended to be primarily for pumping water—especially those associated with the numerous salt works in New Hanover and Brunswick counties.

. . . As an architectural type, the post mill is distinguished from the tower mill or smock mill by having a body mounted and turning on an upright post. A ladder from the ground to the housing was used to enter the mill, and a "tail pole" protruded through the ladder. The end of the tail pole away from the housing rested in the center of a large wheel which could be pushed along a metal track laid in a circle around the windmill. When the wind shifted directions, the miller could raise the ladder, push against the tail pole, and thus turn the mill housing so that the sails would face into the wind regardless of the direction from which it was blowing.

The windmill's movable housing enabled it to operate at all times except when the winds were calm; and the sails on the mill's arms could be furled when the mill was idle, unfurled when the mill was ready for use, or reefed or adjusted so that the amount of sail unfurled ideally suited the velocity of the wind then blowing. If the arms of the windmill turned too fast in a strong wind, the friction from the millstones would scorch the meal; so it was important to maintain the optimum grinding speed. In the isolated coastal settlements which depended on the windmills for bread, long periods of calm could deplete a community's supply of flour or meal. In such times it was common for the coastal people to pray for wind just as they would pray for rain in a drought.

Perhaps the overwhelming preference for the post mill in coastal North Carolina was due to the fact that it was less expensive to build than the tower mill and could be constructed primarily of materials readily available to the coastal inhabitant. A minimum of parts would have to be imported, and in addition the post mill could easily be taken down and moved to a new location if necessary. If the owner found his milling venture unprofitable, he could sell the post mill to a new owner without having to sell the land on which it was situated. If the mill had been a tower mill, the owner would have had to part with both his mill and at least some of his land. One post mill at Ocracoke is reported to have been moved across Pamlico Sound to the Lake Mattamuskeet area. Perhaps there were also other reasons why the post mill appealed to Tar Heel millers.

The design of the post mill was always subservient to the machinery. Its economic housing resulted in a very functional building, and as engineering techniques became more refined the windmill achieved an average efficiency of 14 horsepower. The main challenge in building a post mill was to keep a stable balance. The problem of balance became more complicated when the mill was in motion and receiving the pressure of the wind. Improperly balanced mills tended to tilt slightly forward or backward. If it tilted forward, the mill was called "head sick," or if it tilted backward it was called "tail sick."

Post mills erected to grind corn for the local plantation or the personal use of the plantation owner, his slaves, or farm hands were called "plantation mills." Those erected to grind corn for the general public were called "custom mills." Some combined both purposes, and were called "plantation-custom mills." The owner of the custom mill did not buy or sell grain. Rather, he received his income in the form of a toll which he extracted from the grain he milled. For most nineteenth-century North Carolina windmill operators, the toll (or miller's portion) appears to have been one peck of meal for each bushel ground.

It is ironical that the windmill in North Carolina most often fell a victim to that which it most depended on. Without wind, the windmill was useless; with too much wind . . . the windmill often became a helpless victim. Of those windmills whose destruction is documented, most were blown down by severe storms. Because of the windmill's exposed position out in the open, it was also a frequent victim of lightning. . . . Still others fell victim to long abandonment and decay.

Perhaps the overall demise of the windmill on the Tar Heel coast may be attributed to the introduction of steam- and gas-powered mills, the introduction of the metal windmill for pumping water, and the improved transportation which made reasonably cheap, imported flour and meal more generally available to coastal communities. . . . I have found the following distribution by counties

Carteret	65
Hyde	24
Dare	21
Onslow	11
Camden	7
Tyrrell	4
Beaufort	4
Perquimans	4
Craven	3
New Hanover	3
Pamlico	2
Pasquotank	2
Currituck	2
Brunswick	2
Chowan	1

Sharpies, Shad Boats, and Spritsail Skiffs

MARK TAYLOR 1984

Until well into the twentieth century much of the Outer Banks was accessible only by water. Almost all the boats used for transportation, fishing, or recreation were built locally from material, such as lightweight juniper (Atlantic white cedar), that was readily available in the maritime forests or on the nearby mainland. A few expert craftsmen built boats on a full-time basis and enjoyed the freedom to experiment, but most local boats were built by working watermen with plenty of other things to do. In the nineteenth century the interplay of innovation and practicality created three popular but noticeably different sailing craft—the sharpie, the shad boat, and the spritsail skiff. The following article, originally published in *Wildlife in North Carolina*, relates an apparent revival of interest in these native boats.

IT'S A BLUEBIRD day as we sail out of Harkers Island in the early morning. Bill Newbold handles the tiller while Hank Murdock—resembling a benevolent, bespectacled Ahab in yellow oilskins—leans against the foredeck and watches for crab pots.

"We'll set a gill net for bluefish off Core Banks, and then go check our crab pots," said Newbold. "It's early, but there might be some blues moving."

We tack across Core Sound and drop 200 yards of gill net perpendicular to Core Banks. In older times the net would have been made of heavy tarred cotton twine, but today a lightweight monofilament net snakes out of a large box mounted on the stern as we run downwind. As the marker buoys pop over the side, Newbold changes course for the eastern tip of Harkers Island and starts a small outboard motor mounted on a side bracket as we drop sail.

"Normally I wouldn't do this, but the wind is dying and we've got 40 crab pots to check," he hollered. "We usually do everything but run the crab pots under sail."

Bill Newbold and Hank Murdock, both of Harkers Island, are reviving a classic North Carolina tradition—commercial fishing from a sailing sharpie. Both men are retired, and when Newbold moved to Harkers Island six years ago he decided he wanted to try fishing from a sharpie after learning about the area's maritime heritage.

"I've always wanted to fish from a sailboat, so I had Karl Muller of Harkers Island build me this 26-foot sharpie in 1981. Although I've done a lot of commercial fishing, I had never sailed before. I knew Hank Murdock well, though, and he's an excellent sailer. We decided to try fishing together, and found we made an excellent team. One man handles the net or pots while the other sails the sharpie."

Newbold and Murdock are part of a large renaissance in traditional boats. Until recently, most small working sailing craft were neglected by historians and contemporary boatbuilders. Small fishing boats lack the romance of larger vessels, such as clipper ships, or the elegance and speed of yachts and racing boats. Interest in traditional boats has revived, however, and most of what we know about the early boats of North Carolina is due to the work of the Hampton Mariners Museum in Beaufort.

"It's surprising how little we know about the traditional, sail-powered work boats that were used in most areas well into this century," said Michael Alford, Curator of Maritime Research at the museum, who has been studying traditional North Carolina boats for over 20 years. "Most of these boats were fished hard and then discarded, so few original boats remain. Work boats were also generally built by individual fishermen, and the builder usually carried the plans in his head. The men who built and sailed these boats are rapidly disappearing, and when they are gone a fascinating slice of history will die with them."

Alford and the museum staff have developed working plans for several traditional boats through interviews with aging fishermen and boatbuilders, and by measuring and "taking the lines" of the few original boats that remain. Although there were literally dozens of different types of boats used in North Carolina from the 1700s through the early 1900s, three classic sailing craft either evolved in or have strong links to North Carolina coastal waters. These are the sharpie, the shad boat, and the Carolina spritsail skiff.

The sharpie from which Bill Newbold fishes would have been a common sight in North Carolina at the turn of the century. Thousands of these boats were used along our coast, but they were most common in the Beaufort and Morehead City areas. North Carolina fishermen prized the sharpie for its seaworthiness, large cargo capacity, and open work area. And best of all, especially in Core and Bogue sounds, the shallow-drafted vessels seemed almost capable of sailing on a heavy dew!

There has probably never been a boat better adapted to the shoal waters of North Carolina than the sharpie. Ironically, the sharpie was not developed in North Carolina, but was introduced to the state from the North.

"A Rhode Islander named George Ives introduced the sharpie to North Carolina in 1875," said Alford. "Sharpies were widely used for oyster tonging and net fishing in Long Island, and Ives felt that these boats were well-suited to North Carolina. He was heavily involved in the seafood and fishing industries in coastal North Carolina, and brought a 34-foot sharpie down to Beaufort. Local fishermen were skeptical of the seaworthiness and sailing characteristics of Ives' sharpie until it beat the fastest fishing boat in Beaufort in a race in heavy weather. Then, they were quick to adopt the boat as their own. Within five years, there were over 500 sharpies being used in the Beaufort area."

The sharpie is characterized by a plumb or even inverted stem, straight sides, a flat bottom across the beam (there is considerable curve or "rocker" in a sharpie hull fore and aft), and a rounded stern. The boats were usually sailed with a double-masted, leg-of-mutton spritsail rig. This ancient sail plan lacks the low-swinging boom used on most sloops today, but instead features a spar called a "sprit" that extends diagonally across the sail. No standing rigging is needed to support the mast, and the sprit offers plenty of headroom—a feature much appreciated by lone fishermen who hauled nets and handled the boat at the same time.

North Carolina fishermen also found that the sharpie could be built easily and quickly—most fishermen could build one in three to four weeks. Locally available hard pine, oak, cypress, and "juniper" or Atlantic white cedar produced a boat that was inexpensive, solid and exceptionally durable. Sharpies of all sizes were built in North Carolina, but most ranged from 26 to 36 feet. The smaller ones—from 26 to 28 feet—were usually handled by one man and could carry 75 to 100 bushels of oysters. Larger models were usually worked by two men, and could carry 150 to 175 bushels of oysters.

"Changing times also contributed to the popularity of the sharpie," said Alford. "Improved transportation systems in North Carolina created a large market for shellfish and seafood after the Civil War, and the sharpie was a workhorse of a boat that could help meet this demand. The large, open work area offered plenty of room for handling nets or hauling fish, and the rounded, half-decked stern was convenient to work around while fishing or tonging for oysters. Smaller sharpies were generally used for oystering or fishing for mullet, spot, croaker, trout, flounder, and other species. Larger ones—usually around 35 feet—were also used for fishing. Some transferred the catch from smaller sharpies to fish houses on the shore. Many of these larger models were 'buy boats' that roamed the sounds buying fresh fish and shellfish from individual fishermen in smaller boats. Sharpies of all sizes were also used extensively in the menhaden industry, which was developed by several former Rhode Island soldiers who had served in occupied Beaufort during the Civil War."

By the late 1880s Tar Heels had added a few touches of their own to the design. Some innovative fishermen had tried using large sharpies to "dredge" or drag for oysters in the sounds, but found that the spritsail lacked the power needed to pull a heavy, iron oyster dredge. They replaced the spritsail with more powerful double-masted, gaff-rigged mains and topsails commonly used on coasting schooners, and the Core Sound schooner-sharpie, commonly called a "Core Sounder," was born. Most of these vessels were from 40 to 45 feet long. The largest Core Sounder was the *Prince*, a 63-footer built in Beaufort in 1899.

"Core Sounders were used much like Chesapeake Bay skipjacks," said Alford. "During the fall and winter, a four or five man crew dredged for oysters. In the summer the boats hauled freight. The Core Sounders often ran North Carolina fish to the West Indies and returned with sugar, molasses and rum. They also served as 'buy boats' for fishermen, and hauled general cargo in local waters."

Ironically, the man responsible for the introduction of the sharpie to North Carolina is also partially responsible for its demise. George Ives is generally credited with being one of the first to install a small gasoline engine in a sharpie in the early 1900s, and dwindling numbers of sailing sharpies were built after the turn of the century. The huge Core Sounders continued to run into the 1930s, often stripped of their rigging and delivering freight under power in local waters. However, the sharpie lives on in the Harkers Island boats and Core Sound trawlers and shrimpers that make our coast so picturesque today. The round stern, flat bottom amidships, and straight bow of these boats betray their sharpie lineage.

The shad boat is another North Carolina boat design—as beautiful a vessel as has ever graced our waters. It has its roots in the log dugout canoes used by coastal Indians. Early settlers modified these Indian dugouts by splitting them down the middle, adding a broad plank for a midsection that often included a carved keel, and joining the sections with ribs made of twisted tree roots. These boats were called "kunners," which is probably a corruption of the Indian word for "canoe." Small kunners were paddled or rowed, and larger kunners were equipped with a spritsail.

In the early 1870s a boatbuilder named Washington Creef of Roanoke Island went the kunner one better. Local shad fishermen needed boats to work their pound nets, which were large weirs made of wooden stakes that ran perpendicular to the shore. Large schools of migrating shad intercepted these nets as they traveled along the shore, and were diverted into holding pens called "pounds." The ideal boat for working a pound net was under 27 feet so it could enter the pound and remove the fish. It also had to be shallow-drafted, seaworthy, and capable of hauling a heavy load. In addition, it should carry a large spread of sail so that it could work in the light breezes of summer.

Creef began by making a half-hull model of a small round-bottomed boat with a sharply pointed bow, shallow keel, and a square stern. The keel and garboards (planks adjacent to the keel) of the boat were carved from a single log—as in a kunner—but the hull was finished with carefully joined planking. He rigged the boat with a spritsail, but added a single innovation—a small "flying topsail" was attached to the top of the mast and operated independently of the other sails. This topsail enabled the boat to catch the slightest puff of wind coming in over the treetops when it was working a pound net close to shore.

"Shad boats were prized by fishermen because of their seaworthiness, comfort, speed and graceful lines," said Alford. "Unlike sharpies, shad boats were difficult to build, and a large group of boatbuilders who specialized in shad boats soon developed around Roanoke Island."

To build a shad boat the boatmaker first felled a huge white cedar tree, and hauled both the main log and stump back to the building site. The main log was carved into an elongated-Y that formed the keel and bottom boards called "garboards"—of the boat. The stump was split into sections and taken to a sawmill in Elizabeth City where it was cut into two-inch slices on a huge bandsaw. These slices were to form the ribs and stem of the boat. Referring to his half-model the builder selected a stem and ribs that matched the contours of the model. These were fastened to the log keel and garboards. Then, the boat was carefully planked so that the planking met the log keel and garboards in a graceful curve. Finally, the boats were painted white or gray and a colorful stripe was added along the gunwales. This was unusual because most North Carolina work boats were devoid of ornamentation.

The construction of shad boats changed around the turn of the century. Builders switched to using dead-rise planking (planks met the smaller keel at an angle instead of faring the planking into the single log that formed the keel and garboards) because large trees had grown scarce, and plank ribs replaced the natural crooked ribs and stem cut from stumps. Many of these shad boats were built for waterfowl hunting clubs on the Outer Banks, and the last shad boats made in North Carolina were built around 1930 by the Dough family of Roanoke Island for the Church Island Gun Club on Currituck Banks.

Fishermen who owned original shad boats prized them for their legendary speed, and the boats were often used for smuggling liquor during Prohibition.

Fortunately, about a dozen original shad boats remain, and these boats are still being used under power by commercial fishermen in the Manteo area. "All of the remaining shad boats are of the original design with the one-piece, log keel and garboards," said Alford. "Some of these boats are probably a century old. The boats that were built later with deadrise planking didn't hold up as well, and have all disappeared."

The Carolina spritsail skiff is another classic design that evolved in our waters, and this boat was often called the "mule of the coastal fisherman." Most skiffs ranged from 16 to 22 feet and were used for clamming, oystering, crabbing, fishing and general transportation.

The deadrise hull of the spritsail skiff had one unique feature—it lacked a keel.

The center planks of the shallow, V-bottomed hulls met in a single seam which swelled to form a watertight joint. This reduced the draft of the hull considerably—a 20-footer drew only four to six inches of water with the centerboard up.

"The deadrise Carolina spritsail skiff was an excellent work boat and a very fast sailer," said Alford. "These boats carried a large spread of sail, and fishermen often raced their boats for pleasure on Sunday afternoons and holidays. However, there were differences in the design of these boats throughout the state. In the rough open waters of Albemarle Sound, for example, freeboard was increased and side decks were added to deadrise skiffs to make them better sea boats. Some Carolina spritsail skiffs were also built along sharpie lines. These boats had the flat bottom, straight sides and plumb bow of the sharpie but lacked a round stern. They had a shallower draft than a deadrise skiff, but weren't as fast or as seaworthy."

These boats were not used only for casual fishing and pleasure sailing, however. A 20-foot spritsail skiff routinely hauled several fishermen, a large net, and up to a thousand pounds of fish or shellfish. In fact, Hank Murdock lives next to an elderly man on Harkers Island who raised a family net fishing, oystering, crabbing and clamming from a small spritsail skiff.

Until recently, traditional North Carolina boats were found only in aging photographs and fading memories. The original sharpies and spritsail skiffs are gone, although a few rotting hulks probably lay undiscovered in remote marshes and creeks. Only a handful of shad boats remain to remind us of a time when tough men sailing small boats wrested a living from the water.

Happily, a new day is at hand. The work of the Hampton Mariners Museum has prompted a surge of interest in traditional boats, and gleaming white sharpies and spritsail skiffs built for recreational sailing are now docked amidst sleek fiberglass yachts on the Beaufort waterfront. Many people are also watching Bill Newbold's fishing with keen interest. He was recently featured in *National Fisherman*, a trade journal for the commercial fishing industry, and some knowledgeable observers feel that Newbold is proving that traditional sail-powered work boats such as the sharpie and spritsail skiff have a place in the future of commercial fishing. When I accompanied him, we returned to the dock with two boxes of crabs and a large tub of bluefish. On the run back to Harkers Island he quietly told me about his fishing as we watched Core Banks turn golden in the late afternoon sun.

"I began fishing with the sharpie for the joy of fishing from a classic boat, but I've found it to be a very practical boat for inshore fishing today. Like most fishermen, I go after whatever is in season. Much of my work is clamming, and I just beach the boat on a bar and get out. Since this boat draws only 8 inches of water with the centerboard up, she is ideal for oystering and crabbing in shallow waters.

She'll also haul a load—I once brought in three tons of fish, although that was kind of risky. She's also a good sea boat. We fish in winds up to 35 knots, and in the spring and fall we go five to 15 miles offshore and set gill nets for spot, croaker and Spanish mackerel.

"Of course, there are some limitations to fishing under sail. We can't go as far as a power boat, and have to allow extra time in case the wind doesn't cooperate. However, fuel costs are minimal and this boat is very simple—there's nothing on it that I can't fix myself. A few years ago when fuel prices jumped, Hank and I were making money when most fishermen weren't. We're either revisiting the past or welcoming the future—depending on what happens to the price of fuel."

Bread-and-Butter Fishing

JAN DEBLIEU 1987

Commercial fishing has long been a major source of income for Outer Bankers. Someone once described this occupation as "just like shooting craps, only more risky." There is no guarantee of a good catch or a good season or a good year, and there are no price supports to cover the bad times. Like farming, commercial fishing is cyclical. Species caught in great numbers one year fail to appear the next. And if that is not enough to worry about, as pollution and loss of habitat reduce the number of fish, the commercial fisherman faces more and harsher restrictions on when, where, and how he fishes, along with growing opposition from environmentalists and sport fishermen. In the following piece, taken from her *Hatteras Journal*, Jan DeBlieu gives a vivid description of the business of commercial fishing as practiced by the fleet based in Hatteras village in the late 1980s.

IN THE HARSHEST months of winter most of Hatteras Island slumps deep into solitude, insulating itself from a crippling northwest wind. At dawn a weak sun rises in a cloudless sky. A cold, blue current pushes south past Rodanthe, flat and foamless like a giant glacial lake. The cottages are empty, the windows boarded, the water pumps drained. By early January the traffic on Highway 12 has thinned to a trickle. . . .

Offshore, gray trout bunch together, hanging in the waters near Avon until the full onset of cold forces them south to the lee of Cape Point. A migratory species, they spend their summers as far north as Cape Cod, but by Thanksgiving they have begun to reach Hatteras, one of their primary wintering grounds in the East. Millions of fish swim near the bottom in water as deep as a hundred feet. They press closely together in schools that may be as narrow as a small house or as broad as a football field. Sometimes they startle at the sound of a boat overhead and split into smaller schools, darting only a few yards before settling down. And the past two winters, the roar of workboats has become increasingly common in the waters within twelve miles of shore.

For the fishing fleet of Hatteras village, winter is a reversal of the norm, a season of long days and short nights. By dawn, up to eighty boats have passed through the narrow channel at Hatteras Inlet. The captains and mates who fish them will not return home until the day's catch has been packed, which is frequently not until midnight or later. On the deepest nights of the year, gill-net boats bump against the docks of Hatteras village, and conveyors carry trout and bluefish to packing-house tables to be culled into sizes, weighed, packed in ice, and shipped to market. Winter, with its cutting winds and feeble light, is the season of aching muscles, shivering limbs, and swelling hands—of bread and butter fishing.

By 9 P.M. eight boats had unloaded their catches at Risky Business Seafood, and three more waited at the dock. From a small room off the main packing area came the constant clickety-clickety-clickety of a staple gun. The woman using the gun could not be seen behind the tiers of waxed cartons she had assembled and marked with the letters MGT medium gray trout. In the center of the fish house, a metal conveyor belt dropped stiff, gaping trout onto a second belt to be sorted into bins according to size.

For nearly six hours Steve Bailey, the owner of the fish house, had stood at the second belt culling fish. His hands darted quickly across the table, flipping trout into bins and other species into wire baskets. The room was wide with a low ceiling, and a dank smell rose from a drainage hole in the cold cement floor. On each side of the conveyor, a scale with a large dial hung from a rusty chain. Bailey, the two men shoveling ice behind him, and a woman working at a scale all wore oilskins—bright-orange waterproof overalls—and yellow slip-on sleeves, plus several layers of clothing to protect them from the damp, salty air. Above the squeak of the conveyors and the scrape of shovel against ice, a radio blared the whine of country fiddle and pedal steel.

The flow of trout trickled and then stopped. Bailey glanced up, annoyed. "C'mon, c'mon," he hollered in a husky voice, "let's have some fish."

Out by the dock a tall, muscular man dipped a shovel into a mass of trout that lined the deck of a forty-foot boat, a typical workboat in the Hatteras fleet. There was no flying bridge, just a square-topped cabin with one seat. Toward the stern a reel four feet in diameter held a coil of monofilament gill net—the drop net, as it is called in these parts. It would take the man close to an hour to empty the boat. He shrugged once as if trying to loosen his shoulders, then resumed a mechanical shoveling. The conveyor carried trout up a steep incline, through a washer, and dropped them by ones and twos onto the belt where Bailey waited. "Let's get some more cartons," he yelled, looking around him. "Need more ice. Let's go, let's go, keep it up."

Earlier that evening I had stopped in the fish house to watch a boat being packed. I was handed a pair of oilskins and told to get to work; a crew member had failed to show up. It was a night in early March, but it could have been any evening from Thanksgiving to Easter, the typical beginning and end of drop-net season. I pulled on the clammy, oversized oilskins, cinched them with a belt, and began shoveling ice, first into a large plastic wagon and then into boxes packed with fish. A short time later I was sent to the small room to make cartons. For the next two hours, until the regular crew member arrived, I surrounded myself with pillars of cardboard.

Making cartons is the easiest job in the fish house, the task generally assigned to newcomers, especially women. To spend an evening packing fish requires strength, stamina, and at least a modicum of speed. To pack fish night after night all winter requires more than fortitude—it requires a willingness to ignore pain and exhaustion for five or six dollars an hour. When fishing is slow, the packers work for only three or four hours at a stretch. But more frequently crews begin about 3 P.M. and work past midnight, until every boat has been emptied.

The most taxing jobs are bailing fish from the boat and stacking cartons, but any of the chores become excruciating after twelve straight hours. In addition to aching back muscles and arms, the packers may suffer from fish poison, an inflammation of the joints that comes from being stuck by the spiny fins of certain species, including trout and bluefish. Although they wear nylon gloves to protect their hands, many fish packers cannot close their fists for most of the winter.

Fifty pounds of fish are put in every carton. As a bin on the rim of the culling table fills, a worker lets up a small gate so that the fish slide into the metal scoop of a scale. The scale needle pushes past forty pounds, then to forty-five, forty-eight. A large fish is added or a small one taken out, until the needle is as close as possible to fifty pounds. The worker tips the load into a carton to be surrounded with ice, and the carton is stacked on a pallet. All the while the captains and mates stand by, drinking beers, not talking much, keeping an occasional eye on the scales.

On the dock a balding captain I knew only as Steve was chopping meat from the tail of a monk fish he had caught with the trout. His face and hands were deeply tanned, a striking contrast to the pasty complexions of the workers inside. The thick lips of the monk fish protruded from pink, blubbery folds. "Cute, isn't he?" Steve asked.

"You guys do good today?" A man who worked in a nearby fish house sauntered up.

"Pretty fair. Fifty boxes. Do better if the price weren't so low." Fifty boxes equaled a hundred cartons, or five thousand pounds. That day the boats would receive fifteen cents for each pound of medium trout. The mate and the captain would each get a fourth of the take, after expenses.

"You guys didn't catch so many fish, price wouldn't be so low."

"Them guys from up north didn't run their mouths on the radio, price wouldn't be so low. The whole damn world knows when we set a net on a school of fish. Including the dealers." Steve slung the head and spine of the monk fish over the edge into dark, oily water.

Somewhere in the darkness two other boats waited, one with its mate and captain catnapping on board. Steve's boat was nearly empty, a half-hour sooner than I had expected. I watched as the last trout traveled up the conveyor. Steve stepped inside, where three pallets of dripping cartons awaited his inspection. The woman at the scales was counting the cartons. She had sturdy shoulders and a round, handsome face. A diamond pendant hung in the hollow of her neck. "All right, I got fifty-two boxes," she said. "You want to count them?"

"Nah, I trust you guys."

Bailey appeared in the doorway of his office and handed Steve the fisherman a pink ticket. The fisherman looked at it, nodded once, and said, "Thanks much." There was nothing, neither satisfaction nor disappointment, in his voice. There is not much room for shows of emotion in the business of fishing. Strength, machismo, and sometimes anger, but seldom joy or sadness. It is almost as though, by denying themselves the luxury of feeling, the fishermen cushion themselves against the exhaustion that is a daily part of their trade.

The mate started hosing down the decks. Bailey was already gearing up for the next load, wiping off the scales and calling for more ice and cartons. A man pushing a whirring forklift deftly transferred the three pallets to a loading platform outside to be put in a refrigerated truck. Another boat, and then another, and then four or five hours' sleep before the Pamlico Sound crabbers would start coming in about 9 A.M., and it would all begin again.

In the morning when the first drop-net boats cross the bar at Hatteras Inlet, the sun is still two hours from rising. On the marine radio channels, captains pass information about the condition of the inlet, the roughest water they will encounter all day. Even the most seasoned fishermen occasionally entertain thoughts of losing their boats in Hatteras Inlet. The radio throbs with static and chatter.

"How's she looking out there?"

"There's a breaker right in the middle of the inlet, but if you ride it fast through the middle shouldn't be no problem t'all."

"Looks like it's smooth outside. Pretty fishing."

"Pretty cold, I'll tell you that."

"Okey-doke, I'm going on through."

Once past the inlet they chart a course for Diamond Shoals, the treacherous shoals off Cape Point. If the trout have moved to the south side of the point, the boats will run only two to three miles offshore and ten or twelve miles north. But early in the winter, when the schools congregate off Avon, the boats must travel as far as twenty miles north. For the slowest of the Hatteras fleet, the trip can take as long as three hours, one way.

All the while, the captain monitors a small screen that shows readings from a sonic depth-finder, watching for marks that appear when the boat passes over a school of fish. At the captain's signal the mate tosses out a round float, the reel begins to grind, and a web of net feeds out with the force of water behind the boat. The mate stands by, controlling the speed of the reel with his shoulder or hand. One side of the net sinks under the weight of lead pellets. The other side, tethered to a series of floats, pulls toward the surface to form a free-floating underwater fence. As fish swim into it, their heads poke through the weave; their gills push through, but their bodies will not fit. They can swim neither forward nor back.

Some boats "soak" their nets for a half-hour or an hour, hoping to trap a school on the move. Others retrieve them after only a matter of minutes. As the reel grinds in, the captain and mate pull on nylon or rubber gloves and pluck the fish from the net as fast as they can. Many fishermen use an L-shaped metal pick to stretch the mesh open, but some work the fish free with their hands. The quicker they pick the nets, the sooner they can reset them or return to harbor. The boat rolls with the swells, the breeze blusters and calms. On cold days spray freezes on the upper deck.

It is an independent means of making a living, fraught with physical danger and financial risk. And it is one of the few ways small commercial operators can make enough to survive.

"Hello-o-o to the *Bette G*. What'cha readin' there, Rudy?"

"Nothin' but a bunch of bait. Not a fish in the sea today."

"Marked a school awhile back, but damned if I can set on 'em."

"Hello-o, *Mamacita*. You got anything goin' there, Big Bill?"

On and on all day, with captains switching channels to withhold information from certain boats and share it with their friends. On and on, as lines of fish appear on the screen, splitting into small groups at the sound of the boat, swirling like leaves caught in a current, vanishing just as fast. . . .

The gill-net fishermen discovered that sonic depth-finders could greatly simplify the search for tightly bunched schools of trout, and the instruments soon became standard equipment on Hatteras boats. Offshore fishing was still considered chancy, especially in the winter when storms and high winds could keep the boats in port for a week or more. To make up for lost days, the two-man crews had to bring in good catches—forty boxes or more—and they had to fish virtually every day they could, even when a period of fair weather lasted for ten straight days. But fuel cost less than a dollar a gallon, and the price of trout seldom fell below twenty cents a pound. By 1980 at least thirty Hatteras boats were making more than half their yearly income during the four months of drop-net season. And news of their luck was spreading.

Over the next four winters the size of the Hatteras drop-net fleet swelled, with boats coming to the village for the winter from as far as Morehead City and Stumpy Point, until the local captains and mates grumbled about the stiff competition. No one knew whether the great schools of trout could be depleted by overfishing; but year after year they returned. The winter of 1984–85 proved to be one of the richest seasons to date. By December 1, 1985, ninety-nine of the boats in Hatteras Harbor were rigged with hydraulic reels and gill nets. With so many fishing crews, any cooperative spirit disappeared. Offshore, the boats kept each other in sight, watching and waiting until a captain ran across a school of fish. As soon as one boat began to feed out a net, four or five others crowded around, sometimes setting their rigs so close that the currents would sweep them together and a single trout would be caught in two nets. . . .

"I've seen some bad fishing weather, some cold fishing weather," Steve Bailey said, "but I can't remember a winter's stayed this warm this long. The mackerel never even got this far south."

We were sitting in the living room of Bailey's house, huddled indoors during an early January storm. The house, a 1920s single-story residence with high ceilings and a broad front porch, was a cozy haven in a strengthening breeze. In the corner of the living room a television flashed clips of a basketball game, and in the refrigerator a six-pack of Bud cooled next to a bowl of gritty oysters. Everything was as it should have been on a blustery winter afternoon. Everything except the direction of the wind, which for three days had blown hard and warm from the southwest. Because of the angle of the channel, a southwest wind makes Hatteras Inlet so rough that few boats dare to cross the bar. Temperatures were in the 50s, but the ocean hovered near 60, uncharacteristically warm for midwinter.

Autumn's strange fishing had continued past the first of the year. For nearly three weeks in November and December the commercial fleet of Hatteras had trolled without luck for king mackerel, even as the boats based at Oregon Inlet each brought in ten boxes a day—$800 at the prevailing price of eighty cents a pound. "The boys here just kept hanging around thinking all they needed was one good northeast blow and the mackerel would be here, but they never did get into them thick like they did last year," Bailey said. "You never know when king mackerel will turn up. They usually show up sometime, though, and they didn't. Not this year. The hurricane screwed everything up. That's what it is. After the hurricane there wasn't a fish caught around this village for a month. By anyone. Now we're packing some fish—a hundred forty, a hundred fifty boxes a night—but that's nothing like it'll be, trout ever show up good."

The scarcity of mackerel had kept Risky Business with no business during what normally would have been one of its best months. As the newest of five packers in Hatteras village, Bailey is discovering constantly just how risky the trade can be. The daily prices Risky Business offers are determined by Bailey's partner, Willie Etheridge III, a Wanchese dealer who places the fish packed by Bailey with wholesale markets in Chicago, Philadelphia, Boston, and New York. The partners have tried to attract fishermen, Bailey said, by offering higher prices than other packing houses as often as they can.

Bailey is a likable man of unusual energy and animation. He arrived in Hatteras village in 1979 with Brownie Douglass, an old college friend. Both men had recently separated from their wives and were looking for an out-of-the-way place where they could settle down and fish. The cape was regaining its reputation as a rich fishing ground, and each year new boats filled the slips of Hatteras Harbor. The two men purchased a forty-two-foot workboat, the *In-Det*, and set out to dropnet, bottom fish, and troll for king mackerel.

Five years later Bailey quit fishing to run Risky Business. The first winter he survived on two and three hours of sleep a night and worried constantly about equipment breakdowns, undependable crew members, and fishermen who talked of quitting him to pack with someone else. His friends grew concerned that he would drop from exhaustion and the pressures of trying to turn a profit. The stress came not only from long hours and hard labor, but from constant reminders that Bailey had switched sides in the quarrelsome relationship between fishermen and packers. Where fishermen are quietly suspicious of each other, they are vociferous about their distrust of dealers. To hear fishermen tell it, the Wanchese dealers make an easy living by sitting in warm offices, talking on the phone, and cutting deals on fish for which captains and mates have risked their lives. It is a point of view Bailey clearly resents.

"I got into this partly because I think some fishermen do get screwed at the packing house," Bailey said. "I think we can cut these guys a fair deal and still make some money. We do cut 'em a fair deal, but they're not ever going to tell you that.

"I get paid a packing fee, so much money for each box of fish I send to Chicago or Philly or New York. If I pack fish, I know I'm going to make what's mine. But I can go out and fish all week and not come home with much of anything, except money for my expenses. Say you're fishing one day and you get in the trout thick. And Joe and Charlie get in the trout thick too. The price was forty cents when you left the dock, but when you get back in it's ten cents because everybody caught fish that day. It's always the price that counts. And it's the dealer that sets the price, depending on where he can send his fish.

"It's a game, you know what I'm saying? The dealer's got to be sly. If you end up with a glut of trout, you can't call the Fulton Fish Market in New York City and say, 'I've got fifteen hundred boxes of trout; what'll you give me for 'em?' They'll give you a nickel, which means the fishermen don't get much at all. But if you've got fifteen hundred boxes and you call Chicago and say, 'Well, maybe I can get you three hundred boxes,' and you call New York and say, 'Okay, I can probably let you have five hundred boxes,' if you spread 'em out like that the price stays up and everybody's better off."

"Are you glad you quit fishing?"

He nodded vigorously. "I like packing fish, and I'm good at it. If the fishermen bring me fish that aren't pretty, I won't pack 'em. If there's fish to be packed, I'll do it all night. That's what fishing is, you know? You work when there's fish. If there's no fish, you ride to the beach, have a party. There is no 'typical'—typical week, typical catch—and there is no guarantee. There's just fish. If you're lucky."

Ones of a Kind

From cattlemen to crab pickers, entrepreneurs to engineers,
politicians to publicists, the Outer Banks has been home to more
than its share of interesting individuals, both native and adopted.
Some are remembered only in oral lore. Other characters, such as
"Pharaoh" Farrow of Hatteras Island, who was reputed to have had an
eleven-year-old bride and an as yet undiscovered buried treasure, have
entered the lower reaches of press coverage. Still others have received
fuller treatment in print. It would be impossible to do them all justice.
What follows, then, is just a sample of the last-named category.

Stanley Wahab, Tar Heel of the Week

WOODROW PRICE 1955

In 1750 a member of the North Carolina Colonial Council described Outer Bankers as "a set of people who live on certain sand Islands lying between the Sound and the Ocean, and who are very Wild and ungovernable." To these adjectives later observers have tended to add quaint, crude, inbred, and slow-witted. But, in fact, many Outer Banks natives have had illustrious careers in medicine, education, government, business, and other fields.

The "Tar Heel of the Week" feature of the Raleigh *News and Observer* was in its infancy when it called attention to Ocracoke industrialist Stanley Wahab. The author of the following article was an enthusiastic fisherman and Ocracoke-lover who rose from reporter to managing editor of the *News and Observer* before retiring to the Down East section of Carteret County.

IF PEOPLE FIND Robert Stanley Wahab of the Island of Ocracoke to be an unusual character, it would not be altogether surprising. In his veins runs the blood of pirates and the blood of Arabs, and the mixture could scarcely be expected to produce the commonplace.

He was born at Ocracoke on February 3, 1888, the son of Hatton Wahab of the Life Saving Service, since become the United States Coast Guard; and of Martha Ann Howard Wahab. Hatton Wahab, according to family tradition, descended from an Arabian sailor who was cast ashore on Ocracoke from a shipwreck in the early 1700s. Martha Ann Howard came down the line from the Howard who served as quartermaster aboard the ship of Edward Teach, better known as Blackbeard the Pirate.

Now 67 and in the autumn of his career, Stanley Wahab can look back upon a full life, some of which was spent at sea in the manner of his forebears, except that no pirating was involved. He has been an oysterman, a sailor, an accountant, a public school teacher, a leader in the business world and the entrepreneur of an air service. He has been and still is a real estate man, a promoter and a hotel owner. For decades he has been prominent in the political and economic life of the coastal region.

He looks out upon the world now from behind exceedingly thick lenses and a big cigar. His voice booms across the waters of Silver Lake from the rail of the Community Store as he tells visitors of Ocracoke's past and predicts of its future. He stands a bit over six feet and weighs a bit over 200 pounds and, except on those occasions when he is off tending to some of his enterprises farther up the Banks, he usually is around the lake front when the *Dolphin* comes in each afternoon with its load of mail and passengers from the mainland.

As might be expected for anyone growing up on an island such as Ocracoke, the water always has played a big part in Stanley Wahab's career. It brought his paternal ancestor to the Island. The water also brought ashore his first school books and a little later in life it set him forth on the journey which was to lead him into accounting and, eventually, into the leadership of a prosperous business enterprise.

His books, a reader and a geography, came to him from his uncle, Thomas W. Howard, who found them with other books floating in the ocean surf after the wooden ship, *Pioneer*, went aground and broke up just off Ocracoke in 1889.

He used the two shipwrecked books for private lessons from the Rev. W. E. Hocutt, a Methodist minister, and while attending public school in the village. From 1899 to 1903 he lived at the north end of the island, while his father was assigned to Cedar Hammock Life Saving Station there, a station which now is more than 100 yards out in the ocean as a result of beach erosion.

His island schooling done, Stanley spent the winter of 1903–4 catching fish, clams and oysters. In June of 1904 he went to sea aboard the menhaden schooner, *Fanny Sprague*, which fished the Atlantic coast from Delaware to Massachusetts. The next year found him serving as a seaman on *Dredge Number Three* of the Norfolk Dredging Company, and January, 1906, found him back on his beloved Island.

Oystering was hard that winter but it led Stanley to his big break in life. He was out after oysters one day when a luxurious steam yacht went ashore on Swash Shoal in the sound. The captain came ashore to sign up a couple of seamen to replace two who had seen the breakers in Ocracoke Inlet and promptly decided the time had come to abandon ship. Stanley signed up and went aboard the *Tech*, which was owned by T. Coleman du Pont.

On a long southern cruise with the industrial magnate, Stanley now recalls, "we were not treated like crew members but more like guests."

Stanley's boss, T. Coleman du Pont, persuaded him to enter business school, telling the Ocracoker that the du Pont company employed many graduates of Goldey Business College in Wilmington, Del. Stanley took the du Pont advice and invested his savings of $475 in a business course there. He finished the course a year later and was offered $40 a month as clerk in the office of John J. Rascob, who later became a multi-millionaire with du Pont.

At the same time, Stanley received an offer of $12 a week with a provision company in Wilmington and he took it instead of the du Pont job. "This," he says now, but without regret, "was perhaps a bad decision."

He had his business education and it led him to jobs with Swift & Company and

Wilson & Company in Philadelphia and in Atlantic City, N.J., before he returned to Ocracoke in 1910 to become principal of the public school in the same building where he had studied a few years before. The next year, he married his childhood sweetheart, Fanny McWilliams, who died a year later.

In 1912, Stanley served as principal of the Lake Landing school in Hyde County and the same year he ran unsuccessfully for the office of county register of deeds. When his first political endeavor ended in failure, he borrowed $15 from his father and departed Hyde to seek his fortune elsewhere.

There followed a stint in the accounting department of the Newport News Shipbuilding and Drydock Company and six or seven years as a commercial course teacher in Maury High School in Norfolk. While he was teaching, Stanley took a correspondence course in accounting and an extension course in law, and his studies enabled him to open his own accounting office. Meanwhile, he married Lucille Grandy of Norfolk and they had three children: Robert S. Wahab Jr., now a lawyer at Virginia Beach; Wilson H. Wahab, now a lawyer in Norfolk; and Lillian E. Wahab, who is now teaching school in Norfolk.

He practiced accounting from 1920 to 1924, when he became comptroller for a big retail chain corporation with general offices in Baltimore. Three years later he quit that job to strike out on his own. He had his big idea. Let him tell about it:

"Along about 1927, many independently owned retail stores were complaining about encroachment of the large chain store corporations. I started thinking and had this idea—Independently owned stores should adopt a plan of operation which would have all the benefits of chain store operation, including pooled or mass buying, accounting, advertising, merchandising. All of this to be supervised by a general office, without the independent stores being necessarily identified as having these advantages.

"In August, 1927, with the assistance of an outstanding friend who had vast experience in chain store merchandising, we organized the Retail Stores Service, Inc., with headquarters in Baltimore. We began operation with 13 independent furniture stores and increased in number of store members even during the depression years of 1930–33. The association proved to be practical and profitable to member stores and also to the Retail Stores Services, Inc."

When impaired sight caused Stanley to sell out his share in 1947, this thriving enterprise had 342 member stores in the United States and now it has over 500.

While Stanley prospered, he remembered Ocracoke. He returned frequently to the Island, and, beginning in 1932, he launched a campaign to develop Ocracoke as a summer resort. He bought 1,000 acres of land on the island, 300 of which he later deeded to the government as part of the Cape Hatteras Seashore National Park. He built a hotel. He acquired another building which he transformed into an inn. He led in the organization of groups which built the electric and ice plants. He built up a number of summer cottages.

His second wife died in 1924 and he has since married again, this time to Myra Edwards of Belhaven. They stay in the old Wahab home on the shore overlooking Silver Lake and she helps him tend to his many enterprises. With the privilege of a man who has done much and now is content to take life a little easier, Robert Stanley Wahab is living, as he puts it, "along these shores of contentment and happiness, where life is worth living and living is at its best."

The Mighty Midgetts of Hatteras

DON WHARTON   1957

It is not true that every other person on Hatteras Island is named Midgett. Every third person, maybe, but not every other one. Even so, throughout the history of the U.S. Coast Guard and its predecessor the Lifesaving Service, it has been unusual not to find at least one Midgett, or Midgette, in every station on the island, ready to risk his life for those in peril on the sea.

Don Wharton, prolific author of everything from adventure novels to this *American Mercury* article, visited and wrote about the Outer Banks so often that he was made an Honorary Tar Heel.

THIRTY MILES NORTH of Cape Hatteras, N.C., the Graveyard of the Atlantic, the Honduran freighter *Omar Babun* was in distress in the night. The ship was tossing in rough seas, her cargo broken loose. Before daybreak she struck a bar 250 feet from the Hatteras shore and was stranded there, helplessly pounded by huge waves from the open Atlantic. Then in the half-dark the Coast Guard, alerted by radio, arrived on the beach. They fired a line to the ship's bow, set up a breeches buoy and one by one pulled all 14 of the ship's crew over the boiling surf to safety.

The Coast Guardsman who discovered the stranded ship was Ellery Midgett II; the surfman who fired the line . . . was Edward Midgett; and the boatswain's mate who helped direct this 1954 rescue was Edison Midgett. None of these men is close kin, but they are all members of a fabulous family which for nine decades has been rescuing mariners along North Carolina's Outer Banks. . . .

Midgetts were saving lives long before the Coast Guard had jurisdiction over the brave men watching our coasts. As surfmen and station keepers in the old Life-Saving Service of the 1870's, the family was represented in a dozen stations along the Outer Banks. Today three Coast Guard stations are headed by Midgetts, and elsewhere Midgetts serve in the ranks. At one station I found two Midgetts, at another a Midgett who at one time had four brothers in the Coast Guard, at still another a commanding officer who said, "This is the only station I've ever served at that didn't have a Midgett."

Ordinarily, any family is proud to have one member win a hero's medal. But over the years ten Midgetts . . . have been awarded Life-Saving Medals of Honor.

. . . On December 22, 1884, the barkentine *Ephraim Williams* was spotted five miles off Cape Hatteras, wallowing in a sea running "mountains high" and flying a distress signal. Immediately John Midgett and five other men shoved off in their surfboat. First they had to cross the immense breakers on the inner bar. Then, nearly half a mile out, they had to hold their boat in check in the seething, foaming surf of the outer bar, wait for a comber to flatten out, row madly before the angry water could rear itself again. The surfboat's whole interior could be seen from the shore as she mounted the seas, almost tumbling over backward. The crew then had to pull four miles across what official reports termed "the most tumultuous sea that any boat ever attempted on that bleak coast."

They took nine men off the *Ephraim Williams*, and though the surfboat was now almost gunwale deep, somehow Midgett's men rowed the five miles back through the tremendous seas. The records called it "one of the most daring rescues by the Life-Saving Service since its organization."

It wasn't the first for the Midgetts. Three years before, Bannister Midgett was keeper of the Chicamacomico station on Hatteras Island when the schooner, *Thomas J. Lancaster*, was stranded. The ship was breaking up, the captain's children had been washed overboard, his wife and others were lashed to the port fore-rigging. With a 65-m.p.h. wind blowing, Bannister worked all night and finally got a surfboat out to the schooner, where he plucked six survivors from the rigging. This rescue was aided by another Midgett, Stanley, who wasn't even in the Life-Saving Service but was hauling wood nearby when he saw help was needed.

Another medal winner was Levene Midgett, son of Joseph, who was in the Life-Saving Service, and father of the late Levene, Jr., who served in the Coast Guard. In 1931 Levene, Sr., then keeper of the Hatteras Inlet station, took a crew out in a severe storm to rescue five fishermen whose trawler, *Anna May*, had swamped and sunk on the shoal. The fishermen were clinging to the mast, swaying in the tumultuous sea which tossed spray and shells a hundred feet into the air. They were shouting and waving when Midgett's boat approached, along with a second boat under Bernice R. Ballance, another Outer Banker. Suddenly the mast swayed too far, toppling the seamen into the breakers. Instantly Midgett and Ballance took their surfboats into the seething breakers and saved them all.

Levene was then 41. He had been in the Coast Guard since 1917, and was to serve on until 1953. Once, at Chicamacomico station, he had 16 men under him, 11 of them Midgetts. During World War II, when 87 ships were lost off the Outer Banks, two thirds of them to submarines, Levene Midgett often spent 18 hours a day cruising in a power surfboat, searching for survivors. On one search every member of his seven-man crew was a Midgett. . . .

If the name of any one Midgett stands above the others it's Rasmus. In a little weather-beaten country store far down the lonely Hatteras spit you can see the gold medal given Rasmus by the Secretary of the Treasury: "To Rasmus S. Midgett for Rescuing Single-Handed Ten Men from the Wreck *Priscilla*, Aug. 18, 1899." Here is what Rasmus Midgett did that day:

The 643-ton barkentine *Priscilla* was driven onto shoals off Hatteras Island in a hurricane. The captain's wife and son, the mate and the ship's boy were swept overboard. The hull broke in two. The after part, with ten survivors, settled a hundred yards from shore, in a dark, thick mist. Heavy waves were pounding it to pieces.

Rasmus, patrolling on a horse, heard the cries of the shipwrecked men, made out part of the vessel, quickly calculated that it would take three hours to get help from the station—too long. So Rasmus, a 48-year-old man, ran into the churning water, worked his way toward the wreck, yelled for a man to jump. As each one leaped, Rasmus seized him and dragged him to shore. Seven times he did this, then learned there were three more seamen on the ship, too bruised to move. This time he worked all the way to the wreck, grabbed a line and pulled himself up to the deck. He found one helpless man and got him ashore before a breaker could sweep them out to sea. He made the harrowing round-trip three times. His feat has been called "unparalleled in the annals of lifesaving."

In the early years many Midgetts, as well as other Outer Bankers, went into the Life-Saving Service to get cash. Times were hard and the meager pay ($40 a month for half a year, and $10 for each off-season rescue) was better than fishing. Most of the Midgett families lived in shacks behind the dunes, built of lumber salvaged from wrecks. They had only a horse or cow, a few poor acres of Hatteras Island, sometimes a small boat and a fishing net. Life-saving eventually became a tradition with them, and today many households can boast four generations of men in the Coast Guard and its predecessor service. One of Rasmus' sons was in the *Mirlo* rescue. The four Midgetts decorated along with him had seven sons in the Coast Guard. Ellery Midgett of the *Omar Babun* rescue had a father, grandfather, great-grandfather and great-great-grandfather in lifesaving. When Graves Midgett told me that he was one of five brothers in the Coast Guard, he felt compelled to explain about the sixth brother: bad eyesight.

Cap'n Ban and the Infernal Engine

BEN DIXON MACNEILL   1958

Many details of Bannister Midgett's biography are either subject to dispute or missing altogether. For example, as a boy he may or may not have run in the Chicamacomico Races, and he may or may not have been shown in the engraving of that event in *Frank Leslie's Illustrated Newspaper*. He may or may not have been illiterate and may or may not have eaten a raw duck on a dare. But there is no doubt that he was a first-rate waterman or that he distinguished himself by skill and fearlessness during his long career in the U.S. Lifesaving Service. Nor is there any doubt that he was colorful in public and private life. The author of the following piece, another distinctive character who continually straddled the fence between journalism and public relations when dealing with his adopted Outer Banks, seldom let obsession with accuracy impede the telling of a tale. Although his 1958 book *The Hatterasman* won the Mayflower Award for nonfiction, he admitted, "I am not a historian and this is not a history." The following account of how technological advance intruded on his quiet domain must therefore remain suspect; but it is a good yarn.

EVIL CAME. It came in a box, together with a book, which those of his crew who confessed an ability to read said were instructions for use and operation. The box contained what was called a naphtha engine, and the papers which came with it said that the engine was to be installed in such and such a boat and, after the directed tests were had, a full report was to be submitted. In writing, of course.

Bannister Midgett was filled with disgust and dismay. He had the Islander's inherited distrust of steam, though he had not long been born when the Horn of Gabriel sounded first above the Sounds. But he had seen enough of steamboats during that war which left him illiterate to last him a lifetime. He remembered, with gleeful chortling, that day when the Yankees gave out of steam, and a lot of Confederates, with sailboats, surrounded the steamless craft and took every man jack of the crew prisoner and maybe took them off down the Sound somewhere and drowned them like they should have done. . . .

It is not unlikely that if Bannister Midgett had had only the orders from afar off, from Washington itself, to contend with, he would have, as was generally his custom, ignored the box altogether and at a suitable time dumped it into the ocean. But there was his crew's curiosity about what was in the box, and what was in the accompanying book. Every day, among themselves and just within his hearing, they discussed the engine and the book, and they wondered what it would do if they installed it in a skiff, like the book said, and started her up.

When these tactics got them nowhere and the box and its baleful content just stood there, they shifted into a tack. They began to wonder, privately and among themselves, of course, whether Captain Ban was afraid of it. Bannister Midgett had, it is remembered, uncommonly keen hearing and his ears were, even in the Leslie picture—if indeed it is he—astonishingly big. They protruded widely beyond the reach of his impressive black whiskers.

There came a day when this passive resistance and this not wholly passive insistence could stand no more. Bannister Midgett bellowed very loudly and blasphemously and the crew took up the box, the book, and the skiff, and they went down to the Sound shore. They put down the skiff with its stern protruding into shallow water. The Keeper was a handy man with tools and he had directed the building of the station house, and the installation of the propeller, or wheel, was no problem.

Bannister Midgett worked alone, and near by the crew sat with the book. This was one of the very earliest naphtha engines, made in an era in which the word "gasoline" had not been contrived. It was a very crude engine, gearless and reversible. It had a single cylinder, and the directions in the book were as simple as the mechanism itself. The crew sat on the bank and read out of the book, beginning with Instruction One, and continued down the roster of procedures. It took most of the day, and the only comment Bannister Midgett had to make was, "What does it say next?"

Toward the middle of the afternoon the installation had come down to that section, "How to Start Naphtha Engine." Foul-smelling fuel was decanted into the opening appointed to receive it and the engine was, in so far as they could know from reading in the book, ready to be started, when Bannister Midgett asked the final and critical question, "What does it say now?" They read to him out of the book.

And then the engine started with such a roar as had not been heard hereabout since the unlethal bombardment at the Battle of Chicamicomico . . . years earlier. Somewhere or other Bannister Midgett must not have been paying full attention to the scholarly members, the reading members, of his crew. The engine started in reverse and the propeller bit hungrily into the water. Before he had time to consider what was happening, the boat was plumb out of the harbor, plumb out of range of his mentors on the shore.

Ahead, fifteen or so miles, lay the dimly outlined shore of the mainland, over about Paine's Creek, and the skiff was headed there, stern-first. Ashore the crew ran hither and yon, some wading out into the water as deep as their knees, and all shouting. Their words were shredded by the counter-roar of the godless, implacable engine that was hurling him westward, Paine's Creekward, at a fearful velocity. He was unable to determine what he should do next, or what the book would have recommended. But somehow the damnable piece of evil had to be silenced, stopped.

Even now, sixty years after the ill-starred advent of the naphtha engine, no prudent Islander will get wading-distance from the shore in a motor-driven boat without an oar handy. There was an oar in the skiff and Bannister Midgett knew the uses of an oar, even new and not-yet-tried uses. He took up the oar and with the butt of it, about half a mile outward bound, he beat the engine into submission. No vestige of it remains, but it is doubtful that even its designer and builder could have ever induced it to run again.

The oar survived practically intact, and with it Bannister Midgett rowed himself back to the shore. He beached the skiff and spoke briefly to his crew before he strode away toward the station, which he had built and which he commanded thirty-six years. "Some of you that can write, write them a letter and say the damned thing is no good for this country. And get the damned thing out of that skiff."

Old Quork

CHARLES HARRY WHEDBEE   1966

The Outer Banks has been fortunate in an abundance of storytellers, and in the recent period of rapid change it has needed them all. But the best known of the lot was neither a native nor a full-time resident, and he practiced his craft with a typewriter. Using his Nags Head cottage as summer headquarters, Greenville jurist and television personality Charles Harry Whedbee collected and embellished countless local tales and produced five published volumes of them before his death in 1992. The piece below appeared in his 1966 book *Legends of the Outer Banks and Tar Heel Tidewater*.

NEARLY EVERYTHING is motorized today. With the speed and comparative ease of automotive transportation one tends, if one is not careful, to whiz past some of the most fascinating legends of our past.

For instance, as you pass swiftly southward today over the paved roads that link Kitty Hawk to Kill Devil Hills to Nag's Head and soar up and over storied Oregon Inlet on the magnificent Bonner Bridge and onward past Pea Island to Hatteras Island, it is not even necessary to slacken your speed before you reach Hatteras Inlet itself, where the pavement stops at the ferry slip.

Even the ferry trip is a short and easy one, and you roll ashore on the northern end of Ocracoke Island with only some thirteen miles remaining between you and Ocracoke Village itself. Nearly every one of those thirteen miles has its own legend, and you are now truly traversing fabulous territory.

If you slow your pace now and look sharply, you will notice by the side of the highway an official sign of the North Carolina Highway Department bearing the words: "Old Quork Point." As is the case with most of the place names on these Outer Banks, thereby hangs a tale—a legend that many of the inhabitants will assure you is quite true.

It is well known and clearly remembered here that "Old Quork" was the name of a man, a castaway, who, like so many others, had washed up on Ocracoke Island the survivor of a shipwreck and had elected to remain there among the friendly and courageous people who had helped him to survive. This Old Quork was apparently a person of Arabian origin. His skin is said to have been of a sort of light gold color, and his name such an outlandish mixture of contradictory and guttural sounds that the nearest the native tongue could come to pronouncing it was to mimic the sound the croaker fish makes. So "Quork" he became, and this was soon lengthened to Old Quork because of his strange and outlandish habits and mannerisms. Thus he was known for the rest of his natural life.

This newly arrived citizen soon developed into a mighty fisherman. He quickly learned the skills and the methods the Islanders had developed for making their living from the ocean. They were generously willing to teach, and he was avidly eager to learn. It was not long before he owned his boat, having made a sharp trade with the widow of a fisherman who had died ashore of an undiagnosed ailment at the ripe old age of 94. The boat was almost as old as her former owner, but she was soundly built and was both seaworthy and seakindly.

Old Quork was quick of hand and as sure-footed as a cat. So far as could be told, he was not afraid of anything that walked, crawled, or swam. That part of his make-up the Bankers could understand and appreciate, but there were other facets of his personality of which they were dubious. As a matter of fact, there were some who, even then, were vaguely suspicious of Quork's extraordinary good luck with a net. There were those who wondered out loud just why the sharks never got into his nets and tore them, why the trash fish seemed to avoid his seine, and how it was that he seemed able to make better hauls singlehandedly than other boats could make even by working together.

The thing, however, that disturbed his fellow fishermen most was the fact that Old Quork had no religious feelings whatsoever. His complete lack of any sense of reverence for an almighty power shocked and outraged these people who had in their time known and respected Moslems, Buddhists, and Hindus—all reduced to the common denominator of castaways but all holding to their own particular kind of belief in an omnipotent deity.

And so it transpired that on the morning of February 6, 1788, just one month to the day after Old Christmas had been celebrated (and it is still celebrated in the village of Rodanthe on Hatteras Island), Old Quork put out in his fishing boat from a point of land near Ocracoke Village. He had his nets in order and neatly folded in the stern of his boat. His sails were spread to the freshening wind, which the old-timers had predicted would ripen into a full gale before the next high tide. As always, he sailed alone, and it was not long before his boat disappeared over the horizon.

As the day wore on, and the weather worsened, fears were felt for Quork, and some concern was expressed for his safety. He was a queer one, all right, but none could deny that he was a brave and able fisherman, and the Ocracokers certainly did not wish him any harm. It was with some sense of relief, then, that they spied his boat headed again for the shore. She seemed low in the water, and she seemed to be making unusually heavy weather of it, but she was traveling at a goodly speed, and soon Quork brought her through the inlet and into the calmer waters of Pamlico Sound. As he tied up at the public dock, the reason for the boat's trim became apparent. She was literally loaded to the gunwales with various sorts and sizes of good, marketable fish.

Rejoicing in Quork's continued good luck, his neighbors helped him unload his catch. Seldom had they seen such a harvest of good fish. There were trout, flounder, bluefish, and mullet. There were spot, croaker, redfish, and drum, but not a single trash fish in the lot. When they were loaded onto the shore end of the dock, they made a great pile. You could almost see the wheels turning in Quork's head as he tried to compute his profit on this one haul.

By now the wind had quickened into a half-gale, and the breakers at sea were growing larger and larger. They were also commencing the familiar roar that characterizes some of the winter storms in this area. The fishermen were congratulating themselves upon getting Quork's boat unloaded before the Sound became too rough for such work, when what did they behold to their surprise but Quork himself refolding his nets, refilling his drinking-water jugs, and obviously preparing his sails for a return to the worsening sea.

Noticing the wild light in his eyes, they tried to persuade Old Quork that it was foolhardy to risk a return trip to sea in the face of such weather. Strongly did they remonstrate with him and, overlooking his past coolness to them, begged and pleaded with him, pointing out that the sea was already too rough, that it was bound to get much worse rather than better, and that it would be flying in the face of the Almighty Himself to put out needlessly in such weather.

According to the legend, Old Quork responded with a scornful laugh and continued his preparations. Finally, all being ready aboard his ancient craft, Old Quork, it is said, stood up in the stern sheets of his boat and, fully aware of his audience on the wharf, shook his fist at the threatening heavens, and defied God. "If there is a God up there, show Yourself now," roared Old Quork. "I, Old Quork, am a greater god than any so-called Heavenly Father; and by the devil and with Satan's help and protection, I will put out to my fishing grounds, and I will come back with an even bigger catch before this day is done!" Then, with a flourish, Quork cast off his mooring lines, hoisted his mainsail, and, with lee gunwale almost awash, conned his small boat toward the wild waters of the inlet.

Aghast, his neighbors watched as he successfully and almost miraculously traversed the inlet and reached the open sea. So far, his fantastic luck was holding. Amazed, the watchers saw him alter his course and trim his sails as he headed his wildly bucking and pitching vessel into the very eye of the worsening storm.

Some say that just before he sailed out of sight—a lone figure in the driving rain and spume—they heard a high, mocking laugh that carried to the watchers on the shore even above the roar of the wind. Others declare that it sounded to them more like the scream of a human in mortal terror.

Be that as it may, Old Quork was never seen again, dead or alive. Nor was any fragment of his boat or his nets ever found. On all of Ocracoke Island there was only the great pile of fish to show that he had ever lived there. That pile of fish stayed right there, too, until it got so ripe it had to be shoveled into the Sound to make a feast for the crabs.

This is the story of Old Quork. This is the man the point was named for. And if you wonder if Ocracokers really believe this yarn, just try to get certain ones of them to go fishing on February 6, any year. You will not be able to force or bribe them even to set foot in a boat, much less to venture out on the water. Of course, some of the young ones will, but they get dark and forbidding looks from their elders. "Old Quork Day" is a day remembered in their folklore with apprehension and fear.

The name you read on the highway sign as you approach Ocracoke Village marks the very point from which Old Quork is said to have sailed out in his boat. They call it Old Quork's Point, and if you decide to try a little flounder gigging on that point some February 6—and if you get back—drop me a line and let me know how you came out.

Les and Sally Moore, Pioneers

JERRY BLEDSOE   1975

Life on the Outer Banks has never been easy. Rewarding, even idyllic, but never easy, especially in the vicinity of Cape Lookout. After all, it was the residents of Shackleford Banks, just west of the Cape, who were the only Bankers to engage in the hazardous business of shore whaling. But after a succession of hurricanes devastated the area in the 1890s, residents loaded their surviving houses on boats and barges and fled to the mainland. Much later the last residents of Portsmouth followed suit, leaving the forty-mile stretch of the Banks from Ocracoke Inlet to Beaufort Inlet with no permanent inhabitants. Why, then, would anyone leave the mainland to live at the isolated Cape? Columnist Jerry Bledsoe, in his 1980 book *Just Folks: Visiting with Carolina People*, was able to provide some insight into the motives of two pioneers who did.

THEY CAME like pioneers, motivated by the same dreams that pioneers have always dreamed: to get away, to build new opportunities.

And now they must face the harsh truth that pioneers inevitably face. Time and events have caught up with them.

Sally Moore smiles and her whole face smiles, a maze of crinkles. "We have completed 15 years," she says. "We're starting our 16th."

For all those years, Les and Sally Moore have been the only permanent residents of Cape Lookout (the Coast Guard station has a small detachment of men who are rotated regularly). They have had 20 miles of primitive island to range over, all the solitude they ever dreamed about, but surprisingly, they find they have to explain to a lot of people why they chose such a life. Sally tries.

"Well, I guess we're just outback people to begin with. It was getting too crowded on Atlantic Beach."

Les and Sally met in Morehead City during World War II. She had lived in the area all her life. He had been born and reared in Idaho. He now likes to tell people that "I was just born a long ways from home." He was in the service when they met and married, and after the war, they opened a small motel on Atlantic Beach.

Cape Lookout seemed the natural place to go when they began to feel crowded on Atlantic Beach. It was close by but it was wild and isolated and it offered the potential to support a small business because of the regular traffic of sport fishermen in the area.

Les and Sally sold their motel and bought nearly six acres at the cape, not far from the lighthouse. It was high land for the Outer Banks, a good eight feet above extreme high water.

They had built a small houseboat and they lived on that as they began to build their new home. They did all the work themselves, hauling materials from Morehead City on a barge. They started from the water and worked inward, building a dock before starting their first building. It was hard work.

During the process, a hurricane named Donna caught them on the island and gave them a good idea of what their new life might hold in store. They rode it out in an old fishing shack that stood on their property.

"It was cotton-pickin' bad," Sally recalls. "It was a bad night. I think it was the hardest wind I've seen in my life."

Their complex now includes the dock, the main building that serves as store and home, four adjoining cabins that they rent on a daily basis, usually to fishermen, several out buildings and a field full of fishermen's jalopies.

Business has been good enough to allow them to stay, and Les and Sally seldom leave the island for the simple reason they can't think of any place they'd rather be, even for a short time. Les hasn't even been to Morehead City in more than two years, except once when he had to pass through on the way to an appointment at a veterans' hospital. They keep in touch with the rest of the world by radio.

Les and Sally have weathered with the elements, their skin becoming leathery and deeply lined, and as they weathered it was almost as if they became part of the island itself. They love it deeply. . . .

She is tending the store on this day. Les is out helping another man build a house on the island. The store offers soft drinks, beer, sandwiches, some canned foods, fishing tackle, and assorted odds and ends. Mostly, though, it offers shelter for the great (and not for sale) collection of beautiful old bottles, shells, anchors, driftwood and other treasures Les and Sally have gathered from the beaches through the years.

As Les and Sally became a part of their island, they became acutely aware of their place in it and their responsibility to it.

"Ever since this country has been here," Sally says, "people have taken from it and never put anything back. Well, we're trying to put something back. We planted sea oats seed, American beach grass, up here where people said it wouldn't grow, and yucca. We planted trees galore. All the tall pines you see, we planted.

"They're all doing well, and we've got the prettiest crop of cedars you ever saw coming up from the birds. That's why we get so cotton pickin' mad when we see people over here with guns."

People with guns come all the time. They come to shoot birds and other creatures, to kill just for fun. "They kill all kinds of birds," Sally says. She and Les have no special authority on the island but they do feel free to administer harsh lectures to the gun toters, which they do whenever they spot them. Their concern for the island's wildlife extends beyond the birds, however. Consider the turtles.

Every year when the loggerhead turtles, lumbering giants weighing up to 900 pounds, wallow ashore to lay their eggs, Les and Sally get up early each morning and scour the beaches for signs that they have arrived. The turtles sometimes lay their eggs in places where the tide will wash over the nests, and if that happens the eggs won't hatch. If the tide doesn't get the eggs, gulls or people often do. "Hardly any of them ever hatch and get to the water," says Sally.

Les and Sally see to it that the turtles at least get a chance to live. They find the nests, dig up the eggs and rebury them in a safe spot next to their store. Then, just before they're supposed to hatch, they dig them up again, bring them inside and let them hatch in an ice chest. Late at night, Les takes the little turtles out to sea and sets them on their way with a big headstart in life. They have been doing that for years, and Sally keeps careful records. "We've just had 135 that hatched out," she says thumbing through her record book. "Let's see how many eggs we've got left . . . 556 eggs left. We hope to get at least 500 live turtles out of that and we might just do it. They're just as cute as they can be. They're precious . . . and they're becoming extinct. People are taking the beaches from them. All of our wildlife is like that. Nature is just being taken away from them. They're just as much a part of this world as we are, and they've got a right to live."

Soon, though, the turtles probably will have to fend for themselves once again. Les and Sally doubt they'll be able to stay at Cape Lookout. The island is to become a national seashore and their property is to be taken. They don't like it very much.

"I'd love for it to stay the way it is," Sally says. "There are few places left that aren't ruled and regulated to death, and I suppose this is the last outpost where there's good fishing."

But they know it is coming and that there is nothing they can do about it. Now, they say, they're just in a state of limbo, not knowing exactly what will happen or when. They may be given lifetime rights to remain on their property after it is taken, but they won't be able to operate their business. And without the income from the store and cottages, they say, they won't be able to stay. Beyond that, they have no idea where they would go or what they would do.

"I don't know," Sally says, shaking her head. "Where would we go? I don't know. We'd be like fish out of water. There isn't any place."

August, 1975
Cape Lookout, North Carolina

★   ★

IN THE SPRING of 1979, nearly a year after Les and Sally Moore were forced out of their home at Cape Lookout, I visited them at the house they had bought in Morehead City and found them still living out of boxes.

"We're sorta lost, Jerry," Les said.

We sat at the kitchen table, surrounded by stacks of bulging cardboard boxes, and talked about adjusting.

"The sky," Sally said. "I miss the sky. We used to have the whole sky."

"Here we have to look straight up," Les said. "Don't get us wrong. It's pretty here. We got some little squirrels about to eat us out of house and home."

The house they bought is well away from the water. It is small and old and not much to look at, but the lot has huge live oak trees and room enough for a garden, something Sally couldn't have on the island. Les has been ripping the house apart to remodel it, adding a new room at the back for Sally's shell and bottle collections and other beachcombing treasures.

"I went back to the cape about a month after we left," Sally told me, "and of course I cried and it tore me all to pieces."

Neither has been back since. They have, in fact, been avoiding the water. "Haven't even been fishing," said Sally. "The water is going to have to become separate. If we can't divorce ourselves from that water, then we just can't get along."

"Coming inland like this makes the whole basis of life completely different," Les said. "We had lived on the water since '46."

Sally looked at Les and tried to smile. "When we first left, I was awfully concerned that Les would have difficulty getting adjusted and, by golly, here it is me. I've taken a sewing course and started a garden. Try to get an interest every day.

"But every full moon I can feel it. I'll be sittin' here and say, 'It must be full moon,' and I'll look at the calendar and it is and I'll think, 'Lord, the shoals are out at the cape,' and I'd love to be there. Oh, I loved to prowl the shoals. But I'll just have to get out of that."

Ad Man, Con Man, Photographer, and Legend

VERA A. EVANS   1978

The northern Banks faced a crisis after World War II. Commercial waterfowling was dead, and recreational hunting was in decline. Several commercially valuable species, such as the shad, had been overharvested, and new fisheries had yet to be exploited. The army and navy had closed most of their bases, and the Coast Guard was boarding up many of its historic stations. Demobilized soldiers and sailors returning home had few prospects of work. But with typical resilience, the area turned to tourism as its new main source of income, though it had difficulty at first competing with longer-established resorts. Just when outside help was most needed, along came Aycock Brown, the perfect man to put the Outer Banks on the map. The newly formed Dare County Tourist Bureau hired him as its director in 1952, a position he held for the next twenty-six years, much of the time doubling as publicity director of *The Lost Colony* production. The explosive growth of tourism on the northern Banks and the enduring popularity of the play attest to how well he did both jobs. The item below, reprinted from *Tar Heel* magazine, is an attempt to sum up the career of this man who told the rest of the world about the Outer Banks.

THE BEACH stretches away, wide, warm and drenched with sunshine—just the sort of day for a young and shapely miss to acquire a sun tan.

Sure enough, one is stretched out on a colorful towel, her golden color deepening attractively. She is dozing peacefully, unaware of the role she is about to play.

Over the dune's rise appears the strange figure of a man. Tall, cranelike, a Southern planter panama topping his elongated face, an assortment of cameras strung about his neck, this apparition spots the sleeping beauty.

Before a very few minutes have elapsed, the famous photographer-publicist, the Outer Banks huckster, the extraordinary Charles Brantley Aycock Brown is chatting easily with the young lady, has moved her so that she is posed fetchingly beside an unusual piece of driftwood and has her focused in his camera.

The pretty sunbather will be amazed to find herself and her driftwood in newspapers across the country, further insuring that the Outer Banks of Dare County will become as familiar to the residents of Oshkosh as of Ocracoke—thanks to the genius of Aycock Brown.

That particular genius lies in Aycock's unerring sense of the story to be found in the most commonplace as well as the most dramatic scenes, people and happenings.

"You can find something unusual in just about everything," said the director of the Dare Tourist Bureau from behind a desk so cluttered that he seemed in imminent danger of burial beneath the tottering stacks of glossies, brochures and other evidence of his trade.

No one can exactly pinpoint what his trade is. He has been described variously as a serious photographer and publicist—which he is—and an ad man, con man, unpublished guidebook and coastland legend—which he is also.

But whatever he is, his outstanding success stems from his knack for seeing

things just a little differently and seeing them through the lens of his camera—
then knowing how and where to market his product.

Aycock began his career back in the 1920's working as a newspaper jack-of-all-
trades, from printer's devil to editor. Finding these activities none too satisfying,
he became a press agent and landed a job on, of all places, Ocracoke Island, as
publicity man for the old Pamlico Inn.

"Jonathan Daniels of the *News and Observer* told me I'd better not take the job,"
Aycock recalled, smiling. "He said there wouldn't be more than one or two stories
on the island."

Aycock proved Daniels wrong, many times over. He wrote up the island characters, embellished a few of the local legends and made news of the cattle that
roamed the marshes and the mosquitoes that bit them.

During his tenure in the press agent job, he met and married Esther Styron, an
Ocracoke girl, and she became his devoted companion until her death last year.

The Depression interrupted Brown's island idyll, and he and Esther were forced
to leave to find work. Their journeyings took them to Philadelphia, where Aycock
labored on a dredge, a distinctly distasteful job, the publicist recalls, making a de-
cidedly long face. Back he went to newspaper work, taking over the Beaufort News
until World War II broke out.

During the war, he served in Naval Intelligence, covering the North Carolina
coast as a special agent. . . .

After the war, Aycock set up a freelance publicity operation in New Bern. It was
then that the late Bill Sharpe, head of the North Carolina News Bureau, came into
his life.

Sharpe persuaded Brown to add publicity for *The Lost Colony* to his operation
and that was the beginning of his love affair with Dare County. In 1952, a group of
businessmen picked Aycock to direct, first, the Dare Chamber of Commerce and
then the Dare Tourist Bureau. Twenty-six years later, he is still directing—from the
same WPA-built, paintpeeled building, in the same tiny office with pretty much
the same pictures on the wall.

Bubbling along during this smorgasbord of occupations was the developing
sense of what it is that makes a photograph stand out.

"When all else fails, put a child with a dog or kitten in the picture," Aycock
grinned, "You can't go wrong there."

This seeming oversimplification is quite basic to Brown's nose for news, however.

"Now you take this," he said, pushing aside a mound of brochures, photos and
like impedimenta to pull out a copy of *Aycock Brown's Outer Banks*. Published in 1976,
the volume is a remarkable tribute to the man.

Eighteen editors, journalists and photographers have tried to explain the genius of Aycock Brown, with varying degrees of success. Throughout all, serious and tongue-in-cheek, runs an almost wistful note, a "wish-I-knew-the-trick, the old scoundrel" message. "Aycock," they seem to say, "is unique, darn it!"

Flipping through the pages of his book, Aycock reveals the something that makes him unique. It gets right back to that story he wants to tell.

"See here," he said, pointing to a picture of a pretty girl on the beach, seashell held to her ear. "Now that's what everybody can relate to on a beach—girls, seashells, sand. They immediately get the feel of the warm sun and the water. Makes them want to head for the Outer Banks!" He laughs in his staccato fashion.

He flipped another page and there was one of his prize-winning pictures—a shipwreck just offshore, crashing surf almost obscuring the doomed vessel and a helicopter with a rescued crew member dangling over the treacherous sea.

"I just happened to be there," Aycock said modestly, revealing another basic in the publicist's successful career. Wherever something is happening, the rangy figure of Brown, some sort of hat clapped on his head, cameras swinging, is bound to be around.

He was around the night the astronauts first walked on the moon, and his keen sense of the dramatic put together another prize-winning photo.

"We were at the Wright Memorial to watch the first walk on the moon," Aycock remembered. "We'd rented some TV's and there were maybe a thousand people there.

"After it was all over, when I was on my way home, there was the picture—the moon right over the Wright Memorial, where it all began.

"That really told a story," he said.

The picture and the story were right there before him when Brown made those photos. Other times, he makes the picture happen.

It may be a crowd of people pressing around some celebrity, a governor perhaps. Aycock, head bent as he peers into his box-like camera, like a snorkeler swimming through a school of fish, waves and pushes bodies aside until he has his quarry fully in focus. Then he may add a deft touch or two—switch the pretty girl to the middle, find the governor's first grade schoolteacher in the crowd to pose with him, or get him to pick up an attractive youngster—and there's his picture.

He shifts the crowds hovering around a big catch of fish just unloaded on the dock in the same way. Instead of a burly male with rod and reel, however, he may pick a four-year-old tyke and give her a fish as large as she is. More likely, he'll find a shapely onlooker in abbreviated swimwear and snap her with a monster creature.

Aycock can ride through the wildlife refuge and see a line of snow geese marching two by two. Captioned "goosestepping," it's an eyecatcher. He can take a picture of his old friend Sam Jones leaning on a fence which surrounds a grave bearing fresh flowers. The story happens to be that it is Jones' horse buried in that plot.

Vehicles stuck in the sand, hurricanes' aftermath, camellias in full bloom, an old Coast Guardsman and his dog sitting in the sun, all are grist for Aycock's mill. Turn the subject a little more this way, catch a fleeting expression, even photograph a pretty girl mirrored in a pair of sunglasses lying on the sand—and Aycock has a picture which will spread across the nation's newspapers like a sensational murder story.

This year *The Lost Colony*, Paul Green's outdoor drama, will begin its 38th season and will count its one-millionth visitor. This remarkable record, making the Paul Green musical drama the granddaddy of all the outdoor shows, owes much to Aycock Brown.

Tirelessly, he has attended performances, finding among the audience someone of note or perhaps a pair of identical twins or a family party of several generations. "If these interesting people all come to *The Lost Colony*," Aycock's pictures seem to say, "What are you waiting for?"

It's as if Aycock implanted a tape recording in a million heads. "Outer Banks? I hear it's a fabulous place—*The Lost Colony*, great fishing, beautiful beaches, girls likewise, interesting historic spots, good bird watching, gorgeous flowers—we plan to take our next vacation there."

Some say Aycock is slowing down a little, taking it a bit easier, acting more like his seventy-four years, but it's hard to know how such rumors get started.

He's still up in the Elizabethan Gardens to photograph North Carolina's First Lady, Carolyn Hunt, chinning with the widow of a direct descendant of Sir Walter Raleigh's half brother and just about capturing the latter's English accent on film. At a recent boat commissioning in Wanchese, he was seen climbing the rigging until he was balanced precariously on the top of the vessel's bridge, aiming his camera down at the notables lined up on the deck below for the ceremony.

It's just turned summer, too, so of course he's on the beach.

"Just move over this way, next to this shipwreck," he'll be saying to a lovely lass. "Look out to sea, as if you were dreaming of long ago and where this ship came from."

Click. There you have the Outer Banks story wrapped up in one picture—drama, history, sand, sun, and a beautiful young lady.

Someone in Oshkosh will see it in his morning newspaper and the tape will be activated—"The Outer Banks . . . ah, yes. . . ."

A Time to Reap

WILLIAM RUEHLMANN   1986

Louis Midgett has all the qualifications to be a representative Outer Banker. He has the right name, though he seems as unsure as everyone else about whether it needs an "e" tacked onto the end, as in the telephone book and in the piece below. He was born at Skyco on the west side of Roanoke Island where steamships called, and he was reared at a hunting club, on the beach south of Nags Head— surrounded by vast areas of marsh and duck ponds. He has displayed the versatility that helps Bankers thrive in this place of extremes, serving with distinction in the U.S. Coast Guard, then effortlessly shifting gears to take on an ambitious horticultural project started and overseen by women. All the while, he has been active in civic affairs and has maintained a variety of interests, from sports, to education, to wildlife conservation. Here is a profile of "Dare County's favorite gardener," originally published in the Norfolk Virginian-Pilot.

JACK FROST freaked.

It is supposed to be the dying time of year, the drought-sucked moment of Shakespeare's "sere and yellow leaf." Instead the grounds of the Elizabethan Gardens in Manteo, N.C., explode in red and green and gold, bird-sung, fountain-splashed, ivy-fastened. The sweet scent of spearmint cuts across wind-crisped herbs like a savory scimitar in a season commonly credited for few flowers or none.

These 10 acres of God's neon are the occupational back yard of Louis Midgette, for almost three decades superintendent of this space, now retiring regretfully from an endeavor long entrenched in his affections.

"You can feel the listening in this place," Midgette said, strolling hedged paths and needle-carpeted alleys of the quiet spot he planted. "It's where the colonists walked. The watering is why I haven't been to church for two months.

"You have to be here on Sundays."

Midgette may have missed services, but it is possible to reflect that here, after his fashion, the horticulturist has been conducting another kind of chapel. Fennel, primrose, yarrow; smoke-tailed squirrels among the hydrangea; bright red Show-Biz roses. These are the emeralds of autumn.

"I've asked myself again and again over the years why I gave up my own things and put the Gardens ahead. I never yet have been able to answer. But when I come here in the evening alone with nobody else around, and I see the rabbits shooting out, and the foxes come, and the coons poke up, I feel special, like it was mine.

"Everywhere I look is where I dug a hole and put something in."

The Elizabethan Gardens, designed for the Garden Club of North Carolina and maintained with the cooperation of the state, endures as a living memorial to English settlers who came to America between 1584 and 1587 and "walked away through the dark forest into history." Open year-round from 9 A.M. to 5 P.M. on Roanoke Island beside the *Lost Colony* complex, the lush grounds abound in lovingly cultivated regional flora, from elephant-eared tobacco to spidery Virginia creeper to soft, bowl-big camellias, bursting pink-purple as if still adorning milady's ruffed 16th century bosom. Since 1958 Midgette, a former Coast Guard warrant officer, has been as fixed a Fort Raleigh feature as the night symphony of waterside cicadas.

"I didn't feel like I'd ever leave all this," the 68-year-old superintendent conceded, touching a finger to one perfect Queen Elizabeth bud provided from Her Majesty's own plot by the British ambassador eight years back. "It takes so much care. But I've been talking about retirement for five years now.

"I want to do some things with my wife and children and grandchildren before I get sick or something."

Still . . .

Midgette turned his collar to the beginning rain, put both hands in his pockets and sighed.

"The days when I plant," he admitted, "I feel better."

The Elizabethan Gardens office of Louis Midgette looks more like a boiler room out of his marine engineering past than the fecund focal point for creative botany. The steel desk is gray, the filing cabinet is gray, the shelves, shoring up quantities of Windex, 6–12 insect repellent and slug-killing Snarol pellets, are gray, gray, gray. A rust-pocked sign sits in one corner:

"DANGER—Keep Off Birdbath."

Between the old green dial phone and the fuse box sits Midgette, silver-haired, bespectacled, Naugahyde-skinned, with two items in front of him. One is a delicate peach-colored rose, the gift of a friend. The other is a 12-year-old greenhouse fan he's trying to fix.

"You have to be pretty well organized in your work schedule," admits the superintendent, who even as he speaks is planning with his staff of five to put in 8,000 new white, gold, rose and blue pansies. "We try to keep something blooming all year 'round. That's what makes so much work.

"You get hardened to it; you're able for it.

"It's amazing what an older guy can do."

Isn't it. When Midgette is not routinely logging 65-hour weeks at the Gardens, fertilizing, pruning, planting, he is running the Dare County Board of Education, of which he has been chairman 18 years, and directing the local Boys Club. Midgette has kept the statistics for the Manteo High football team over a quarter of a century and run concession stands at the *Lost Colony* since 1960. Then there is the little matter of maintaining his personal 1,000-acre wildlife preserve nearby, abounding in snow and Canada geese, osprey, blue wing teal and green cottonmouth moccasins.

That's what he does to relax.

"After I finish at the Gardens I go over and feed the ducks myself."

The preserve and its cultivation earned him the Governor's Conservation Award in 1978.

"I began at an early age to love the things of nature," Midgette recalls. "When I'm out there is when I feel content, looking across the marshland. Just bein' a part of it."

He was born in Skyco, south of Manteo, the only child of a commercial fisherman. His father went to work for former Kentucky Lt. Gov. Jules Day, who built the Skyco Lodge and Goose Wing Club on the Outer Banks, stamping grounds then for the likes of Jack Dempsey and Vice President John Nance Garner. The elder Midgette managed the properties; Mrs. Midgette ran the housekeeping staff.

Growing up on resort properties was a rich experience for a youngster in love with the outdoors. Wild horses and cattle abounded on the beaches; deer and bear choked Mill Tail Creek. Midgette rode a red stallion named Mac and packed a 12-gauge pump gun.

"Guide Tucker Daniels from Wanchese treated me nice. He always had time for this 9-year-old boy who wanted to go hunting. 'Louis,' he'd say, 'one day I'm gonna take you.'

"So one time during the holidays he took me out to this battery, a juniperplanked, water-tight box you'd sit in with the tip of your head at the water surface and decoys all around. I had a simple double-barreled gun, and Tucker told me to keep my head down, and the flock was coming. I raised up and killed my first greenhead mallard drake.

"I was so happy."

Midgette still smiles at the memory, but he also shakes his head over it.

"I used to want to kill Canada geese," he says. "Now I try to raise 'em. I've seen how hard it is for 'em to survive the predators, the coons and the hawks after the eggs, the snapping turtles and bass when they hatch; there's so many odds against wild things, even before man gets to shoot 'em.

"I just don't have any feel for it anymore.

"I've had enough huntin'.

"I'm on their side these days."

Midgette graduated from Manteo High when he was 16. Went to college at the

University of North Carolina, Chapel Hill. Enlisted in the Navy at the outset of World War II.

"I failed the physical," he remembers. "Nearsighted. So I memorized the eye chart and went into the Coast Guard."

Midgette spent the war aboard sub chasers and frigates stalking the Wolf Pack in the North Atlantic. He married his wife, Dora, in 1943. They have three children: Louis Jr., 40, a forester; Robert, 36, a physical education teacher; and Nancy, 33, a housewife.

The Coast Guardsman remained in the service, mustering out at last in 1958 after serving on east coast buoy tenders and cutters. He wanted to devote himself to gardening, propagating azaleas at his Norfolk home on the Lafayette River. At one time Midgette had 200 roses in his yard.

"I always had a feel for plants, you know; in the service it was my way of getting away from steel and diesel engines."

Then Midgett's mother, president of a North Carolina horticultural club, came to her retired son with a modest proposal.

"We're trying," she explained, "to build this garden. . . ."

Midgette calls it fate.

"I said, 'Well, yeah, I can help you.' Something was pulling me to come this way. Not money.

"I just had a feeling it was what I was supposed to do."

In 1950 Mrs. Charles Cameron, chairman of the Roanoke Island Historical Association, and Mrs. Inglis Fletcher, an historical novelist, were showing Sir Evelyn Wrench, founder of the English Speaking Union and friend of the Royal Family, the Fort Raleigh site of Virginia Dare's birth. Wrench remarked it might be appropriate to construct a garden in commemoration of the colonists who came to the New World in the 1580s. Cameron and Fletcher took the idea to the Federation of North Carolina Garden Clubs; by 1953 land had been leased with the intention of building nature trails on it.

The family of John Hay Whitney, former ambassador to the Court of St. James, donated statuary and ornaments, lions couchant, balustrades, stone piers. Ground was cleared in 1956 for a design by landscape architects Umberto Innocenti and Richard Webel. When Midgette arrived in 1958, the memorial was little more than a few crape myrtles in sand, but he had the premonitory feeling that "this was going to be something."

Midgette helped with an ambitious planting plan.

Things grew.

The Elizabethan Gardens burgeoned to a sense-dazzling Eden on Roanoke Sound.

"I thought I'd be here a little while. That was 28 years ago. I got into it.

"I spent a lot of time planting."

An understatement. In the beginning Midgette knew so little he tied colored rags to plants to distinguish male from female. But by the end of his first 10 years at the Gardens, the superintendent was single-handedly propagating 5,000 to 8,000 new plants annually.

"I never had a night where I didn't go over in my mind at bedtime what I was going to plant the next day."

Lemon balm, sparkleberry, Devil's walkingstick. White-fringed orchids, rattlesnake plantains, Jacks-in-the-pulpit. Geraniums.

Hibiscus.

Impatiens.

Pink lady slippers.

A shaped floral world took form in the manner of Hampton Court, south of London—"formal, but not too."

Helen Hayes admired the Elizabethan Gardens. So did Lady Bird Johnson, twice. And Princess Anne of England herself.

"It's uplifting to plant and think about the beauty you're going to get," says Midgette.

And now, effective Jan. 31, the man who has not had a vacation in two years and not many for 28 will step down as superintendent. He will spend time with his family, travel some. He will feed the ducks.

Not easy.

"Now I just feel I ought to," Midgett says. "Writing the letter was tough. But one of these days I won't be able to work, and it's better to get somebody else in here before that happens.

"I just hope they'll find someone special to do this, someone who will love it.

"As I have."

His work with boys and the School Board continues, pursuits not so far removed from gardening as one might think.

"I get a lot of satisfaction," admits conservator Louis Midgette, "from watching things grow."

The Last of the Currituck Beach Cowboys

LORRAINE EATON   1989

Settlers drifting down from Virginia in the late 1600s found the Outer Banks nearly ideal for raising livestock because the numerous islands needed no fencing and held few large predators. Although free range was abolished on most of the barrier chain in the 1930s, one Currituck Banks native resisted the demands of tourists and government regulators and remained a stockman well into the 1990s. He even introduced a breed of livestock unknown to his ancestors. Since this article appeared in *Outer Banks Magazine*, Ernie Bowden has yielded to growing pressure and given up the ranching business. Lately he has concentrated on politics as an elected member of the Currituck County Board of Commissioners.

THIS ISN'T THE Wild, Wild West. In fact, the Outer Banks is just about as far east as you can get, short of taking a dip in the salty Atlantic. Yet there are places on the Outer Banks where you might question your eyesight or your sanity or both.

Steers plodding through the sand, swatting greenhead flies. Buffaloes, bigheaded, lumbering across the dune.

This is Carova Beach.

Placing a hairy muskrat-skin boot on one knee, Ernie Bowden, 64, settles comfortably into a chair in the living room of his oceanfront home in the desolate dunes near the North Carolina–Virginia border.

Straightening his gray felt Stetson, he pauses for a moment, and gazes out the salt-stained window at the sand and the sea. Today, this seasoned coastal cowboy is down to 95 head of cattle, but he can recall a time not so long ago when tourism was unheard of on the northern Outer Banks, and raising livestock was a way of life.

Back in the first third of this century, before he was old enough for his own mount, Bowden remembers countless sweltering summer days when he and his sidekicks would spend all day chasing livestock from marshes, woods, and underbrush, and then onto the beaches, where the animals would be headed off by men on horseback galloping in the soft sand.

"Sometimes, there would be 30 or 40 kids running barefoot on that beach," he said. "The sand was so hot in the summer that you had to develop a process where you would dig a place a few inches deep, down to where it was cool. Then you'd stand in the hole on one foot until the other cooled off.

"And then you'd run another hundred yards and repeat the procedure."

Once on the beach, the herd would be contained by a human fence of children.

Then, one by one the men would inventory the herd, cutting the ears of unmarked animals in a variety of designs: slashing the tips off, adding a curve, a triangular gash, or a hole.

It was branding, Outer Banks style.

Today, the sight of a cowboy galloping across the beach on a half-wild mare, snug in a crude saddle of cross wood and leather, would doubtless turn a lot of heads. But there was a time when many Outer Bankers earned a considerable part of their living raising livestock.

. . . Deeds dating back as early as 1676 specified that when land was sold, a portion of the livestock went with it. Other historians have called the cattle drives of the late 1700s, from North Carolina into Virginia, a forerunner of the "Wild West."

And roaming herds, fenced in only by the sound and sea, had an effect on Outer Banks architecture which lasts even to this day.

Just after the Civil War, Nags Head's summer resort scene shifted from cottages built on stilts over the sound, to the newly-in-vogue oceanfront. It was only natural for wandering cows and pigs to seek out the shade provided by the new oceanfront cottages perched on stilts above the sand. It was also only natural for their companions, the ever-present fleas, flies, and ticks, to find their way through the floorboards.

The 19th century solution was to build latticework screens around the pilings. Today, the latticework provides a decorative effect.

Though few reminders remain of the era of the open range on the Outer Banks, old timers remember well when cattle easily outnumbered people, even during the summer months.

"Cattle ranching was quite an industry on this beach from the late 1800s to the 1930s," said Bowden, who was born and raised on the northern Outer Banks. "When I was a kid, I bet there were 3,000 head of cattle from False Cape to Carova."

"When you're talking livestock on the beach, you're talking everything," said Leland Tillett, 76, of Wanchese, who also grew up on the cattle-filled Currituck beaches. "There were hogs, pigs, sheep, cows, steers—and back in those days they roamed everywhere. Every bit of this beach was used as a free pasture—every bit of it. And the mainstay was the northern beaches."

The land, the natives say, was as suited for cattle ranching back then as it is for a tourist mecca today.

"The beach was a lot different then from what is here now," Bowden recalled. "It was flat, with no vegetation, just sand and shells on the beach."

"If there was one blade of grass on the beach," Tillett agreed, "the livestock would stomp it down on their way to the ocean and stomp it down again on their way back." Instead, lush pastures were provided by the verdant inland marsh.

In the early 1900s, this East Coast barrier island must have been a curious variation of the infamous Wild West. Tillett can't remember anyone ever having spurs; these barefoot cowboys used their sand-toughened heels. Instead of tooled leather, Outer Bankers' saddles were either homemade or World War I surplus. There were no blacksmiths, since horseshoes were hardly necessary in the soft sand and marshes. And a cattle drive, often as not, came to an abrupt end at the edge of the sound, where the livestock were prodded aboard boats and barges. The cows were different too, as different from their western counterparts as the barefoot cowboys that herded them.

"Mostly they were long-horned humpbacked scraggly lookin' cattle," Tillett said of the old-time coastal cattle herds. "Not beefy lookin' at all."

"It didn't matter a bit what they looked like though," he added. "The main thing you wanted was a calf each year. My grandmother aimed to sell 100 calves every summer for $10 to $15 a head, and that was a good price in those days."

As in today's tourist industry, summer marked the busiest time of year for the cattle ranchers on the Banks. Following spring calving, the yearlings would be rounded up, earmarked, and either trucked or floated to bustling livestock markets in downtown Norfolk.

Tillett remembers the massive three-day cattle drives which started at dawn at Oregon Inlet and ended just south of the Virginia border near the Wash Woods Coast Guard Station. To make sure they didn't miss a head, the cowpokes split up, some riding the beach and others scouting the marshes.

"They would start early in the morning because a lot of the cows would go to the ocean to get away from the mosquitoes," Tillett said. "They'd be easy to get because they would be right on the beach. When it got to be light, the man in the marsh would start getting more cattle to run out because they would get hungry and go back up there to eat."

Often the drovers would camp overnight at Tillett's grandmother's place, near . . . Penny's hill. He remembers that the holding pen there was big enough for 200 or 300 head of cattle.

By the time the drive reached Wash Woods, there would sometimes be hundreds of cattle lumbering across the wide, white beaches, their long-winded moan mixing with the sound of crashing waves.

Due west of the Wash Woods station, now an area of scattered summer cottages, Tillett recalls a huge holding pen where calves destined for market would be led onto barges headed for Knotts Island. Still others would be loaded into trucks owned by Norfolk wholesale cattle dealers.

"They'd be waiting with old Model A trucks, 1928, 27, 26, somewhere in there,"

Tillett recalled. "They'd load up six or seven calves and drive back along the waterline all the way to Norfolk."

Tillett's grandfather, Leon White, "a man who was smart, pretty tight, and not really well thought of, but who knew how to squeeze a dollar," had his own method of moving cattle: a 50-foot wooden sailboat named the *Jubilee*.

On market days, White would dock the boat near the family homestead at the base of the New Currituck Inlet channel, a finger of water surrounded by marsh that Tillett said was once six feet deep but today "isn't deep enough to float a black duck in."

Loading the cargo of live cattle was an ordeal. First, the *Jubilee* would be secured flush with the bank, and tied off to nearby pines. The toughest job, Tillett recalls, was boating obstinate steers that could weigh upwards of 1,000 pounds. But the method they devised was simple, calling mainly for strength, courage, and determination.

To begin, a pair of ropes was tied to the cantankerous steer. Next, two men, one in front and one behind, would guide the snorting and stamping animal toward the gunwales of the *Jubilee*. When they got near enough, one man would jump over the side of the boat and run to the bow, forcing the steer to tumble over the hull.

"If the animal fell and broke a leg it didn't matter," said Tillett. "They were going to market anyway."

Loading the calves was easier, Tillett remembers. First, someone would grab a calf by the snout and the ear, leading the animal to the edge of the boat. Then, another drover would grab the calf's tail and hoist the young animal to the deck. To aid in navigation, the livestock were then tied to the deck and forced to lie down.

Still, when the sheets were hoisted and *Jubilee* set sail across the Currituck Sound, she must have been a sight to behold. With Leon White at the helm and a crew consisting of a contingent of his 10 daughters and 3 sons, the one-masted boat would be laden with a cargo of livestock, fish, muskrats, eels. In his quest for profit, White even loaded bones of deceased cattle that young Leland Tillett would pick up along the beaches. The sun-bleached bones were destined for northern factories where they would be made into buttons and fashionable ladies' corsets.

"He'd bring anything that would bring a nickel," Tillett said.

Destined for Norfolk, they'd sail up the North Landing River, and then hook up with a sidewheeler tug for the remainder of the trip to Water Street, the hub of the Tidewater livestock market.

Long after the days of the *Jubilee*, Tillett remembers going to market with his grandmother on their bi-monthly hog deliveries. "There would be dead hogs in the back seat wrapped in bed-sheets, and we'd ride up the beach to 17th Street (in

Virginia Beach) in her 1923 Model A, always running on low tide and always get-ting stuck."

But there was other work for the barrier island cattle ranchers, aside from get-ting their products to market. Throughout the mild part of the year, salt grass was harvested and stored for the harsh winter months. Sheep had to be sheared, cows milked, and horses watered.

And in the early 1930s, the federal government started the Rocky Mountain spotted fever tick-eradication program, a mandatory requirement that added con-siderably to the ranchers' workload.

"We had to herd up all the livestock—cattle, sheep, and hogs—and run them through this thing they called a dipping vat," Bowden recalled.

The dipping vat, according to Bowden, was a dunking system where the cattle were forced up a chute that dropped off into a six-foot-deep pool of foul-smelling, oily green insecticide.

"A dark-colored cow would plumb disappear," Bowden said. "Then it would come walking up the steps on the other side."

After all the livestock in the area had been dipped, a visiting government veteri-narian would check each animal for signs of the deadly parasite.

"You had to have three consecutive clear inspections before they considered you tick-free," Bowden recalled. "If there was one tick on one cow you would have to start over again."

Evidence of those summers is still visible on the Tillett property near Penny's Hill. Further south on Hatteras Island, another dipping vat is intact but barely visible amidst the brush behind Cape Hatteras School in Buxton.

The decade of the 1930s brought both trying and exciting times to the Outer Banks. The government's spotted tick program came and went. In 1933, a pair of hurricanes raged through the area just a month apart, destroying homes and killing livestock. A fledgling tourist industry was becoming more and more estab-lished. And hundreds of the New Deal's Civilian Conservation Corps workers came to the Outer Banks to build more than 100 miles of oceanfront dunes, from Carova to Ocracoke.

The new dune line indirectly dealt a devastating blow to the Outer Banks live-stock industry. Shortly after hundreds of tender young shoots of Carolina beach-grass were planted to stabilize the dunes, the State of North Carolina outlawed open grazing with the Livestock Act of 1934.

"North Carolina officials felt livestock running at large and grazing would de-stroy that beach grass," Bowden said. "Of course, not many people here owned the grazing land; it belonged to the large hunt clubs. Not many people could make that capital investment so they divested the livestock."

Quite rapidly, the number of livestock producers on the Currituck Outer Banks dwindled from about 50 down to seven or eight, according to Bowden. . . .

But hanging on to a vestige of an earlier time is modern-day rancher Ernie Bowden, a man who has continued to raise cattle and horses on property that is destined to become an expensive, if isolated, vacation community, accessible only by foot or four-wheel drive.

Though his ranch in the sand-locked community of Carova is 13 miles from a paved road, Bowden keeps the farm running by leasing unbuildable marshland from developers and through sheer ingenuity.

And at 64, Bowden no longer runs barefoot through the marshes scaring up strays. Today he rides the range in a beat-up four-wheel-drive pickup, always dressed in a yoked shirt, worn denims, a wide-brimmed Western hat and one of several pairs of leather boots: alligator, ostrich, muskrat, or just plain cow leather.

Though the dress is similar, ranch headquarters in Carova Beach is strikingly different from the red barns, shiny silos, and wide open pastures of inland farms. At the sandy center of Ernie's operation is a corrugated metal building surrounded by rusting house trailers, ancient automobiles, an assortment of hulking industrial-yellow equipment, flat-bed trailers, giant trash bins, and even a crane.

"The old house trailers people give to me when they replace them with houses," Bowden said. "You learn to keep everything on this beach—every wheel and tire, every part of a motor—everything."

Regardless of his isolation from his cattle-raising colleagues, Bowden manages to run a sophisticated farm known as a "cow-calf" operation. He breeds calves and sells them to feeder operations, mostly in Texas, where they are fattened up to slaughter weight and then sold to slaughter houses.

In early 1989, Bowden had almost 100 cows, calves, and sires, including hybrid Cenipoles imported from the Virgin Islands and a number of creamy white French Charolais. In their company, wandering the pastures, are also 14 registered quarter horses, a 30-year-old pony, a few stray goats and pigs, and a mess of assorted cats.

But aside from the location of Bowden's farm, three-quarters of a mile west of the often stormy Atlantic, the most startling facet of his livestock operation are the majestic purebred buffalo that occasionally can be spotted in the marshes, grazing languidly alongside the cows.

Bowden brought the beasts to Carova Beach a few years ago to breed with his cattle. He was aiming for "beefalo," an animal that is five-eighths cow and three-eighths buffalo and yields considerably more "beef" than regular cattle.

Success came in 1986, with the birth of the first beefalo. A second success followed in January 1989, when one of his buffalo gave birth to the first purebred buffalo calf ever to be born on the Outer Banks.

"Hasn't been one born within anyone's immediate memory, so far as I know," he said.

Today, three curly-headed buffalo and two beefalo roam the 3,000-acre range.

But even in Carova, where people generally ignore unconventional behavior in both man and beast, a stray cow or buffalo found grazing in someone's front yard still raises eyebrows, especially those of summer visitors.

"They never seem to stray except in the summer." he said, his grin revealing a row of white even teeth. "And they never go into people's yards except on the weekends when people are here. Then they either call me or call the sheriff and say, 'That Ernie Bowden's cows are in my yard again.' They all know who they belong to."

Raising cattle on the Outer Banks is easier in warm weather than during the period from early December through late March, when week-long blasts of northeast wind prohibit cattle from grazing. During the winter months, Bowden uses his faithful front-loading tractor to fill the livestock troughs with anywhere from a half-ton to three tons of grain each day.

Going to market 1980s-style means loading 30 or so calves into one of his trailers and driving them to Virginia along the sandy roads. It's hard work, and these days Bowden is the only one doing it.

"Today, there's not enough profit in the cattle business to hire somebody to help," Bowden said. "Today, you need to have hard-road access to have the business. I'm sure I'll be the last one to raise livestock on this beach."

The subject of a road is often a topic of heated debate in these parts. And Bowden, a former Currituck County commissioner who never hesitates to speak his mind, is certain that there will never be a paved road leading into Carova.

His opinion is based on the fact that the community is located between the Currituck National Wildlife Refuge (created in 1984) to the south and Virginia's False Cape State Park and the Back Bay National Wildlife Refuge to the north. A fence, from the ocean and deep into the dunes, traces the state line, keeping vehicular traffic off the Virginia lands.

Only about 50 long-time Carova residents, including Bowden. have keys to a gate that allows the short trip through the state and federally owned lands to Virginia Beach and civilization. Those without keys are forced to make the 130-mile trip inland by way of the Wright Memorial Bridge.

But even those with keys are restricted. Travel is limited to the hours from 5 A.M. to midnight and Bowden has vehemently opposed the regulations, maintaining they are a violation of his rights as a United States citizen.

That rugged brand of individualism so symbolized by the West also seems to have its Eastern counterpart here on the Outer Banks. If not an outright outlaw,

Bowden is certainly a man willing to stand by his convictions, even if it means going to jail. He has spent a total of 58 days behind bars, after being arrested twice for violating the curfew.

"I felt that was a very unproductive part of my life," he said. "I have no more respect for their laws now than I did then."

If the range wars put an end to open cattle ranching in the West, here on the East Coast different forces are at play. What was once considered scrub land, not good for much else except cattle ranching, is now becoming the rage among real estate investors. As demand for vacation property continues to drive prices up, cattle ranching is being driven out.

Never mind that there's no road. It doesn't matter that few banks are willing to finance. And even though it costs an average of 20 percent more to build a house because building materials must be brought in by four-wheel drive . . . property values in Carova Beach have increased in the past four years, in some cases by almost 500 percent.

Although Carova Beach, North Swan Beach, and Swan Beach lands were sub-divided some 20 years ago, it's only recently that renewed interest has been shown in completing the development of this secluded area. Soon, the stampede won't be a herd of cattle, but land-hungry investors looking for new seaside opportunities in an ever-dwindling market.

"People look at it as the last frontier," said David Weybright, a sales associate with RE/MAX Island Realty. "There's not a pretty lot in Duck that is as beautiful as the lots in Carova. I take people up there and they either love it or they hate it. There's no in between. But no matter what, they're amazed."

Partially due to the ever-increasing development pressures and recent government acquisition of the windswept beaches flanking Carova, Bowden said he has been forced to cut back his herd from a high of 400 head of cattle in the late 1960s to early 1970s to the 85 he has today.

But still the aging cowboy is dedicated to this waning way of life, one he has known since childhood. Regardless of encroaching development and the pitfalls of running a ranch accessible only by four-wheel drive, Bowden vows to continue raising buffalo, cows, and horses on the Currituck Banks as long as he is able.

Cattle ranching runs strong in the Bowden blood, and Ernie will doubtless be remembered in chronicles of the Outer Banks as the last of the Currituck Beach cowboys.

The Crab Picker

ELIZABETH LELAND 1992

Blue crabs are among the favorite local delicacies served in Outer Banks restaurants, but this was not always so. A report on the commercial fisheries of North Carolina in the 1880s stated that blue crabs, also known as channel crabs, were very abundant along the coast but not in great demand. "The fishermen take them in immense numbers in their drag-nets while fishing for sea-trout, mullet, and other fish, and consider them a great annoyance, and it is difficult to remove them from the nets," the report said, adding that "they kill nearly all that are captured in this way, by a blow from a stick carried for the purpose, and then throw them away, or use them as manure." Once they caught on, though, blue crabs became important to the local economy and provided seasonal employment for many watermen and their wives and children. Today there are two quite different crab fisheries, one in which large numbers of soft crabs, many of which molt in modern, labor-intensive "shedders," are shipped to market alive, mostly in the spring, and the other in which hard crabs are steamed, picked, packed, and sold by weight. In her book *Our Vanishing Coast*, Elizabeth Leland profiled a *mainland* woman so proficient at picking hard crabs that the College of the Albemarle hired her to teach the craft to young Outer Bankers.

JOSEPHINE SPENCER'S callused hands fly across the table. She jerks the claws off a cooked crab, rips off the bright orange back, scoops out the eggs, cuts off the legs, then carefully picks out the delicate white meat. "I love to pick crabs," Spencer says, her bright brown eyes never even looking down to see what her hands are doing. Less than a minute and she's on to the next crab.

Spencer is a crab-picking expert. She's been making a living at it for more than thirty-five years. She says that while people don't get rich in her line of work, "you don't stay broke once you learn how to pick 'em."

She picks her crabs in Wanchese, an out-of-the-way corner of Roanoke Island. "They put a timer on me one time long ago," she brags. "I used to be able to pick seventy-five pounds a day. I slowed down since I got older. Everything I do is fast. Everybody says that, even about my housework."

Spencer grew up in Engelhard on Pamlico Sound, where most of the state's forty crab houses are located. Crabs are big business on the North Carolina coast. Fishermen caught more than 31.8 million pounds in 1988, valued on the docks at more than $7 million. It's such a good business in the area that a local college hired Spencer to train more workers. Her job comes with a title: Crab-picking Instructor of the College of the Albemarle.

Spencer began picking at age seventeen, the year after she married. She worked in crab houses in Engelhard . . . before the college sent her to St. Elmo's Crab Company in Wanchese to teach others to pick crabs.

In an age of automation, there's still only one way to pick crabs, and that's by hand. There's an art to it. The toughest part is making sure to pick only the meat. . . . "If the crab is cut deep enough," Spencer says, "you always get good clean meat. That's what I tell them. I check out every pound. Oh my gracious I like to work with the meat. . . . Not that I couldn't quit. I'm an ordained minister."

Spencer always works with the same four-inch stainless-steel knife. No other knife will do. She sits on a chair in front of a long stainless-steel table. At five-foot-three, she's too short to reach the floor of the concrete-block building, so she rests her feet on a spare block.

Nineteen-year-old Lisa Barnett works across the table. Her face contorts in frustration as she slowly picks at a crab. There's none of the joy Spencer radiates when she's finished picking, when she flashes a smile so broad it reveals two gold teeth.

"I don't like this," Barnett admits. . . . "I can only do ten pounds a day."

"Oh my gracious," Spencer says. "You can do more than ten pounds, Lisa."

"I can. But I don't."

Patty Jarvis, co-owner of Mattamuskeet Seafood . . . says she expects each worker to pick twenty pounds in an eight-hour day. Most pickers get paid by the pound, at the going rate of $1.25 to $1.50 per pound. If they're good, the arrangement generally works out better than minimum wage. But Donald Caroon, the owner of St. Elmo's Crab Company, where Spencer teaches, pays his trainees by the hour instead of by the pound. They go through about two thousand pounds of crabmeat a day, compared with ten thousand pounds at Mattamuskeet Seafood.

"It's slow going," Spencer says of her trainees. "But they'll catch on."

Freddie Barnes shovels a load of crabs onto the table. Then he stares at Spencer. "I just like to sit here and watch her," he says. "She can put on a good show. She can pick and do a whole lot of talking." And singing, too. Spencer is as likely to break into a rendition of "God Has Smiled on Me" as she is to scold another worker that "the Bible says he who has no sin casts the first stone."

By the end of the day, she's as aromatic as the crabs she picks. "Your whole skin smells," she says. "You really got to take a good bath. My husband, he can't stand the smell. Now, crab picking has become a part of me. I don't eat many. I been working in seafood so long crabs isn't one of my favorites. I just like to pick 'em."

Visitors Leave Their Footprints

There seems to be something about the Outer Banks that attracts
all kinds of people, a good many of whom have stayed around long
enough to make their distinctive marks. There was the sixteenth-
century explorer and artist John White, who lost his daughter and
granddaughter on Roanoke Island but left us the earliest known
pictures of local plants, animals, and people. There were two brothers
from Ohio who mastered flight near the village of Kitty Hawk at the
very same time that an obscure employee of the U.S. Weather Bureau
was sending messages through the air, between Roanoke Island and
Buxton, ushering in the age of radio communication. These and others
were outlanders who made lasting and distinctive marks on the Outer
Banks and the world.

The Governor Returns

JOHN WHITE 1590

John White was sent over by Sir Walter Raleigh in 1587 as governor of a colony that was to have been planted on the shores of Chesapeake Bay. But by his own admission he could not prevent the sailors under his nominal command from depositing his colony instead on Roanoke Island, where Ralph Lane's colony had failed the previous year. Under pressure, White reluctantly returned to England for supplies in August, leaving behind his daughter, Eleanor Dare; his newborn granddaughter, Virginia Dare; and more than 100 others. The attack of the Spanish Armada and other misfortunes back home prevented him from completing his mission for three years, and when he finally reached the island again he was little more than an unwelcome passenger in a flotilla assembled mainly to plunder Spanish shipping. White arrived off the Outer Banks on August 15, 1590, but additional bad luck (including the drowning of seven companions) delayed his setting foot on Roanoke Island until August 18—Virginia Dare's third birthday. The editors of the third edition of Richard Hakluyt's *Principal Navigations* modernized some spelling and typography in the following selection, which were further modernized for this book.

THE 15 OF AUGUST towards evening we came to an anchor at Hatorask, in 36 degr. and one third, in five fathoms water, three leagues from the shore. At our first coming to anchor on this shore we saw a great smoke rise in the Isle Roanoak near the place where I left our colony in the year 1587, which smoke put us in good hope that some of the colony were there expecting my return out of England.

The 16 and next morning our 2 boats went a shore, & Captain Cooke, & Cap. Spicer, & their company with me, with intent to pass to the place at Roanoke where our countrymen were left. At our putting from the ship we commanded our master gunner to make ready 2 minions and a falcon well loaden, and to shoot them off with reasonable space between every shot, to the end that their reports might be heard to the place where we hoped to find some of our people. This was accordingly performed, & our two boats put off unto the shore, in the admiral's boat we sounded all the way and found from our ship until we came within a mile of the shore nine, eight, and seven fathom: but before we were half way between our ships and the shore we saw another great smoke to the southwest of Kenricks Mounts: we therefore thought good to go to that second smoke first: but it was much further from the harbor where we landed, then we supposed it to be, so that we were very sore tired before we came to the smoke. But that which grieved us more was that when we came to the smoke, we found no man nor sign that any had been there lately, nor yet any fresh water in all this way to drink. Being thus wearied with this journey we returned to the harbor where we left our boats, who in our absence had brought their cask ashore for fresh water, so we deferred our going to Roanoak until the next morning, and caused some of those sailors to dig in those sandy hills for fresh water whereof we found very sufficient. That night we returned aboard with our boats and our whole company in safety.

The next morning being the 17 of August, our boats and company were prepared again to go up to Roanoke, but Captain Spicer had then sent his boat ashore for fresh water, by means whereof it was ten of the clock aforenoon before we put from our ships which were then come to an anchor within two miles of the shore. The admiral's boat was half way toward the shore, when Captain Spicer put off from his ship. The admiral's boat first passed the breach, but not without some danger of sinking, for we had a sea break into our boat which filled us half full of water, but by the will of God and careful steerage of Captain Cooke we came safe ashore, saving only that our furniture, victuals, match and powder were much wet and spoiled. For at this time the wind blew at Northeast and direct into the harbor so great a gale, that the sea brake extremely on the bar, and the tide went very forcibly at the entrance. By that time our admiral's boat was hauled ashore, and most of our things taken out to dry, Captain Spicer came to the entrance of the breach with his mast standing up, and was half passed over, but by the rash and undiscreet steerage of Ralph Skinner his master's mate, a very dangerous sea brake into their boat and overset them quite, the men kept the boat some in it, and some hanging on it, but the next sea set the boat on ground, where it beat so, that some of them were forced to let go their hold, hoping to wade ashore; but the sea still beat them down, so that they could neither stand nor swim, and the boat twice or thrice was turned the keel upward, whereon Captain Spicer and Skinner hung until they sunk, & were seen no more. But four that could swim a little kept themselves in deeper water and were saved by Captain Cooke's means, who so soon as he saw their oversetting, stripped himself, and four other that could swim very well, & with all haste possible rowed unto them, & saved four. They were 11 in all, & 7 of the chiefest were drowned, whose names were Edward Spicer, Ralph Skinner, Edward Kelley, Thomas Bevis, Hance the surgeon, Edward Kelborne, Robert Coleman. This mischance did so much discomfort the sailors, that they were all of one mind not to go any further to seek the planters. But in the end by the commandment & persuasion of me and Captain Cooke, they prepared the boats: and seeing the Captain and me so resolute, they seemed much more willing. Our boats and all things fitted again, we put off from Hatorask, being the number of 19 persons in both boats: but before we could get to the place, where our planters were left, it was so exceeding dark, that we overshot the place a quarter of a mile: there we espied towards the north end of the island the light of a great fire through the woods, to the which we presently rowed: when we came right over against it, we let fall our grapnel near the shore, & sounded with a trumpet a call, & afterwards many familiar English tunes of songs, and called to them friendly; but we had no answer, we therefore landed at daybreak, and coming to the fire, we found the grass & sundry rotten trees burning about the place. From hence we went through the woods to that part of the island directly over against Dasamongwepeuk, & from thence we returned by the water side, round about the north point of the island, until we came to the place where I left our colony. . . . In all this way we saw in the sand the print of the savages' feet of 2 or 3 sorts trodden in the night, and as we entered up the sandy bank upon a tree, in the very brow thereof were curiously carved these fair Roman letters CRO: which letters presently we knew to signify the place, where I should find the planters seated, according to a secret token agreed upon between them & me at my last departure from them, which was, that in any ways they should not fail to write or carve on the trees or posts of the doors the name of the place where they should be seated; for at my coming away they were prepared to remove from Roanoke 50 miles into the main. Therefore at my departure from them in An. 1587 I willed them, that if they should happen to be distressed in any of those places, that then they should carve over the letters or name, a cross + in this form, but we found no such sign of distress. And having well considered of this, we passed toward the place where they were left in sundry houses, but we found the houses taken down, and the place very strongly enclosed with a high palisade of great trees, with curtains and flankers very fort-like, and one of the chief trees or posts at the right side of the entrance had the bark taken off, and 5 foot from the ground in fair capital letters was graven CROATOAN without any cross or sign of distress; this done, we entered into the palisade, where we found many bars of iron, two pigs of lead, four iron fowlers, iron saker-shot, and such like heavy things, thrown here and there, almost overgrown with grass and weeds. From thence we went along by the water side, towards the point of the creek to see if we could find any of their boats or pinnace, but we could perceive no sign of them, nor any of the last falcons and small ordnance which were left with them, at my departure from them. At our return from the creek, some of our sailors meeting us, told us that they had found where divers chests had been hidden, and long since digged up again and broken up, and much of the goods in them spoiled and scattered about, but nothing left, of such things as the savages knew any use of, undefaced. Presently Captain Cooke and I went to the place, which was in the end of an old trench, made two years past by Captain Amadas: where we found five chests, that had been carefully hidden of the planters, and of the same chests three were my own, and about the place many of my things spoiled and broken, and my books torn from the covers, the frames of some of my pictures and maps rotten and spoiled with rain, and my armor almost eaten through with rust; this could be no other but the deed of the savages our enemies at Dasamongwepeuk, who had watched the departure of our men to Croatoan; and as soon as they were departed, digged up every place where they suspected any thing to be buried: but although it much grieved me to see such spoil of my goods, yet on the other side I greatly joyed that I had safely found a certain token of their safe being at Croatoan, which is the place where Manteo was born, and the savages of the island our friends.

When we had seen in this place so much as we could, we returned to our boats, and departed from the shore towards our ships, with as much speed as we could: For the weather began to overcast, and very likely that a foul and stormy night would ensue. Therefore the same evening with much danger and labor, we got ourselves aboard, by which time the wind and seas were so greatly risen, that we doubted our cables and anchors would scarcely hold until morning: wherefore the captain caused the boat to be manned with five lusty men, who could swim all well, and sent them to the little island on the right hand side of the harbor, to bring aboard six of our men, who had filled our cask with fresh water: the boat the same night returned aboard with our men, but all our cask ready filled they left behind, unpossible to be had aboard without danger of casting away both men and boats: for this night proved very stormy and foul.

The next morning it was agreed by the captain and myself, with the master and others, to weigh anchor, and go for the place at Croatoan, where our planters were: for that then the wind was good for that place, and also to leave that cask with fresh water on shore in the island until our return. So then they brought up the cable to the capstan, but when the anchor was almost apeak, the cable broke, by means whereof we lost another anchor, wherewith we drove so fast into the shore, that we were forced to let fall a third anchor: which came so fast home that the ship was almost aground by Kenricks Mounts: so that we were forced to let slip the cable end for end. And if it had not chanced that we had fallen into a channel of deeper water, closer by the shore than we accompted of, we could never have gone clear of the point that lieth to the southwards of Kenricks Mounts. Being thus clear of some dangers, and gotten into deeper waters, but not without some loss: for we had but one cable and anchor left us of four, and the weather grew to be fouler and fouler; our victuals scarce, and our cask and fresh water lost: it was therefore determined that we should go for Saint John or some other island to the southward for fresh water. And it was further purposed, that if we could any ways supply our wants of victuals and other necessaries, either at Hispaniola, Saint John, or Trinidad, that then we should continue in the Indies all the winter following, with hope to make 2 rich voyages of one, and at our return to visit our countrymen at Virginia. The captain and the whole company in the admiral (with my earnest petitions) thereunto agreed, so that it rested only to know what the master of the *Moonlight* our consort would do herein. But when we demanded them if they would accompany us in that new determination, they alleged that their weak and leaky ship was not able to continue it; wherefore the same night we parted, leaving the *Moonlight* to go directly for England, and the admiral set his course for Trinidad.

Gray-Eyed Indians

JOHN LAWSON   1714

John Lawson's lively *New Voyage to Carolina* makes several references to the Outer Banks and speculates on the fate of the Lost Colony. Some of Raleigh's colonists spent considerable time on what is now Hatteras Island, keeping watch for ships, gathering shellfish, and trading with the natives. It would be a wonder if they did not also sire a few children by native women. By Lawson's time, the remnant of the Indians living on the Banks had been reduced to soliciting handouts of food from the proprietary government. Before the end of the eighteenth century, they had vanished. The following selection is taken from the 1967 edition, edited by Hugh T. Lefler, who modernized some spelling and typography and made the bracketed insertions. Further modernization has been done for this book.

THIS PART OF CAROLINA is faced with a chain of sand-banks, which defends it from the violence and insults of the Atlantic Ocean; by which barrier, a vast sound is hemmed in, which fronts the mouths of the navigable and pleasant rivers of this fertile country, and into which they disgorge themselves. Through the same are inlets of several depths of water. Some of their channels admit only of sloops, brigantines, small barks, and ketches; and such are Currituck, Ronoake, and up the sound above Hatteras: Whilst others can receive ships of burden, as Ocracoke, Topsail Inlet, and Cape Fear. . . .

The first discovery and settlement of this country was by the procurement of Sir Walter Raleigh, in conjunction with some public-spirited gentlemen of that age, under protection of Queen Elizabeth; for which reason it was then named Virginia, being begun on that part called Ronoake Island, where ruins of a fort are to be seen at this day, as well as some old English coins which have been lately found; and a brass gun, a powder horn, and one small quarterdeck gun, made of iron staves, and hooped with the same metal; which method of making guns might very probably be made use of in those days, for the convenience of infant colonies.

A farther confirmation of this we have from the Hatteras Indians, who either then lived on Ronoake Island, or much frequented it. These tell us, that several of their ancestors were white people, and could talk in a book [read], as we do; the truth of which is confirmed by gray eyes being found frequently amongst these Indians, and no others. They value themselves extremely for their affinity to the English, and are ready to do them all friendly offices. It is probable, that this settlement miscarried for want of timely supplies from England; or through the treachery of the natives, for we may reasonably suppose that the English were forced to cohabit with them, for relief and conversation; and that in process of time, they conformed themselves to the manners of their Indian relations. And thus we see, how apt human nature is to degenerate.

I cannot forbear inserting here, a pleasant story that passes for an uncontested truth amongst the inhabitants of this place; which is, the ship which brought the first colonies, does often appear amongst them, under sail, in a gallant posture, which they call Sir Walter Raleigh's ship; and the truth of this has been affirmed to me, by men of the best credit in the country.

The Nag's Head Picture of Theodosia Burr

BETTIE FRESHWATER POOL   1813

In early January 1813 the schooner *Patriot* disappeared en route from Georgetown, South Carolina, to New York. A severe storm had struck the Carolinas soon after the *Patriot* sailed, and before long rumors circulated that she had wrecked on the Outer Banks with no sign of crew or passengers. It is odd that no one seems to have tried very hard to substantiate these rumors, for the *Patriot* carried Theodosia Burr Alston, daughter of former vice president Aaron Burr and wife of South Carolina governor Joseph Alston. Most writers of succeeding generations have overlooked the weather, the British (with whom the United States was then at war), and a multitude of infamous hazards to navigation. They fixed blame instead on the allegedly piratical Bankers. Although Bettie Freshwater Pool was no geographer (in the following selection she places Kitty Hawk "a few miles below Nags Head"), she cut a memorable figure as raconteur, novelist, teacher, and literary historian in her native Pasquotank County. This piece from her 1905 collection *The Eyrie and Other Southern Stories* has been mined countless times.

THE SAND DUNES of North Carolina have long been famous as the scene of marine tragedies. The bleaching ribs of some of the stateliest craft that ever plowed the deep bear testimony to the ravages of old ocean. The English merchantman, the Portuguese galleon, the Dutch brigantine, the Spanish treasure ship, the French corvette, the Norwegian barque, representatives of every maritime nation on the globe, are scattered over the beach . . . their grisly skeletons protruding from the sands like antediluvian monsters in some geological bed.

This narrow strip of sand, winding like a yellow ribbon between the inland sounds and the sea, presents a curious study to the geologist. For years it has been gradually sinking, and at the same time becoming narrower, until now its average width is not more than a mile; and, the libertine waters of the great sea not seldom rush across the frail barrier to embrace those of the Albemarle. . . .

The ornithologist may here find much to interest him, and the conchologist revel in a paradise of shells. But the nautilus, pale and pearly, and the delicate blush of the sea conch, have small influence on the rude nature of the native "banker." Isolated from the world on this barren waste of shifting sand the "banker" of a hundred years ago was almost a barbarian. His savage instincts not only made him consider all flotsam and jetsam his lawful property, but induced him to use every means to lure vessels ashore, for purposes of plunder. And when a wreck occurred, the wreckers held high carnival. The sparse population turned out "en masse," and with demoniac yells, murdered without remorse the hapless victims who escaped the raging surf. Nags Head, a favorite summer resort along the coast, was named from a habit the "bankers" had of hobbling a horse, suspending a lantern from its neck, and walking it up and down the beach on stormy nights, impressing the mariner with the belief that a vessel was riding safely at anchor. Through this device many a good ship has gone down and much valuable booty secured to the land pirates.

The "bankers" of to-day are different beings from their ancestors of a century ago. Fellowship with enlightened people has had a humanizing influence, and they are now good and useful citizens. . . .

In the winter of 1812 there drifted ashore at Kitty Hawk, a few miles below Nags Head, a small pilot boat with all sails set and the rudder lashed. There was no sign of violence or bloodshed; the boat was in perfect condition, but entirely deserted. The small table in the cabin had been spread for some repast, which remained undisturbed. There were several handsome silk dresses, a vase of wax flowers with a glass covering, a nautilus shell beautifully carved, and hanging on the wall of the cabin was the portrait of a young and beautiful woman. This picture was an oil painting on polished mahogany, twenty inches in length and enclosed in a frame richly gilded. The face was patrician and refined: the expression of the dark eyes, proud and haughty; the hair dark auburn, curling and abundant. A white bodice cut low in the neck and richly adorned with lace, revealed a glimpse of the drooping shoulders, and the snowy bust, unconfined by corset.

The wreckers who boarded the boat possessed themselves of everything of value on board. The picture, wax flowers, nautilus shell and silk dresses fell into the possession of an illiterate banker woman, who attached no especial value to them.

This picture, which has since attracted so much attention, hung on the wall of a rude cabin among the North Carolina hills for fifty-seven years. In the year 1869, it fell into the possession of the late Dr. William G. Pool, a prominent North Carolina physician. Dr. Pool was a man of marked individuality. He had the tastes of an antiquarian, was literary, cultured, and noted for his remarkable conversational gifts. While summering at Nags Head, he was called upon to visit professionally the old banker woman referred to above. He was successful in his treatment of the case, and knowing the circumstances of his patient, would accept no payment for his services. In her gratitude for his kindness, the old woman insisted upon his accepting "as a gift," the portrait hanging on the wall of her cabin. When questioned concerning its history, she related the facts above mentioned. This she did with apparent reluctance, possibly suppressing many interesting details that might have thrown more light upon the subject. Her husband had been one of the wreckers who boarded the pilot boat, and the picture and other articles referred to had been his share of the spoils. Her story was, that the wreckers supposed the boat to have been boarded by pirates, and that passengers and crew had been made to "walk the plank." The picture and its strange history became a subject of much interest and conjecture to Dr. Pool. Artists pronounced it a masterpiece, and the unmistakable portrait of some woman of patrician birth.

Chancing one day to pick up an old magazine in which appeared a picture of Aaron Burr, Dr. Pool was forcibly struck by the strong resemblance between it and the portrait in question. Like a flash it occurred to him that this might be a likeness of Theodosia, the ill-fated daughter of Aaron Burr. Eagerly he compared dates and facts, until be became thoroughly convinced that he had found a clue to that mysterious disappearance, which is one of the most awful tragedies of history. A brief account of this discovery was published in the New York Sun, and immediately letters innumerable were received by him asking for more particulars.

Photographs of the portrait were sent to the numerous members of the Burr and Edwards families, and almost without exception the likeness was pronounced to be that of Theodosia Burr. Charles Burr Todd, the author, and Mrs. Stella Drake Knappin, descendants respectively of the Burr and Edwards families, visited

Dr. Pool's residence on Pasquotank river for the purpose of examining the portrait. They were both convinced that it was a likeness of Theodosia Burr.

The wife of Col. Wheeler of Washington, D.C., who is a daughter of Sully, the famous portrait painter, and is herself an artist, compared a photo of the Nags Head picture with a likeness of Theodosia Burr in her possession. She at once perceived that both features and expression were identical.

There was probably no woman in America at the time of Theodosia Burr's death, more universally known and admired than she. Her high social rank, her beauty, her genius, her accomplishments, as well as her heroic devotion to her father in the dark days of his disgrace and banishment, had made her a prominent figure and had won for her the admiration of thousands.

When Aaron Burr upon his return from exile sent for his daughter to visit him in New York, she decided to make the voyage by sea. Her health had been almost completely wrecked by grief over her father's disgrace, and the recent death of her only child, young Aaron Burr Alston. It was thought that a sea voyage might prove beneficial. She accordingly set sail from Georgetown, S.C., in the *Patriot*, a small pilot boat, December 30th, 1812. Days and weeks passed, but Aaron Burr waited in vain for the arrival of his daughter. Months and years rolled away and still no tidings came. The *Patriot* and all on board had completely vanished from the face of the earth, and the mystery of its disappearance remained unsolved for more than half a century.

Governor Alston did not long survive the loss of his beloved wife, and Aaron Burr, in speaking, years afterwards of his daughter's mysterious fate, said that this event had separated him from the human race.

Let us now compare dates and facts: A pilot boat drifts ashore during the winter of 1812 at Kitty Hawk, a few miles below Nags Head. There are silk dresses in the cabin, and other indications that some lady of wealth and refinement has been on board. There is a portrait on the wall of the cabin that has been pronounced by artists and members of her family to be a likeness of Theodosia Burr.

The *Patriot* was lost during the winter of 1812. On the voyage from Georgetown, S.C., to New York, it would pass the North Carolina coast. The sea at this time was infested by pirates. A band of these bold buccaneers may have boarded the little vessel and compelled passengers and crew to "walk the plank." Becoming alarmed at the appearance of some Government cruiser, they may, from motives of prudence, have abandoned their prize.

This theory is not mere conjecture. Years ago two criminals executed in Norfolk, Va., are reported as having testified that they had belonged to a piratical crew who boarded the *Patriot*, and compelled every soul on board to "walk the plank." The same confession was made years subsequently by a mendicant dying in a

Michigan almshouse. This man said he would never forget the beautiful face of Theodosia Burr, as it sank beneath the waves, nor how eloquently she pleaded for her life, promising the pirates pardon and a liberal reward if they would spare her. But they were relentless, and she went to her doom with so dauntless and calm a spirit, that even the most hardened pirates were touched.

I cannot vouch for the truth of these confessions which have appeared from time to time in print, I only introduce them as collateral evidence in support of the banker woman's story. The *Patriot* was supposed to have been wrecked off the coast of Hatteras during a terrific storm which occurred soon after it set sail. This, however . . . has never been substantiated by the slightest proof.

Our Winds Are Always Steady

JOSEPH J. DOSHER, WILLIAM J. TATE,
WILBUR WRIGHT, ORVILLE WRIGHT   1900

By the summer of 1900, while eminent scientists around the world raced toward the elusive goal of manned flight in heavier-than-air craft, Wilbur and Orville Wright— high-school dropouts running a bicycle shop in Dayton, Ohio—had also become "afflicted with the belief that flight is possible to man." They decided to try their own ideas about powered flight by designing and building a man-carrying kite. Their next step was to find the right place to fly it, one that was isolated and windy, with hills overlooking flat expanses free of trees and other obstructions. Maps showed that the Outer Banks was isolated, and information provided by the U.S. Weather Bureau confirmed that Kitty Hawk was windy; so Wilbur wrote to the weather station there for details. He received two replies. The first, from Joseph J. Dosher, the operator of the station, whetted the brothers' appetite; the second, an unsolicited testimonial from William J. Tate, the Kitty Hawk postmaster, convinced them that the place deserved investigation. Wilbur, the elder brother, went to see for himself and soon began writing back with his findings. The first two selections below were taken from Fred Kelly's *Miracle at Kitty Hawk*; the other two, from *The Papers of Orville and Wilbur Wright*, edited by Marvin McFarland.

Joseph J. Dosher to Wilbur Wright, August 16, 1900

In reply to yours of the 3rd, I will say the beach here is about one mile wide, clear of trees or high hills and extends for nearly sixty miles same condition. The wind blows mostly from the north and northeast September and October. . . . I am sorry to say you could not rent a house here, so you will have to bring tents. You could obtain board.

William J. Tate to Wilbur Wright, August 18, 1900

Mr. J. J. Dosher of the Weather Bureau here has asked me to answer your letter to him, relative to the fitness of Kitty Hawk as a place to practice or experiment with a flying machine, etc.

In answering I would say that you would find here nearly any type of ground you could wish; you could, for instance, get a stretch of sandy land one mile by five with a bare hill in center 80 feet high, not a tree or bush anywhere to break the evenness of the wind current. This in my opinion would be a fine place; our winds are always steady, generally from 10 to 20 miles velocity per hour.

You can reach here from Elizabeth City, N.C. (35 miles from here) by boat direct from Manteo 12 miles from here by mail boat every Mon., Wed. & Friday. We have Telegraph communication & daily mails. Climate healthy, you could find good place to pitch tents & get board in private family provided there were not too many in your party; would advise you to come any time from September 15 to October 15. Don't wait until November. The autumn generally gets a little rough by November.

If you decide to try your machine here & come I will take pleasure in doing all I can for your convenience & success & pleasure, & I assure you you will find a hospitable people when you come among us.

Fragmentary Memorandum by Wilbur Wright, circa September 13, 1900

Left Dayton Thurs. eve. at 6:30 over Big Four and C.& O. Arrived at Old Point about six o'clock P.M. the next day, and went over to Norfolk via the steamer *Pennsylvania*. Put up at the Monticello Hotel. Spent Saturday morning trying to find some spruce for parts of machine, but was unsuccessful. Finally I bought some white pine and had it sawed up at J. E. Etheridge Co. mill. Cumpston Goffigon, the foreman, very accommodating. The weather was near 100 Fahr. and I nearly collapsed. At 4:30 left for Eliz. City and put up at the Arlington where I spent several days waiting for a boat to Kitty Hawk. No one seemed to know anything about the place or how to get there. At last on Tuesday left. I engaged passage with Israel Perry on his flat-bottom schooner fishing boat. As it was anchored about three miles down the river we started in his skiff which was loaded almost to the gunwale with three men, my heavy trunk and lumber. The boat leaked very badly and frequently dipped water, but by constant bailing we managed to reach the schooner in safety. The weather was very fine with a light west wind blowing. When I mounted the deck of the larger boat I discovered at a glance that it was in worse condition if possible than the skiff. The sails were rotten, the ropes badly worn and the rudder-post half rotted off, and the cabin so dirty and vermin-infested that I kept out of it from first to last. The wind became very light, making progress slow. Though we had started immediately after dinner it was almost dark when we passed out of the mouth of the Pasquotank and headed down the sound. The water was much rougher than the light wind would have led us to expect, and Israel spoke of it several times and seemed a little uneasy. After a time the breeze shifted to the south and east and gradually became stronger. The boat was quite unfitted for sailing against a head wind owing to the large size of the cabin, the lack of load, and its flat bottom. The waves which were now running quite high struck the boat from below with a heavy shock and threw it back about as fast as it went forward. The leeway was greater than the headway. The strain of rolling and pitching sprung a leak and this, together with what water came over the bow at times, made it necessary to bail frequently. At 11 o'clock the wind had increased to a gale and the boat was gradually being driven nearer and nearer the north shore, but as an attempt to turn round would probably have resulted in an upset there seemed nothing else to do but attempt to round the North River light and take refuge behind the point. In a severe gust the foresail was blown loose from the boom and fluttered to leeward with a terrible roar. The boy and I finally succeeded in taking it in though it was rather dangerous work in the dark with the boat rolling so badly. By the time we had reached a position even with the end of the point it became doubtful whether we would be able to round the light, which lay at the end of the bar extending out a quarter of a mile from the shore. The suspense was ended by another roaring of the canvas as the mainsail also tore loose from the boom, and shook fiercely in the gale. The only chance was to make a straight run over the bar under nothing but a jib, so we took in the mainsail and let the boat swing round stern to the wind. This was a very dangerous maneuver in such a sea but was in some way accomplished without capsizing. The waves were very high on the bar and broke over the stern very badly. Israel had been so long a stranger to the touch of water upon his skin that it affected him very much.

Orville Wright to Katharine Wright, October 18, 1900

Our nights in Kitty Hawk are interesting and, were there not so many of them, not unpleasant. A little excitement once in a while is not undesirable, but every night, especially when you are so sleepy, it becomes a little monotonous. This is "just be-fore the battle," sister, just before the squall begins. About two or three nights a week we have to crawl up at ten or eleven o'clock to hold the tent down. When one of these 45-mile nor'easters strikes us, you can depend on it, there is little sleep in our camp for the night. Expect another tonight. We have just passed through one which took up two or three wagonloads of sand from the N.E. end of our tent and piled it up eight inches deep on the flying machine, which we had anchored about fifty feet southwest. The wind shaking the roof and sides of the tent sounds exactly like thunder. When we crawl out of the tent to fix things outside the sand fairly blinds us. It blows across the ground in clouds. We certainly can't complain of the place. We came down here for wind and sand, and we have got them.

We spent half the morning yesterday in getting the machine out of the sand. When we finally did get it free, we took it up the hill, and made a number of ex-periments in a twenty-five-mile wind. We have not been on the thing since the first time we had it out, but merely experiment with the machine alone, sometimes loaded with seventy-five pounds of chains. We tried it with tail in front, behind, and every other way. When we got through, Will was so mixed up he couldn't even theorize. It has been with considerable effort that I have succeeded in keeping him in the flying business at all. He likes to chase buzzards, thinking they are eagles, and chicken hawks, much better.

Today we took the machine about a mile below camp to some small steep hills to try gliding. The wind died out before we got there so all our experiments had to be made with the machine alone—no one on it. We let it up about four or five feet from the brow of the hill and then started it forward over the embankment. We were greatly pleased with the results excepting a few little accidents to the ma-chine. It would glide out over the side at a height of 15 or twenty feet for about 30 feet, gaining, we think, in altitude all the while. After going about 30 feet out, it would sometimes turn up a little too much in front, when it would start back, in-creasing in speed as it came, and whack the side of the hill with terrific force. The result generally was a broken limb somewhere, but we hastily splint the breaks and go ahead. If the wind is strong enough and comes from the northeast, we will probably go down to the Kill Devil Hills tomorrow, where we will try gliding on the machine.

I am sitting on our chicken coop writing this letter. The coop has never had a chicken in it yet, but we hope to have two tomorrow morning. Trying to camp down here reminds me constantly of those poor Arctic explorers. We are living nearly the whole time on reduced rations. Once in a while we get a mess of fish, and if our stuff comes about the same time from Elizabeth City—which stuff consists of canned tomatoes, peaches, condensed milk, flour and bacon & butter—we have a big blowout or, as the Africans would say, "a big full." But it only lasts a day. We are expecting to have a big blowout tomorrow when we get those two chickens. We have just appointed the Kitty Hawk storekeeper our agent to buy us anything he can get hold of, in any quantities he can get, in the line of fish, eggs, wild geese or ducks. We have had biscuits, molasses, coffee, and rice today. Tomorrow morning we will have biscuits (made without either eggs or milk), coffee, and rice. The economics of this place were so nicely balanced before our arrival that everybody here could live and yet nothing be wasted. Our presence brought disaster to the whole arrangement. We, having more money than the natives, have been able to buy up the whole egg product of the town and about all the canned goods in the store. I fear some of them will have to suffer as a result.

Speaking about money reminds me of a pretty good one Tom the fisherman got off a few days ago when I asked him who was the richest man in Kitty Hawk. "Dr. Cogswell," he replied. "How much has he?" I inquired. "Why, his brother owes him fifteen thousand dollars," and the young fisherman thought the question settled. Tom is a small chap . . . that can tell more big yarns than any kid of his size I ever saw. We took a picture of him as he came along the other day on his way home from the beach with a drum almost as large as he. The drum is a salt-water fish.

It is now after eight and "time to be abed." A cold nor'easter is blowing tonight, and I have seen warmer places than it is in this tent. We each of us have two blankets, but almost freeze every night. The wind blows in on my head, and I pull the blankets up over my head, when my feet freeze, and I reverse the process. I keep this up all night and in the morning am hardly able to tell "where I'm at" in the bedclothes. From this on we are going to run the stove at nights—at least from midnight on, which heats up the tent pretty well. In spite of all these little drawbacks, I have been getting in from nine to ten hours of sleep every night— except the storm nights, when I'm either up running around outside the tent or in bed awake (with my clothes on) expecting to see the tent get up and fly away every minute. Them's interesting times, but rather hard on sleep. There is no news here, except that Mr. Calhoun the storekeeper has just sold out and will leave Kitty Hawk tomorrow. He is the most interesting character I have found here. He is an old man, broken down in health, who came here to seek recovery. "It was the greatest mistake of my life," he always tells you, "and I will die here before I am able to get away." He was not greatly beloved by the Kitty Hawkers, but was pretty well liked by us foreigners. I'm out of paper. Will start Tuesday for home.

The Forgotten Pioneer

PATRICK K. LACKEY   1902

In December 1901, Guglielmo Marconi, a young Italian aristocrat, sent the first wireless telegraph message across the Atlantic, stunning the world and putting himself in line for the Nobel Prize. Barely four months later Reginald Aubrey Fessenden, a little-known, middle-aged former assistant of Thomas Edison working for the U.S. Weather Bureau, made comparable breakthroughs in radiotelephony, that is, the transmission of audio signals on a radio-frequency carrier. Having made crude voice transmissions between towers a mile apart on Cobb Island, Maryland, in 1900, Fessenden built a more advanced three-station network stretching from Cape Hatteras north to Cape Henry, Virginia. In April 1902, at his headquarters on Roanoke Island he received musical notes sent from his southernmost tower, and before long he was "talking with Hatteras." The Wright brothers conducted their revolutionary experiments in flight on the north banks at Kitty Hawk and achieved enduring fame. Fessenden laid the foundations of modern radio and television during the same period a short distance away but has been nearly forgotten, as the author of this 1992 article for the Norfolk *Virginian-Pilot* learned.

AT THE BEGINNING of this century, only six miles separated the work sites of the "Fathers of Flight" and the "Father of Radio Broadcasting."

At the sand dunes of Kill Devil Hills, Orville and Wilbur Wright mastered flight.

Just across Roanoke Sound, at the northern end of Roanoke Island, Reginald A. Fessenden made the scientific breakthroughs that led to the world's first radio broadcast.

While practically everyone has heard of the Wright brothers, the bike builders from Ohio, the public quickly forgot Fessenden after he died in 1932 at age 65.

He deserves to be remembered.

Without Fessenden, or someone else as bright and pigheaded, there would be no rock radio, no MTV, no PBS, for many of his discoveries and inventions still are used in radio and television.

Early in 1902 he made the first wireless broadcast of musical notes, from an antenna near Buxton on Hatteras to an antenna at Roanoke Island, about 50 miles away.

"It was a companionable thought" wrote Fessenden's wife, Helen, "that in this element, the air, two men not so many miles away from us were achieving mastery in one form while we at Manteo were achieving mastery in another."

Many of Fessenden's most significant discoveries were made during his 20 months on Roanoke Island, beginning in January 1901.

In a letter from Manteo to his patent attorney dated April 3, 1902, Fessenden made this amazing report:

"I have more good news for you. You remember I telephoned about a mile in 1900 (on Cobb Island in the Potomac River)—but I thought it would take too much power to telephone across the Atlantic. Well I can now telephone as far as I can telegraph, which is across the Pacific Ocean if desired. I have sent various musical notes from Hatteras and received them here with but 3 watts of energy, and they are very loud and plain, i.e., as loud as in an ordinary telephone."

At that time, other wireless-communications experimenters were still sending the dots and dashes of Morse Code.

Fessenden had not yet fired messages and music across the ocean, but he knew he could.

Four years later, working at Brant Rock, Mass., he would make the world's first wireless two-way transatlantic telegraphic and voice transmissions. People in Scotland and Massachusetts conversed over the air. The world shrank.

And on Christmas Eve of 1906, again at Brant Rock, he would make his most famous broadcast, the one encyclopedias call the first radio broadcast in history. Unlike his earlier transmissions, including ones on Roanoke Island, the Christmas Eve broadcast was announced in advance.

In an article hailing Fessenden as the "father of radio broadcasting," Science Digest magazine described the 1906 broadcast this way.

"Fessenden played Handel's 'Largo' on the phonograph and Gounod's 'O Holy Night' on his violin. There were songs, speeches and the reading of a poem."

Astonished radio operators at sea heard music over their sets for the first time, and the broadcast was picked up as far south as Norfolk. Thus, the first radio performer on an instrument was Professor Fessenden, and the first radio singer was his wife. Talk about a tough trivia question!

In Manteo, Fessenden was employed by the U.S. Weather Bureau, which hoped he could develop a method of wireless communication by which weather data could be transmitted rapidly on the East Coast.

During that period, he had an antenna at Cape Henry, Virginia Beach, though most of his transmissions were between Hatteras and Roanoke Island.

After he quit the Weather Bureau and left Roanoke Island, he lived and worked a while in the Ocean View section of Norfolk, before heading north to Massachusetts.

Fessenden is no household name for a number of reasons, besides the usual one that the public's attention span for scientific matters is as narrow as it is short.

Working against Fessenden ever becoming famous was the fact that he usually was far ahead of his time. One of the first of his more than 500 patents was for a parking garage with ramps and hoists like ones used today, but the patent expired long before garages were needed.

Also, while other inventors like the wealthy Italian Guglielmo Marconi had publicity machines, Fessenden was highly secretive, for fear of having his inventions stolen before they were patented.

Furthermore, Fessenden, a tall redhead, was at times a hot-tempered jerk. In the book *The Continuous Wave: Technology and American Radio, 1900–32,* author Hugh G. J. Aitken wrote that the following adjectives were commonly used to describe Fessenden:

"Vain, egotistic, arrogant, bombastic, irascible, combative, domineering."

According to Aitken, Fessenden was known to repeatedly tell one of his most valuable employees, "Don't try to think, you haven't the brain for it."

A lengthy master's thesis was written on Fessenden's feud with his boss at the Weather Bureau. Fessenden quit the bureau in September 1902 and left Manteo for Norfolk even as his boss was attempting to fire him for insubordination and other crimes repugnant to a bureaucrat.

And one final reason for his obscurity: He made himself unpopular with major communications companies by suing them for patent infringements. One target was RCA, then the world's largest communications company.

Sailors may well have heard of Fessenden. His nautical inventions include a sonic depth and distance finder called a fathometer, the wireless compass, the turbo-electric drive for battleships, and various submarine signaling devices.

The World War II destroyer escort ship *Fessenden* was named after him. And of course scientists and other inventors never forgot him.

In 1929, *Scientific American* magazine awarded him the Scientific American Medal "for outstanding achievement in the field of marine safety."

In Fessenden's *New York Times* obituary, Elihu Thomson, then head of the General Electric Company's main laboratories, described Fessenden as "the greatest wireless inventor of the age—greater than Marconi."

Fessenden was born Oct. 6, 1866, in Quebec, Canada, the son of an Episcopal rector who was far from wealthy.

He graduated from high school at age 14 and taught college courses while attending college for four years.

At age 19, he moved to Bermuda and became the principal and only teacher of a small school. Two years later he left for New York, determined to work for Thomas Alva Edison. Starting at a low position as inspector and tester, Fessenden finally was hired at age 21 to work with Edison in the laboratory. For most of the next three years, he served as Edison's chief chemist.

He then worked for a subsidiary of Westinghouse and as a professor of electronics, first at Purdue University and then at the school that became the University of Pittsburgh, before being hired early in 1900 by the weather bureau.

His first success on his new job was the transmission of a voice for one mile on Cobb Island, Md., after which he moved his operation to Manteo.

He and Helen lived in a hotel there, and he trekked four miles each day to his work station on Croatan Sound.

The only biography of Fessenden was written by Helen and titled *Fessenden— Builder of Tomorrows*. Nary a negative thought about Fessenden is contained in the book. Helen described his work this way;

"Under Fessenden, work became an adventure; goals were set, preposterous and beyond the borderland of possibility. The men were in that constant state of mental gymnastics advised in *Alice Through the Looking Glass*—'practice believing so many possible things before breakfast.'

"The tasks set might seem like trying to grasp beautiful bubbles but marvelously, the bubbles held, were brought down to earth and one by one linked to perform the appointed miracles."

Radio waves, or electromagnetic waves, had been discovered in 1888, by the German physicist Heinrich Hertz.

They were miraculous. The British physicist Sir William Crookes wrote of them four years later:

"Rays of light will not pierce through a wall, nor, as we know only too well, through a London fog. But the electrical vibrations of a yard or more in wave length . . . will easily pierce such medium, which to them will be transparent.

"Here, then, is revealed the bewildering possibility of telegraphy without wires, posts, cables, or any of our present costly appliances."

In 1895, Marconi sent messages in dots and dashes. But in 1899, his wireless messages remained erratic, and the maximum transmission distance was 35 miles. There was no means of tuning, so only one transmitter could work in an area at a time.

Marconi's system worked by turning a device off and on. Hence speed was impossible, as was the transmission of voice and music.

Realizing that voices and music could never be transmitted via broken radio waves, Fessenden learned to piggyback voice and music onto continuous waves and invented a sensitive method for detecting and receiving the waves when they arrived.

In other words, he invented the first precise radio tuner. By turning one dial, he could home in on a specific frequency, the same way people today spin a dial to get a specific radio or television station.

After quitting the weather bureau in a huff, Fessenden went in with two Pittsburgh bankers to form the National Electric Signaling Co., which later was bought by RCA in order to obtain Fessenden's patents.

Fessenden spent much of his later life suing others for patent infringements. His two original partners ended up bankrupt.

Like many other geniuses, he seemed to have no head for business. He sought to use others' money while retaining complete control of all projects and pursuing whatever lines of thought interested him.

To say the least, he did not have Thomas Edison's practical streak. Still, he would obtain half as many patents as Edison.

Although more than 100 boxes of Fessenden's working papers and other materials are stored in the North Carolina State Archives at Raleigh and his drawings and blueprints take up another 30 or so large cases there, two key questions are unanswered:

What were the first words spoken over a wireless telephone?

For all anyone knows, someone gave the temperature and humidity or complained about the mosquitoes.

Did the Wright brothers and Fessenden ever meet?

Michael Lewis Everette, a radio engineer for the North Carolina Highway Patrol, wrote a master's thesis on Fessenden and has read most of the materials by or about him.

He wrote in his thesis:

"It is quite likely that Fessenden was a visitor at the Wright camp, and that the Wrights may have visited the Fessenden team, although no record exists of such contacts in Fessenden's papers. Fessenden was on exceptionally cordial terms with the Wrights in later years, offering in 1911 to collaborate with them in the development of a new and more efficient engine for their airplanes. (Nothing came of the offer.) A rare and beautiful engraved Christmas card sent him by the Wrights, apparently in 1919 or 1920, is found among his papers."

While a museum has been erected in honor of the Wright brothers, there are only two physical indications Fessenden ever visited the Outer Banks.

One is a historical sign on N.C. Route 12 in Buxton. It says: "Radio Milestone. From near here in 1902, R. A. Fessenden sent the first musical notes ever relayed by radio waves. Received 18 miles north." The distance given is about three times too short.

The other indication is a concrete slab visible at low tide in Croatan Sound, about 300 yards off the northwest shore of Roanoke Island, near the U.S. Route 64/264 bridge leading toward Raleigh. That slab held the boiler used to power the transmissions.

At one point, a wood tower more than 100 feet high was erected at Buxton, but no evidence of it remains.

Efforts to memorialize Fessenden have been made over the years without success.

But Congress last year appropriated $5.6 million for the National Park Service to expand the Fort Raleigh National Historic Site on Roanoke Island. That money will not be enough to purchase the site of Fessenden's experiments immediately, but the Park Service plans to buy that 73-acre parcel as part of the expansion within the next few years and to memorialize Fessenden in some way. A park ranger has been assigned to learn as much about Fessenden as possible.

One thing seems crystal clear. The slogan for Dare County, which encompasses Kill Devil Hills and Roanoke Island, is no exaggeration: "Land of Beginnings."

The first English attempt at a permanent New World settlement was on Roanoke Island.

Later came the Wright brothers.

And Fessenden.

The Campers at Kitty Hawk

JOHN DOS PASSOS   1903

The Wright brothers' success on the bleak sands near Kill Devil Hill was so improbable that their competitors and detractors soon began to intimate that certain features of the Wright Flyer or ideas behind their advances had been stolen. Eventually cranks and civic boosters from Connecticut to New Zealand advanced claims for earlier flights by favorite sons. John Dos Passos, an innovative and influential novelist of the American Lost Generation and, in the first part of his career, an eloquent leftist, fell into neither category. Although he clearly disapproved of the uses that industrialists and military men found for the airplane, his admiration for the Wrights and their achievement was undiminished. But sometimes even Dos Passos, the Harvard-educated champion of the common man, betrayed class prejudice by mistaking Orville and Wilbur for hobbyists who had discovered the secret of flight while "tinkering" during holidays at the beach—as he does in the following selection from *The Big Money*, the final volume of his *U.S.A.* trilogy. In fact, the Wrights were self-taught scientists and inventors every bit the equal of Franklin or Edison. Only after years of painstaking preparation, systematic experimentation, careful observation, and dauntingly slow progress did they realize their dream of flight.

ON DECEMBER SEVENTEENTH, nineteen hundred and three, Bishop Wright of the United Brethren onetime editor of the Religious Telescope received in his frame house on Hawthorn Street in Dayton, Ohio, a telegram from his boys Wilbur and Orville who'd gotten it into their heads to spend their vacations in a little camp out on the dunes of the North Carolina coast tinkering with a homemade glider they'd knocked together themselves. The telegram read:

SUCCESS FOUR FLIGHTS THURSDAY MORNING ALL AGAINST TWENTY-ONE MILE WIND STARTED FROM LEVEL WITH ENGINEPOWER ALONE AVERAGE SPEED THROUGH AIR THIRTYONE MILES LONGEST FIFTYSEVEN SECONDS INFORM PRESS HOME CHRISTMAS

The figures were a little wrong because the telegraph operator misread Orville's hasty penciled scrawl

but the fact remains

that a couple of young bicycle mechanics from Dayton, Ohio

had designed constructed and flown

for the first time ever a practical airplane.

After running the motor a few minutes to heat it up I released the wire that held the machine to the track and the machine started forward into the wind. Wilbur ran at the side of the machine holding the wing to balance it on the track. Unlike the start on the 14th made in a calm the machine facing a 27 mile wind started very slowly. . . . Wilbur was able to stay with it until it lifted from the track after a forty-foot run. One of the lifesaving men snapped the camera for us taking a picture just as it reached the end of the track and the machine had risen to a height of about two feet. . . . The course of the flight up and down was extremely erratic, partly due to the irregularities of the air, partly to lack of experience in handling this machine. A sudden dart when a little over a hundred and twenty feet from the point at which it rose in the air ended the flight. . . . This flight lasted only 12 seconds but it was nevertheless the first in the history of the world in which a machine carrying a man had raised itself by its own power into the air in full flight, had sailed forward without reduction of speed and had finally landed at a point as high as that from which it started.

A little later in the day the machine was caught in a gust of wind and turned over and smashed, almost killing the coastguardsman who tried to hold it down;

it was too bad

but the Wright brothers were too happy to care

they'd proved that the damn thing flew.

When these points had been definitely established we at once packed our goods and returned home knowing that the age of the flying machine had come at last.

They were home for Christmas in Dayton, Ohio, where they'd been born in the seventies of a family who had been settled west of the Alleghenies since eighteen fourteen, in Dayton, Ohio, where they'd been to grammarschool and highschool and joined their father's church and played baseball and hockey and worked out on the parallel bars and the flying swing and sold newspapers and built themselves a printingpress out of odds and ends from the junkheap and flown kites and tinkered with mechanical contraptions and gone around town as boys doing odd jobs to turn an honest penny.

The folks claimed it was the bishop's bringing home a helicopter, a fiftycent mechanical toy made of two fans worked by elastic bands that was supposed to hover in the air, that had got his two youngest boys hipped on the subject of flight

so that they stayed home instead of marrying the way the other boys did, and puttered all day about the house picking up a living with jobprinting,

bicyclerepair work,

sitting up late nights reading books on aerodynamics.

Still they were sincere churchmembers, their bicycle business was prosperous, a man could rely on their word. They were popular in Dayton.

In those days flyingmachines were the big laugh of all the crackerbarrel philosophers. Langley's and Chanute's unsuccessful experiments had been jeered down with an I-told-you-so that rang from coast to coast. The Wrights' big problem was to find a place secluded enough to carry on their experiments without being the horselaugh of the countryside. Then they had no money to spend;

they were practical mechanics; when they needed anything they built it themselves.

They hit on Kitty Hawk,

on the great dunes and sandy banks that stretch south towards Hatteras seaward of Albemarle Sound,

a vast stretch of seabeach

empty except for a coastguard station, a few fishermen's shacks and the swarms of mosquitoes and the ticks and chiggers in the crabgrass behind the dunes

and overhead the gulls and swooping terns, in the evening fishhawks and cranes flapping across the saltmarshes, occasionally eagles

that the Wright brothers followed soaring with their eyes

as Leonardo watched them centuries before

straining his sharp eyes to apprehend

the laws of flight.

Four miles across the loose sand from the scattering of shacks, the Wright brothers built themselves a camp and a shed for their gliders. It was a long way to pack their groceries, their tools, anything they happened to need; in summer it was hot as blazes, the mosquitoes were hell;

but they were alone there

and they'd figured out that the loose sand was as soft as anything they could find to fall in.

There with a glider made of two planes and a tail in which they lay flat on their bellies and controlled the warp of the planes by shimmying their hips, taking off again and again all day from a big dune named Kill Devil Hill,

they learned to fly.

Once they'd managed to hover for a few seconds

and soar ever so slightly on a rising aircurrent

they decided the time had come

to put a motor in their biplane.

Back in the shop in Dayton, Ohio, they built an airtunnel, which is their first great contribution to the science of flying, and tried out model planes in it.

They couldn't interest any builders of gasoline engines so they had to build their own motor.

It worked; after that Christmas of nineteen three the Wright brothers weren't doing it for fun any more; they gave up their bicycle business, got the use of a big old cowpasture belonging to the local banker for practice flights, spent all the time when they weren't working on their machine in promotion, worrying about patents, infringements, spies, trying to interest government officials, to make sense out of the smooth involved heartbreaking remarks of lawyers.

In two years they had a plane that would cover twentyfour miles at a stretch round and round the cowpasture.

People on the interurban car used to crane their necks out of the windows when they passed along the edge of the field, startled by the clattering pop pop of the old Wright motor and the sight of the white biplane like a pair of ironingboards one on top of the other chugging along a good fifty feet in the air. The cows soon got used to it.

As the flights got longer

the Wright brothers got backers,

engaged in lawsuits,

lay in their beds at night sleepless with the whine of phantom millions, worse than the mosquitoes at Kitty Hawk. . . .

Aeronautics became the sport of the day.

The Wrights don't seem to have been very much impressed by the upholstery and the braid and the gold medals and the parades of plush horses,

they remained practical mechanics
and insisted on doing all their own work themselves,
even to filling the gasolinetank.

In nineteen eleven they were back on the dunes
at Kitty Hawk with a new glider.
Orville stayed up in the air for nine and a half minutes, which remained a long
time the record for motorless flight.
The same year Wilbur died of typhoidfever in Dayton.
In the rush of new names: Farman, Blériot, Curtiss, Ferber, Esnault-Peltrie,
Delagrange;
in the snorting impact of bombs and the whine and rattle of shrapnel and the
sudden stutter of machineguns after the motor's been shut off overhead,
and we flatten into the mud
and make ourselves small cowering in the corners of ruined walls,
the Wright brothers passed out of the headlines
but not even headlines or the bitter smear of newsprint or the choke of smoke-
screen and gas or chatter of brokers on the stockmarket or barking of phantom
millions or oratory of brasshats laying wreaths on new monuments
can blur the memory
of the chilly December day
two shivering bicycle mechanics from Dayton, Ohio,
first felt their homemade contraption
whittled out of hickory sticks,
gummed together with Arnstein's bicycle cement,
stretched with muslin they'd sewn on their sister's sewingmachine in their own
backyard on Hawthorn Street in Dayton, Ohio,
soar into the air
above the dunes and the wide beach at Kitty Hawk.

Foreword to The Lost Colony

PAUL GREEN   1937

Beginning in the 1890s, residents and visitors gathered each year on August 18 at Fort Raleigh on the north end of Roanoke Island, to celebrate Virginia Dare Day, the anniversary of the first English birth in America. In the 1920s local school administrator Mabel Evans started to enliven the proceedings with historical pageants, but as 1937 drew near there were calls for a more sophisticated observance of Virginia Dare's 350th birthday. In 1931 Elizabeth City journalist W. O. Saunders approached Paul Green, a North Carolina native and Pulitzer Prize–winning dramatist, about writing a play on the 1587 English settlement. By early the next year they and others had incorporated the Roanoke Island Historical Association to plan a suitable commemoration. RIHA eventually hired Green to write the play that he and Saunders had discussed. Green had toyed with such a project earlier and had visited Roanoke Island in search of inspiration. When he returned to the topic and to the spot in 1937, he set out to create a peculiarly American dramatic form, blending history, historic setting, prose, poetry, music, song, dance, and pantomime. The result of this experiment in "symphonic drama," The Lost Colony, was an immediate sensation and a milestone in the development of American musical theater. Though intended to last but a single season, the play has been on the boards every summer since, except during World War II.

I

Back in 1921 when I was a student at the University of North Carolina and trying to turn out one-act plays fast enough to equal the measure of Professor Frederick Koch's inspiration, I got to thinking about the story of Sir Walter Raleigh's tragic lost colony as subject matter for a play. So I decided to go down to Roanoke Island on the coast and look around at the original site of the colonization attempt. I set out from Chapel Hill and traveled by bus and train to Beaufort, thence up Pamlico Sound by mailboat, and finally made the latter part of my journey across the open inlet by hiring a fisherman and his little motorboat—in all a distance of some three hundred miles. I still remember that fisherman, a muscular old fellow, sturdy and craggy and coming back to me now in visualization like that old man Ernest Hemingway wrote about recently in his great sea story. He sang a song to me as we went across. I still can remember some of the words—

"Oh, haul away, bully boys,
   Oh, haul away high-o,

We'll wipe away the morning dew
And then go below."

It was night when I arrived at the little town of Manteo. I got a room at a local boarding house, and early the next morning started walking up the sandy road through the forest toward the place known as Fort Raleigh four miles away. I plodded along in the . . . sand, and the sun was coming up in its great holocaust of flame when I got to the little grove of pines and live-oaks on the edge of [the] Sound and stood beside the small squat stone erected in 1896 to Virginia Dare, the first English child born in the new world. I wandered around in the woods. I idly plucked some sassafras twigs and chewed them, and thought upon that band of hardy pioneers who, three hundred and thirty-four years before, had come to this spot to build a fort, a bastion, a beachhead for the extension of the English-speaking empire across the sea. In a holly tree a mocking bird trilled his timeless note.

I thought of the hardships that these people had suffered, of the dark nights, the loneliness, the despair and frustration here, desolate and forgot by Queen Elizabeth in her concern with her Spanish war in England faraway. In my mind I could hear the cries of the sick and hungry little children, see the mothers bending above their rough home-made cribs as their little loved ones twisted and turned in their fever and their fret. And what anguish, what heartache and homesickness! And ever the anxious expectant look toward the eastern sea where never the bright sail of a ship was seen nor the mariner's cheer was heard, to tell that help was nigh. Night after night, day after day, only the murmur of the vast and sheeted waters, only the sad whispering of the dark forest to break upon their uneasy dreams.

Yes, here on the very spot where I stood, all this suffering and pain had happened, all this had been endured.

II

I came away charged with inspiration to write a drama on the lost colony. Back in Chapel Hill I promised "Proff," as we all affectionately called Professor Koch, to have a piece for his playwriting class come the next week. I turned out a one-acter for production in the University Forest Theatre. It told an imaginary story of Virginia Dare and how she grew up and lived in the wilderness among the Indians, falling in love with Chief Manteo's son and marrying him—a forest idyll. But the class didn't think much of it. Proff Koch didn't care for it either, though he smiled and said it had good points. By that time I thought it was pretty rotten. Somewhere along the line my inspiration had petered out. I had come home and started reading too much in the literature of the subject, I guess. One piece that had stuck in my mind was a long poem by a North Carolina author which told the made-up legend of how Virginia Dare, as a beautiful young woman, had been turned into a white doe by the spell of an angry Indian suitor and how she had been mistakenly shot by the arrow of her own true lover, another Indian brave—only returning to her beautiful maidenly self in the throes of death.

I threw the play away, and turned back to writing furiously about the poor whites and the Negroes of my native county in Eastern North Carolina.

III

Ten years later I was teaching philosophy in the University of North Carolina. One day there came a knock on my office door and W. O. Saunders, of Elizabeth City, North Carolina, entered. Saunders was the editor of an active paper in his town, known as the *Independent*. At that time he was famous locally, not for his editorship of a liberal and outspoken paper or as a contributor of articles to *Collier's Magazine*, but for his recent pioneer activity of walking up and down Broadway in New York City in the mid-heat of summer, wearing pajamas and carrying a sign advocating a change to sensible summer clothing for the comfort of the American male.

Saunders explained to me that he had been in Germany some months past and had seen the great Bavarian outdoor religious play at Oberammergau.

"Paul," he said, "we've got to have something like that in North Carolina. And I've got an idea."

Then he went on to say that the story of Sir Walter Raleigh's lost colony, he thought, would make a good drama. "I hear you've already written something about it," he said. I told him I had tried a piece on Virginia Dare, but it hadn't worked out.

"You see," he said, "1937 will soon be here. This will mark the 350th anniversary of the colony and the birth of Virginia Dare also. We ought to have a great exposition—something like the Jamestown Exposition of 1907. We could move a tribe of Indians down to Roanoke Island, let them carry on farming, raise tobacco, set their fishing weirs, just the way they did at the time Sir Walter sent his colony over. We could have every man on the island grow a beard and the people could wear the dress of three centuries ago." He got excited, his eyes shone. "It would be the biggest thing ever to hit North Carolina," he said. "We would get nation-wide, even world-wide publicity for it."

We talked some more and finally agreed to have a meeting down in the little town of Manteo on Roanoke Island. The date was set for three weeks later, and my wife and I drove down there overland, and in the crowded courthouse the project of doing a drama was initiated. The idea of a full-blown exposition seemed by this time to be too ambitious an undertaking. Also we were realizing that the Carolina fishermen wouldn't take to the idea of growing beards and wearing doublet and hose.

W. O. Saunders made a speech that night. I made a talk. But the audience still seemed rather cold and unenthusiastic. Suddenly from the back of the hall a bell-like voice rang out, the voice of United States Senator Josiah William Bailey. He and Lindsay Warren, who was then a Congressman and later became Comptroller General of the United States, were down at nearby Nags Head on a fishing expedition. They had come over to the courthouse meeting and sat in the back unrecognized. Now Senator Bailey got up, strode down the aisle and delivered a speech that soon had everybody eager for activity. He made it quite clear to us that Roanoke Island was the true inspiration for Shakespeare's play, *The Tempest*. And then he quoted several parts of the play in a voice that sent the chills running up and down our backs.

"When Shakespeare wrote 'Come unto these yellow sands,' " he went on, "he had in mind the sands of Roanoke Island. No doubt about it. The tragedy of the lost colony that happened on this island inspired the pen of the immortal Shakespeare to write one of his finest and most imaginative plays. This is a sacred spot here, people. Let us put on a drama, our drama, here at this patriotic shrine where those brave pioneers lived, struggled and died. Yes, let us tell their story to the world."

IV

After this, committees were set up, meetings held, and the Roanoke Island Historical Association was reactivated.

One of the meetings I especially remember. It was in Raleigh, and the governor and a number of legislators were present. The newly-appointed promotion man arrived with a Hollywood-looking secretary on each arm and a big scrolled map drawn up, which he exhibited triumphantly, showing the whole of Roanoke Island's thousands of acres of land cut up in lots all numbered and ready for sale. We had to get rid of him.

And I felt the old feeling of that early summer morning ten years before, coming back to me. A group of North Carolina and Norfolk, Virginia, businessmen agreed to raise the necessary funds for building the amphitheatre and producing the play. I got busy writing it.

This time let me hold true to the stimulation of my subject matter. Let me keep ever before me the sense and image of this group of tragic suffering people—more than a hundred and twenty of them—men, women and children who had fared forth from England on that fatal day in 1587 to brave the turmoil and terror of the vast and raging sea in search of their destiny, these the keepers of a dream. Away with all secondhand sources—let it come prime, let it come raw.

And I would forget the baby Virginia Dare except as one of the items in the whole dramatic symphony. Don't worry because the father's name Ananias must cause a dramatic emphasis different from that of history. These didn't matter. The main thing was the people. For these were the folk of England, the folk of our race—these who now must labor with their hands to wrest from cryptic nature her goods and stores of sustenance, or die, these who had to live with their feet in the earth and their heads bare to the storms, the wind and sleet and the falling fire from heaven. Flood and drought and hunger were their lot, their minds and spirits a prey to the nightmare fear and horror of the dark and impenetrable wilderness around them.

And yet out of this testing, this straining and tension here on these lonely shores, this being hammered on an anvil of God, there must emerge the faith that lies native in them as workers, as believers, as spiritual beings who lift their eyes in awe to the great Presence riding the lightning flashes down the sky, the Power that breathes in earthquakes and the bellowing of the storm, or sweetly sings His pleasure to them in the birds of spring and smiles His joy in the flowers by the road. Yea, out of this play must come a sustaining faith, their faith, a purified statement of aim and intent, of human purpose, or then all was waste and sacrifice made vain.

And so here on these yellow muted sands of Roanoke Island, let my hero, John Borden Everyman, speak out in the play on the night he and his companions are to disappear into the vast unknown out of our sight forever—let him speak the words which are his credo and our credo as self-reliant and valiant men—"Hear that once Sir Walter said, the victory lieth in the struggle, not the city won. To all free men it standeth so, he said. And by the death of our friends and companions and those who lie buried in this ground, let us swear our consecration to the best that is in us. Let the wilderness drive us forth as wanderers across the earth, scatter our broken bones upon these sands, it shall not kill the purpose that brought us here! And down the centuries that wait ahead there'll be some whisper of our name, some mention and devotion to the dream that brought us here."

And let there be music, always music on which the story might ride.

V

Thus I struggled with the drama, trying to make it say something worthy of the lost and vanished people about whom it was written.

Then as the months went by, the economic depression settled on down in its deadening freeze of the nation's sap and vitality. By this time hundreds of pledges had been made, amounting to a total, I was told, of some two hundred thousand dollars. But not one cent was ever collected from these sources. Still, W. O. Saunders and his associate, D. B. Fearing of Manteo, kept working, riding, talking, promoting the idea of the drama, and even going to Washington to confer more than once with Senator Bailey, Congressman Warren and others.

Finally the agencies of the WPA, the C. C. Camp, and the Federal Theatre came into being. Through them and with the cooperation of the North Carolina Historical Association, the Roanoke Island Historical Association, and the Carolina Playmakers our project at last was realized. And with Samuel Seldon as director and Frederick H. Koch as advisory director, the play opened for its first annual summer run on the night of July 4, 1937.

Lifestyles

Life has always been different on the Outer Banks. It had to be, because of the isolation if nothing else. As a result, the people of the Outer Banks have done things in a distinctive fashion. From the creation of perhaps the first European laboratory in North America to the rise and decline of the district school, and the observance of Old Christmas at Rodanthe, here are examples of how Outer Bankers managed to do things their own way.

America's First Science Center

IVOR NOËL HUME   1585

Whole forests of pulpwood have been devoted to poetry, prose, drama, and fiction about the 1587 Lost Colony, whose chief attraction is that it remains a loose end of history. The Ralph Lane colony of 1585–86, about which a great deal less has been written, was by no means an undistinguished warm-up exercise for the later enterprise. It was the first English colony in what is now the United States. It produced the first accurate maps, drawings, and descriptions of the Eastern Seaboard. Its roster included Thomas Harriot, who stood with Francis Bacon and a few others at the pinnacle of late-Tudor science. No wonder, then, that the Lane colony also occasioned the first scientific investigations of natural resources in this part of the world. The recent discovery of the site where some of this work occurred is a matter of scientific as well as historical interest. In the piece below, from *Colonial Williamsburg* magazine, the man who made the discovery offers a heartening account of learning something new from an important site that had seemed played out. Ivor Noël Hume is a former head archaeologist at Colonial Williamsburg and author of *Here Lies Virginia* (1963), *A Guide to Artifacts of Colonial America* (1969), *Martin's Hundred* (1982), and *The Virginia Adventure* (1994).

EVERY ARCHAEOLOGIST dreams that just once in his life he'll find treasure. Mine substituted copper for gold and antimony for silver, and it came not from a sunken galleon or an Egyptian tomb but from Roanoke Island on the Outer Banks of North Carolina. There, in 1585, English and European scientists unpacked the equipment that would help determine the future course of American history. For me, finding the place where they set up their laboratory was to be the most exciting in a lifetime of discoveries.

Rarely, if ever, can one point to a piece of ground and say of it that the decisions reached there hundreds of years ago would impact today on the lives of us all. But a little patch of sandy soil on Roanoke Island is just such a place. Had the Elizabethan scholars working there concluded that Virginia held no economic promise, we might have had no Jamestown settlement in 1607 and no Williamsburg; indeed, no British presence south of New England. Instead, the southern British colonies would almost certainly have been settled by Spaniards—and Virginia might now be a Spanish-speaking, independent country akin to those of Central America.

I first visited Fort Raleigh National Historic Site in the summer of 1957. Part of the Park Service's Cape Hatteras National Seashore, it featured the reconstructed, star-shaped fort whose remains had been known as long ago as 1817, when President Monroe visited the island. A ranger pointed to the grass-covered earthwork and told us "This was the fort built in September 1585 by Ralph Lane, the first governor of Virginia."

"Virginia?" asked a puzzled tourist. "But we're in North Carolina."

The ranger gave no hint that he had heard the question countless times before. The Elizabethan English, he explained, claimed the eastern seacoast from Cape Fear to Maine, and called it all Virginia.

"The fort's not very big," somebody muttered.

"How many people were there?" somebody else wanted to know.

We were told 108, though not all of them lived in the fort. That seemed just as well. Only about 50 feet wide within its earth rampart, a couple of dozen would have been plenty.

My archaeologist wife Audrey knew much more than I did about Ralph Lane's "new Fort in Virginia" and the story of Queen Elizabeth's "Lost Colony." She had read about it as a child and discovered that she shared the same birthday as Virginia Dare, the first English girl born in America. So thrilled by the mystery of the 1587 colonists' disappearance was Audrey that she begged her parents to change her name to Virginia. Little did she know that she would one day be standing where it had all happened or that, later still, she would play a major role in reassessing what was known about the site.

When we first saw it, the earthwork was only seven years old. It had been reconstructed in 1950 following excavations directed by the father of historical archaeology in America, Jean C. "Pinky" Harrington. But he wasn't the first to dig there. In 1849 a visitor reported the finding of "glass globes containing quicksilver, and hermetically sealed." What became of them, nobody knows. But someone had unwittingly discovered the first relics of the metallurgical laboratory that we were to identify more than a century later. Union soldiers, camped nearby after the February 1862 Battle of Roanoke Island, had dug more holes in search of treasure—until ordered away by their commanding officer. Thirty-four years later still, Talcott Williams, an amateur archaeologist from Philadelphia, cut several trenches, some as much as nine feet deep, and although he found the site to be "singularly barren of debris" he pronounced it to be the right place.

That was enough to justify the Roanoke Colony Memorial Association, which had already bought the site, to erect a marker recording the birth of Virginia Dare and recalling that

THESE COLONISTS WERE THE FIRST SETTLERS OF THE ENGLISH RACE IN AMERICA. THEY RETURNED TO ENGLAND IN JULY, 1586, WITH SIR FRANCIS DRAKE.

The Association also erected a wooden fence to outline the fort—which was good thinking. Without it, nobody would have known where it had been, for nothing remained but the barely visible depression of its ditch.

The colonists who went back with Drake had been on the island little more than nine months, during which time they had turned the resident and neighboring Indians from "gentle, loving, and faithfull" friends into implacable enemies. With villages burned and their king beheaded, the Algonkian Indians of Roanoke Island were no longer considered "voide of all guile and treason." Instead, the English now saw them as heathen and dangerous savages, a perception that would color Europeans' relations with Native Americans throughout the colonial centuries. That, coupled with the failure of promised supply ships to arrive from England, prompted Governor Lane to hitch a ride home.

England-bound after successfully attacking Spanish bases in the Caribbean, Drake had anchored off the North Carolina Outer Banks to deliver seized hardware and artillery, along with scores of Central American Indians and more than 200 black slaves he had freed from the Spaniards and who, he thought, would be helpful to the Roanoke colonists. Instead, neither window frames and cannon from St. Augustine nor a massive free labor force were what the colonists had in mind. Passage home was all they wanted.

Even as Lane and Drake negotiated, a hurricane of prodigious force raked the coast and scattered the fleet. Thunder shook the heavens, lightning stabbed the waves, hailstones the size of eggs rained down, and from time to time waterspouts linked sky and sea in murderous embrace. Although the worst had passed over by the time the hundred or so settlers loaded themselves and their baggage into the open boats, the weather was still "so boisterous" and the boats so often driven aground that sailors rowing them out through the Outer Banks shoals threw much of the baggage overboard to lighten the load.

The losses caused much lamentation at the time and would become an enigma to baffle future historians and archaeologists. How much did the fleeing colonists take away with them, and how much never reached the ships? To put it another way: How much was left behind for us to find?

A few weeks later the supply fleet did arrive. Its admiral, Sir Richard Grenville, found the place deserted, and left behind a tiny, 15-man garrison to hold the island for England....

Attacked by the Indians, with their storehouse in flames and their officer dead, they fought their way to their boat . . . never to be heard from again. So ended the second English attempt to sustain a colony on Roanoke Island.

The third group arrived in August 1587, under the governorship of artist John White, whose daughter was married to fellow colonist Ananias Dare—the parents of my wife's would-be namesake—Virginia. Because the fate of White's people is unknown and because, for the first time, the settlement was home to women and children, the Lost Colony is the one that everyone remembers. But theirs, as the Park Service ranger told us, was not the fort that we were looking at. It had been built by their predecessors in 1585. John White's colonists lived inside a large stockade that he described as built from "great trees, with cortynes [walls] and flankers very Fort-like. . . ."

It was those words that sent me back to Roanoke Island in 1989. I was then doing research on Virginia's fort at Jamestown, which in 1610 had been described in very similar terms. I had also learned that the only description of Lane's earlier defenses called them a "wooden fort of little strength," a structure that John White found to have been "taken downe" when he arrived in 1587. So where did the re-constructed earthwork fit into the sequence?

A solution had seemed in sight in 1965 when Pinky Harrington had returned to the site to investigate a "brick path" found by a Park Service maintenance crew lay-ing a water pipe. The path turned out to be a cluster of bricks dumped into one of three pits, all of them inside a square wooden structure whose supports Harring-ton thought had been provided by conveniently located trees. Built barely 20 feet from the earthwork, Harrington called it "an outwork to Fort Raleigh" but was careful not to be more specific.

Twelve years later, after Colonial Williamsburg's archaeological team found the 1620 fort at Wolstenholme Towne, Park Service historian Phillip Evans noticed that the postholes of its watchtower almost exactly paralleled Harrington's out-work. Was it possible, Evans asked, that he had found a corner of Ralph Lane's wooden fort?

Excavations to try to find out were resumed in 1983, but although the digging yielded more broken pottery reportedly of the right period, it did nothing to solve the outwork enigma.

If that really was a corner of Lane's wooden fort or even, as Harrington had sug-gested, an outwork to the close-by earthwork, in military terms one would have been in the way of the other. At least that was how I read it. And what about the potsherds?

The Park Service report listed fragments of "Salt-Glazed stoneware," Spanish majolica, and two sherds from a shallow dish or pan "similar to a type of stone-ware known as basaltware." This last was worrying because black basalt wares date from the 18th and not the 16th century. "Maybe," I told Audrey, "if we were to go down to the park and take a look at this stuff, we might spot something that our predecessors have missed."

Never one to refuse a trip to the beach or the prospect of a chartered fishing trip, Audrey agreed. Although our request had meant bringing the artifacts back from the Park Service's regional center at Tallahassee, Superintendent Thomas Hartman agreed.

It turned out that the "Salt-Glazed stoneware" wasn't salt-glazed stoneware. The sherds were fragments of rough-surfaced metallurgical crucibles. The Spanish majolica proved to be from English or Netherlandish ointment pots used by apothecaries, and the "basaltware" dish pieces came from a globular stoneware bottle made in Normandy in the 16th century. This last was identical to a partially complete example that Harrington had found in his 1965 outwork dig.

As she put the last piece back in its bag, Audrey looked at me and asked, "Are you thinking what I'm thinking?"

"We should take another look at Harrington's finds?"

"I believe so," she replied.

And so we did. The range of his European pottery was virtually identical to the 1983 discoveries—crucibles, ointment pots, plus sherds from more than one Normandy flask of a shape used by distillers. And then there were the bricks. Many of the bats were heavily burned at one end, and several had been ground down so that one side was deeply concave. Harrington had speculated that the shaping had resulted from using the soft, sandy bricks for sharpening tools and weapons.

"I wouldn't mind betting," I said, "that they are from the round openings in the furnace."

The pieces of the puzzle were beginning to fit together. The 1585 settlers sent out by Sir Walter Ralegh had included a scientific team headed by Thomas Hariot— astronomer, mathematician, oceanographer, surveyor—in short one of the finest minds of the Elizabethan Age. He was there to assess the commercial potential of the New World, and when he returned with Drake in 1586, he would begin work on the report that still stands at the cornerstone of American natural history. Titled *A briefe and true report of the new found land of Virginia* and illustrated with engravings from drawings by John White, it provided Europeans with their first detailed look at the Native Americans of the new continent's southeast coast.

With Hariot went a crew of miners to search for marketable metals led by "minerall man" Joachim Gans, a Jewish metallurgist from Prague who had gone to England in 1581 to help improve its outmoded copper smelting industry. This was a blue-ribbon team, and like most scientific research efforts today, quality of mind brushed aside barriers of race, religion, or national origin—except for Jesuits and Spaniards who, to the English, were the devil's kin.

That copper was likely to be Virginia's principal mineral had been established in 1584 after Ralegh had sent out two exploratory ships. Their returning captains had reported that the senior Indians wore "red pieces of copper on their heads," and that the king's brother wore "a broade plate of golde, or copper, for being unpolished we knew not what metall it should be." Believing that where there was copper there might well be silver and even gold, Ralegh and his backers made sure that the expedition's scientific component would be the very best.

As Audrey and I examined the bricks and pottery fragments, we knew that we were seeing something amazing. These were not trash from Lane's or the Lost Colony's village; they were the relics of America's first scientific evaluation.

The next day, at the end of the promised but only marginally successful fishing trip, I asked the boat's mate his name.

"I'm Billy Coppersmith," he said.

Never before having heard of anyone named Coppersmith, I was convinced that here was an omen. "Somehow," I told Audrey, "we've got to find the money and the people to dig again at Fort Raleigh."

Pinky Harrington's impeccable report on his earlier excavations had recorded finding two lumps of smelted copper, one in the silt of the fort's ditch and the other under the remains of its rampart. He correctly deduced that one piece had been deposited before Ralph Lane's fort was built and the other after it was abandoned. The sequence had to be right. But what about the timing? We know from a letter that Lane wrote on September 3, 1585, that his "New Fort in Virginia" was in existence before Gans and his helpers had any copper to process. That a lump of it lay on the ground before the earthen rampart was piled on top of it had to mean that the earthwork was of later date. But if so, how much later?

Although more digging might prove beyond doubt that the reconstructed earthwork was not Lane's fort, Superintendent Hartman agreed to allow new excavations to be launched by the Virginia Company Foundation and under my direction. Preliminary testing in the spring of 1991 showed what Harrington already well knew: The site had been severely mutilated by a wide variety of disturbances that began when the Civil War soldiers dug their holes. Not only that, when the modern intrusions had been removed, what remained were two extremely friable layers of sandy loam and clay whose testimony could be destroyed by a single misdirected shovel. This was to be surgical work, and only the most experienced surgeons would be good enough to do it.

Rather than following the usual practice of assembling a team of anthropology students and a couple of trained supervisors, I called on the services of most of the good excavators who had worked with me over the years in Williamsburg, people who were now professors and directors elsewhere and used to watching others do the dirty work. They would be the people down on their knees with the trowels and the dustpans. It was to be a remarkable team, and on one day when Pinky Harrington and his archaeologist wife Virginia joined us, we realized that we had four generations of America's foremost historical archaeologists assembled on the site.

But as the spoil heaps grew higher than the earthwork's rampart, I found it increasingly hard to sustain the team's morale. Every area we opened had been disturbed by someone. Trenches for water and electric lines crisscrossed the site. Harrington's excavation trenches were cut by the 1983 digging; the remains of a 1936 road taken up in 1950, and the bed for a still existing walkway, all combined to thwart us. And the weather was getting worse.

A nor'easter had pounded the Outer Banks on the dig's first days, forcing the crew to flee in the dark from their beach house as water rose in their living room. Now, as the last digging day dawned, another storm was approaching—and still we had found nothing we could be sure hadn't been disturbed. And then just before noon, we did.

Because it lay on one of his 1965 survey lines, Harrington had left a narrow strip of ground undisturbed, and by some miracle the 1983 excavators had stopped two inches above it. Pressed into the sandy subsoil were more than a hundred artifacts, broken crucibles, pieces of Normandy flasks, a badly burned Indian bowl that looked as though it had been used in distilling, and pieces of chemical glassware—the oldest English glass yet found in the New World.

There were other things too, tiny chips of European flint, a scattering of iron scale perhaps used, as contemporary accounts said, in the making of a high refractory mortar to secure the elements in distilling apparatus. And there were fragments from Indian pipes—doubtless relics of the first English smokers' experience of what they would describe as "drinking" tobacco.

Virginia Company president William Kelso, who found the pipe fragments, recalled that tobacco smoking in England is believed to have started with the 1585 expedition. "Maybe these are the prototypes for all the millions of clay pipes that came after," Bill suggested. And he may well have been right.

There was more to come: a broad scattering of charcoal and one tiny fragment of coal indicative of two different kinds of fuel used in Joachim Gans's mineral assaying furnace, and there were seeds and nuts from longleaf pine and shagbark hickory that may have been among the plants being distilled by Hariot to test their pharmaceutical and commercial properties. We had found the working floor of what amounted to an interdisciplinary analytical laboratory.

Although Martin Frobisher's earlier expeditions, first in search of the Northwest Passage to the Orient and then for Baffin Island's elusive gold, had included their own German "mineral man," I felt justified in calling what we were finding colonial America's first science center.

But before we could complete the excavation, the threatened nor'easter arrived. The rain came down and so did the overnight tents put up to protect the hallowed ground. The next morning we finished clearing the exposed layer and called for volunteers to return to finish the work in 1992. Two weeks of disappointment were instantly forgotten.

The second season expanded our investigation into the reconstructed fort, where we found more of the same: more crucible fragments, more Normandy flasks, and a lead seal bearing its owner's initials—the first letters found on the site since 1590 when John White returned in a vain search for his lost colonists and saw the word CROATOAN carved on a post of their abandoned palisade.

Although the seal is of a type used by clothiers and merchants and so may not bear the initials of one of the first English American colonists, we fervently hoped that it did. Heavily encrusted with sand, the first letter was obscured, but the second appeared to be an L. Immediately we thought of expedition leader Ralph Lane. But when Colonial Williamsburg conservator Carey Howlett was able to remove some of the sand, it was clear that the first initial had to be either a J or more probably an H—but not an R. Alas, although there are two J. L. candidates, John Linsey in 1585 and James Lasie in 1587, no H. L. is listed on the rosters of either expedition.

Now the research shifts from the earth to a modern laboratory in Albany, New York, where metallurgical scholars Drs. Robert Ehrenreich and Peter Glumac will try to interpret what we have found. Did a lump of smelted copper from the floor come from an American or a European mine? Is a bar of antimony the product of trade with the Indians, or did Joachim Gans bring it with him as a flux to separate silver from copper?

And what mineral traces lie hidden in the dross-coated crucible sherds?

No matter what the answers may be, it is clear that Sir Walter Ralegh's scientists reached Roanoke Island with state of the art equipment and put it to use in a roughly built lab that was anything but ideal.

And what of the reconstructed fort?

Because the earthwork's entrance faces west, conventional archaeological wisdom has dictated that the 1585–1587 village must lie beyond it—an assumption bolstered by finding Elizabethan artifacts extending in that direction. . . . If the fort had nothing to do with Lane's settlement . . . then one is free to look for the village in another direction.

"Yes, but where do we start?" Bill Kelso asked.

"Not we," I replied. Audrey had been adamant that after 43 years I had directed my last excavation. "It's your turn now," I told Bill. "But if I were you, I'd begin over there."

The Contraband Colony

HORACE JAMES 1864

Soon after Roanoke Island fell to the Burnside Expedition and became U.S. territory once more, refugees from all over northeastern North Carolina began to congregate there. Some were brought in by Union soldiers. Others made their own way. A few were free blacks, but most were liberated or runaway slaves, still legally the property of their masters and therefore contraband of war, like horses or boats. As the population of the island grew, conditions worsened. In the spring of 1863, not long after the Emancipation Proclamation had rendered the island even more attractive by making it free soil, Major General J. G. Foster put the Reverend Horace James in charge of all the blacks in the parts of North Carolina under Union control. James quickly set about building a proper settlement for the refugees on Roanoke Island, one of the few places in eastern North Carolina safe from Confederate guerrilla raids. Affected by James's sense of urgency, his operatives cut acres of timber to provide material for the refugees' dwellings and dismantled a number of unoccupied buildings. As the black men of fighting age volunteered for military service, James arranged for their dependents to receive a rudimentary education and employment in various types of work. The colony reached a peak population of nearly 3,100 by the end of the war, but despite its size and promise it was broken up by 1867.

WITHIN A MONTH after assuming the Superintendency of the Blacks in North Carolina, I was ordered by Major General J. G. Foster, then commanding the Department, to establish a colony of negroes upon Roanoke Island. The good or ill success of this experiment ought to be credited as well to the mind which originated the enterprises as to those who were entrusted with its execution. It was General Foster's purpose to settle colored people on the unoccupied lands, and give them agricultural implements and mechanical tools to begin with and to train and educate them for a free and independent community. It was also a part of his plan to arm and drill them for self defence. This was in May, 1863. The bill to enlist colored soldiers did not pass Congress until the 16th of July following. . . .

Colored soldiers were first recruited here by Brig. Gen. E. A. Wild, on the 19th day of June, 1863. They freely and enthusiastically volunteered, to the number of nearly one hundred. The writer recollects spending one whole night with General Wild, in adjusting, on Quartermaster's papers, the accounts of these soldiers against the Government for previous labor, which accounts have not been settled to the present day.

This was the first company of colored troops raised in North Carolina, and so far as I know, the first in the country. Since that time a recruiting officer has resided at the island, and a large number from this locality have joined the army.

This removal of the vigorous young men, who would have worked upon the soil, and fished in the Sounds for the support of the colony, necessarily changed the character of the enterprise, converting it into an asylum for the wives and children of soldiers, and also for the aged and infirm, where the children might be educated, and all, both young and old, be trained for freedom and its responsibilities, after the war.

For such an asylum our forces held no other suitable or safe place in the State. Not a square mile of territory (excepting Hatteras Banks,) lying outside of the interior fortifications of New Berne, Beaufort, and Morehead, but has been repeatedly overrun by rebels and guerrillas during the past year. Even Roanoke Island was seriously threatened for a few days, when the Ram Albemarle seemed about to take possession of the Sounds.

I went North in June, 1863, under orders from Gen. Foster, "to procure materials and implements with which to furnish the projected colony with an outfit," and in a few weeks raised in New England and New York between eight and nine thousand dollars. It was most cheerfully given, and the donations were accompanied with many expressions of good-will towards the works and of hearty interest in the colored people. Especially did the Freedmen's Associations at Boston and New York render efficient aid. . . .

I returned from the North in July, 1863, accompanied by female teachers, and furnished with large supplies, to find that Gen. Wild had been ordered, with his negro troops, to Charleston S.C. He left New Berne on the 30th of July, with his brigade of 2,154 men—among them the flower of Roanoke Island—bearing the beautiful banner of the Republic which had been presented by the colored ladies of New Berne to the First North Carolina Regiment, Col. James C. Beecher.

Gen. Wild being no longer able to act in North Carolina, Maj. Gen. J. J. Peck, at the suggestion of Gen. Foster, issued the following order, devolving upon me the duty of superintending the organization of Roanoke Island, and conferring more ample powers.

General Orders No. 12
Headquarters Army and District of North Carolina
New Berne, N.C., Sept. 10, 1863.

In accordance with the views of the Major General commanding the Department of Virginia and North Carolina, Chaplain Horace James, Superintendent of Blacks for the District of North Carolina, will assume charge of the colonization of Roanoke Island with negroes.

The powers conferred upon Brig. Gen. Wild, by General orders No. 103, Headquarters Department of North Carolina, 18th Army Corps, are hereby transferred to Chaplain James. He will take possession of all unoccupied lands upon the island, and lay them out, and assign them, according to his own discretion, to the families of colored soldiers to invalids and other Blacks, in the employ of the Government, giving them full possession of the same, until annulled by the Government or by due process of United States law. The authority of Chaplain James will be respected in all matters relating to the well-fare of the colony. . . .

The work was now prosecuted with vigor, though with little outside aid for some time. With compass, chart, and chain, and a gang of choppers, the old groves of pine, gum, holly, and cypress were penetrated, crossed and recrossed and the upper, or northern, end of the island was laid out in acre lots, and at once assigned to families. Nothing could exceed the enthusiasm of these simple people, when they found themselves in possession of a spot they could call their own.

To be absolute owners of the soil, to be allowed to build upon their own lands cabins, however humble, in which they should enjoy the sacred privileges of a HOME, was more than they had ever dared to pray for. It was affecting to hear the old men and women declare how fervently they blessed the Lord, that their eyes were permitted to see this unexpected sight. The woods now began to ring with blows from the woodman's axe, and to gleam at night with the fires which consumed the refuse vegetation, swept off in clearing the forests.

It was never intended to give these people FARMS at Roanoke, but only a homestead, and a garden spot for each family. There were sufficient reasons for this, in that the island is not large enough to divide into farms for any considerable number of people. The land is not rich enough for profitable farming, though it will produce vegetables, grapes, and other fruits in abundance and variety. And again, invalids, aged people, and soldiers' wives and children could not be expected to improve more than a single acre. This was the plan of the settlement. Broad, straight avenues were laid out, 1,200 feet apart, up and down the island, nearly parallel with its shores and parallel with one another, which were named "Roanoke Avenue," "Lincoln Avenue," "Burnside Avenue," &c. At right angles with these were streets, somewhat narrower than the avenues, and 400 feet apart, numbered "First Street," "Second Street," &c., &c., in one direction from a certain point, and "A Street," "B Street," &c., in the other direction.

This arrangement divided the land into parallelograms or sections, containing each twelve one acre lots, square in form, every one having a street frontage. Along these the houses were disposed, being placed in lines and all at the same distance from the street. The lots were neatly enclosed, and speedily improved by the freedmen, soon making "the wilderness and the solitary place glad" at their coming. Wives and children with alacrity united with the men in performing the work of the carpenter, the mason, and the gardener. So zealous were they in this work, as to spend, in many cases, much of the night in prosecuting it, giving no sleep to their eyes until they could close them sweetly, under their own dear roof-tree.

A good supply of lumber being indispensable when one would build a town, I purchased at the North a valuable steam-engine and saw-mill, thus using the larger portion of the funds which had been secured in aid of the freedmen. But as the mill could not be made immediately available, logs and boards split by hand were used at first, and chimneys of the Southern style were constructed of sticks and clay. A few sawed boards for floor, door, and window, were sometimes obtained in a boat expedition across the Sound, to Nagg's Head, Oregon Inlet, or Croatan, and thus their mansions were completed. A proud day was it for Mingo, or Luck, or Cudjoe, when he could survey his home as a thing accomplished, and sit at night by its blazing firelight and see the dark shadows of his wife and children dance upon the cabin wall. And this, too, in a Slave State! his old master living, perhaps, at the south end of the island! Listen to his song:

"De yar ob Juberlo am come!"

Major Gen. B. F. Butler, on succeeding to the command of the Department, issued that important order No. 46, organizing the Department of Negro Affairs, confirming the doings of his predecessor, and providing with a wonderful prescience, for all the exigencies likely to occur in the enrollment, employment, support and care of the colored people. Under this regime, the work at Roanoke prospered more and more.

At one time, during the winter of 1863–4, there was a degree of suffering on the island from insufficient shelter. This was when a thousand or fifteen hundred persons at one time were sent there by Gen. Wild, not returned from the South, the result of a raid through the northern counties of the State. But the new comers were soon domiciliated, as comfortably as their predecessors had been before.

The number of colored people now on the island, as ascertained by the recent census, is three thousand and ninety-one (3,091). Of these, 1,295 are males, and 1,796 females; 1,297 are children under fourteen years of age, of whom 710 are girls, and 587 boys; 1,794 are fourteen years of age or upwards, of whom 708 are males, and 1,086 are females; of these 708 males, only 217 are between the ages of 18 and 45, the proper military age, and the larger portion of these, even, are exempts on account of physical disability, showing that 491, or seventy per cent of the adult males, are either in the immature period of youth, or in the decline of life.

These statistics indicate, with sufficient clearness, what may be expected of these people, and what is, at present, their industrial force.

If remunerative employment could be given to the women and older children it would be a blessing to them. Household cares do not sit heavily upon people who live in almost primitive simplicity.

Some kind of domestic manufacturing, supplied to them as a regular business, would not only train them to habits of industry, but raise them above the level of mere field hands. To substitute an occupation which requires skill, and taxes ingenuity, for one which is coarse and plodding is to confer a lasting benefit. In this view spinning and weaving have been encouraged. Some of the better mechanics on the island have manufactured spinning wheels for sale, doing it without the use of a lathe, and making a very good article. Many of the women can card, spin, and weave. They might succeed in willow work, if the material could be easily procured. I have had a quantity of osier willow slips planted on Roanoke, hoping to introduce, by and by, this species of industrial labor. The Friends in Philadelphia, among their many benefactions to the negroes in this District, have sent out some complete sets of shoemakers' tools, the use of which is understood by several of the freedmen on the island. The same is true of coopers' tools, and to a much larger extent; for the turpentine business, the leading pecuniary interest of North Carolina, has made them familiar with the making and mending of barrels. It is common to find colored men acquainted with splitting and shaving shingles, and not a few are constantly engaged in this business, selling them at from $3.00 to $7.00 per thousand. . . .

Like all people who live near navigable waters, the negroes at Roanoke are fond of boats, and know how to manage them. Some few of them are respectable boat builders. About one hundred of the most active men on the island are employed in Government works by the Quartermaster and Commissary of the Post. Some two hundred more have been kept at work a large portion of the year upon the fortifications of the island. More than one hundred were sent, in September last, to Bermuda Hundred, to labor upon "Dutch Gap Canal" and elsewhere.

These occupations, with the toil expended upon their own premises, have kept the men generally employed, and given to the colony an aspect of industry, The few, in every community, who are incorrigibly lazy, and who deliberately intend to eat their bread in the sweat of another's face, undoubtedly have their representatives here. Considering the antecedents of these people, who can wonder at it?

Roanoke Island is favorably located for carrying on fisheries, especially of herring, mullet, blue-fish, and shad. These have heretofore furnished one of the principal means of subsistence to the inhabitants. Preparations were made to pursue this business for the advantage of the colony; but the shad season in 1864 was much less productive than usual, the nets being broken and destroyed by ice and storms in the early spring.

Mr. Holland Streeter was entrusted with the charge of this business, and has pursued it, with a small gang of fishermen, through the year. Up to Jan. 1st, 1865, the income of the fisheries, as reported by Mr. Streeter, was $1,404.27. It is expected to be much larger during the approaching season, if the elements prove propitious.

The mill before alluded to was substantially erected, near the military Headquarters of the island, during the spring and early summer, and has now been for several months in successful operation. The engine is of seventy horse-power, carrying several circular saws, a turning lathe, and a grist mill. Its capacity to produce the different styles of lumber, and to convert grain into the form so widely used by the negroes, and indeed by all the Southern people for food, makes it a positive addition to the wealth and resources of the island, and as valuable to the whites as to the blacks. . . .

A pioneer teacher from the North landed on the island, Oct. 16th, 1863, and for more than three months labored alone and unattended, living in one log cabin, and teaching in another, with most commendable zeal and self-denial.

This was Miss Elizabeth James, a lady sent out by the American Missionary Association. On the 25th of January, 1864, Miss Ella Roper arrived, who was followed, on the 20th of February, by Mr. S. S. Nickerson, and a little later, by Miss Mary Burnap, transferred from a school in New Berne.

After the fall of Plymouth, and the flight of our teachers from that locality, Mrs. Sarah P. Freeman, and her daughter, Miss Kate Freeman, took up their abode upon the island. Mrs. Freeman and Miss James remained through the summer vacation, and did great good in ministering, as judicious matrons, to the various wants of the islanders. Since the schools were reopened, the corps of teachers has been enlarged by the addition of Miss Esther Williams and Mrs. Nickerson to the number. The wants of the island are not yet fully supplied. Besides the 1,297 children under fourteen years of age, many of the adults are eager to be taught to read and write, and will not be denied. Add to this the distribution of donated clothing, visitation of the sick, writing letters for the women to their husbands or sons in the army, and their own domestic cares, and one may readily decide whether from ten to twenty dollars per month, would tempt teachers to do this works in banishment and obloquy, if their minds were not glowing with enthusiasm and their hearts penetrated with benevolent love. The colony would have been more promptly supplied with schools but for the want of suitable school rooms and quarters for teachers. The only abandoned house on the island was fitted up for a teacher's home, and will accommodate five or six. Its former occupant is in the rebel army. Since the mill began to produce lumber, schoolhouses and teachers' quarters have been, or are being, erected, sufficient for all our purposes.

An Industrial School and an Orphan Asylum have been projected, and will be built, it is hoped, during the present winter.

An attempt was made, early in the year, to give the colonists an idea of governing themselves. A "council" of fifteen leading individuals was appointed, and instructed to meet and consult for the common welfare, and be a medium through which the rules and orders of the Superintendent of Negro Affairs and of the military authorities might be communicated and enforced. This was intended to be the germ of a civil government. But the plan proved unsuccessful in the main. The "councilors" were too ignorant to keep records, or make and receive written communications, were jealous of one another, and too little raised in culture above the common people to command their respect, at least while the island is under military rule. To fit these people for republican self-government, education is the prime necessity. The sword to set them free, letters to make them citizens.

The whites, who lived to the number of about four hundred on Roanoke Island previous to this rebellion, did not, for the most part, abandon their homes. They hastened, after the capture of the island, to take the oath of allegiance, which some of them have faithfully kept in its spirit, others only in "the letter which killeth." The truly loyal among them have appreciated the necessity which compelled the Government to take possession of their uncultivated lands for a negro settlement, and have accepted the fact with patriotic submission. But the other class, whose loyalty is so ill-disguised as to reveal the "copper," are loud in their complaints of the "nigger" and the "abolitioners." They would be glad to drive the colored people and their friends from the island. And this too, when, by their own confession, their estates are worth more by four or five hundred per cent than they were before the war, and their island home has been lifted from an ignoble obscurity into honorable prominence and commercial importance. The average value of the wood and waste lands, on which the colony has been settled, was only two dollars ($2.00) an acre before the war. The "nigger" will yet be the making of these poor people.

The question is sometimes asked, whether the Freedmen's colony on Roanoke Island has proved a success? The answer may be gleaned in part from the statements already made. If by success is meant complete self-support, the question must be answered in the negative. Its insular and isolated position far removed from any centre of population, the necessity of clearing the lots assigned, which were all wild land, the smallness of the garrison, furnishing but little employment to the people as laundresses, cooks, and servants, the partial failure of the shad fisheries, and above all, the transfer into the army of most of the laboring men, have made it necessary to feed the larger portion of the colonists at the expense of the Government.

But this is done in obedience to military orders in the case of all wives and children of negro troops, and is to be considered a part of their compensation.

In every other aspect except that of "rations," the colony has met and exceeded expectations.

It has proved a safe and undisturbed retreat for the families of soldiers, who were nobly defending our flag at Petersburg, Charleston, and Wilmington.

It has instructed many hundreds of children and adults to read and spell, and to value knowledge as the means of elevating them and their race, and assuring to them the blessings of freedom forever.

It has made three or four thousand human beings useless as "chattels," by breathing into them new hopes and aspirations, and fitting them to go forth from this Patmos, where they have been inspired with the spirit of liberty, and teach the same divine apocalypse to their brethren, now in "Confederate" bonds.

It has helped to develop the resources of a somewhat remarkable island. Here landed, in 1585 and 1587, two colonies of Englishmen, sent out by Sir Walter Raleigh, which became utterly extinct in the short period of two years, leaving only some rude fortifications now overgrown with trees, by which to recognize this first attempt to settle America from our fatherland. The Freedmen's colony has done better than Sir Walter's. Within a period of about twelve months, the settlers have built five hundred and ninety-one (591) houses, which, with the improvements made upon their lots, are estimated to be worth $75.00 a piece. One of them was recently sold for $150.00. Adopting the lower figure, here is a money value of forty-four thousand three hundred and twenty-five dollars . . . a sum large enough to have purchased the whole island three years ago, with all the improvements of two hundred years, under the rule and culture of its white inhabitants.

It has multiplied the value of real estate thirty-seven times in a single year, at least in the estimation of the negroes who occupy it, and has led the native whites to ask almost fabulous prices for the lands which they still retain.

It has furnished important manufacturing facilities to the island and its vicinity, by introducing valuable steam-power, and opening stores for trade, which will survive the war, and become elements of prosperity and sources of wealth.

The colored population of the island would have been much less dependent upon the Government, if the Government had more fully met its engagements with them. Immediately upon the occupancy of Roanoke Island by the Union troops, the negroes began to be employed by the Quartermasters, the Surgeons, the Engineers, and other Government officers, upon verbal promises to pay, at rates varying from $8.00 to $25.00 per month. In the frequent changes of command which came over the island, their accounts were transferred from officer to officer, and usually in a very imperfect form. Oftentimes they were never rendered at all, but the laborer was deliberately swindled out of his earnings by some officer leaving the service, who thought this a brave transaction, and "good enough for the nigger" and his friends. At the commencement of Gen. Butler's administration in North Carolina, these people were led to believe that their just dues would be paid them. The several Superintendents of Negro Affairs, were made special commissioners to audit carefully these accounts, and present them at Headquarters for payment. Accordingly a roll of labor was made up for Roanoke Island, with care and painstaking, making use of all the scattered materials at command, and comparing them, when possible, with the testimony of the parties. This Report Roll embraced unsettled accounts amounting to EIGHTEEN THOUSAND FIVE HUNDRED AND SEVENTY DOLLARS AND SEVEN CENTS. This sum of money in circulation on Roanoke Island would make greenbacks tolerably plenty over its limited area of twelve miles by three or four. The most unsatisfactory manner in which these accounts were kept by the officers under whom the work was done, which was practically encouraged by the vacillating policy of the government toward the negroes at that time, is probably the reason for their nonpayment. Fearing that it never will be paid, I have exhorted the freedmen to consider this loss as one of their sacrifices for freedom; as something that they should willingly bear for the country's good; and which is in part made up to them by the fostering care of the government over their families and more than compensated by their assured freedom in all time to come.

Roanoke Island is the key of six charming estuaries, whose ready navigation by small vessels and light draft steamboats, must needs make them hereafter the seat of a profitable commerce, in cotton, corn, turpentine, rosin, tar, timber, fish, oysters, wood, reeds, cranberries, and grapes. The Roanoke fisheries, alone would yield fortunes every year if pursued in a business-like manner. The scuppernong grape, which is a native of North Carolina, if planted in vineyards and cultivated scientifically, might be made to produce on Roanoke alone, an income of $100,000 annually. It grows here spontaneously, and without enrichment of the soil, and yields, perhaps, the most delicious white wine that ever tempted the palate. I have corresponded with parties at the North, who are ready to commence its culture here as soon as the way is open.

Some persons have predicted that the government would fail to confirm to the Freedman the rights and privileges they enjoy in these homesteads on Roanoke

Island. I cannot believe it. These people are wards of the government. It is an element of our glory as a nation, that we can crush out a slave-holding rebellion with one hand, and sustain a liberated people with the other. The person, be he white or black, who has taken an acre of piney woods, worth two dollars in the market, and increased its value thirty or forty fold by his own labor in a single year, certainly deserves well of his country, and should be permitted to enjoy, while he lives, the fruits of his industry. When a "Bureau of Freedmen's Affairs" is created by Congress, it may well look to this matter.

Sir Walter Raleigh's El Dorado, where gay cavaliers hoped to discover mines of gold, but only found starvation and an early grave, may yet fulfill, under the magic touch of freedom, the expectations of its early settlers. Its evergreen woods, its picturesqué dales, its wave-kissed shores may yet, under the skillful appliances of labor, and the stimulus of republican institutions, be the abode of a prosperous and virtuous people, of varying blood, but of one destiny, differing, it may be, in social positions but equal before the law, a happy commonwealth, in which Ephraim shall not envy Judah, and Judah shall no longer vex Ephraim.

The Eye of the Tempest

JOEL G. HANCOCK   1906

Like most of the Outer Banks, Harkers Island was long spared many dubious benefits of mainland life, such as denominational squabbling. Even after the first resident minister (Northern Methodist) arrived in the 1870s, the island entertained a variety of itinerant preachers, to whom the Methodists often lent their chapel. The storm of 1896 started an exodus across the sound from Core and Shackleford Banks that the San Ciriaco Hurricane of 1899 accelerated, and the population of Harkers Island quadrupled in just a few years. Natives and newcomers alike welcomed the missionaries that the Church of Jesus Christ of Latter-Day Saints added to the explosive mixture in 1898, but differences over theology soon descended into violence. Egged on by the Reverend Thomas Morgan, the new Methodist minister, who denounced Mormons as "worse than devils . . . lower than hogs and dogs," one faction set fire to the Mormon meetinghouse in January 1906, while most of the Latter-Day Saints congregation attended a "candy pulling" party. As a result the church hierarchy recalled its elders, leaving the isolated flock to fend for itself. Three elders paid a discreet visit that July, hoping that hostility had subsided, but almost immediately it came to a head again. Joel Hancock, who is both a Mormon and a native of Harkers Island, pieced together the following account of the climactic confrontation for *Strengthened by the Storm*, his 1988 history of this troubled and fascinating period.

AFTER LEAVING Harkers Island in early February of 1906, Elder William Petty was named President of the North Carolina Conference. In that capacity, he kept in frequent contact with his friends at Harkers Island. He was scheduled to complete his mission and return home at the end of July. As that time drew near, the Saints at the Island urgently appealed for him to visit with them before taking his departure. They assured him that matters had improved and that he and his companions would be safe during their stay. Though the Reverend Morgan had recently returned to the Island, the members were confident that a short visit by the missionaries would not create a breach of the peace. Regardless of what might have been threatened in the past, they promised to ". . . protect the Elders with their lives if necessary."

Elder Petty eventually decided to honor their request and he arrived at Harkers Island at 9:30 in the evening of Tuesday, July 3, 1906. Traveling with Elder Petty were Elders Arthur W. Anderson, who, like Petty, was from Emery, Utah, and John A. Berrett, who had just arrived in the area after being transferred from the Georgia Conference. Elder Berrett had been designated to succeed Elder Petty as President of the North Carolina Conference.

The Elders were met at Morehead City by Tom Styron, Augustus Nelson, and Johnnie Guthrie. Arriving at Harkers Island at 9:30 that evening, they were greeted "with open arms" by a large party of the Saints at the home of Willie Willis. Willie's wife, Lillie, had prepared supper for the guests and they received their friends from all over the Island until well after midnight. This was the first visit of Mormon Elders since they had been removed from the Island on February 6, and the members were delighted at the opportunity once more to partake of the presence of their spiritual leaders. Elder Petty was unprepared for the emotion displayed at the gathering.

"The men were on the shore and the sisters were in the house. I have never witnessed such a handshaking and hugging in all my life. Oh how glad the poor, distressed Saints were to see some Elders. . . . When I stepped into the door and saw all the people I was instantly bewildered. It was truly a happy meeting and one to be remembered by all who witnessed it."

It was agreed that evening that a meeting should be held the next morning, and that if all went well, further meetings might be scheduled. At 10:00 in the morning of Wednesday, July 4, the Saints gathered again at Willie Willis'. The meeting was very well attended and proceeded without incident, so another was held at Jim and

Rachel Lawrence's home that afternoon at 3:00. The Reverend Morgan was conducting a revival at the same time. After the close of the latter service a note was delivered to the Latter-day Saint congregation. In it they were warned that, ". . . if they did not take the Elders away from the Island by 8 o'clock that night, there would be trouble." The members decided to ignore the injunction and to proceed with the plan of having their guests spend that evening at the home of Oscar and Armecia Brooks.

The Elders and their many hosts walked the two miles along the shore to the westard where they were treated to a large supper by Armecia Brooks. After the meal, all went out on the porch where the members and Elders joined together in singing the songs of Zion on a beautifully clear summer's evening. Perhaps they assumed that on their country's most special holiday, a day dedicated to the celebration of freedom, they might be spared the religious intolerance their common ancestors had fought and struggled to overcome.

In spite of the apparent tranquillity and solemnity of the occasion, their peace was suddenly shattered. Just after nightfall Armecia Nelson came running from the eastard with news that the ". . . mob had already gathered for the purpose of carrying out their threats made during the day." There were only eight men among the crowd still gathered at the Brooks' home, but all immediately ". . . pledged their lives for the protection of the Elders if they would but remain." Armecia reported that the mob ". . . numbered twenty-five to thirty men, armed and full of mean whiskey." That description was indication that the mob included some "troublemakers," in addition to the sectarian fanatics. A quick counsel among the members decided that ". . . it would be folly to attempt to defend themselves against such a fiendish gang of lawbreakers, and so they withdrew to the mainland in a small boat. . . ."

The three Elders were transported across Straits channel to Marshallberg by Cicero Willis, his brother-in-law James, and by Oscar Brooks' youngest son, Gordy. At Marshallberg they were granted refuge by the family of Eugene and Ruth Guthrie. . . .

The missionaries were carried back to Harkers Island by Cicero Willis and David Brooks early the following morning, Thursday, July 5. David was the eldest of Oscar and Armecia's sons. Upon arriving, they learned that no one had been disturbed during the previous night. The Elders therefore decided to travel back to the east end of the Island. Two days earlier they had made an appointment to hold a 10:00 [A.M.] meeting there at the home of Willie Willis.

Elders Petty, Anderson, and Berrett, and their accompanying party had walked for about a mile when they were met again by Armecia Nelson, this time accompanied by her brother Thomas. The pair had run at full speed from their home at the eastard to warn the Elders that the mob had reassembled and "were laying along the beach and waiting." They advised that the group was armed and angry and should be considered dangerous. And they added that this time the mob was being led by the Reverend Thomas Morgan, himself.

Once more it was agreed that discretion might be the better part of valor and again the missionaries prepared to leave the Island rather than risk a confrontation with an angry mob. They began to retrace their steps back to the westard and headed for the home of Oscar Brooks where they intended to secure passage off the Island. But they soon observed one of their enemies in a "sharpie," or skiff, out in the water. He had a large flag attached to the center mast of the boat and apparently was ready to send signals to his accomplices still on the shore.

When the man keeping lookout eventually lowered his flag, it summoned the mob that the Elders had turned around and that the attackers should begin their pursuit. For just a few minutes later, Thomas Nelson, though already exhausted from his previous effort, again overtook the Elders to warn that the mob was on its way. He then hurried on ahead of the party to warn the Saints at the westard as to what was happening. Then, in what seemed like little more than a moment, ". . . about thirty or thirty-five men and six or eight women came up the shore like so many cannibals in pursuit of their favorite prey."

The missionaries and their escorts ran for their lives along the shore towards Rush Point where they hoped to find help. It was more than a little ironic that the very spot that had been the site of so many Latter-day Saint baptisms in the previous seven years now was to be the scene of a violent confrontation.

At almost the same instant that the fleeing missionaries reached the Point, they were greeted on the one hand by Thomas Nelson and a band of approximately thirty Saints, mostly women and children. On the other side they saw the mob, led by the minister, which just then was about to overtake them. The ensuing stand-off there at the water's edge could have lasted for no more than a few minutes; yet it must have seemed like an eternity. Some of the members sought to place themselves between the mob and the missionaries, hoping to shield them from an expected attack. The Elders even walked out into the water toward where Joseph Willis' boat was now headed in their direction. Suddenly, several of the mob broke through the barricade of bodies and made directly for the Elders.

At that point Thomas Nelson rushed forward and issued forth a challenge that immediately earned him a place of honor among the most exalted heroes of the Latter-day Saints at Harkers Island. Standing directly between the missionaries and their attackers, he shouted with a voice loud enough to rise above the din of the crowd, "I'll take you on one at a time, or all at a time, but you're not going to touch these Elders!"

Thomas Nelson's defiant challenge forestalled the mob long enough to allow Joseph Willis and David Brooks to arrive and safely convey the Elders to Morehead City. Elder Petty later wrote that as the missionaries departed they did so,

> . . . amid the heartbroken sobs, and terrified screams of the women and children . . . [as] the human degenerates, led by the minister, renewed their threats in shrieking tones which could be heard by the brethren as they sped away. And upon their ears also fell all the vile epithets that a cursing and sacrilegious tongue could utter, from the mouths of that savage band. What a contrast met [our] eyes as we sailed away; between the handful of hated, despised and persecuted, yet law-abiding and God-fearing people; and the band of vile wretches at their side who all were counted as good Christians, whose professed religion constituted the violation of law, a disregard for human rights, and the inclination and desire to commit the blackest deed known in the category of crime.

As the Latter-day Saint missionaries sailed away, the mob next turned on the members who remained at the shore. "You have heard the 'woice' of your last Mormon Elder," they boasted as Joseph Willis' small sailskiff disappeared over the horizon. They went on to assert that no further "Mormon meetings" of any type would be tolerated in the future. They concluded by declaring, "You have built your last church on Harkers Island. If you go to any church and hear any preaching, it will be in one of ours!"

The heartbroken women and children left at the shore could do little but stand and listen to the boastful taunts of their adversaries. Finally, Letha Brooks stepped forward, pulled off her bonnet, folded it in her hand, and looked the leaders of the mob squarely in the eyes. With all the determination left in her weary body she uttered forth the words of a Latter-day Saint hymn, "Kill this body if you will, but my soul will shine on Zion's hill."

Wild Goose Chase

REX BEACH 1921

Early visitors to the Outer Banks, beginning with the Raleigh colonists in the 1580s, almost always made note of the vast quantities of wildfowl wintering in the area, including geese, brant, swan and a variety of ducks. It was probably inevitable that sportsmen would discover this hunters' paradise, and not long after the Civil War northerners began buying up tracts of land and building clubhouses, many of them gargantuan by local standards.

By the first part of the twentieth century many local men were employed by the clubs as caretakers or guides. Others, having rigged up for hunting with their own blinds, batteries, decoys, and skiffs, catered to unaffiliated hunting parties. More often than not, their wives made extra money by providing room and board for the visitors.

One of those attracted to Pamlico Sound by the goose hunting was the novelist, humorist, and adventure writer Rex Beach. In his book *Oh, Shoot!* he recounted one memorable exploit he shared with fellow writers Grantland Rice and Max Foster; "Duke and Duchess, two English setters of breeding"; and a guide identified only as Ri.

OCRACOKE, center of the goose-hunting industry, is a quaint New England village pitched on the outer rim of Pamlico Sound, and it hovers around a tiny circular lagoon. The houses are scattered among wind-twisted cedars or thickets of juniper and sedge, and most of them possess two outstanding adjuncts—a private grave-yard and a decoy pen. All male inhabitants above the age of nine are experts on internal-combustion engines, for motor boats are everywhere except in the back yards. Of distinctive landmarks there are four—one lighthouse, one colored man, and two Methodist churches. Ocracoke has tried other negroes, but likes this one, and as for religion, it will probably build another Methodist church when prices get back to normal.

Now, for the benefit of any reader genuinely in quest of information, a word as to the kind of hunting here in vogue and the methods involved. First, understand that this stormy Hatteras region is the Palm Beach of the Canada goose and his little cousin the brant. Ducks winter all along the Atlantic coast, but Pamlico Sound marks, roughly, the goose's southern limit. Here each wary old gander pilots his family; here he and his mate watch their young folks make social engagements for the following season.

There is no marsh or pond shooting, for the wild fowl frequent the shallow waters of the sound and it is necessary to hunt from rolling blinds, stake blinds, or batteries. The rolling blind I have described—it is used only on cold drizzly days in the late season when the geese have chilblains and gather on the dry bars to compare frost bites. A stake blind resembles a pulpit raised upon four posts, and is useful mainly in decoying inexperienced Northern hunters. Green sportsmen stool well to stake blinds, for they are comfortable, but a wise gunner shies at them as does a gander. He knows that the real thing is a battery.

This latter device may be described as a sort of coffin, but lacking in the creature comforts of a casket. It is a narrow, water-tight box with a flush deck about two feet wide, to three sides of which are hinged large folding wings of cloth or sacking stretched upon a light wooden framework. It is painted an inconspicuous color; heavy weights sink it so low that its decks are awash. The sportsman lies at full length in it, and his body is thus really beneath the level of the water. When it is surrounded by a couple hundred dancing decoys, the hunter is effectually hidden from all but high-flying birds. To such as fly low, the rig is a snare and a delusion; not unless they flare high enough to get a duck's-eye view do they see the ace-in-the-hole, and then it is usually too late.

Battery shooting requires some little practice and experience. One must begin by learning to endure patiently the sensations of ossification, for to rest one's aching frame even briefly by sitting up, or to so much as raise one's head for a good look about, is a high crime and a misdemeanor. It completely ruins the whole day for the guides, who are comfortably anchored off to leeward in the tender, and affords them the opportunity of saying, later:

"You can't expect 'em to decoy to a lump. If you'd of kep' down, you'd of got fifty birds to-day."

And that is not the only discomfort. All batteries are too small, and some of them leak in the small of the back. If the wind shifts or blows up, they sink before the guides arrive. For years I tried to adapt myself to the existing models, but failed. I fasted until my hips narrowed to an AA last; I wore the hair off the top of my head; my body became rectangular, and still I did not fit. I have had rubber-booted guides stand upon my abdomen and stamp me into my mold, as the barefoot maidens of Italy tread the autumn vintage, but, no matter how well they wedged me in, some part of me, sooner or later, slipped. The damp salt air swelled me, perhaps; anyhow, I bulged until from a distance I looked like a dead porpoise, and the ducks avoided me.

Tiring of this, I had a large box built. I equipped it with a rubber mattress and pillow, and now I shoot in Oriental luxury. But, even under favorable conditions, to correctly time incoming birds, to rise up and "meet them" at precisely the right instant, is a matter of considerable nicety. One must shoot sitting, which is a trick in itself, especially on the back hand, and ducks do not remain stationary when surprised by the apparition of a magnified jack-in-the-box. They are reputed to travel at ninety miles an hour, when hitting on all four, but that is too conservative. Start the goose flesh on a teal's neck, for instance, and he will leave your vicinity so fast that a load of shot needs short pants and running shoes to overtake him.

I have lain in a double box alongside of experienced field shots and picked up many valuable additions to my vocabulary of epithets. I have seen nice, well-bred, Christian gentlemen grind their teeth, throw their shells overboard, and send for better loads, even smash their guns in profane and impotent rage. That is, I have seen them perform thus when I myself was not stone blind with fury.

We shot for a couple of days, off Ocracoke, while we were waiting for Grant, but the weather was warm and we had little luck; then the bottom fell out of the glass and, in high hopes of a norther, we ran up the banks to our favorite hunting grounds. As we pulled into our anchorage, the bars were black with wild fowl; through our field glasses we could see thousands, tens of thousands, of resting geese; up toward Hatteras Inlet the sky was smudged with smoky streamers which we knew to be wheeling clouds of redheads. Before we had been at rest a half hour, the wind hauled and came whooping out of the north, bearing a cold, driving rain; so we shook hands all around. All that is necessary for good shooting on Pamlico is bad weather. It looked as if we had buried our jinx once for all.

Our party had grown, for we had picked up the hunting rigs at Ocracoke — they were moored astern of us, launches, battery boats, and decoy skiffs streaming out like the tail of a comet. All that day and the next we watched low-flying strings of geese and ragged flocks of ducks beating past us, while we told stories or conducted simple experiments in probability and chance. In the latter I was unsuccessful, as usual, for I simply cannot become accustomed to the high cost of two small pair.

The second morning brought a slight betterment of conditions; so we set out early, Max in search of shelter behind a marshy islet, while I hit for the outer reefs. After several attempts, Ri finally found a spot where a mile of shoals had flattened the sea sufficiently to promise some hope of "getting down."

While we were placing the battery, Grantland Rice arrived in a small boat from Ocracoke. He was drenched; he had been four days en route from New York, and he was about fed up on rough travel. Through numb, blue lips he chattered; "You're harder to find than Stanley."

I directed him to the houseboat and told him where to obtain comfort and warmth — third bureau drawer, left-hand corner, but be sure to cork it up when through — then explained that Max had put down a double box and was waiting for him.

"The weather to kill geese is weather to kill men," I assured him. "You're in luck to arrive during a norther like this."

"Any nursing facilities aboard the boat?" Grant wanted to know.

I assured him with pride that we were equipped to take care of almost anything up to double pneumonia, and that if worse came to worst and his lungs filled up, we could run him over to the mainland, where he could probably get in touch with a hospital by mail.

My battery managed to live, with the lead wash strips turned up, but the gale drove foam and spray over me in such quantities that I was soon numb and wet—the normal state for a battery hunter. Members of the Greely expedition doubtless suffered some discomforts, and the retreat from Serbia must have been trying, but for 100-per-cent-perfect exposure give me a battery in stormy winter weather.

However, I managed to collect a fair number of birds before dusk, when, in answer to my feeble signals, the guides rescued me. They seized me by my brittle ears, raised me stiffly to my heels, then slid me, head first, into the tiny cabin of the launch, as stokers shove cordwood into a boiler. By the time we got back to the boat I could bend my larger joints slightly and I no longer gave off a metallic sound when things fell on me.

The other boys had not fared so well. They had been drowned out, their battery had been sunk without trace, and they had nothing to show for their day's sport except a clothes line full of steaming garments and a nice pair of congestive chills. Otherwise it had been a great day, and we looked forward to more fun on the morrow.

But how vain our hopes! As usual, the weather was unparalleled. Once again it surprised the oldest inhabitants. That night the wind whipped into the south, drove all the water off the bars, then fell away to a calm, and the temperature became oppressive. The wild fowl reassembled in great rafts where we could not get at them; we lay in our batteries, panting like lizards and moaning for iced lemonade, while the skin on our noses curled up like dried paint. The only birds we got were poor half-witted things, delirious with the heat.

Such conditions could not last—the guides assured us of that—and they didn't. The next day it rained, and a battery in rainy weather is about as dry as a goldfish globe. Now, a strong man with an iron will may school himself to lie motionless while he slowly perishes from cold, for after the first few agonizing hours there is comparatively little discomfort to death by freezing, but I defy anybody to drown without a struggle.

But why drag out the painful details? We had not interred our jinx. One day a hurricane blew out of the north and piled the angry waters in upon us, the next it shifted, ran the tides out, and left us as dry as a lime burner's boot; the third it rained or fogged or turned glassy calm. Grizzled old veterans from the Hatteras Life-saving Station rowed out to tell us that such weather was impossible and threatened to ruin their business, but what could you expect under a Democratic administration? One morning, Ri outlined a desperate plan to me, and I leaped at it. Away inshore, across miles of flats, we could see probably a million geese and twice that many ducks enjoying a shallow footbath where no boat could approach them.

"Let's leave the launch outside, wade our rig up to their feedin' ground, and dig it in. It'll take a half day of hard work, but there's goin' to be a loose goose flyin' about three o'clock, and you can shoot till plumb dark. We'll leave the box down and wade back."

It sounded difficult, so we tried it, towing the empty battery behind us. The big decoy skiff dragged like an alligator, but we poled, waded, shoved, and tugged until we came to where the bottom was pitted and white with uptorn grass roots. Here we dug a hole deep enough to sink the box—no easy job with a broken-handled shovel—put out our stools, and then the men shoved the empty boat away.

Tons of wild fowl had gone out as we came in, but soon after I lay down they began returning. First there came a pair of sprigs, then a pair of black ducks. The black mallard is my favorite—he is so wary, so wise, and so game. He can look into the neck of a jug, and he fights to the last. When the hen dropped, the drake, as usual, flared vertically. Upward he leaped in that exhibition of furious aerial gymnastics peculiar to his breed; then, at the top of his climb, he seemed to hang motionless for the briefest interval. That is the psychological instant at which to nail a black duck. As he came down, fighting, I was up and overboard after him. The water was shallow, but I splashed like a sternwheeler, and I was wet to the waist before I had retrieved that cripple.

Next I glimpsed a long, low line of waving wings approaching, and flattened myself to the thickness of a flannel cake, thrilling in every nerve. Never did twenty geese head in more prettily. They had started to set their pinions, and I was picking my shots, when one of the decoys, a young gander in the Boy Scout class, cracked under the nervous strain and began to flap madly. He flared the incomers, and I failed to get more than two.

I made haste to gather up the dead birds and lay them on the battery wings; then I moved the shell-shocked gander to the head of the rig. But before I could get him anchored, distant honks warned me, and I ran for cover. Of course, I tripped over decoy lines—everybody does. I did Miss Kellerman's famous standing, sitting, standing dive, but there was still a dry spot between my shoulder blades when I plunged kicking into the battery. I was too late, however, and the flock went by, out of range, laughing uproariously at me.

Then up from the south came a rain squall, and I stood with my back to it, shivering and talking loudly as tiny glacial streams explored parts of my body that are not accustomed to water. During the rest of the afternoon, cloudbursts followed one another with such regularity that my battery resembled a horse trough, and when I immersed myself in it it overflowed. But between squalls the birds flew. When a bunch of geese pitched in at my head and I downed five, I fell in love with the spot and would have resisted a writ of eviction.

When the guides appeared at dark I had a pile of game that all but filled the tiny skiff which they had thoughtfully brought along. By the time we had loaded it with the dead birds and the crate of live decoys it was gunwale deep, so we set out to wade back to the launch, towing it behind us.

Night had fallen; fog and rain occasionally obscured the gleam of our distant ship's lantern. Other lights winked at us out of the gloom, and although they were miles away, nevertheless they all looked alike; so, naturally, we got lost. We headed for first one then another twinkling beacon, and altered our course only when the water deepened so that we could proceed no farther without swimming.

I have been successfully lost where you would least expect it, but never before had I been lost at sea with nothing whatever to sit down upon . . . and after an hour or two I voted it the last word in nothing to do. I can think of no poorer way of spending a rainy December night than chasing will-o'-the-wisps round a knee-deep mud flat the size of Texas, with an open channel between you and the shore.

I presume we waded no more than twenty-five miles—although it seemed much farther—before we found the launch and collapsed over her gunwale like three wet shirts. Then, just to show that things are never as bad as possible, the engine balked.

I asked if there was plenty of gas and if the spark was working, and, receiving the usual affirmative answer, I dissolved completely into my rubber boots. Ri was probably quite as miserable as I, but he began to scrub up for the customary operation. He removed the motor's appendix, or its Fay and Bowen, and ran a straw through it, the while we could see frantic flashes of the houseboat's headlight.

I felt an aching pity for Max and Grant. What a shock to them it would be to find us in the morning, frozen over the disemboweled remains of our engine, like merrymakers stricken at a feast of toadstools. They were men of fine feelings; it would nearly, if not quite, spoil their whole trip, even though they divided my dead birds between them.

But the machine made a miraculous recovery, and at its first encouraging "put" a great warmth of satisfaction stole through me. After all, it had been a wonderful day.

Human endurance, however, could not outgame that weather. The evening finally came when the boys announced that their time was up, so, after supper, we sent the small boats up to Ocracoke on the inside and fared forth into the dark sound.

As we blindly felt our way out from our anchorage, we ran over a stake net, picked it up and wrapped it around our propeller, and grounded helplessly on the edge of the outer bar. There we stuck. Examination showed a very pretty state of affairs. The net with its hard cotton lead line had wedged in between the propeller and the hull, and disconnected the shaft—a trifling damage and one that could have been repaired easily enough had we possessed a deep-sea diving outfit or a floating dry dock. But, search our baggage as we might, we could find neither. That's the trouble about leaving home in a hurry, one is apt to forget his dry dock.

Just to show us that he was still on the job, old J. W. Jinx arranged a shift in the wind. It had been calm all day; now a gale came off the sound and held us firmly on the reef. Pamlico began to show her teeth in the gloom, and with every swell we worked higher up on the bar and the boat bumped until our teeth rattled. We were several miles offshore, without any sort of skiff; it began to look as if we had about run out of luck and might have to hunt standing room somewhere in the surf. However, a yacht had made in near by on the day before, and, thanks to our searchlight, we managed to get a rise out of her. She sent a launch off, and it finally towed us back to shelter.

By this time it was midnight and the duties of host rested heavily upon me. I could with difficulty meet the accusing eyes of my guests, and, although I had ex- hausted my conversational powers, I hung close to them for fear of the cutting, unkind things they would say if I left them alone.

The next morning, Mr. Scott, owner of the neighboring yacht, prompted by true sportsman's courtesy, towed us back to Ocracoke, and as we went plunging down the sound in a cloud of spray we realized that the weather had hardened up and the birds were beginning to fly. The sky was full of them; we could hear the noise of many guns—a sound that brought scalding tears to our eyes.

I simply could not bear to leave just as the show had begun; so I reread my wife's last letter, and, finding it only moderately cool, I took the bit in my teeth and declared it my intention to stick long enough to change defeat into victory, even if I had to sleep in the woodshed when I got home,

"Better stay on for a few days," I urged the boys. "It will be dangerous to sit up in a battery to-morrow; the birds will knock your hats off. A blind man could kill his limit in this weather."

I had not read their mail, but I understood when they choked up and spoke tear- fully about "business." While I pitied them sincerely, a fierce joy surged through my own veins; nothing now could hinder me from enjoying a few days of fast, furi- ous shooting. The birds were pouring out of Currituck; there would be redheads, canvasbacks, teal—every kind of duck.

As we tried to work the house boat into the lagoon at Ocracoke, where we could get her out on the ways and count the fish remaining in that fragment of net, an Arctic tornado hit us and blew us up high and dry on a rock pile. It was a frightful position we now found ourselves in, for we had such a list to port that the chips rolled off the table—and we all felt lucky.

But the storm had delayed the mail boat and my companions were forced to remain over another day. The courage with which they bore this bitter disappointment was sublime; they sang like a pair of thrushes as they feverishly unpacked.

Conditions were ideal the next morning and we were away early. Having put down my rig in shallow water, where I could wade up my own birds, I sent the launch back to the village. This promised to be a day of days, and I wanted to get the most out of it.

Almost immediately the ducks began flying, and several bunches headed in towards me. I was puzzled as to why they changed their minds and flared, until a cautious peep over the side showed a small power-boat threshing up against the wind. It had already cost me several good shots, but there was nothing to do except wait patiently for it to pass. However, it did not pass; in spite of my angry shouts and gesticulations it held its course until within hailing distance. Then the man in the stern bellowed:

"Telegram!"

Now, mail is bad enough on a hunting trip, but telegrams are unbearable, and I distrust them. Nobody ever wanted me to stay away and enjoy myself so urgently as to wire me; therefore I openly resented this man and his mission. By the time he had handed me the message I had made up my mind to ignore it, reasoning rapidly that it could by no possibility be of importance, and if it were—as it probably was—I could do nothing about it before the mail boat came that night. Hence it was futile to permit my attention to be distracted from the important business of the moment.

I thanked the man, then urged him, for Heaven's sake, to beat it quickly, for, in the offing, flocks of geese were noisily demanding a chance to sit down with my decoys, and just out of range ducks were flying about, first on one wing then on the other, waiting for him to be gone.

But that telegram exercised an uncanny fascination for me. I lacked the moral courage to destroy it, although I knew full well if I kept it on my person I would read it—and regret so doing. Things worked out just as I had expected. I yielded and—my worst apprehensions were realized. The message was from my wife, but beyond that fact there was nothing in its favor, for it read:

"Your secretary has forged a number of your checks and disappeared. Total amount unknown, as checks are still coming in. Presume you gave him keys to wine cellar, for they, too, are missing. Wire instructions quick. Am ill, but stay, have a good time, and don't worry."

I stared, numb and horror-stricken, at the sheet until I was roused by a mighty whir of rushing pinions. Those ducks had stood it as long as possible and were decoying to me, sitting up. Through force of habit my palsied fingers clutched at my gun, but, although the birds were back-pedaling almost within reach, I scored five misses. Who can shoot straight with amount of loss unknown and certain precincts unheard from? Not I. Those broadbills looked like fluttering bank books.

And the keys to the wine cellar missing! That precious private stock, laid in for purely medicinal purposes, ravaged, kidnapped! A hoarse shout burst from my throat; I leaped to my feet and waved frantically at the departing boatsman, but he mistook my cries of anguish for jubilation at the results of my broadside, waved me good luck, and continued on his way.

As I stood there striving to make my distress heard by that vanishing messenger, geese, brant, ducks, and other shy feathered creatures of the wild poured out of the sky and tried to alight upon me, or so it seemed. They came in clouds and I shooed them off like mosquitoes. One would have thought it was the nesting season, and I was an egg.

I read again that hideous message as I undertook to reload, but I trembled the trigger off and barely missed destroying my left foot—my favorite. Never in the annals of battery shooting has there been another day like that. Those ducks reorganized and launched attack after attack upon me, but my nerve was gone, and the most I could do was defend myself blindly.

I did spill blood during one assault, and I was encouraged until I found that I had shot one of Ri's live decoys. Beyond that, the casualties were negligible, and when the guides came to pick me up they had to beat the blackheads out of the decoys with an oar.

As we pulled out of Ocracoke at dawn the next morning, the town was full of dead birds, and visiting sportsmen with eager, feverish eyes were setting forth once more for the gunning grounds. But we hated them. Flocks of geese decoyed to the mail boat whenever it hove to or broke down, and we hated them also.

Upon my arrival home I found a wire from Ri reading:

Too bad you left. Nathan killed fifty birds the next day and he can't hit a bull with a spade.

However, take it by and large, it was a fine trip and a good time was had by all.

Bring Back the Old Deestric' Skule!

VICTOR MEEKINS   1933

Early residents of the Outer Banks concerned about their children's education found it necessary to teach them at home or get help from more-literate neighbors. In time, however, people began to find it advantageous to band together, build a one-room school, and hire a teacher for a few months a year. By the first quarter of the twentieth century there were about as many little schools as there were little churches on the Outer Banks, each a source of community pride. School districts were formed with authority to levy taxes for additional construction, though much of the money for operating expenses continued to come from various fund-raising activities. Finally, the state took over the responsibility for school operation, and soon the rage for consolidation began. Victor Meekins, Manteo's longtime outspoken editor-publisher, preferred things as they had been before consolidation, and he said so clearly in the following article from *The State*.

IN WRITING THIS, I realize that I am laying myself open to the challenge of being a reactionary, a radical and a stumbling block in the path of progress. But that doesn't make any material difference, so far as I am concerned.

I rise to the defense of the district school; the old-time deestric' skule—which knew how to build characters, as well as stuffing boys and girls with the fundamentals of education. It has vanished, and today we've got a smooth-running educational machinery which has about it . . . as much individuality as a cider mill or a sausage grinder. I'm ag'in these professional "bang-arounds," living off the money which poor taxpayers have to put out. In case you don't know what a "bang-around" is—he's one of those efficiency and educational experts whose sole interest—were he to be frank about it—is to get an easy job, without having to put out very much work.

I was ten years old before I went to school. My teacher was a local woman, who had grown up in our community. She knew us just as intimately as did our own mothers. She was responsible to all of the patrons of the school. She had to keep her mind on her business; to know the individual peculiarities of every person in the district. She had to be on her toes to produce results. She didn't dare stay out until the wee morning hours, because such tactics would bring down upon her head the scorn and abuse of her neighbors. The type of young men with whom she kept company was known and noticed by the public. They must pass the test of public approval as weighed by all the patrons of the school.

Our district school was the one community interest that united every person in the neighborhood in a wholesome and happy civic spirit and in a common cause. It was financed by the labor of the folks who were our neighbors. It was a source of pride to every person. Not a man or a woman who didn't gladly give a day's labor to repair or paint or tidy up the building and grounds. There was no division or difference of opinion when it came to doing things for the district school.

Many times, the folks would gather for an ice cream social or similar entertainment, and wholeheartedly spend liberally from their pocket change. It was the custom to treat, and the young folks would treat the old people who were unable to buy for themselves. Cakes were sold, and chicken suppers were raffled off—all for the purpose of raising money for a worthy cause: maybe to paint the building, make repairs, buy desks or supplement the school library. All of the young bucks enjoyed those occasions, and enjoyed spending their money. Much more so than they now enjoy paying taxes for school purposes.

I recall when I finished my studies in that little district school, and when it became necessary for my companions and myself to depart therefrom and trudge four miles to the larger school in town; to continue our studies and to make new associations and learn new things. We walked those miles without a murmur, and we had a better time trudging along the road than now do the children of our neighborhood, who ride in big, shiny busses. The exercise was good for us.

Came the time when the march of progress—if you want to call it that—sidetracked our little school. It was in the interest of economy, they said, yet it cost more to transport the children to the consolidated school than the teacher's salary had been. It was in the interest of efficiency, they said, yet few of the pupils got through high school. None of them has gone through college. Half the young boys dropped out after a while, but failed to go to work, and many of them are not yet doing anything at all that is gainful.

Taxes went up, however, despite all of this so-called efficiency and economy in our educational system. We all went wild on the subject of consolidation, myself included. All of our children were going to receive a wonderful education, and as a result, all of them would prove to be prosperous and happy men and women. What a disillusionment!

Strangers now come to every community to teach the children. They know nothing of local conditions, or of local problems. They know nothing of the background of their pupils. The whole thing is a machine-made sort of a proposition, with all individuality completely smothered. Gone is the old community camaraderie and good fellowship: gone is the old wholehearted spirit of contribution of money, of time and of materials. Gone is that laudable local pride in making that one local institution the best it could be, because it meant the best for our children.

Worst of all, gone far from their homes for an entire day—day after day—are the little children who should be nearby and under the care and watch of their parents, instead of being subjected to the coarser contacts with larger children at the consolidated schools. And, with all this, there has arisen a great parental indifference—a great decline in parental aid. No more strict supervision of homework—in most cases, no homework at all.

Instead of that community pride, which the old district school used to arouse, we now have almost continuous bickering and squabbling about bus transportation and other things of that nature.

You may be able to systematize the growing of your crops; to regulate your acres, to control production, to breed all your livestock from pedigreed sires and to kill off all the culls. You may paint your barns, fences and outbuildings. You may budget your income, control your bank account and regulate your vitamins, calories and capsules, but you cannot systematize, standardize and bulldoze for long an entire commonwealth, or any political subdivision thereof, when it comes to education. Education of the human mind must not be of the sausage-mill type: it must be suitable to the individual needs. And how in the world are you going to give proper individual training when your teachers, coming from foreign parts and knowing nothing about the pupils whom they instruct, are placed in charge of your consolidated schools?

Let's take the rope off the taxpayers' neck. Let's have some more wholesome, corn-fed education, properly sandwiched between the right amount of work and seasoned with the grains of commonsense. Let's let the taxpayer stand on his feet awhile, eased of his present excessive burdens, so that he may have a chance to catch his breath. Let us go back to the old-fashioned district school for a while, and put some of the hard-driving efficiency experts, the district supervisors and the educational "bang-arounds" back to looking in the south end of a mule, for which they apparently are better qualified, if we must judge them by their works.

Hatteras Highway

BILL SHARPE 1952

Bill Sharpe began publicizing the Outer Banks when he headed the North Carolina Office of Tourism in the 1940s, and he continued to do so after buying *The State* magazine from its founder, Carl Goerch. On his early trips to Hatteras Island, driving on the Banks was a sometimes dangerous, sometimes exciting, but seldom unremarkable experience. Whether you sank into a gravel bed while driving between the tidemarks, came to an abrupt stop negotiating the deep sand tracks that passed for a road, buried your car to its chassis avoiding an oncoming car, or bogged down simply backing off the ramp of the little ferry at Oregon Inlet, each trip was an adventure. As the asphalt strip running the length of the island neared completion, Sharpe reminisced in this piece for *The State* about the era drawing to a close.

BACK IN 1936, a bewildered motorist, struggling through the sandy ruts of the Outer Banks, stopped on top of the great flat near Pea Island where a WPA worker was building sand fences.

He wanted to know which road to take to Hatteras.

"Take road 108," he was told.

A half-hour later, after following one auto track in the sand after another, he had circled back and approached the same man. "Which road did you tell me to take to Hatteras?" he asked.

The boy wearily pointed to the maze of ruts. "Take 108. There's 108 roads to Hatteras."

Morris Burrus, of Hatteras, told it mirthfully. It is a lot funnier to a motorist today than it was to the badgered and laughed-at beach traveler of 1936.

There'll be a road all the way to Hatteras soon, and it isn't any joke. It's a real, paved highway, the solution to one of North Carolina's most unusual engineering problems.

To most people—native and traveler—who for years have groped their way along old 108, the new highway is a success story. But to others, the highway not only is not a joke; it is a grim door slammed shut upon another fragment of the vanishing frontier.

The slow ferry landed you on the south side of Oregon Inlet and you were upon a finger of sand which pointed in a general southeasterly direction. As you headed south, the surf broke upon a lonely beach on your left, and on your right, Pamlico Sound swiftly widened into the vast inland sea which it is, until the continental mainland was pushed far to the west, and you rode a tight rope of sand to the ends of the earth. . . .

There was a choice of routes. At low tide, most people "rode the wash," which is the business of driving your car with the left wheels almost, but not quite, in the ocean, and if there were no wind-made camel-back humps, and if the sand was hard and firm, as it usually was, this was a fine speedway.

Or you took the inside, a "road" composed of the most recent set of ruts made by those who preceded you. It was a road by custom only; it had neither right-of-way or maintenance. An old driving rule on the Outer Banks is to follow the most auto tracks, no matter where they lead; it is a good rule today, and will be good until the last stretch of pavement on the new highway is completed.

Those first 20 miles of driving from the ferry had a lot to do with determining whether you were suited for the Outer Banks or not. No matter where you went, the dull roar of the surf always was in your ears. Except for Pea Island Coast Guard station (until recently manned by the only all-negro life guard crew in America) there was not a habitation in that first 20 miles. There are no "rural" people on the Banks. Simple and inconvenient as life is on the island, it is no place for hermits, and people live in tight little villages—seven of them—all located on the sound (west) side. It is not possible on the Banks to get very far away from the ocean, but the villagers are as far from it as geography permits.

For the most part, they spent their lives on that side, so as you drove down the Banks, you had an ocean and a beach all to yourself. It is a beautiful beach, highly exposed and disturbing under the threat of a hurricane, because it offers no hope of shelter, but benign on a sunny day and under a moderate wind. Your car would throw up an almost continual cloud of shore birds—an astonishing variety, bird fans say—in front of you.

The remnants of old wrecks protruded from the beach. The sands covered and uncovered them at the will of the winds. At the coast guard stations, which once were more numerous than they now are, you could talk to the men who saw these crafts come ashore. In the records you could read which of your companions were the heroes of those disasters; and in some instances you would see the medals and citations given by our own and by foreign governments to these sturdy surfmen, living out their careers in these lonely posts.

For every mile there is a wreck, for every wreck a deed of heroism, and for every deed a dozen enchanting stories.

If you took the "inside" you would encounter the villages of Rodanthe, Waves, Salvo, Avon and Buxton before reaching the Cape itself. If you traveled the beach you would never know that these communities were just a little way to your right. At the Cape—or the Point, as it is called there—the Outer Banks continue stubbornly out into the Atlantic, but now under water, and now forming Diamond Shoals, the greatest area of quicksand in the world. Over these shoals the water seethes and hisses in bad weather, throwing spray high in the air. The shoals comprise the most dangerous navigational hazard of the American seaboard, and it is said that only one vessel ever to strike on them ever came off alive—and she drifted off, mysteriously, after her crew had taken to their boats. . . .

At the Cape, the shore line turns almost due west to be terminated by Hatteras inlet. Also west of the Cape, the land rises to an altitude of 90 feet, and here is Cape Woods, or Trent, a thick growth of pines, myrtle, yaupon. In this forest is the village of Buxton, a place of perhaps 500 people. Even in a country which, to its natives, is without compare, Buxton is exalted. It contains many retired people—principally those who have seen service in the Coast Guard or some other branch of government service. The island as a whole has a large proportion of pensioners. It is only a few miles from here to your journey's end—the village of Hatteras, itself.

On this island are perhaps 2,000 persons. It would be a mistake to call them lotus eaters, for this is largely a barren island and the elements are as often stern and forbidding as they are pleasant. With the exception of Trent Woods, Hatteras is as exposed as the deck of a ship uneasily anchored in an uneasy sea. Although a sand fixation project of the '30's has encouraged growth of grass, shrubs and some scrubby pines north of Buxton, the island's geography is still in a state of flux.

But those who have lived on Hatteras like it. For many others, it has been a secret retreat from the distractions of the mainland.

If the island was neglected so long by road-builders, it always was overlooked by less beneficent improvements. It lacks a drugstore, and for a long time had no doctor, but it also had no neon signs, juke boxes or a jail. Until a couple of years ago, the nearest law was at Manteo, but there was less crime and disorder in the seven island villages in a year than there was in Manteo and Nags Head on a lusty weekend. The only telephone was in the Coast Guard service. There were no luncheon clubs and consequently no luncheon club speakers, and political orators found the arduous trip not worth taking. There were no bridge clubs, mayors, city councilmen, health officers, traffic congestion or traffic lights.

There was a great lack of hurry and bustle. There aren't many places to go on the island, and most natives have been to them already. There are few excuses for scheming around to make money, because there is little of it to be made. The difference between the richest man on the island and the poorest man is slighter than in any community we know. You don't keep up with the Joneses, because there are no Joneses to keep up with, either literally or metaphorically. But there is no squalor on the banks; if there is, it doesn't appear to be poverty in this environment.

Sport fishing is good in this territory and also waterfowl hunting, and it is the excuse most people use to go there, though you can swim on a good beach. Beyond that, you have to improvise your own recreation. The weather, in spite of the well-founded slanders heard about it, is good on the whole. It is about 12 degrees warmer in winter and cooler in summer than it is at the closest mainland weather station.

Naturally, a highway to such a special place would be kind of special. And the highway being built from Oregon Inlet to the village of Hatteras is one of the most unique ever attempted. This one is being constructed according to specifications laid down by the wind and the sea. Contractors who have punctured mountains and spanned gorges soon learned that damp sand in a northeaster is more formidable than granite and space.

The banks are being conquered with their own sand, which is an ingredient in the asphalt base of the highway. The Ballengers found the sand fine for beachcombers, but lousy for roadbuilding. So liquid asphalt, made by mixing naphtha in it, was substituted for the hot asphalt usually used on road beds. When the naphtha evaporated, only the asphalt was left, and the sand was found suitable when used this way.

How to elevate the road was a major problem for Ballenger Paving Company of Greenville, the contractors. Experience showed that attempts to defy the elements failed, and so engineers conspired to make the road live in compatibility with the water. Northeasters sometime bring high waves in from the ocean; southwesters flood the area from the other side—the sound. . . .

There were special problems, too. The project may go down in history as the only one in which a barge sank at a point about where the curb would be on a large inland highway. The barge, loaded with trucks, a caterpillar tractor, and other equipment, sank in about nine feet of water in December, 1947. Using a diver and huge cranes, Ballenger recovered their equipment and marked it down as just another hazard of the contract.

The new road has been proceeding in links. The 17.3 mile link between Hatteras and Avon was finished in August 1948. The link between Avon and Rodanthe—17.8 miles—is almost complete.

Work began on the 12.4 miles between Rodanthe and the south shore of Oregon Inlet in January 1952, and is due for completion "sometime before the summer is over."

So here's the way it is: Those who want their Hatteras with comfort and convenience and with all the good things a highway can bring, will have to wait a little while.

Those who want to see a simpler, more rugged Hatteras they'll never see again, had best get going. Fast!

Old Christmas

JAN DEBLIEU 1987

Every writer worth his salt learns that if he writes about the Outer Banks long enough, he must eventually address three topics: the Lost Colony, the Wright brothers, and Old Christmas at Rodanthe. Historic sites, archaeological discoveries, reams of written material, and legions of experts help ensure a steady supply of informative or thought-provoking things to say about the first two. But since it was turned into a weekend holiday for the sake of greater attendance, the Old Christmas celebration has provided little to see or write about and has seemed not to warrant all the publicity that it gets. A good writer can usually find interesting details and draw important lessons from mundane events. As she proved in her book *Hatteras Journal*, from which the following piece is taken, and in subsequent books and articles, naturalist Jan DeBlieu, a Delaware native now living in Dare County, possesses these enviable abilities.

EVERY JANUARY on Hatteras Island, a week or so after most families have packed up the duties and indulgences of the holidays, the residents of Rodanthe hold a celebration known as Old Christmas. It is simultaneously a meeting of friends and a curious gathering of people with little in common but their hometown and perhaps their last names.

Old Christmas has been observed in Rodanthe on the Saturday closest to Epiphany for at least a hundred years. It is said to have had its beginnings in 1752, when England adopted the Gregorian calendar and shortened the calendar year by eleven days. According to legend, the towns of Hatteras Island were not informed of the change until decades later, and then they refused to abide by it. Whether or not the legend is true, a tradition has evolved whereby the townspeople of Rodanthe spend Christmas Day with relatives in Waves, Salvo, or southern parts of the island, then throw a party in the Rodanthe Community Center to observe the holiday a second time. The celebration is planned for local families, and although tourists are welcomed, they seldom grasp the significance of the event. Moreover, many tourists are reluctant to attend, for Old Christmas has the reputation of being a drunken brawl.

It once was customary for the men of Hatteras Island to settle their grudges against each other once a year with a fist fight after dinner on Old Christmas. The custom seldom led to anything but a few brief sparring matches, and until recent years the celebration generally was held without incident. In the 1970s, however, it became common for men looking for a brawl to arrive in Rodanthe just before dark on Old Christmas. Frequently the men were not from Hatteras Island but from mainland communities or the northern reaches of the Outer Banks, and they started picking fights as soon as they got into town. The altercations ruined the holiday for some island residents. Even though Old Christmas has been held peacefully for the past several years, a few local families refuse to attend.

On January 4, the day of the 1986 celebration, no one expected any violence. Several weeks before, family circumstances had made it necessary for me to move to Atlanta for most of the winter, but I had managed to return to Rodanthe for the weekend of Old Christmas. Late in the afternoon I wandered down the gravel road to the community center, a small, white building that once served as the town's single-room schoolhouse. The festivities were to have started at 1 P.M. with an oyster shoot, but it was nearly 2:30 when the first guns began to fire. On the far side of a patio, sheets of plywood had been fastened to a chain-link fence and painted with orange streaks to delineate the target zones. A knot of heads bent over a stack of paper targets that someone had spread on the hood of a car. Several of the targets were untouched; the marksmen had missed them completely. One target had a hole only a quarter-inch from the black bull's-eye. Maggie Smith, a thin woman with a strong chin and a ski cap covering a crop of dark hair, looked up from the targets and shrugged. "Looks like JoBob gets the oysters again," she said. It was the third time JoBob Fagundes, a local merchant, had won. The men standing around her grunted and moved off.

Beside Smith was a twelve-gauge shotgun and a box of shells. She is Mac Midgett's sister, and she seemed at ease chatting with a half-dozen local men who stood on the fringe of the group. "C'mon," she coaxed. "Who's next? Three bucks for a shot at a half-bushel of Stumpy Point oysters, the best oysters around."

I walked around the community center to where two men—both Midgetts— were stringing fishing net around a patio and stoking an oversized roaster with charcoal and wood. The roaster had been fashioned from a rusty oil drum cut in half and hinged on one side. Long tables with rough plywood tops had been placed around it. As bushels of oysters finished roasting, the men would shovel them onto the tables for the crowd to shuck and eat. The coals would not be ready for a half-hour, and I wandered inside.

The tiny dance hall had begun to fill, and the instruments for a bluegrass band were set on stage. The dancing would come later; now was the time for visiting. At the door Louell Midgett, an Ocracoke native who lives in Rodanthe with her husband, collected money and hugged friends as they entered. She saw many of them several times a month, but it was Old Christmas, after all. I rounded a corner to the building's small kitchen and was enveloped by Virginia O'Neal, the postmistress, before I even saw her. "Merry Old Christmas," she beamed, hugging me tighter. She wore a Christmas-red skirt and jacket, with a holly-green pin on her lapel. Her face shone with a gracious, happy beauty. Around were her friends from the Fairhaven Methodist Church—older women named Midgett, O'Neal, Hooper, and Gray—all in holiday clothes with festival smiles on their bright-red lips.

At a string of tables just off the kitchen, several women supervised a group of young children. These were the wives of the fishermen who congregated in a corner of the dance hall, smoking and leaning back, their crossed arms resting on ample bellies. I scanned the hall, finding scores of faces I did not recognize. It seemed many people had come from towns on the southern part of the cape. I waved to Mac Midgett and pushed my way toward the patio door. As I did, a stout woman with a wide face and large, stylish glasses caught my arm. "Jan." I looked at her blankly. "I'm Joyce Rucker."

Ersie Midgett's only daughter. I pumped her hand and smiled. As a young girl she had slept in the upstairs bedroom I would later use as an office. At the age of twelve she had huddled inside the yellow frame house as a brutal wind wrenched it from its foundation. Standing behind her were her brothers, Stockton and Anderson, dressed nattily in plaid slacks. "I'm surprised to see you here," I said. It had not occurred to me that Ersie's children would attend Old Christmas.

"We wouldn't miss it for the world," Rucker said. "This is still home in some ways. But my, it's changed. Every year there are more strangers. There's no way to stop more people from coming here. The island's growing, and in many ways it's good that we have the kinds of amenities we have now. It was hard to live the way we did, with no electricity or roads. We have a movie theater in Avon now. I never thought I would live to see a movie theater open in Avon."

A few minutes later I left her to get some oysters. Ersie's children were among the wealthiest and most controversial figures on Hatteras Island. They had made a substantial portion of their money by selling land. Tonight they would rub elbows with fishermen who were slowly losing their livelihoods to pollution and powerful sports-fishing lobbies. During the past ten years the people of Hatteras have divided themselves into two bitter camps, one that wants to preserve the cape's rugged desolation and a second that is working to build a string of glitzy resorts. Among the crowd in the community center were people who had grown up as cordial neighbors, and who now were entangled in disputes over the boundaries of their land. The real estate speculators were winning the fight—or at least were making the most money and gaining the most political clout. But the development of Hatteras was not to be a topic of discussion. Not here, not on Old Christmas.

Outside, a batch of oysters had just finished cooking. A wiry man with curly, brown hair opened the lid of the roaster. Steam cascaded into the night. "Who wants oysters?" he hollered. "You want oysters, you got to make some noise."

A few of us whooped.

"Pretty slack," he said, spreading the oysters across the table in front of me. I picked one up, twisted an oyster knife to pop open the gritty shell, and sucked down the tender flesh. I downed a dozen more and went inside, where the band had begun to play.

The dance floor was filling with people of all ages and physiques, some twisting, some dancing a jerky version of the fox trot. A fisherman with the build of a concrete block held up an arm to twirl his wife, who in her forties still had the figure and toothy smile of a debutante. A thick-bodied elderly couple waltzed in the middle of the floor, bumping buttocks with the people around them. On the sidelines, women leaned their heads close together to talk above the music, and teenage girls shyly watched the dancers. I picked my way through to the other side and halted near Louell Midgett, who was still standing guard at the door. "Interesting party, isn't it?" I said.

"We usually have a good bit of fun," she said, smiling. "If I were you I'd stand back against the wall a bit. Old Buck's getting ready to come in."

Old Buck is a kind of Old Christmas Santa Claus, a mythical wild bull. It is said that many years ago Old Buck impregnated every cow in Buxton Woods and terrorized local farmers until a hunter finally shot him. His spirit lives in the marshes and hammocks of Rodanthe. I had expected him to be personified by a mounted cow head, but the creature that stomped through the door had no eyes, nose, or mouth, just two horns and a piece of cowhide mounted on top of some long, sturdy object, probably a piece of wood. His lumpy back was covered by a green Army blanket, beneath which protruded two sets of legs in blue jeans and men's boots. People crowded into the smoky hall, yelling and clapping, stomping their feet.

A red-faced and jovial man led the cow into the room with a tether. "Look out, Old Buck's wild," he yelled in a gravelly voice. "He's wild tonight."

I pressed myself against the wall as the four legs beneath the blanket kicked and clomped past me. Old Buck was not only wild, he was bent on knocking down as many people as he could. The crowd screamed with laughter and scrambled for cover, some people jumping into the laps of friends who had managed to find seats on the edge of the dance floor. As one man crouched down for a picture, the bull hit him broadside and sent him reeling across stage. Fifteen seconds later Old Buck had jostled his way outside and vanished for another year.

Seldom had I laughed so hard. The crowd caught its breath as the band swung into "Truck Driving Man" for the third time. The celebration had peaked. People drifted outside, calling good-byes into the crisp night air. I had begun searching for my coat when the wiry man who had tended the oysters grabbed a microphone from the band. "Okay, I want all the children cleared out of here," he said, "because this is an adult's night. And us adults are gonna fight."

"No we're not," said a large fisherman standing next to me.

I did not stay around to hear the shouting match that followed. Later I learned that the man had been calmed by friends and that violence had been avoided for another year. Barring hangovers, the town awoke the next day in good spirits. The only apparent casualty was a red pickup that had somehow missed the road and landed on its side in a muck-lined drainage ditch.

Sources

First Impressions

"Contact," by Giovanni da Verrazzano, from Susan Tarrow, "Translation of the Cèllere Codex," in Lawrence C. Wroth, *The Voyages of Giovanni da Verrazzano, 1524–1528* (New Haven and London: Yale University Press, 1970), 135–36. Reprinted by permission of Yale University Press.

"Traffic with the Savages," by Arthur Barlowe, from Richard Hakluyt, ed., *The Principal Navigations Voyages Traffiques & Discoveries of the English Nation* . . . (London, 1600; 3rd ed., Glasgow: James MacLehose & Sons, 1903), vol. 8, 299–301, 304–6.

"The Dividing Line," by William Byrd, from William K. Boyd, ed., *William Byrd's Histories of the Dividing Line betwixt Virginia and North Carolina* (Raleigh: North Carolina Historical Commission, 1929), 38–50.

"Antebellum Nags Head," by Gregory Seaworthy (George Higby Throop), from *Nags Head; or, Two Months among "the Bankers"* (Philadelphia: A. Hart, late Carey and Hart, 1850), 22–26, 37–39, 79–80, 159–61.

"Three Weddings at Hunting Quarters," by Nathaniel H. Bishop, *Voyage of the Paper Canoe: A Geographical Journey of 2500 Miles from Quebec to the Gulf of Mexico, during the Years 1874–5* (Boston: Lee and Shepard, 1878), 196–203.

"A Visit to Ocracoke," by Carl Goerch, from *Ocracoke* (Winston-Salem: John F. Blair, 1956), 38–45. Reprinted by permission of John F. Blair, Publisher.

The Natural Environment

"Native Agriculture," by Thomas Harriot, from Richard Hakluyt, ed., *The Principal Navigations Voyages Traffiques & Discoveries of the English Nation* . . . (London, 1600; 3rd ed., Glasgow: James MacLehose & Sons, 1903), vol. 8, 361–64.

"Market Gunning," by H. H. Brimley, from Eugene P. Odum, ed., *A North Carolina Naturalist: H. H. Brimley, Selections from His Writings* (Chapel Hill: University of North Carolina Press, 1949), 17–23. Reprinted by permission of The University of North Carolina Press.

"The Hungry Horde," by Jack Dermid, from *Wildlife in North Carolina*, August 1952, 23. Reprinted by permission of the author.

"Creatures of the Shoals," by Rachel Carson, from *The Edge of the Sea* (Boston: Houghton Mifflin, 1955, 1983), 145–52. Copyright © 1955 by Rachel L. Carson,

© renewed 1983 by Roger Christie. Reprinted by permission of Houghton Mifflin Co.

"A History of Blues," by Joel Arrington, from *Wildlife in North Carolina*, December 1984, 23–27. Reprinted by permission of the author.

Man versus Nature

"The Opening of Oregon and Hatteras Inlets," from William L. Welch, "An Account of the Cutting through of Hatteras Inlet, North Carolina, Sept. 7, 1846," *Bulletin of the Essex Institute* (January 1885), 37–42.

C. O. Boutelle, "Extract from letters . . . relating to the new inlets formed . . . in 1846," *Report of Superintendent of the Coast Survey . . . .* U.S. Senate Exec. Doc. 6, 30th Congress, 1st Session (Washington, D.C.: Government Printing Office, 1847), 76–77.

"The *Worst* Light in the World," by David D. Porter, from U.S. Light-house Establishment, *Compilation of Public Documents and Extracts from Reports and Papers relating to Light-houses . . . 1789 to 1871* (Washington, D.C.: Government Printing Office, 1871), 736–38.

"The Sand Wave," from "Sand Waves at Henlopen and Hatteras," by John R. Spears, *Scribner's Magazine*, October 1890, 510–12.

"Project Nutmeg," by Captain Howard B. Hutchinson, USN, from "Project Nutmeg" (final report, classified January 28, 1949), 50–54.

"Man's Impact on the Barrier Islands of North Carolina," by Robert Dolan, Paul J. Godfrey, and William E. Odum, from *American Scientist*, March–April 1973, 161–62. Reprinted by permission of *American Scientist*.

"Saving Nags Head Woods," by Michael Godfrey, from *Wildlife in North Carolina*, December 1981, 2–8. Reprinted by permission of the author.

"Cape Lookout National Seashore: A Return to the Wild," by Michael E. C. Gery, from *Outer Banks Magazine*, 1992–93 annual, 37–41, 86. Reprinted by permission of *Outer Banks Magazine*.

Ships and the Sea

"Shipwreck off Hatteras," by Sarah Kollock Harris, from *North Carolina Booklet*, July 1921–April 1922, combined issue, 90–100.

"The Foundering of the USS *Monitor*," by William Frederick Keeler, from Robert W. Daly, ed., *Aboard the USS Monitor: 1862: The Letters of Acting Paymaster William Frederick Keeler, U.S. Navy, to His Wife, Anna* (Annapolis: U.S. Naval Institute, 1964), 253–60. Reprinted by permission of Naval Institute Press.

"The Wreck of the USS Huron," by Joe A. Mobley, from *Ship Ashore! The U.S. Lifesavers of Coastal North Carolina* (Raleigh: North Carolina Division of Archives and History, 1994), 53–64. Reprinted by permission of the author.

"The Wreck of the Bark Josie Troop," from *Annual Report of the Operations of the United States Life-Saving Service for the Fiscal Year Ending June 30, 1889* (Washington, D.C.: Government Printing Office, 1891), 34–37.

"Wreck of the Schooner Sarah D. J. Rawson," from *Annual Report of the United States Life-Saving Service for the Fiscal Year Ending June 30, 1905* (Washington, D.C.: Government Printing Office, 1906), 38–40.

"The Ghost Ship Mystery of Diamond Shoals," by John Harden, from *The Devil's Tramping Ground and Other North Carolina Mystery Stories* (Chapel Hill: University of North Carolina Press, 1949), 1–10. Reprinted by permission of The University of North Carolina Press.

"When the Ship Hit the Span," from *Ribbon of Sand: The Amazing Convergence of the Ocean and the Outer Banks*, by John Alexander and James Lazell, 192–201. © 1991 by the authors. Reprinted by permission of Algonquin Books of Chapel Hill.

"The Pea Island Lifesavers," by David Wright and David Zoby, from *Coastwatch*, May–June 1995, 3–9. Reprinted by permission of *Coastwatch*.

War on the Banks

"Of Captain Teach alias Blackbeard," by Captain Charles Johnson, from *A General History of the Pyrates*, ed. Manuel Schonhorn (Columbia: University of South Carolina Press, 1972), 77–83.

"The Rendezvous at Hatteras," by William Morrison Robinson Jr., from *The Confederate Privateers* (New Haven: Yale University Press, 1928), 101–15.

"Lincoln Hears the News," by Carl Sandburg. Excerpt from *Abraham Lincoln: The War Years*, by Carl Sandburg (332–33), © 1939 by Harcourt Brace & Company and renewed in 1967 by Carl Sandburg, reprinted by permission of the publisher.

"The Chicamacomico Races," by Evert A. Duyckinck, from Evert A. Duyckinck, *National History of the War for the Union, Civil, Military and Naval. Founded on Official and Other Authentic Documents* (New York: Johnson, Fry, and Co., 1862), vol. 1, 549–50.

"The Battle of Roanoke Island," by George Washington Whitman, from Jerome MacNeill Loving, *Civil War Letters of George Washington Whitman* (Ph.D. dissertation, Duke University, 1973), 57–61. Reprinted, with changes, by permission of Special Collections Library, Duke University.

"The Mirlo Rescue," by John Allen Midgett, from official wreck report in Nell Wise Wechter, *The Mighty Midgetts of Chicamacomico* (Manteo, N.C.: Times Printing Co., 1974), 33–36. Reprinted by permission of Times Printing Company.

"I Wore a Dead Man's Hand," by Aycock Brown and Ken Jones, from *Male*, October 1955, 17, 78–79.

Making a Living

"The Petition of Legal Pilots of Ocracoke Bar," by John Williams et al., from William L. Saunders, ed., *Colonial Records of North Carolina* (Raleigh: Josephus Daniels, 1890), vol. 9, 803–4.

"The Wild Horses, Their Qualities and Habits," by Edmund Ruffin, from *Agricultural, Geological, and Descriptive Sketches of Lower North Carolina and the Similar Adjacent Lands* (Raleigh: Privately printed, 1861), 130–33.

"The Last Whale Killed along These Shores," by Grayden Paul and Mary C. Paul, from *Folk-Lore, Facts and Fiction about Carteret County in North Carolina* (Privately published, 1975), 10–14. Reprinted by permission of Grayden M. Paul, Jr.

"Yaupon Factory," by H. H. Brimley, from *The State*, December 17, 1955, 9–11. Reprinted by permission of *Our State*.

"A Record Catch," by Old Trudge (Carl Goerch), from *The State*, November 4, 1944, 1–4, 22. Reprinted by permission of *Our State*.

"Pumping and Grinding," by Tucker Littleton, from *The State*, October 1980, 8–12. Reprinted by permission of *Our State*.

"Sharpies, Shad Boats, and Spritsail Skiffs," by Mark Taylor, from "Traditional Boats of North Carolina," *Wildlife in North Carolina*, July 1984, 20–27. Reprinted by permission of the author.

"Bread-and-Butter Fishing," by Jan DeBlieu, from *Hatteras Journal* (Golden, Colorado: Fulcrum, 1987), 149–67. Reprinted by permission of Fulcrum Publishing, Inc., 350 Indiana St., Suite 350, Golden, CO, 80401, (800) 992-2908.

Ones of a Kind

"Stanley Wahab, Tar Heel of the Week," by Woodrow Price, from Raleigh *News and Observer*, May 29, 1955. Reprinted by permission of *The News and Observer*.

"The Mighty Midgetts of Hatteras," by Don Wharton, from *American Mercury*, August 1957, 45–49.

"Cap'n Ban and the Infernal Engine," by Ben Dixon MacNeill, from *The Hatterasman* (Winston-Salem: John F. Blair, 1958), 231–34.

"Old Quork," by Charles Harry Whedbee, from *Legends of the Outer Banks and Tar Heel Tidewater* (Winston-Salem: John F. Blair, 1966), 57–63. Reprinted by permission of John F. Blair, Publisher.

"Les and Sally Moore, Pioneers," by Jerry Bledsoe, from *Just Folks: Visitin' with Carolina People* (Charlotte, N.C.: East Woods Press, 1980), 35–39. Reprinted by permission of Down Home Press.

"Ad Man, Con Man, Photographer and Legend," by Vera A. Evans, from "Charles Brantley Aycock Brown: Ad Man, Con Man, Photographer and Legend," *Tar Heel*, July–August 1978, 9–10, 44–45. Reprinted by permission of the author.

"A Time to Reap," by William Ruehlmann, from Norfolk *Virginian-Pilot*, November 19, 1983. Reprinted by permission of *The Virginian-Pilot*.

"The Last of the Currituck Beach Cowboys," by Lorraine Eaton, from *Outer Banks Magazine*, 1989–90 annual, 22–27, 83–84. Reprinted by permission of *Outer Banks Magazine*.

"The Crab Picker," by Elizabeth Leland, from *Our Vanishing Coast* (Winston-Salem: John F. Blair, 1992), 139–41. Reprinted by permission of John F. Blair, Publisher.

Visitors Leave Their Footprints

"The Governor Returns," by John White, from Richard Hakluyt, ed., *The Principal Navigations Voyages Traffiques & Discoveries of the English Nation . . .* (London, 1600; 3rd ed., Glasgow: James MacLehose & Sons, 1903), vol. 8, 414–19.

"Gray-Eyed Indians," by John Lawson, from *A New Voyage to Carolina*, ed. H. T. Lefler (Chapel Hill: University of North Carolina Press, 1967), 68–69. Reprinted, with changes, by permission of The University of North Carolina Press.

"The Nag's Head Picture of Theodosia Burr," by Bettie Freshwater Pool, from *The Eyrie and Other Southern Stories* (New York: Broadway Publishing Co., 1905), 18–25.

"Our Winds Are Always Steady"

"Joseph J. Dosher to Wilbur Wright" in Fred C. Kelly, ed., *Miracle at Kitty Hawk: The Letters of Orville and Wilbur Wright* (New York: Farrar, Straus & Young, 1951), 25. Reprinted by permission of Farrar, Straus & Giroux, Inc.

"William J. Tate to Wilbur Wright" in Fred C. Kelly, ed., *Miracle at Kitty Hawk: The Letters of Orville and Wilbur Wright* (New York: Farrar, Straus & Young, 1951), 25–26. Reprinted by permission of Farrar, Straus & Giroux, Inc.

"Fragmentary Memorandum by Wilbur Wright circa September 13, 1900" in Marvin W. McFarland, ed., *The Papers of Wilbur and Orville Wright* (New York: McGraw-Hill, 1953), vol. 1, 23–25.

"Orville Wright to Katharine Wright, October 18, 1900" in Marvin W. McFarland, ed., *The Papers of Wilbur and Orville Wright* (New York: McGraw-Hill, 1953), vol. 1, 37–40.

"The Forgotten Pioneer," by Patrick K. Lackey, from "Pioneer of the Air," *The Carolina Coast*, September 13, 1992, 4–7. Reprinted by permission of *The Carolina Coast*.

"The Campers at Kitty Hawk," by John Dos Passos, from *The Big Money* (New York: Harcourt, Brace and Co., 1933, 1934, 1935, 1936), 278–85. Reprinted by permission of Elizabeth H. Dos Passos.

"Foreword to the Lost Colony," by Paul Green, from *The Lost Colony: Roanoke Island Edition* (Chapel Hill: University of North Carolina Press, 1954), iii–viii. Reprinted by permission of the Paul Green Foundation and the Roanoke Island Historical Association.

Lifestyles

"America's First Science Center," by Ivor Noël Hume, from *Colonial Williamsburg*, Spring 1994, 14–28. Reprinted by permission of the author.

"The Contraband Colony," by Horace James, from *Annual Report of the Superintendent of Negro Affairs in North Carolina, 1864* (Boston, 1865), 21–34.

"The Eye of the Tempest," by Joel G. Hancock, from *Strengthened by the Storm: The Coming of the Mormons to Harkers Island, North Carolina, 1897–1909* (Morehead City, N.C.: Campbell & Campbell, 1988), 109–29. Reprinted by permission of the author.

"Wild Goose Chase," by Rex Beach, from *Oh, Shoot! Confessions of an Agitated Sportsman* (New York: P. F. Collier & Son, 1921), 17–38.

"Bring Back the Old Deestric' Skule!" by Victor Meekins, from *The State*, October 28, 1933, 3, 18. Reprinted by permission of Our State.

"Hatteras Highway," by Bill Sharpe, from *The State*, July 12, 1952, 3–5, 19. Reprinted by permission of Our State.

"Old Christmas," by Jan DeBlieu, from *Hatteras Journal* (Golden, Colo.: Fulcrum, 1987), 168–74. Reprinted by permission of Fulcrum Publishing, Inc., 350 Indiana St., Suite 350, Golden, CO, 80401, (800) 992-2908.

Index